WOLFGANG AMADEUS MOZART

GARLAND COMPOSER
RESOURCE MANUALS
(VOL. 16)

GARLAND REFERENCE LIBRARY
OF THE HUMANITIES
(VOL. 910)

GARLAND COMPOSER RESOURCE MANUALS

General Editor: Guy A. Marco

1. *Heinrich Schütz: A Guide to Research* by Allen B. Skei

2. *Josquin Des Prez: A Guide to Research* by Sydney Robinson Charles

3. *Sergei Vasil'evich Rachmaninoff: A Guide to Research* by Robert Palmieri

4. *Manuel de Falla: A Bibliography and Research Guide* by Gilbert Chase and Andrew Budwig

5. *Adolphe Adam and Léo Delibes: A Guide to Research* by William E. Studwell

6. *Carl Nielsen: A Guide to Research* by Mina F. Miller

7. *William Byrd: A Guide to Research* by Richard Turbet

8. *Christoph Willibald Gluck: A Guide to Research* by Patricia Howard

9. *Girolamo Frescobaldi: A Guide to Research* by Frederick Hammond

10. *Stephen Collins Foster: A Guide to Research* by Galvin Elliker

11. *Béla Bartók: A Guide to Research* by Elliott Antokoletz

12. *Antonio Vivaldi: A Guide to Research* by Michael Talbot

13. *Johannes Ockeghem and Jacob Obrecht: A Guide to Research* by Martin Picker

14. *Ernest Bloch: A Guide to Research* by David Z. Kushner

15. *Hugo Wolf: A Guide to Research* by David Ossenkop

16. *Wolfgang Amadeus Mozart: A Guide to Research* by Baird Hastings

WOLFGANG AMADEUS MOZART
A Guide to Research

Baird Hastings

GARLAND PUBLISHING, INC. • NEW YORK & LONDON
1989

Library of Congress Cataloging-in-Publication Data

Hastings, Baird.
    Wolfgang Amadeus Mozart: a guide to research / Baird Hastings.
        p.   cm. — (Garland composer resource manuals; vol. 16)
    (Garland reference library of the humanities; vol. 910)
    Includes index.
    ISBN 0–8240–8347–4 (alk. paper)
    1. Mozart, Wolfgang Amadeus, 1756–1791—Bibliography.
I. Title.   II. Series: Garland composer resource manuals;
v. 16.
ML134.M9H34   1989
016.78'092'4—dc19   88–21294
                                                                     CIP
                                                                     M N

Printed on acid-free, 250-year-life paper
Manufactured in the United States of America

To Lily

CONTENTS

Acknowledgments   xi

Preface   xiii

Introduction and Lacunae   xv

Illustrations   xxiii

1. PROFILE
   Chronology of Mozartean Events and Celebrations, 1756–1956   3
   Geographical Register of Towns Mozart Visited   17
   Iconography, including Commentary   19

2. MOZART'S COMPOSITIONS, EDITIONS, MOZARTIANA, AND SOURCES
   Introduction   27
   Collected Editions   28
   Publishers of Early Editions   31
   Facsimile Editions   36
   Sources of Music and Mozartiana   43

3. MOZART'S WRITINGS
   Letters   71
   Documents   72

4. BIBLIOGRAPHY   75
    General Publications   76
    Specialized References   83
        Commentary
        Letters (Editions)   86
        Teaching   88
    Background
        Historical and Cultural   90
        Musical Influences   93
    Biography   97
        General   98
        Specialized Biographical Subjects, including Travel and
                Miscellaneous Topics   107
        Colleagues and Contemporaries   110
        Family and Friends   116
        Followers   119
        Miscellaneous   121
        Freemasons   123
        Illnesses and Death   124
    Music
        General and Stylistic Matters, including Commentary
                on Editions and Sources   125
        Performance Practice   142
            Mozart and Other Composers   145
            Mozart's Compositional Procedures and Techniques   148
        Vocal Music
            General   151
            Religious Works   152
            Secular Vocal Music   154
            Operas/Dramatic Works
                General   155
                Decorators of Mozart's Operas, 1768–1791   156
                Alphabetical by Title   162
            Texts   178
        Instrumental Music
            General   178
                Chamber Music (primarily Strings)   179
                Orchestra Music (except Concertos)   180

Piano and Keyboard Music (including
    Concertos) 184
String Music (including Concertos) 188
Wind Music (including Concertos) 189
Films and Videos 191
    Operas 192
    Other Films 198
    Commentary 203

5. ALPHABETICAL DICTIONARY OF MOZART'S
    CONTEMPORARIES (AND OTHERS IN
    HIS WORLD) 205

Appendixes

I.   Pupils (Chronological List) 353
II. Patrons, Vienna, 1784 (Alphabetical List) 359
III. Alphabetical Lists of Characters and Identifiable Locales
    in Mozart's Works 365
IV. Lists of Organizations and Publications Concerned with
    Mozart and His Music 375

Index of Authors, Editors, and Translators 395

Index of Names 407

Index of Works 411

ACKNOWLEDGMENTS

As this volume aims toward the better understanding of a great figure in the western world, I recognize over 100 Mozart scholars of the present as well as noted pioneers of the past, and wish to mention here persons who particularly assisted in making this publication better: Lily Hastings; Rudolph Angermüller; Fran Barulich; Ann Basart; Barry S. Brook; Tony Cardillo; Deborah Davis; Inge Dupont; Karl Geiringer; Boris Goldovsky; Jane Gottlieb; Thema Hecht; Leslie Kamtman; Marie Ellen Larcada; James N. Lewis; Klaus Liepmann; Sarah Lipsett-Allison; Lacey McDearmon; Guy A. Marco; Stephen Roe; John Shephard; and Hugh Williams.

I hope that each reader who finds a significant error, or a pathway I have not included, or an important new emphasis, will communicate with me in order that the next edition can be improved.

PREFACE

While the Table of Contents, supplemented by the Indexes, should enable readers to find references pertaining to their particular needs, a few words on how to use this book might be useful.

1. Note that the *Profile* provides guidance on many historical, chronological, geographical, and pictorial questions.

2. *Mozart's Compositions* includes lists of works, editions, and publishers, as well as collectors, sources of the music, and other Mozart material. Collectors' names are not indexed.

3. *Mozart's Writings* evaluates various editions of letters and other prime documents.

4. *Bibliography*, arranged alphabetically within topics, includes classic and recent, as well as general and specific, items necessary for an overall study of Mozart, his times, and his music. As every scholar knows, it is difficult to separate overlapping areas.

5. *Alphabetical Dictionary of Mozart's Contemporaries* should be very useful for research on all levels (although some dates are approximate).

Appendixes list the chronological list of pupils, the alphabetical list of patrons in 1784, the alphabetical list of characters in Mozart's operas, the alphabetical list of identifiable places in dramatic works, and the lists of organizations devoted to Mozart. A complete list of Mozart's relatives and a list of Mozart scholars today were omitted for technical reasons.

A note on the spelling—while attempting not to be arcane or inconsistent, and to use the spellings of names as the persons preferred, I admit to variations, engendered particularly by authors who adopt spellings other than those presently used.

Philosophically, I wish I had time to research many mysteries. Practically, it is time to encourage new scholars who will bring expanded dimensions to our understanding of Mozart. Meanwhile, as Bruno Walter said, it was a privilege.

Baird Hastings
27 January 1989

INTRODUCTION

In research there can be no final word for very long. There are statistics, there are probabilities, and there are insights. In this pioneer guide in English I am attempting to provide a balanced introduction to the world of Mozart and his music, as seen through the careful and admiring eyes of those who in the past have come closest to the heart of the man and the soul of his work. While of course recognizing the historical advance in Mozart research as it has proceeded for more than a century and a half, I certainly believe the "classics" are entitled to continued credence, on occasion far more than the "dernier cri." Many have noted that "to ignore history is to force us to repeat it." Also, bibliographical studies are like road maps. They indicate ways to get from one place to another, acquiring information. As a traveler who has used many maps, I offer you an informed guide, and I wish you a rewarding journey. As you find and appreciate new landmarks on your journey, I hope you will enlighten me in turn.

Given the large number of publications on the subject, this guide must be selective. There have been two excellent extensive German bibliographies: Keller's in 1927, and that of Schneider and Algatzy in 1962, as well as shorter ones in various languages. Both Keller and Schneider and Algatzy will be discussed in Section 4 (as will the other volumes mentioned in this Introduction). Many of the most valuable volumes are out of print, and thus it is important to include their pertinent entries in the present volume, as well as a number of entries (current and historical) which have been part of Angermüller's careful continuation volumes of bibliography.

The present work retains useful features of its predecessors as it offers a survey of Mozart research, scholarship, and publications up to 1983 (with additional information on many subjects through 1988) which, used in connection with the latest (1964) Köchel catalogue of Mozart compositions (or the 1980 *New Grove's Dictionary* summary of that catalogue), will enable individuals to chart their particular courses. Careful study of 19th-century sources of relevant facts has been made by Otto Erich Deutsch, Alfred Einstein, and Alexander Hyatt King, as well as Robert Eitner, all of whom are discussed in this volume, to whose insight all current researchers are indebted. The author of this volume has seen all numbered items except for those with an asterisk (*) after the entry; the annotations cite the source of information.

Although my initial idea was that a full chronology would be an invaluable asset to this research guide as an outline to where Mozart was when, the fact that Deutsch, Schneider and Algatzy, and Eibl all offer chronologies (in differing forms) has made our Chronology of Mozartean Events and Celebrations a convenience readily available rather than a unique necessity. Persons Mozart knew—the hundreds who were important to him and his music in one way or another—are listed in Section 5. Performers of his music are included, as are composers appreciated by Mozart or noteworthy for their involvement with his music (particularly in his lifetime), while contemporaries (some famous), who are not known to have been involved with him or his work are not included. The most important later figures in the development of Mozart's world are included.

The facts of Mozart's biography are not all known, nor is it likely that they ever will be. Particularly troubling are the problem of his worsening finances (when he appeared to be earning a satisfactory living in Vienna) and the mystery of his untimely death; our section on lacunae notes other avenues of indicated research activity. Readers will find the Profile useful in connection with the evaluation of Mozart's works as well as the biography, and the many fascinating letters of Mozart and his family offer a key to understanding both his life and his surroundings. The most important and extensive studies of Mozart and his works have been written by Jahn in German and by Wyzewa and Saint-Foix in French. (The recent comprehensive study by the Massins invents more problems than it solves.) And works which commit Mozart mayhem or are pastiches do not properly belong within the limits of this guide. The biography of Mozart is of utmost importance and is furnished with far more facts than that of Shakespeare, yet as we strive to learn more about both Mozart and his works, we know that whatever the biography may reveal, it is the compositions that will matter most, in their revelations to generations and generations.

Generally, where an important writer has written a book, one can assume he has taken into consideration articles he and his colleagues have written prior to that date, even if he or she does not refer to every possible item. However, because we are forced to be selective, it is appropriate to remind researchers that the absence of a particular "Mozart subject" in these pages should not be construed to mean that the subject has never been covered or that I have overlooked it; more likely this subject has not been covered authoritatively (or possibly even creditably).

In major subjects I have tried to include one or more monographs presenting the facts, often from different points of view. Where no monograph is available, I include one or more articles, when appropriate. In specialized subjects, an article may often be all that is available. In the end, a researcher will find his or her own way, bolstered by this guide, the Köchel catalogue, the letters, the bibliographies, the yearbooks, and the appropriate articles. Whatever gaps there may be in my outline, which has been developed with the gracious cooperation of a number of authorities, may be remedied by careful reference to the many sources presented as resources. The alert researcher will always find new and effective ways to approach basic subjects, as well as new avenues to open up on his or her own.

NMA, the *Neue Mozart Ausgabe*, is published by Bärenreiter, located in Kassel. Its address is Heinrich Schütz Allee 31, D 3500, Kassel-Wilhelmshöhe, Federal Republic of Germany.

In addition to the volumes already mentioned, I have searched the New York Public Library catalogue, the *National Union Catalogue*, the *Music Index*, the *Reader's Guide to Periodical Literature*, the *Mozart Jahrbuch*, *Mitteilungen der Internationalen Stiftung Mozarteum* (Salzburg), *Acta Mozartiana*, the *Neue Mozart Ausgabe*, *RISM*, *RILM* (through 1982), as well as bibliographies in standard reference works and monographs in English, German, French, Italian, and occasionally in Spanish, Russian, Japanese, Danish, Swedish, Hungarian, Czechoslovakian—some in translation.

Because I wish to make this volume as nearly self-sufficient and convenient to use as possible, I am using very few abbreviations of any kind—essentially only those literary abbreviations known to every reader who has taken a course in English literature—plus the very few Mozart musical abbreviations such as K^6 and K^3 for the sixth and third editions of the Köchel catalogue.

In compiling a research book on Mozart, I proceed humbly on the broad shoulders of Jahn, Köchel, Wyzewa and Saint-Foix, Einstein, Deutsch, King, and Grove. As time passes we assemble material of value to performers and historians but at the same time find it difficult to place certain facts in proper perspective, as we lose contact with the roots from which they spring. May this volume encourage us to advance our quest for Mozart and inspire further research which will make his mysteries and magic more valuable to today's fragmented society, as we come to understand more than merely the outline of the Mozart achievement. (Available ISBN and Library of Congress classification numbers are included as a convenience to readers.)

Lacunae

Lacunae in Mozart research are of at least three dimensions.

Questions of aesthetics—Mozart's classicism and his romanticism—various important influences on Mozart other than musical ones (what he read, what he saw, whom he spoke to, etc.)—naturally discussed on the basis of 18th-century evidence and not 20th-century hindsight.

Particular biographical episodes that need clarification in themselves or that have definite relationships to his works. For example,

Mozart saw death as a close observer in the case of his mother, four children (and a pet parakeet), and in his own rapid decline in the fall of 1791. Another area that would profit from further research is his attitude toward religion and ethics.

Musical questions that would benefit from deeper study and elucidation where possible, including Mozart's methods of composition. Mozart's family tree still needs research.

The first dimension touches on Mozart's place in music of the 18th century—a period of enlightenment and reaction, of incipient revolution—and, in fact, of his place in all of western history.

The large body of surviving letters of members of the Mozart family reveals personal involvement and how Mozart was touched by many ideas and ideals of his time. Although love, forgiveness, and liberty abound as primary themes in his operas, Mozart's early death prevented the imprint of violent revolution from having a direct effect on his outlook and his music. In this connection it is appropriate for us to reflect that Mozart's admired and beloved Joseph Haydn remained calm during the decade of the 1790s and appeared to dissociate himself from violence the more he approached his last years. We have no way of knowing whether Mozart's response to the horrors of war would have paralleled that of Haydn, or of Beethoven (whose reactions were more intense). Further studies could bring understanding of Mozart's reactions to *Sturm und Drang*, his reconciliation of religion and Freemasonry, and other pertinent philosophical issues.

Particular elements under biography can be explored further with the help of notes found in the splendid edition of letters of the Mozart family prepared by Bauer, Deutsch, and Eibl (#559), and many contemporary resources are now being investigated and made available—without recourse to such extraneous and misleading avenues as Freud and Marx. Research into the lives and works of numerous figures listed in Section 5 of this volume (such as Wenzel, Süssmayr, and members of the Swieten circle) will illuminate areas of biography, particularly as they also take advantage of what we know of Mozart's travels. The question of Mozart's professional and emotional relationship to his pupils, particularly ladies, has not yet been considered fully, nor have his finances. Although a basic character understanding of Mozart's father, wife, and cousin seems to have been established, a revision may well be needed, when his many friends and connections are understood better, as neither Leopold nor Constanze was nearly as one-sided as certain biographers seem to indicate. (This writer is still sifting through biographical evidence relating the creation of *Così fan tutti* to Mozart's personal life.) A biography of Mademoiselle Jeunehomme would almost certainly contribute useful details to our understanding of Mozart's life and works from 1777 to 1780.

Further investigation of Mozart's method of composition following the important results discussed by Plath and Tyson, etc., should be revealing on several levels. Questions of authenticity, orchestration, performance practice, methods of composing, form, and tonality all need further consideration. While wars and other upsetting activities have displaced our cultural assets, more Mozart remains to be found—and continued search for lost music could result in finding many of the more than twenty additional compositions we know he wrote. Particular projects include the unravelling of the mystery of the wind concertante; perhaps an authentic copy can be located in France or elsewhere. Finally, despite the justly acclaimed clarification of numerous works as a result of the NMA, the instrumental and vocal works which have more than one authentic copy (or perhaps multiple sketches) should continue to have attention focused on them that will enable performers to have available all the proper evidence to present the works faithfully to the public. Publishing a complete list of sources of manuscripts once the casualties of World War II have been accounted for could yield further biographical and statistical information. An authoritative discussion of the symphonies, bringing up to date the solid research of Saint-Foix and others, is a major desideratum. (Neal Zaslaw is at work on this.)

GARLAND COMPOSER RESOURCE MANUALS

In response to the growing need for bibliographic guidance to the vast literature on significant composers, Garland is publishing an extensive series of research guides. The series, which will most likely appear over a five-year period, encompasses almost 50 composers; they represent Western musical tradition from the Renaissance to the present century.

Each research guide offers a selective, annotated list of writings, in all European languages, about one or more composers. There are also lists of works by the composers, unless these are available elsewhere. Biographical sketches and guides to library resources, organizations, and specialists are presented. As appropriate to the individual composers, there are maps, photographs, or other illustrative matters, and glossaries and indexes.

1. Mozart family portrait by Johann Nepomuk della Croce (1780?). Left to right: Nannerl and Wolfgang at the keyboard, mother (in portrait painted by Deglé, Loronzoni, or Barducci-Hagenauer in Salzburg, c. 1775), Leopold. Mozart Museum, Salzburg.

2.   Constanze Weber Mozart (Nissen) by Hans Hansen (c. 1802).
Mozart Museum, Salzburg.

3. Mozart's children: Franz Xaver Wolfgang and Carl Thomas by Hans Hansen (c. 1798). Mozart Museum, Salzburg.

4.   Tyl Theatre, Prague, where *Don Giovanni* was premiered, 1787.

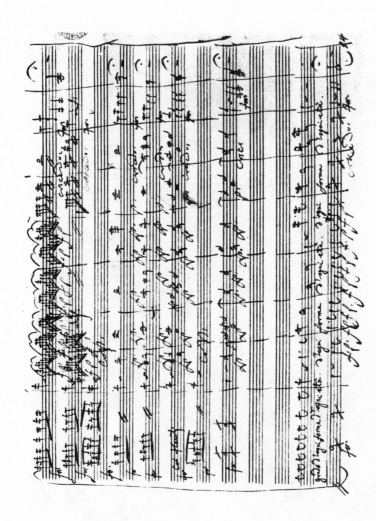

5. Portion of Catalogue aria, Act I, number 4, from *Don Giovanni*, K. 527; composer's original manuscript (reduced). Bibliothèque Nationale, Paris.

6. Prague reconstruction of original set by Josef Platzer, showing scene of Act I, number 4, of *Don Giovanni*.

7. Graveyard scene (Act II) reproduced from piano vocal score of *Don Giovanni*, edited by A. E. Müller for Breitkopf & Härtel, Leipzig, c. 1803. Vignette by Friedrich Bolt, after V. B. Kinninger.

8. Map of Mozart's tours, showing routes of three important tours; the first two tours began in Salzburg, and the third tour began in Vienna. (From *Mozart* by Richard Baker. Copyright (c) 1982 by Thames and Hudson Ltd., London. Reprinted by permission of the publisher.)

Wolfgang Amadeus Mozart

1.
PROFILE

Chronology of Mozartean Events and Celebrations, 1756–1956

References to the Köchel number of Mozart's compositions list K^6 first, then K^3 if appropriate in parentheses.

1756

27 January   Salzburg. Birth of Joannes Chrysostomos Wolfgangus Theophilus Mozart. Augsburg. Publication of Leopold Mozart's *Violinschule*.

1760

Studies clavier pieces with father Leopold, having already played by ear for some time.

1761

Composes first pieces, written down by Leopold.

1762

12 January	Travel to Munich (first of eight visits) for three weeks with father and sister (Nannerl—Maria Anna—Marianne); court presentation.
18 September	Travel to Vienna (first of three visits) with father, mother, and sister; concerts and court presentations.

1763

5 January	Return to Salzburg from Vienna, after a side trip to Pressburg (Bratislava).
9 June	Travel from Salzburg with father, mother, and sister on a trip lasting three and one-half years; concerts and court appearances in most towns. (See Geographical Register and Map.)
12 June	Munich.
22 June	Augsburg (first of five visits).
6 July	Travel to Ulm, Heidelberg, Mannheim (first of four visits), Worms, Mainz (first of two visits).
10 August	Frankfurt (first of two visits).
17 September	Coblenz.
27 September	Travel to Bonn, Cologne, Aachen.
5 October	Travel to Brussels, Liège.
18 November	Paris and surroundings until 10 April 1764 (first of three visits). Admired by royalty (Princesses Victoire, Sophie, and Adelaide, and others), Baron Grimm and his entourage, etc. Mozart's *Clavier and Violin Sonatas*, K. 6-7 published by Marie Charlotte Vendôme (1764) at the expense of Leopold, and dedicated to Madame Victoire (1764). Frequent concerts.

1764

23 April	Arrival in London (via Calais), where Mozart gives numous concerts, performing on the piano, with his family and others. Received by royalty, he sees J. C. Bach and others, composes

symphonies, sonatas, and other works, some of which were published.

1765

24 July	Travel to Lille, where illness forces the family to stay a month.
4 September	Travel to Ghent, Antwerp, Rotterdam.
10 September	Travel to The Hague, where Mozart composes symphonies and sonatas.

1766

January	Travel to Amsterdam.
March	Return to The Hague.
End of March	Travel to Haarlem, Antwerp, Brussels, etc.
10 May	Paris.
9 July	Travel to Dijon, Lyon, Geneva, Lausanne, Bern, Zurich, Schauffhausen, Donaueschingen, Augsburg.
8 November	Arrival in Munich.
29 November	Return to Salzburg.

1767

12 March	Salzburg. Premiere: *Die Schuldigkeit des ersten Gebotes*, K. 35. Mozart composes Part I of three parts.
13 May	Salzburg. Premiere: *Apollo et Hyacinthus*, K. 38.
11 September	Travel to Lambach, then to Vienna, with entire family.

1768

April–July	Vienna. Mozart composes *La finta semplice*, K. 46a (51). Also, a trumpet concerto, and a solo for violoncello (both lost).
September	Vienna. Mozart composes *Bastien und Bastienne*, K. 46b (50). Meets Baron van Swieten.

| December | Travel to Melk, Linz. |

1769

5 January	Return to Salzburg.
1 May	Salzburg. Premiere: *La finta semplice.*
13 December	Travel to Italy with father, via Innsbruck (first of three visits), Rovereto; concerts in many towns.
27 December	Arrival in Verona (first of three visits).

1770

5 January	Verona. Mozart gives first concert at the Philharmonic Academy.
10 January	Travel to Mantua, Milan (first of three visits), Cremona, Parma, Modena.
24 March	Arrival in Bologna (first of several visits). Meets with Padre Martini.
29 March	Travel to Florence. Meets with Thomas Linley.
11 April	Arrival in Rome (host: Uslenghi family).
14 May	Naples.
26 June	Return to Rome, where he completes several compositions, and is made Papal Knight of the Golden Spur.
20 July	Return to Bologna.
September	Begins composing *Mitridate,* K. 74a (87), at the estate of Fieldmarshall Pallavicini.
9 October	Elected member of the Bologna Academy.
13 October	Travel to Milan.
26 December	Milan. Premiere: *Mitridate,* conducted by Mozart; premiere lasts six hours, including three ballet intermezzos composed by others.

1771

| 5 January | Elected a member of Verona Academy. |
| 14 January | Travel to Venice, where Mozart gives a concert on March 5. |

28 March	Return to Salzburg, after stops in Padua, Verona, Innsbruck.
June–July	Salzburg. Composes *La Betulia liberata*, K. 74c (118), and sacred works and symphonies.
15 August	Travel to Italy (second trip) with father, via Innsbruck, Verona.
21 August	Arrival in Milan. Begins composition of *Ascanio in Alba*, K. 111. Several concerts.
17 October	Milan. Premiere: *Ascanio in Alba*.
5 December	Travel to Verona, Innsbruck.
15 December	Return to Salzburg.

1772

14 March	Count Hieronymus von Colloredo becomes Archbishop of Salzburg, succeeding Count Siegmund Schrattenbach (who died).
1 May	Salzburg. Premiere: *Il sogno di Scipio*, K. 126.
9 August	Mozart named concertmaster of Salzburg court orchestra.
24 October	Travel to Italy (third and last trip) with father, via Innsbruck, Verona.
4 November	Milan. Premiere: *Lucio Silla*, K. 135.

1773

17 January	Milan. Premiere: "Exsultate, jubilate," K. 158a (165).
13 March	Return to Salzburg, after short stays in Verona, Innsbruck.
14 July	Travel to Vienna (and Baden) with father; Mozart gives several concerts.
26 September	Return to Salzburg, via Linz, St. Pölten.
December	Mozart composes *Symphony in g*, K. 173dB (183), *Clavier Concerto in D*, K. 175, etc.

1774

March	Mozart composes some incidental music for *Thamos*, K. 336a (345); in 1779 (?) Mozart composed additional numbers for another production.
September	Mozart begins composition of *La finta giardiniera*, K. 196, for Munich.
6 December	Travel to Munich with father.

1775

13 January	Munich. Premiere: *La finta giardiniera*.
7 March	Return to Salzburg with father and sister (Nannerl), who came to attend opera premiere.
23 April	Salzburg. Premiere: *Il re pastore*, K. 206.
April–December	Salzburg. Mozart composes five violin concertos: K. 207, 211, 216, 218, 219.

1776

January–April	Salzburg. Mozart composes three clavier concertos: KI. 238, 242, 246.
18 June	Salzburg. Premiere: *Divertimento in F*, K. 247, composed for Countess Lodron.
21 July	Salzburg. Premiere: *Haffner Serenade*, K. 248b (250), with *March*, K. 249.

1777

January–February	Mozart composes *Clavier Concerto in E flat*, K. 271, and *Divertimento in B flat*, K. 271b (287).
23 September	Travel from Salzburg with mother, on a trip lasting sixteen months.
24 September	Arrival in Munich, where Mozart gives several concerts.
11 October	Arrival in Augsburg, where Mozart gives several concerts and sees his relatives.

30 October	Arrival in Mannheim, where Mozart quickly becomes a member of the Cannabich circle (including Holzbauer, Raaff, Ramm, Wendling). Mozart teaches pupils and gives concerts.

1778

23 January	Mozart goes on a brief concert tour with Fridolin Weber and his daughters, Josepha and Aloysia (new acquaintances).
14 March	Travel from Mannheim to Paris with mother.
23 March	Arrival in Paris, where he composes a *Symphony in D*, K. 300a (297); a *Miserere*, C.14.01 (297a); a *Sonata in D* for keyboard, 311. Gives lessons. Sees Grimm, J. C. Bach, collaborates with Noverre, etc. His music is performed several times at Concerts Spirituels.
11 June	Paris Opéra. Premiere: *Les petits riens*, K. 299b, choreography by Noverre.
3 July	Death of mother in Paris.
26 September	Travel from Paris, on way to Salzburg.
17 October	Arrival in Strasbourg, where Mozart gives three concerts.
6 November	Arrival in Mannheim.
25 December	Arrival in Munich.

1779

15 January	Return to Salzburg, where on January 17 Mozart is named Salzburg court organist.
Spring and Summer	Completes *Mass in C*, K. 317, followed by several symphonies.

1780

First half of year	Composes numerous sacred and secular works. Gives public performances with sister.
5 November	Travel from Salzburg to Munich to compose *Idomeneo*, K. 366.

1781

29 January	Munich. Premiere: *Idomeneo*; father and sister attend performance.
12 March	Travel to Vienna by order of Archbishop Colloredo; henceforth Vienna is home for Mozart. Father and sister return to Salzburg.
May	Resigning from the service of the Archbishop, Mozart moves to a room at the house of Frau Fridolin Weber, although by this time Aloysia (for whom he had composed several arias, and with whom he was in love) was Frau Joseph Lange.
Summer	Mozart begins composition of *Die Entführung aus dem Serail*, K. 384.
September	Mozart moves to a room in the Graben. Gives concerts and instructs keyboard pupils.
24 December	Keyboard competition with Muzio Clementi, before Emperor Joseph II.

1782

Spring	Mozart composes several piano concertos and performs at numerous concerts.
16 July	Vienna. Premiere: *Die Entführung*.
4 August	Mozart and Constanze Weber are married; Leopold Mozart's blessing arrives August 5.

1783

17 June	Birth of Mozart and Constanze's first child (Raimund Leopold); only two of their six children survived.
July–November	Mozart and Constanze visit Leopold and Nannerl Mozart in Salzburg.
	Salzburg. Premiere: *Mass in c*, K. 417a (427) (unfinished), with Constanze singing.
4 November	Linz. Premiere: *Linz Symphony in C*, K. 425.

1784

9 February	Mozart begins keeping a chronological record of all his compositions in a small notebook; the first entry is the *Piano Concerto in E flat*, K. 449.
Spring–Summer	Vienna. Series of important concerts for which Mozart composes new music.
23 August	Marriage of Mozart's sister Nannerl to Baron J. B. von Berchtold zu Sonnenberg (a widower) of Saint Gilgen (near Salzburg).
21 September	Birth of Carl Thomas, Mozart's elder surviving son.
14 December	Mozart joins Vienna Freemason lodge, gradually achieving recognition in the order.

1785

January–February	Meetings and concerts with Joseph Haydn.
11 February	Leopold Mozart comes to Vienna from Salzburg; attends many concerts.
6 April	Leopold Mozart joins Freemasons.
25 April	Leopold Mozart returns to Salzburg.
Summer–Autumn	Mozart gives many concerto performances and composes lieder, including K. 476.

1786

7 February	Schönbrunn Palace. Premiere: *Der Schauspieldirektor*, K. 486.
1 May	Vienna. Premiere: *Le nozze di Figaro*, K. 492.
Summer	Considers English trip, but does not go.
Fall	Composes *Prague Symphony in D*, K. 504.

1787

8 January	Mozart travels to Prague on concert tour with Constanze, Franz Hofer, Marianne Crux (first of four visits).

12 February	Return to Vienna.
7–20 April	Beethoven begins lessons with Mozart but then returns to Bonn.
28 May	Leopold Mozart dies in Salzburg.
10 August	Mozart composes Serenade, K. 525.
10 October	Mozart travels to Prague, with Constanze.
29 October	Prague. Premiere: *Don Giovanni*, K. 527.
16 November	Return to Vienna.
7 December	Mozart is named court chamber composer by Emperor Joseph II.

1788

7 May	Vienna. First performance of revised *Don Giovanni.*
June–August	Mozart composes last three symphonies: K. 543, 550, 551, in E flat, g, and C.
November	Mozart conducts his revision of Handel's *Acis and Galathea*, K. 566, for the Baron van Swieten concerts.

1789

6 March	Mozart conducts his revision of Handel's *Messiah*, K. 572, for the Swieten concerts.
8 April	Travels to Prague with Prince Lichnowsky, where he is contracted for a new opera.
12 April	Travels on a concert tour, to Dresden, Leipzig, Potsdam, Berlin.
4 June	Return to Vienna.
Summer	Money problems begin and plague Mozart for the remainder of his life.
29 September	Mozart composes *Clarinet Quintet in A*, K. 581, and begins *Così fan tutti*, K. 588.

1790

| 26 January | Vienna. Premiere: *Così.* |

23 September   Travels to Frankfurt on concert tour with brother-in-law, violinist-composer Franz de Paula Hofer.
10 November   Return to Vienna.
15 December   Mozart says farewell to Joseph Haydn, who is on his way to England.

1791

January   Mozart composes his last piano concerto, K. 595, also chamber music and dances.
17 June   Mozart composes *Ave verum corpus*, K. 618.
26 July   Birth of Franz Xaver Mozart, known as Wolfgang, Jr., Mozart's younger surviving son.
25 August   Mozart travels to Prague, with Constanze and Süssmayr.
6 September   Prague. Premiere: *La clemenza di Tito*, K. 621.
15 September   Return to Vienna.
30 September   Vienna. Premiere: *Die Zauberflöte*, K. 620.
18 November   Vienna. Mozart conducts his *Kleine Freimaurerkantate*, K. 623.
20 November   Mozart takes to his bed, still composing the *Requiem in d*, K. 626, which he began in July.
5 December   Mozart dies.

1793

2 January   Vienna. First performance of *Requiem*.

1798

Prague. Publication of *Leben des K. K. Kapellmeisters Wolfgang Gottlieb Mozart* by Franz Niemetschek, philosopher and classicist who had known Mozart.
Leipzig. Breitkopf & Härtel begin publication of Mozart's "Complete Works," a project abandoned a decade later.

1799

Offenbach. Johann André and Constanze Mozart enter into an agreement to publish Mozart's works, a project finally abandoned in 1830.

1805

Vienna. Wolfgang Mozart, Jr., performs in concert.

1809

26 June   Pressburg (Bratislava). Marriage of Constanze Weber Mozart to Georg Nikolaus von Nissen.

1826

24 March   Salzburg. Georg Nikolaus von Nissen dies.

1829

29 October   Salzburg. Nannerl (Marianne) von Berchtold zu Sonnenberg dies. (Born 29 August 1751.)

1841

Salzburg. Mozarteum und Dom-Musik established.
Vienna. Mozart Festival on 50th anniversary of the death of the composer.

1842

Salzburg. Constanze Mozart Nissen dies. (Born 5 January 1762.)
Salzburg. Wolfgang Mozart, Jr., conducts his own cantata.

1844

29 July   Karlsbad. Wolfgang Mozart, Jr., dies.

1856

September   Salzburg. Säkularfest of Mozart's works. Several
                   cities also have Mozart festivals.

1858

13 October   Milan. Carl Thomas Mozart dies.

1859

                   Leipzig. Publication of first edition of Otto
                   Jahn's *Mozart* is completed, Breitkopf & Härtel.

1862

                   Leipzig. Publication of Ludwig Köchel's
                   *Chronologisch-thematisches Verzeichnis sämtlicher
                   Tonwerke Wolfgang Amadé Mozarts*, Breitkopf &
                   Härtel.

1863

                   Frankfurt. Mozart Institut, founded in 1838,
                   celebrates its 25th anniversary.

1877

                   Leipzig. First volumes of Breitkopf & Härtel
                   Mozart Collected Edition (GA) appear.

1880

                   Salzburg. Mozarteum formally established for
                   research and as a school.

1891

Vienna, Salzburg, Augsburg, etc., commemorate 100th anniversary of Mozart's death.

1896

Munich. Hermann Levi directs *Così, Figaro,* and *Don Giovanni.*

1906

Salzburg. Festival, featuring *Don Giovanni.*

1910

London. Camille Saint-Saëns performs twelve Mozart piano concertos, with his own cadenzas, in three concerts.

1920

Salzburg. First of the annual festivals devoted primarily to the music of Mozart.

1934

Glyndebourne, England. First annual festival of Mozart operas. Recently this festival has included operas by other composers.

1956

Worldwide celebration of Mozart's 200th anniversary, including the initiation of a new Mozart Collected Edition (NMA).

Geographical Register of Towns Mozart Visited

Alphabetical list of 82 important places, with dates. When date is italicized, it indicates that Mozart gave a concert there. Letter "T" means he attended a performance there.

1.	Aachen	*1763*
2.	Amsterdam	*1766*
3.	Antwerp	*1765, 1766*
4.	Augsburg, T	*1763, 1766, 1777,* 1781, *1790*
5.	Baden	*1766*
6.	Berlin, T	*1789*
7.	Biberbach	*1766*
8.	Bologna	*1770*
9.	Bonn	1763
10.	Bozen (Bolzano)	1772
11.	Brixen	1769, 1770, 1771, 1772
12.	Brünn	*1767*
13.	Brussels	*1763*
14.	Budwitz	1789
15.	Canterbury	1765
16.	Chelsea (London)	1764
17.	Coblenz	*1763*
18.	Cologne	1763
19.	Cremona, T	*1770*
20.	Dijon	*1766*
21.	Dillingen	*1766*
22.	Donaueschingen	*1766*
23.	Dresden, T	*1789*
24.	Florence	*1770*
25.	Frankfurt, T	*1763, 1790*
26.	Geneva	*1766*
27.	Ghent	*1765*
28.	Hall	*1772*
29.	Haarlem	*1765*
30.	The Hague	*1765, 1766*
31.	Heidelberg	*1763*
32.	Innsbruck	*1769, 1771*
33.	Kaysersheim	1778
34.	Kircheim-Boland	*1778*
35.	Lambach	*1767, 1783*

36.	Lausanne	*1766*
37.	Leipzig	*1789*
38.	Liège	1763
39.	Lille	*1765*
40.	Linz	*1762, 1783*
41.	London, T	*1764–1765*
42.	Ludwigsburg, T	1763
43.	Lyon	*1766*
44.	Mainz	*1763, 1790*
45.	Mannheim, T	1763, *1777–1778, 1778, 1790*
46.	Mantua	*1770*
47.	Melk	*1767*
48.	Milan, T	*1770, 1771, 1772, 1773*
49.	Modena, T	*1770*
50.	Munich, T	*1762, 1766, 1775, 1777, 1778, 1779, 1781, 1790*
51.	Nancy, T	1778
52.	Naples, T	*1770*
53.	Nymphenburg	*1763*
54.	Olmütz, T	1767
55.	Padua	*1771*
56.	Paris, T	*1763–1764, 1766, 1778*
57.	Parma	*1770*
58.	Passau	*1762*
59.	Potsdam	1789
60.	Prague	*1787, 1789, 1791*
61.	Pressburg (Bratislava)	1762
62.	Regensburg	1791
63.	Rome	*1770*
64.	Rotterdam	*1766*
65.	Rovereto	*1766*
66.	Saint Germain	1778
67.	Salzburg, T	*1756–1783* (except 1782)
68.	Schaffhausen	1776
69.	Schwetzingen, T	*1763*
70.	Steyr	1783
71.	Strasbourg	*1778*
72.	Stuttgart	1763
73.	Turin, T	1771
74.	Ulm	*1763*
75.	Utrecht	*1766*
76.	Venice, T	*1771*
77.	Verona, T	*1770*

78.	Versailles	*1763–1764*
79.	Vienna, T	*1762, 1768, 1773, 1781–1791*
80.	Wasserburg	*1763*
81.	Worms	*1763,* 1778
82.	Zurich	*1766*

Iconography

The best sources for information on Mozart iconography include the Deutsch-Zenger *Mozart and his World in Contemporary Pictures* (#26) and the essay by Otto Erich Deutsch, "Mozart Portraits," in *The Mozart Companion* (Landon-Mitchell) (#774). Most of the other sources are less reliable; Bory's book, *The Life and Works of Wolfgang Amadeus Mozart in Contemporary Pictures* (#25), reproduces a number of interesting prints along with some spurious and posthumous portraits. Two articles in different volumes of *The Musical Quarterly* are also of considerable interest. The first, by Edward Speyer, is entitled "Notes on the Iconography of Wolfgang Amadeus Mozart" (5,2 [1919]: 175–191); the second, by William Barclay Squire, is entitled "A Spurious Mozart Portrait" (9, 2 [1923]: 211–216).

Below is a chronological listing of the accepted Mozart portraits, with attribution where known, and brief commentary.

1. Lorenzoni, Pietro Antonio (?) (1721–1786)
   The Boy Mozart.
   Oil.
   Dimensions 83.7 x 64 cm.
   Painted in Salzburg (early 1763).
   Portrays Mozart standing by a clavier and wearing a court costume in lilac, trimmed with gold braid.
   Possibly by the Salzburg painter Franz Joseph Deglé (1724–1812); later engraved by L. Sichling (c. 1740–1800). It was bequeathed to the Mozart Museum, Salzburg, by Constanze von Nissen.

2. Carmontelle, Louis Carrogis de (1717–1806)
   Leopold Mozart with Wolfgang and Maria Ana (Marianne, called Nannerl).
   Watercolor.
   Dimensions 33 x 20 cm.
   Painted in Paris (November 1763).
   Leopold stands, playing the violin, and Wolfgang and Nannerl are at the keyboard. Probably the original version, it is housed in the Musée Condé at Chantilly, France.

3. Carmontelle
   The "Paris copy" is housed at the Musée Carnavalet de la Ville de Paris.

4. Carmontelle
   The "London copy" is owned by the National Gallery of London and deposited in the British Museum.
   Several engravings of one or another of the versions have been made, by Jean-Baptiste Delafosse (1721–1775), Thomas Cook (1744–1818), Christiane Mechel (1737–1817), A. Weger (1767–1832).

5. Ollivier, Michel Barthelémy (1712–1784)
   Tea at Prince Louis François de Conti's in the Temple.
   Oil.
   Dimensions 53 x 68 cm.
   Painted in Paris (summer of 1766).
   Shows Wolfgang at the harpsichord preparing to accompany Pierre de Jélyotte. Housed at the Musée du Louvre, Paris; previously at Versailles.

6. dalla Rosa, Saverio (1745–1821)
   Wolfgang (at Verona) at the Keyboard.
   Oil.
   Dimensions 71 x 58 cm.
   Painted in Verona (January 1770) for Pietro Lugiati, receiver-general of Venice.
   Previously believed to have been the work of one of the Cignarolli brothers, it is considered the first characteristic

picture of Mozart. It is in the collection of the heirs of Alfred Cortot (Paris).

7. Anonymous
Miniature on ivory, in leather frame of later date.
Dimensions 5 cm. in diameter.
Painted in Milan (1773?)
Perhaps the work of Martin Knoller (1725–1804), it may be identical to the portrait Nannerl mentioned which showed Mozart in somewhat ill health. It is housed in the Mozart Museum, Salzburg.

8. Anonymous
Miniature on ivory, in an old frame.
Dimensions 4 x 2.8 cm., oval.
Painted in Augsburg (October 1777), or Mannheim (November 1777).
Mozart allegedly gave this doubtful work to his cousin, Maria Thekla. Now in poor condition, it is on loan to the Mozarthaus, Augsburg.

9. Anonymous
Mozart as Knight of the Golden Spur.
Oil.
Dimensions c. 75 x 65 cm.
Painted in Salzburg (1777) for Padre Martini, the original has disappeared. What we have now are two copies—one in the Padre Martini Conservatory, Bologna, and the other (painted in 1926 from the Italian copy) housed in the Mozart Museum, Salzburg.

10. della Croce, Johann Nepomuk (1736–1819)
Mozart Family Portrait.
Oil.
Dimensions 140 x 180 cm.
Painted in Salzburg (late autumn of 1780?).
Shows Wolfgang and Nannerl at the keyboard, with Leopold beside them, and a portrait by Deglé (?) of their mother (who had died in 1778) on the wall. Inheriting this painting from

Nannerl in 1829, Constanze left it to her sons in 1842, and
Wolfgang, Jr., bequeathed it to the Mozart Museum in
Salzburg in 1844, where it is housed today. See illustration 1.

11. Lange, Joseph (1751–1830)
    Mozart (in profile) at the Fortepiano.
    Oil, unfinished sketch.
    Dimensions 34.6 x 29.7 cm.
    Painted in Vienna, 1782–1783 (?). Some authorities now date
    it to 1789.
       A smaller version, since lost, and a portrait of Constanze
    (perhaps the one now in Glasgow) were sent to Leopold by
    Wolfgang in 1783. Deutsch surmises the lithograph in Nissen's
    biography (#632) was based on the smaller version. In 1858
    Mozart's older son, Carl Thomas, bequeathed this work to the
    Mozart Museum, Salzburg.

12. Löschenkohl, Hieronymous (c. 1753–1807)
    Silhouette (in profile).
    Dimensions 8.1 x 5 cm.
    Engraved in 1785 for Löschenkohl's Musik- und Theater-
    Almanach of 1786. A copy is in the Historisches Museum der
    Stadt Wien.

13. Löschenkohl
    Silhouette (in profile).
    Dimensions 5.1 cm. high.
    Profile, engraved after Löschenkohl for the Viennese
    composer-publisher Franz Anton Hoffmeister in 1792. A copy
    is in the Historisches Museum der Stadt Wien.

14. Löschenkohl
    Silhouette (in profile).
    Dimensions 5.3 cm. high.
    Engraved after Löschenkohl for Heinrich Philipp Bossler of
    Darmstadt in 1795, who published it in the *Musikalische
    Realzeitung.* A copy is in the Historisches Museum der Stadt
    Wien.

15. Posch, Leonard (1750–1831)
Medallion (in profile) in red wax.
Dimensions 9 cm. in diameter.
Inscribed to Posch from Wolfgang, Jr., on February 9, 1820, this medallion later was given to the Mozart Museum, Salzburg, by J. Küss. Missing since 1945.

16. Posch
Medallion in plaster.
Dimensions 8.2 x 6.9 cm. oval.
This profile, the original of which was made in Vienna (1788–1789), is part of the Munzen- und Medaillen Collection of the Kunsthistorisches Museum, Vienna. The collection includes a bronze made from the original plaster medallion. When the original plaster medallion was broken during a casting in 1904, a new plaster medallion was made from the bronze casting.

17. Posch
Medallion in boxwood.
Dimension 8.5 cm. oval.
Profile carved by, or after, Posch in May 1789.
Professor Joseph Hyrtl presented it to the Mozart Museum, Salzburg, in 1894.

18. Posch
Medallion in wax, mixed with plaster.
Dimensions 9.8 cm. oval.
This profile was made into a belt buckle for Constanze in Vienna about 1790. In 1857 Carl Thomas Mozart called its likeness to his father "the most perfect." About 1925 the daughter of the Berlin singer, Baroness Natalie Grünhof, presented it to the Mozart Museum, Salzburg. Missing since 1945.

19. Posch
Engraving by Johann Georg Mansfeld the younger (c.1764–1817).
Dimensions 14 x 8.5 cm.

This profile for Artaria, Vienna, dates from 1789. On the lower right side is "An Chloe" K. 524, a song published by Artaria (first edition). Formerly in the collection of Dr. Max Zenger, Munich, the engraving is now in the Mozart Gedenkstätte, Augsburg.

20. Posch
    Engraving by Klemens Kohl (1754–1807).
    Dimensions 13.7 x 9.4 cm.
    This profile was engraved in Vienna in 1793.
    As in 19 (above), sheet music was included in the original. Apparently ordered by Constanze, it was probably intended for the reprint of Friedrich Schlichtegroll's obituary volume on Mozart published in Graz by J. G. Hubeck in 1794, and then purchased by Constanze. In 1798 Constanze sold the printer's plate to Breitkopf & Härtel, who published it in their *Allgemeine musikalische Zeitung* (1806). Formerly in the collection of Dr. Zenger, it is now in the Mozart Gedenkstätte, Augsburg.

21. Posch
    Engraving by Johann Neidl (1776–1832).
    Dimensions 19.8 x 14.7.
    This profile was engraved for Artaria in Vienna in 1800. In the engravings "after Posch" the nose has been altered, especially by Neidl. Formerly in the collection of Dr. Zenger, it is now in the Mozart Gedenkstätte, Augsburg.

22. Stock, Doris (1760–1831)
    Drawing in silver point.
    Dimensions 7.5 x 6.2 cm.
    Profile drawn on ivory paste board, Dresden, April 1789.
    It is in the Musikbibliothek der Stadt, Leipzig.

23. Anonymous
    Watercolor.
    Dimensions 7 x 6 cm. oval.
    Painted in Vienna, c. 1795.

Constanze gave it to Barbara Ployer, one of Mozart's favorite keyboard pupils. Ployer's notebook, containing this portrait and also a page of his music, was in the Mozart Museum, Salzburg, until 1945. Missing since then.

24. Krafft, Barbara (née Steiner) (1764–1825)
    Oil.
    Dimensions 54 x 42 cm.
    Painted in Salzburg, 1819, or earlier.
    Commissioned by Joseph Sonnleithner, the artist used as her model three works supplied by Nannerl: an anonymous miniature in ivory, the family portrait by della Croce, and a copy of the Lange portrait. It is housed in the Gesellschaft der Musikfreunde, Vienna.

Commentary

25. Bory, Robert. *The Life and Works of Wolfgang Amadeus Mozart in Contemporary Pictures.* Geneva: Les Éditions Contemporaines, 1948. 224 pp.

    Useful, revealing, but not always reliable. Indexes. (There is also an edition in French.)

26. Deutsch, Otto Erich, and Max Zenger. *Mozart and his World in Contemporary Pictures.* Kassel: Bärenreiter, 1961. 404 pp.

    Undoubtedly the best single volume. However, portraits by Batoni, Blanchet, Bosio, Duplessis, Grassi, Greuze, Hansen, Helbling, Klass, Kymli, Langenhöffel, Quénédy, Rigaud, Saint-Aubin, Schulz, Tischbein, and others may be considered part of the Mozart legacy, if not the Mozart life.
    See also: Emil Vogel. "Mozart Portraits." *Jahrbuch der Musikbibliothek Peters* (1899). Leipzig: Peters, 1900, 11–37.

27. Thieme, Ulrich, and Felix Becker. *Allgemeines Lexicon des Bildenden Kunstler.* Leipzig: Seaman, 1908–1947. 36 vols.

    Unique art reference work. It covers 18th-century Viennese artists very well.

2.
MOZART'S COMPOSITIONS, EDITIONS, MOZARTIANA, AND SOURCES

Introduction

The 682 compositions by Mozart that are properly authenticated were composed between 1761 and 1791. In addition there are various references to compositions that have been lost, which if retrieved would bring the number to more than 700 works.

There are two authentic contemporary lists of Mozart's works—one by Leopold Mozart for the period 1761–1768, first printed in Nissen in 1828 (#632), and the other by Wolfgang for the period 1784–1791, first printed by J. A. André in 1805–which together cover sixteen of the thirty-one years, leaving a gap in chronological records of fifteen years; a facsimile of Mozart's own listing of his works (owned by the British Library) issued in Vienna in 1938, and again in New York in 1956, is now out of print. Both these invaluable lists are described in King (#768). Programs for a number of works and mention in the voluminous family letters of the pieces make it possible to date many compositions with near certainty. Publishing projects in the early 1800s by J. A. André of Offenbach (assisted in the editing by Franz Gleissner) and separately by the Leipzig firm of Breitkopf & Härtel (with various editors) helped establish an initial chronological listing of Mozart's compositions, the authenticity of which was declared by Constanze Mozart, who was assisted by Abbé Maximilian Stadler, a musician friend of the Mozarts. These banks of information were fundamental to the pioneer biography and work list prepared by

Constanze's second husband, Nikolaus von Nissen (completed and issued after the death of Nissen in 1826 under Constanze's supervision).

The catalogue of Mozart's works was expanded by the research of early Mozart collectors and scholars such as Aloys Fuchs (1799–1853), Leopold von Sonnleithner (1797–1893), Otto Jahn (1813–1869), and above all Ludwig von Köchel (1800–1877). The results of Köchel's expert cataloguing were first published in 1862, and despite important refinements made in the last 120 years (by Alfred Einstein, Otto Erich Deutsch, Alexander Hyatt King, and others), Köchel's catalogue has stood the test of time. It is now in its sixth edition (1964), and if the current renumbering of the appendix seems cumbersome, presumably its organization was dictated by logic.

In 1976 Gherardo Casaglia published *Il Catalogo delle opere di Wolfgang Amadeus Mozart*. Using Köchel's list of the works of Mozart, and also sixteen other lists (which include some compositions widely regarded as doubtful), Casaglia reorders a number of works, rather more drastically than did Wyzewa and Saint-Foix (#647). Although the author gives reasons for re-dating, some of his conclusions are debatable.

The four lists referred to above are: Leopold Mozart: *Werkverzeichniss für Wolfgang Amadeus Mozart* (1768, included in Bauer-Deutsch-Eibl, #559); Wolfgang Mozart *Verzeichnüss aller meiner Werke* (1784–1791); Ludwig von Köchel: *Chronologisch-Thematisches Verzeichnis sämtlicher Tonwerke Wolfgang Amadé Mozarts* (1862); Gherardo Casaglia: *Il Catalogo delle opere di Wolfgang Amadeus Mozart* (Bologna: Compositori, 1976. 444 pp.).

Collected Editions

Prior to the initiation of the *Neue Mozart Ausgabe* (NMA)—in process of being issued by Bärenreiter in Kassel, Germany, since 1955—there were a number of "Collected" editions of the works of Mozart. Publishers are listed chronologically; numbers which are italicized indicate that the person is also listed in Section 5:

28. Magazin de musique (J. P. Spehr, c. 1770–1860?), Braunschweig, 1797–1799.
   Six sections; piano works.

29. Breitkopf & Härtel, Leipzig, 1798–1808?
   Seventeen sections: piano, vocal, some scores, etc.

30. André (Johann A.), Offenbach, c. 1797–1825?
   Chamber works, etc.

31. Artaria & Company, Vienna, c. 1800–1818?
   Chamber works, etc.

32. Hoffmeister (Franz Anton), Vienna, 1802–1807.
   Eleven sections: piano; five sections: chamber works.

33. Chemische Druckerei, Vienna, c. 1803–1814?
   Seventeen sections: reprint of (#29), above.

34. Simrock (Nikolaus), Bonn, 1803-1834.
   Twenty-eight sections: piano, chamber works.

35. Haslinger (Tobias, 1787–1842), Vienna, c. 1810–1840? (partly based on edition begun by Steiner?).
   Thirty-eight sections: piano, lieder, canons.

36. Sieber (Jean-Georges, 1738–1832), Paris (Sieber, père), 1810?
   Chamber works, etc.

37. Janet (Pierre Honoré, c. 1780–1840?) et Cotelle (Alexandre, c. 1790–1858), Paris, 1810?
   Chamber works, etc.

38. Frey (Jacques Josfa, 1781–1838), Paris, c. 1811–1822?
   Miscellaneous.

39. Pleyel (Ignaz), Paris, c. 1803–1829?

   Thirteen sections: piano, chamber works.

40. Steiner (Sigmund Anton, 1773–1838), Vienna, c. 1817 or earlier–1826?

   Thirty-six volumes of piano music, solo or in instrumental or vocal ensemble.

41. Madame Veuve Launer (successor of Carli), Paris, c. 1820–1850?

   Thirteen sections: piano.

42. Richault (Charles Simon, 1780–1860), Paris, c. 1828–1860?

   Chamber works, instrumental music, operas.

43. Coventry (Charles, c. 1800–1850? and John C. Hollier, c. 1800–1848), London, Firm, 1833–1851, succeeded by Novello.

   Piano. In 1848 Coventry published a thematic catalogue of Mozart's works for the piano.

44. Chabal (Jean Louis, c. 1810–1870?), Paris, 1840–1894.

   Chamber works, etc.

45. Breitkopf & Härtel, Leipzig, 1877–1883, with supplements, later revised.

   Collected edition (GA) in twenty-four series.

   Above publication dates (given generally from K[6]) are approximate. Despite devoted research by King (#768), Weinmann (#821), and others, much work on music publishers in the Classic period remains to be done.

Publishers of Early Editions

Listed alphabetically. Köchel numbers are noted, K^6 (K^3). (About 150 compositions were issued in Mozart's lifetime.) Individual early publishers listed in Section 5 have their entry numbers underlined. No modern practical editions are listed.

46. Alberti, Ignaz (c. 1750–1794).
Vienna. Publisher, active 1790s.
First editions: K. 596, 597, 598, libretto to *Die Zauberflöte*.

47. Allgemeine Musikalische Zeitung.
Leipzig. Publisher, active 1790s.
First editions: K. 621a (Anhang 245), etc.

48. André, Johann (1741–1799) & Company.
Offenbach. Composer, publisher, active c. 1797–1825.
Many early editions; Mozart's own *Verzeichniss* (1784–1791), published in 1805 and later reissued.

49. Artaria & Company.
Vienna. Publishers, active 1778–1856.
First editions: K. 387, 123a (381), etc.; also early editions.

50. Bianchi, Giovanni Batista (c. 1740–1800).
Milan. Publisher, active 1770s.
First editions: librettos, *Ascanio*, K. 111, and *Lucio Silla*, K. 135.

51. Bossler, Heinrich Philipp (1744–1812).
Speyer, Darmstadt, Germany. Publisher of music and prints, active 1781–1828.
First editions: K. 285b (Anhang 171), etc.

52. Boyer, Pascal (1743–1794).
Paris. Publisher (associated with Le Menu), firm active c. 1778–1806.
First editions: K. 175, etc.; also early editions.

53. Breitkopfische Musikhandlung.
Leipzig. Publishers, active 1790s.
First editions: K. 486, etc.; also early editions.

54. Bureau des Arts et d'Industrie.
    Vienna. Publishers, active 1801–1823.
    First editions: K. 386b (361); also early editions.
    Early editions: K. 520, etc.

55. Cappi, Johann (1765–1815).
    Vienna. Publisher (successor to A. Q. Witzendorf), active c.
    1802–1824?

56. Chappell, Samuel (c. 1782–1834).
    London. Composer, publisher (first with Cramer & Latour),
    active from 1812.
    First edition: K. 588b (236).

57. Cianchettini, Francis (c. 1770–1830), and B. Sperati (c. 1770–
    1820?).
    London. Publishers, active 1805–1820?
    First editions: K. 504, 543 (score), 550, 551.

58. Diabelli, Anton (1781–1858).
    Vienna. Composer, publisher, active from 1818 (first with
    Johann Cappi, later taken over by Carl Anton Spina, 1790–
    1870, and then by August Cranz, 1789–1870).
    First editions: K. 272a (277), etc.

59. Diesbach, Giuseppe Emanuele (c. 1750–1810?).
    Prague. Publisher, active 1780s.
    First Prague edition: libretto of *Figaro.*

60. Falter, Markarius (1762–1843).
    Munich. Publisher, firm active 1787–1888.
    First editions: K. 385d (314), etc.

61. G. Gombart & Company (c. 1760–1810?).
    Augsburg. Publisher, firm active 1795–1844?
    First editions: K. 247, etc.

62. Götz, Johann Michael (c. 1760–1810?)
    Mannheim. Publisher, active in 1790s.
    First editions: K. 502, 542, 548 (?); also early editions.

63. Gräffer, Rudolf (c. 1740–1800?).
    Vienna. Publisher, active from 1760s.

First editions: K. 47e (53), etc.

64. Günther & Böhme (Johann August).
Hamburg, and Vienna. Publishers, active 1794–1885.
First editions: K. 162; also early editions.

65. Heydenreich, Joseph (1753–1821).
Vienna. Composer-arranger, publisher, active 1796–1821.
First editions include *General-Bassschule* (*Thorough-Bass Manual*), 1796.

66. Heina, Madame Gertrude Brockmüller (1729–1790?)
(married to François Heina, 1729–1790).
Paris. Publisher, active from 1770s.
First editions: K. 229a (354), etc.; also early editions.

67. Hoffmeister, Franz Anton (1754–1812).
Vienna. Composer, publisher, active from 1780s.
First editions: K. 469, etc.

68. Hummel, Johann Julius, & Company (1728–1798).
Amsterdam. Publisher, active 1766–1821.
Berlin. Publisher, active from 1774.
First editions: K. 24, etc.

69. Imbault, Jean Jerôme (1753–1832).
Paris. Publisher, violinist, active c. 1783–1812.
First editions: K. 318, etc.

70. Krausstschen Buchladen nächst Burg.
Vienna. Publisher, active 1760s.
First edition: libretto of *Bastien*, K. 46b (50).

71. Kurzböck, Joseph (c. 1740–1800?).
Vienna. Musician, publisher, active from 1770s.
First editions: libretto, *Figaro*, K. 492; libretto, *La finta giardiniera*, K. 190 (also published by Stecchi & Pagani of Florence).

72. Leuckart, Franz Ernst Christoph (1748–1817).
Breslau. Publisher, active from 1780s.
First editions: uncertain, but many early editions.

73. Lotter, Johann Jakob (1683–1738), and successors.
    Augsburg. Publishers, active 1720–1844.
    First editions: K. 186h (194), etc.

74. Mayr, Johann Joseph (1740–1790).
    Salzburg. Publisher-printer, active 1760s.
    First editions: libretto, *Die Schuldigkeit*, K. 35, etc.

75. Mollo, Tranquillo (1767–1838), & Company.
    Vienna. Publisher, active c. 1784 on.
    First editions: uncertain, but many early editions.

76. Montani, Giovanni (c. 1740–1800?).
    Milan. Publisher, active 1770s.
    First edition: libretto, *Mitridate*, K. 74a (87).

77. Musenalmanach.
    Vienna. Publishers, active 1784–1803.
    First edition: K. 506

78. Musikalische Magazin.
    Vienna. Publishers, active 1784–1816? (directed by Leopold
    Koželuch, 1747–1818; Anton Koželuch, 1752–1805; Ludwig
    Maisch, 1776–1816).
    First editions: K. 620, etc; also early editions.

79. Peters, Carl Friedrich (1779–1827).
    Leipzig. Publisher, active 1813– .
    First editions: K. 512, etc.; also early editions.

80. Rellstab, Johann Karl Friedrich (1759–1813).
    Berlin. Publisher, active 1779–1806.
    First editions: K. 577, etc.; also early editions.

81. Schmiedt & Rau.
    Leipzig. Publishers, active 1790s.
    First editions: K. 386c (407), etc.

82. Schönfeld, Johann Ferdinand von (c. 1750–1810?).
    Prague. Publisher, active from 1780s.
    First editions: librettos, *Don Giovanni* and *La clemenza di Tito*
    (first Vienna edition of *Don Giovanni* libretto published
    1788 by Sordi & Muti).

93. Traeg, Johann (1747–1805).
    Vienna. Publisher, active from 1770s (taken over by Artaria, and Cappi).
    First editions: uncertain, many early editions.

94. Vendôme, Marie Charlotte (and family: mother, husband, daughter).
    Paris. Publishers, active from 1740s.
    Engraver of K. 6, 7, 8, 9.

95. Wappler, Christian Friedrich (1711–1807).
    Vienna. Publisher, active from 1780s.
    First editions: libretto of *Messiah*, etc.

96. Weingand, Johann Georg (c. 1750–1800?).
    Vienna. Publisher, active from 1780s.
    First editions: selection from *Die Entführung*, etc. (*Entführung* libretto first published by Logenmeister of Vienna.)

97. Wenzel, Johann (c. 1750–1810?).
    Vienna. Organist, publisher.
    First editions: K. 543, etc.

98. Williamson, Thomas G. (c. 1740–1800?).
    London. Musician, publisher.
    First editions: K. 10, etc. (1764).

99. Ziegenhagen, Franz Heinrich (1753–1806).
    Vienna. Publisher, text author of K. 619, Hamburg, 1792.

In Section 5 the following Parisian publishers of early editions of compositions by Mozart are also named: Bouin, Cochet, Cousineau, Doisy, Duhan, Erard, Guénin, Jouve, LeRoy, Michaud, Porro, Viguerie, Vogt.

Facsimile Editions

Facsimiles are among the most important tools we have for interpreting faithfully the desires of the composer. Naturally, the composer may have revisionary thoughts which go into the first

83. Schott, Bernhard (1748–1809) & Sohn.
    Mainz. Publishers, from 1770s.
    First editions: piano vocal scores, *Don Giovanni, Die Entführun*
    etc.

84. "Self-publisher" (Mozart and members of his family).
    K. 10, 11, 12, 13, 14, 15, 375a (401), 503, etc.

85. Sieber, Jean-Georges (1738–1822).
    Paris. Musician, publisher, active from 1770s.
    First editions: K. 293a (301), etc.

86. Simrock, Nikolaus (1752–1834).
    Bonn. Publisher, active from 1790s.
    First editions: K. 285a, etc.

87. Societa Tipografica.
    Vienna. Publishers, active 1790s.
    First edition: libretto, *Così fan tutte.*

88. Storace, Stephen (1747–1805).
    London. Composer, publisher, active from 1780s.
    First edition: K. 564.

89. Taubstimmen Institut (Franz Seizer, c. 1750–1800?).
    Vienna. Publishers, active from 1780s.
    First editions: K. 472, etc.

90. Thonus, J. P. von (c. 1750–1810?).
    Leipzig. Publisher, active from 1770s.
    First edition: K. 196.

91. Thuille, Francesco Giuseppe (c. 1750–1800?).
    Munich. Publisher, active 1780s.
    First edition: libretto of *Idomeneo.*

92. Torricella, Christoph (1715–1798).
    Vienna, originally from Switzerland.
    Publisher, active 1775–1786 (taken over by Artaria).
    First editions: K. 465, etc.

edition if it is prepared under his direction, or he may express these thoughts in "production notes" which may or may not be generally available. However, in the absence of significant, contradictory information from the composer later than the original manuscript, a facsimile of the original remains invaluable to performers and to historians, particularly when reproduced clearly at the same size as the original. The selected Mozart facsimile editions that follow are listed chronologically according to the Köchel catalogue.

100. *The Earliest Compositions of Wolfgang Amadeus Mozart*, K. 1, 2, 3, 4, 5, 6, 8, and four pieces believed to antedate K. 1. 50 pp. 22 x 29 cm.

Presented by the Deutsche Mozart-Gesellschaft in cooperation with H. J. Laufer, the compositions were selected from Leopold Mozart's *Nannerl Notenbuch* and detached pages (once) owned by Mr. Laufer. Munich: H. Rinn, 1956. There is a foreword by Ernst Fritz Schmid, an introduction by Edward J. Dent, and a monograph by Erich Valentin (who has also published a full edition of Nannerl's music book with a discussion of the handwriting of Leopold Mozart). Notes. (The compositions reproduced come from the collections of H. J. Laufer, London [since dispersed]; Stadt Bibliothek, Leipzig; Mozarteum, Salzburg; Museum Carolino-Augusteum, Salzburg; Bibliothèque du Conservatoire, Paris.)

101. *Symphony in E flat*, K. 16. Appendix to NMA, IV, 11, 1. 23 x 30 cm. Kassel: Bärenreiter, 1984. 12 pp.

102. "Two Mozart Cadenzas to K. 107." *Journal of the American Musicological Society* 8, 3 (Fall 1955): 212–216.

Greatly reduced facsimiles. Commentary by Hans Moldenauer. (Collection: Hans Moldenauer, Spokane, Washington.)

103. *Violin Concerti* (K. 207, 211, 216, 218, 219) and Adagio (K. 261) and Rondo (K. 261a). Notes; bibliography. New

York: Raven Press, 1986. 23 x 30 cm. 400 pp. ISBN: 0-88167-156-8. ML96.4 M7 no. 30.

The excellent, extensive, occasionally controversial commentary by Gabriel Banat cannot be summarized here, but I hope it can be reprinted inexpensively for the use of every violinist who plays Mozart. (Collections: Berlin Staatsbibliothek; Jagiellonian University Library, Poland [temporary?]; Library of Congress, Washington, D.C.)

104. *Andantino in E flat for Clavier*, K. 236, in "Mozart and Cramer." See King (#768). 1 p.

Facsimile greatly reduced. Commentary by Alexander Hyatt King. (Collection: Berlin Staatsbibliothek.)

105. *Piano Sonata in A minor*, K. 300d (310). Vienna, 1973. 11 pp. 23 x 30 cm.

No commentary. (Collection: Morgan Library, New York.)

106. *Piano Sonata in B major*, K. 333 (315c). Stuttgart: Ichthys Verlag, 1965. 35 pp. 37.8 x 23.3 cm.

Commentary by Karl Julius Marx. (Collection: Berlin Staatsbibliothek.)

107. *Gran Partita in B flat*, K. 370a (361). Washington, D.C.: U.S. Govt. Printing Office, 1970. 98 pp. 27 x 35 cm. ISBN: 0-8444-0173-0.

Penetrating commentary by Alfred Einstein, translated by Jim Newsom. (Collection: Library of Congress, Washington, D.C.)

108. *Symphony Number 35 in D major*, K. 385. New York: Oxford University Press, 1968. 60 pp. 30 x 37 cm.

Commentary by Sidney Beck. (Collection: Morgan Library, New York.)

109. *Allegretto,* K. 385d (404). Frankfurt: Jos. Baer (after 1842, when it was in the André Collection). 1 p. 20 x 26.5 cm. Facsimile reduced 20% from original size.

    This is the second part of an "Andante and Allegretto" composed for Constanze. (Collection: Mozarteum, Salzburg.)

110. C *Minor Mass,* K. 417a (427). Kassel: Bärenreiter, 1983. 146 pp. 25 x 33 cm. ISBN: 3-7618-0622-1.

    Commentary by Monika Hall and Karl-Heinz Köhler, who discuss the creation of the work, and its transformation into *Davidde penitente.* (Collection: Berlin Staatsbibliothek.)

111. Pizka, Hans, ed. *Das Horn bei Mozart. Facsimile Collection.* Kircheim: Hans Pizka, 1980. 276 pp. 23 x 32 cm.

    Facsimile of K. 447 and 495, along with fragments, excerpts, arias. Discussion includes material on eighteenth-century horn players. Facsimiles reduced 10%. Bibliography; discography; no index. (Various collections.)

112. *Piano Concerto in C Major,* K. 467. New York: Dover, 1986. 88 pp. 22 x 29 cm. ISBN: 0-486-24968-9. ML 96.5 M 97.

    Commentary by Jan LaRue and J. Rigbie Turner. Reduced about 15% from original. (Collection: Morgan Library, New York.)

113. *Das Veilchen,* K. 476. New York: Storm Publishers, 1949. 30 pp. including plates and notes. 23 x 30 cm.

    Commentary by Paul Nettl, covering the music and the text (by Goethe). (Collection: Friderike Zweig.)

114. *Rondo for Piano in D,* K. 485. Vienna: 1973. 23 x 30 cm.

    No commentary. (Collection: Morgan Library, New York.)

115. *Der Schauspieldirektor,* K. 486. New York: Morgan Library,
      1976. 89 pp. 27 x 35 cm. ISBN: 0-87598-055-4.

      Commentary by Charles Ryskamp and J. Rigbie Turner.
      (Collection: Morgan Library.)

116. *Piano Concerto in C Minor,* K. 491. Washington, D.C.: Robert
      Owen Lehman Foundation, 1964. 86 pp. 27 x 37 cm.

      No commentary. (Collection: Royal College of Music,
      London.)

117. *Piano Concerto in C Minor,* K. 491. Kilkenny, Ireland:
      Boethius Press, 1979. 86 pp. 27 x 37 cm.

      Commentary by Watkins Shaw and Denis Matthews. A
      welcome edition, as above is out of print.

118. *Rondo for Piano,* K. 494. The Music Forum I (December
      1967): 6-8, plus commentary by Hans Neumann and Carl
      Schachter. New York: Columbia University Press, 1967. c.
      25 x 36 cm., reduced 33% in facsimile.

      (Collection: Carl Schachter.)

119. *Deutsche Tänze,* K. 509. Leipzig: Peters, 1955. 23 pp. 24 x 33
      cm.

      Commentary by Wilhelm Virneisel. (Collection: Berlin
      Staatsbibliothek.)

120. *Rondo for Clavier,* K. 511. Leipzig: Peters, 1955. 2 pp.
      Reduced.

      (Collection: Musikbibliothek Peters.) (Published earlier,
      with K. 485, by Universal Edition, Vienna?)

121. *Serenade, Eine Kleine Nachtmusik,* K. 525. Kassel: Bärenreiter,
      1955. 36 pp. 25 x 34 cm. Commentary by Manfred
      Gorke.

      Although the missing minuet had apparently been seen
      in this century in Italy by Giuseppe Bertolini, it is not in
      the facsimile, nor is any authentic copy extant.

122. *Don Giovanni*, K. 527. Paris: A. G. Maisoneuve, 1967. 273 pp. 25 x 33 cm. Prague version. Unpaged. Commentary by François Lesure. (Collection: Bibliothèque Nationale, Paris.)

123. *Trio for Violin, Clavier, and Violoncello*, K. 542. Munich: Drei Masken Verlag, 1921. 8 pp.* (Collection: Berlin Staatsbibliothek.)

124. *Adagio and Fugue for Strings*, K. 546. Brussels: *Musica Viva*, I, 1 (April 1936).* (Collection: Salzburg, Mozarteum.)

125. *Symphony in C*, K. 551. Kassel: Bärenreiter, 1978. 103 pp. 25 x 33 cm. ISBN: 3-7618-0608-6. Commentary by Karl-Heinz Köhler. (Collection: Berlin Staatsbibliothek.)

126. *"Un moto di gioia,"* K. 579. Vienna: Gesellschaft der Musikfreunde, 1982. 1 p. (Collection: Vienna Gesellschaft der Musikfreunde.)

127. *Kantate, Die Ihr des unermesslichen Weltals Schöpfer ehrt*, K. 619. Stockholm: Gehrmans, 1955. 5 pp. 23 x 30 cm. Commentary by Richard Engländer. (Collection: Upsala University, Sweden.)

128. *Die Zauberflöte*, K. 620. Kassel: Bärenreiter, 1979. 454 pp. 26 x 33 cm. ISBN: 3-7618-0609-4. Spoken dialogue omitted. Commentary by Karl-Heinz Köhler calls attention to Mozart's own revisions. (For further discussion see Michael Freyhan, "Toward the Original Text of Mozart's 'Die Zauberflöte.'" *Journal of the American Musicological Association*, 39, 2 (Summer 1986): 355-380. (Collection: Berlin Staatsbibliothek.)

129. *Requiem*, K. 626. Vienna: Gesellschaft für Graphische Industrie, 1913. 32 pp.

      (Collection: Vienna Nationalbibliothek.)

130. *Ten String Quartets*, K. 387, 417b (421), 421b (428), 458, 464, 465, 499, 575, 589, 590. Washington, D.C.: Robert Owen Lehman Foundation, 1969.

      Reproduced from holograph in the British Museum. No commentary, but Lea Pocket Scores, edition 175, 176, 177, reprints commentary on the works by Alfred Einstein which anyone performing Mozart will treasure. A new facsimile edition of these quartets has been issued by the British Library, 1987. 176 pp. 28.5 x 37.5 cm. ISBN: 0-7123-0137-2. Commentary by Alan Tyson.

131. *The Six 'Haydn' String Quartets*. London: British Library, 1985. 160 pp. 29 x 38 cm.

      Commentary by Alan Tyson. (Collection: British Library, London.)

132. *Cadenzas to Piano Concertos in the Library of St. Peter's, Salzburg.* K. 387a (413), 316a (365), 175, 271, 246. 6 pp.*

      Commentary by E. Mandyczewski.

133. *Esperimento d'esame per l'aggregazione all' Accademia Filharmonica di Bologna* (1770). Bologna: Bornia, 1972. unpaged. 25 x 32 cm.

      Includes: Mozart's original test; corrections by Padre Martini; Mozart's faithful copy; attestation of Padre Martini; minutes of meeting October 9, 1770 accepting Mozart as a member of the Academy.

(N.B. Bärenreiter has announced an ongoing series of facsimiles to include concertos and arias.)

Sources of Music and Mozartiana
Alphabetized by City

It seems advisable to indicate locations of manuscripts, autographs, letters, documents, portraits, even a few notable editions, as well as significant collections of Mozartiana in as comprehensive a manner as possible. For collections in Mozart Societies, readers are referred to Appendix IV. Where available the date of reliable verification is noted. Possible clues as to subsequent location are included. Although in certain entries the listed location and owner are at best questionable, inquiry may produce some information. In any case the heirs, whose street addresses rarely were available, may have some information or material. For a listing of Mozart compositions missing since World War II, see *Mozart Jahrbuch* 12 (1962–1963): 306 ff.

My primary sources have been: Bauer/ Deutsch/ Eibl (1975), particularly for letters; Köchel 6 (1964); Deutsch & Zenger, *Mozart and His World* (1961); Eitner (1904); *The New Grove* (1980); RILM (1971–); RISM: recent Salzburg *Mozart Jahrbuchs* and *Mitteilungen*; NMA. Certainly the greatest Mozart collections are in Salzburg, Vienna, Berlin, Paris, London, and New York (all of which I have visited personally, except Berlin). I suggest that readers wishing to verify information and pursue particular entries in this section write to the nearest Mozart Society (noted in Appendix IV), inquiring as to what pertinent addresses the local experts may have available. (Spellings are in the usual English version, or in the local language.)

ALTHORP, NORTHAMPTONSHIRE, ENGLAND
134. Lord Spencer   Music: K. 520, etc.

ALTONA, GERMANY
135. A. von Bonn   Mozartiana

AMSTERDAM, NETHERLANDS
136. Oud-archief der Gemeent Museum   Mozartiana, 1765 contemporary accounts, etc.

137. Heirs of Willem Mengelberg   Mozartiana
     (In November 1986 the London
     dealer Albi Rosenthal purchased K.
     71c in an auction at Sotheby's from
     the Mengelberg heirs.)

ANSBACH, SWITZERLAND
138. Schlossbibliothek   Mozartiana

AUGSBURG, GERMANY
139. Deutsche Mozart-Gesellschaft   Music: K. 300e
     (includes Mozart-Gemeinde,   (265), etc.,
     Mozart Gedenkstätte)   Letters
140. Staats- und Stadtbücherei (1975)   Letters
141. Stadtarkiv (1987)   Music: sketches
                                           Letters

BASEL, SWITZERLAND
142. Heirs of Braus-Riggenbach   Letters
143. G. Flörsheim (Koch) Collection   Music: K. 380,
     (1975)   etc.
                                           Letters
                                           Documents

144. Geigy-Hagenbach Collection (1975)   Music: K. 375e
                                           (401), etc.
                                           Letters
145. Dr. R. Grumbacher   Music: K. 455, etc.
146. Universitäts Bibliothek   Music: K. 585
                                           (partial)
                                           Letters

BERGAMO, ITALY
147. Biblioteca dell' Instituto Musicale   Mozartiana
     Gaetano Donizetti (1987)

BERKELEY, CALIFORNIA, U.S.A.
148. University of California   Einstein
                                           Collection

BERLIN, GERMANY

149. Deutsche Staatsbibliothek (DDR): Mozart Collection. Begun officially in 1873, the Bibliothek purchased from André what the André family had retained from their original purchase from Constanze. Before World War II there were more than 422 items, including *Così, Die Entführung, Idomeneo* (partial), *Die Zauberflöte,* and *Figaro,* as well as the Fuchs Collection. Oskar Fleischer prepared a catalogue in 1900. See also Preussischer Kulturbesitz, Berlin, for which H. G. Klein prepared a new catalogue in 1982.
    Music: Including symphonies
    Letters
    Mozartiana

150. Staatsbibliothek (Tübingen) — Music

151. Staatsbibliothek (Marburg) — Music

152. Deutsche Staatsbibliothek (DDR) — Letters

153. Heirs of Karl Eckert (1888) — Music: K. 496, etc.

153a. Heirs of Dr. Max Friedlaender (1900) — Mozartiana

154. Heirs of F. A. Grasnick (1888) — Music: K. 516, etc.

155. Heirs of K. E. Henrici (1964) — Music: K.626b/40, etc.

156. Heirs of Frau Jähns (1975) — Letters

157. Heirs of Joseph Joachim — Music: Instrumental (?)

158. Heirs of Herr Liebig (1888) — Mozartiana

159. Heirs of Leo Liepmannsohn (famous antiquarian and dealer) — Various

160. Heirs of Joseph von Radowitz — Music: K. 626b/13

161. Heirs of O. Rauthe — Music: K. 23 (?)

162. Heirs of Ernst Rudorff — Music Mozartiana

163. Heirs of D. Salomon — Letters

164.	Heirs of Philipp Spitta	Music: Instrumental
165.	Heirs of W. Taubert	Music: Instrumental
166.	Theater an der Behrenstrasse	Mozartiana
167.	Wagener Collection	Mozartiana

BEVERLY HILLS, CALIFORNIA, U.S.A.

168.	Ernest E. Gottlieb, dealer	Music
169.	Dr. Myron Prinzmetal (1975)	Music: K. 64 Letters
170.	Heirs of Bruno Walter (1964)	Music: K. 64

BLOOMINGTON, INDIANA, U.S.A.

| 171. | Heirs of Paul Nettl | Music: contemporary copy of *Figaro* in ms. |

BLUDENZ, AUSTRIA

| 172. | Heirs of Theobald Eibl (1888) | Music: K. 198 |

BOLOGNA, ITALY

173.	Archivo di Stato (1975)	Letters, etc.
174.	Liceo Musicale	Portrait
175.	Accademia Filharmonica (Biblioteca Musicale G. B. Martini) Emilia Succi Accademia Filharmonica di Bologna	Music: K. 73v (86) Music: K. 626b/7

BONN, GERMANY

176.	Heirs of Max Cohen & Sohn (1888)	Music: K. 112, etc.
177.	Heirs of Dr. Prieger	Letters, etc.
178.	Heirs of Dr. L. Scheidler	Letters
179.	Heirs of Ludwig Schiedermair (see also #493)	Letters, etc.
180.	Universitäts Bibliothek	Letters

BOSTON, MASSACHUSETTS, U.S.A.
181. Public Library (1975)   Music: K. 404b
                                       (443), etc.
                                       Letters

BRATISLAVA (PRESSBURG), CZECHOSLOVAKIA
182. State Archives (1975)   Music; Letters

BRAUNSCHWEIG, GERMANY
183. Stadtarkiv (1975)   Music: K. 294
                                       Letters

BRESSANONE (BRIXEN), ITALY
184. Archivo di Stato (1975)   Letters

BRNO, CZECHOSLOVAKIA
185. State Archives (1987)   Mozartiana

BRÜNN, GERMANY
186. Professor Dr. Jan Racek   Music: K. 488d

BRUSSELS, BELGIUM
187. Bibliothèque du Conservatoire   Music
      Royale de Musique (1975)   Letters

BUCHAREST, RUMANIA
188. Academy Library (Royal   Music: Cadenza
      Collection)   to K. 385p (414)
                                       Portrait(?)

BUDAPEST, HUNGARY
189. National Museum (1987)   Music:
                                       Contemporary
                                       copy of K. 492,
                                       etc.

CAMBRIDGE, ENGLAND
190. Fitzwilliam Museum (1987)   Music:
                                       K. 27c (267), etc.

191. Mrs. Olga Hirsch Collection   Mozartiana
192. Weisbeck Museum (1975)   Letters

CAMBRIDGE, MASSACHUSETTS, U.S.A.
193. Harvard University Library   Letters,
     (Biblioteca Mozartiana Eric   Mozartiana, etc.
     Offenbacher, now at Harvard,
     includes music, etc.) (1987)

CARLSRUHE, GERMANY
194. Landesbibliothek   Mozartiana

CHANTILLY, FRANCE
195. Musée Condé   Portraits

CHICAGO, ILLINOIS, U.S.A.
196. Roger W. Barrett (1975)   Letters
197. Dr. Max Thorek (1975)   Letters
198. Newberry Library (1987)   Music:
                                         K. 448b (464),
                                         610,
                                         626b/37

CINCINNATI, OHIO, U.S.A.
199. S. M. Doane   Mozartiana

COBURG-GOTHA, GERMANY
200. Heirs of Prince Ernest von Sachsen Music:
                                         K. 375a (448)

COBURG-VESTA, GERMANY
201. Bibliothek (1987)   Music: K. 255,
                                         317c, (328), 320d
                                         (364), 385b (393),
                                         416b (435), 416c
                                         (433), 417a (427),
                                         538, 582, 621

COLOGNE, GERMANY

202. J. M. Heberle — Music: K. 626b/4
203. Musikhistorisches Museum, Heyer Collection (catalogue G. Kinsky) (1975) — Mozartiana
204. Dr. Karl Niessen — Mozartiana

CRACOW, POLAND

205. Biblioteka Jagiellónska (1987) — Music: In 1945 had 120 works; some have since been returned to Berlin and other owners, but as of July 1987, K. 492 and many other works remain in Cracow.

DARMSTADT, GERMANY

206. Hessische Landes- und Hochschulbibliothek (1975) — Letters

DIEPPE, FRANCE

207. Musée Saint-Saëns — Music: K. 320c (445)

DIJON, FRANCE

208. Heirs of M. Clémendot — Letters
209. Archives Municipales — Mozartiana

DONAUESCHINGEN, GERMANY

210. Hofbibliothek (1987) — Music: Contemporary copy K. 492, 555, etc. Letters

DRESDEN, GERMANY

211.	Heirs of Dr. Julius Reitz	Music: Instrumental (?)
212.	Saxon State Library (1987)	Music: K. 73w, etc. Mozartiana

EISENSTADT, AUSTRIA

213.	Esterhazy Castle Archive	Mozartiana

EINSIEDELN, SWITZERLAND

214.	Benediktinerkloster (1987)	Music: K. 297 (sketch)

ERLANGEN, GERMANY

215.	Bibliothek	Mozartiana

ERLAU, HUNGARY

216.	Heirs of J. L. Pyrker von Felsö-Ör (1975)	Letters

FELLBACH bei STUTTGART, GERMANY

217.	Frau Ruth Weiss (1975)	Letters

FLORENCE, ITALY

218.	Archivo di Stato	Mozartiana
219.	Biblioteca Horace de Landau (also London?)	Music: K. 293e
220.	Conservatorio di Musica "Luigi Cherubini" (1987)	Music: K. 492, early copy
221.	Gisella Selden Goth, or heirs	Music: K. 42b
222.	Frau Maria Hummel (1975)	Music: K. 176 (partial) Letters

FORLI, ITALY

223.	Biblioteca Communale (1975)	Letters

FRANKFURT, GERMANY

224.	Heirs of C. A. André	Music (?)
225.	Heirs of Jul. André	Music (?)
226.	Heinrich Eisemann	Music
227.	Stadt Bibliothek (1975)	Letters

FREISING, GERMANY

228.	Bibliothek	Mozartiana

FULDA, GERMANY

229.	Hessische Landesbibliothek (Parts of the André and Henkel collections, formerly at Fulda, are now in the Library of Congress, Washington, D.C.)	Music

GARMISCH-PARTENKIRCHEN, GERMANY

230.	Heirs of Richard Strauss (1975)	Letters

GENEVA, SWITZERLAND

231.	Bibliothèque de l'Université	Mozartiana
232.	Martin Bodmer	Music: K. 168, etc.
233.	Aloys Mooser	Mozartiana

GLASGOW, SCOTLAND

234.	University Library and Gallery (1975)	Letters, Portrait Mozartiana

GLOUSTERSHIRE, ENGLAND

235.	Mr. T. G. Odling (1987)	Music: K. 386 (partial)

GOTTWEIG MONASTERY, AUSTRIA

236.	Bibliothek, including part of Aloys Fuchs Collection (1987)	Music: K. 166f Mozartiana

GRAZ, AUSTRIA

237.	Alfred Doppler Nachlass	Music

238. Professor H. Federhofer   Music: K. 459,
                                             cadenza
239. Landeskonservatorium, including   Music: K. 173c
      Lannoy Collection   (80), etc.

THE HAGUE, NETHERLANDS

240. Gemeente Museum (1975)   Music: K. 32
                                             Letters, etc.
241. Konklijk Huis-Archief (1975)   Letters
242. Herman Jeurisson   Mozartiana
243. Baron von Lucius   Music: 374d (376)

HALTENSBERGSTETTIN, GERMANY

244. Bibliothek   Mozartiana

HAMBURG, GERMANY

245. Frl. Eva Müller   Music: 246c (288)
246. University Theatre Collection   Mozartiana
      (1975)   Letters

HANOVER, GERMANY

247. Stadtbibliothek (Kestner   Music: K. 294
      Collection) (1975)   Letters

HARBURG, GERMANY

248. Bibliothek   Mozartiana

HEIDELBERG, GERMANY

249. H.   Music: K. 185, etc.

HERZOGENBURG, AUSTRIA

250. Bibliothek   Mozartiana

HOLLYWOOD, CALIFORNIA, U.S.A.

251. Karl Klein (1942)   Music:
                                             K. 90a (116)

HOVE, SUSSEX, ENGLAND
252. J. E. Kite   Music: K. 320b
                                       (single leaf)

INGOLSTADT, GERMANY
253. Emerich Collection   Mozartiana

ITHACA, NEW YORK, U.S.A.
254. Cornell University Library (1987) Music: K. 626/36,
                                        44 (sketch)

JERUSALEM, ISRAEL
255. National Library (1987)   Music: K. 430
                                        (424a) (sketch)
                                        Letters

JESI, ITALY
256. Biblioteca Communale (1975)   Letters

KARLSBAD, CZECHOSLOVAKIA (KARLOVY, VARY)
257. State Archive (1975)   Letters

KASSEL, GERMANY
258. Speyer Collection   Mozartiana
     (Kassel is the location of the   (see #433)
     principal office of Bärenreiter,
     publisher of NMA.)

KESZTHELEY, HUNGARY
259. Országos Széchényi Könyvtár   Mozartiana

KLAGENFURT, AUSTRIA
260. Professor Robert Keldorfer   Music: K. 375f
                                        (153), 621a
                                        (Anhang 245)

261. Heirs of Viktor Mayerhofer   Music:
     von Grünbünel   K. 284b (309)

KLOSTERNEUBURG, AUSTRIA
262. Monastery Library   Mozartiana

KØBENHAVN (COPENHAGEN), DENMARK
263. Kongelige Biblioteket (1975)   Letters

KÖNIGSBERG, GERMANY (now Kaliningrad, U.S.S.R.)
264. Staats und Universitäts Bibliothek   Mozartiana
     (Gotthold Collection)
265. Heirs of Count Paul von Waldersee   Mozartiana

KREMSMÜNSTER, AUSTRIA
266. Monastery Library   Music: K. 436,
                                                438, etc.

KROMĚŘÍŽ (KREMSIER), CZECHOSLOVAKIA
267. Statni Zamek (1987)   Music: K. 590
                                                (fragment)

KRUMLOV ČESKÝ, CZECHOSLOVAKIA (near Linz, Austria)
268. Krumlov-Schwarzenberg Collection   Mozartiana

KRUMPENDORF, CARINTHIA, GERMANY
269. J. A. Streicher family (1975)   Letters

KUTTENBERG, GERMANY
270. Bibliothek   Mozartiana

LAIBACH, GERMANY
271. Philharmonische Gesellschaft   Music: K. 332,
     (1888)   etc.

LAMBACH, AUSTRIA
272. Benediktiner Stift Bibliothek   Music: K. 45a, etc.
                                                Mozartiana

LANDAU, GERMANY
273. Heirs of A. Zahn — Letters

LEIPZIG, GERMANY
274. Heirs of Boerner Antiquariat — Music: K. 626/b/14, 43
275. Heirs of A. Cranz, publisher — Mozartiana
276. Heirs of H. Hartung — Music: K. 626/b/5, etc.
277. H. Hinrichson (Peters) — Mozartiana, etc.
278. Kippenberg — Mozartiana
279. Heirs of O. A. Schul — Music: K. 186i (91), 626/b/9, 10
280. Heirs of List & Francke — Music: K. 626/b/3, 6, etc. Mozartiana
281. Stadt Bibliothek — Music: K. 3, etc
282. Stadt Musikbibliothek — Mozartiana Portrait
283. Universitätsbibliothek (1987) — Music: K. 488c (fragment)
284. Professor Wach — Music: K. 312 (?)
285. Herr A. Weigel — Mozartiana

LENINGRAD, U.S.S.R.
286. Institute for Theatre, Music, and Cinematography — Early copies
287. Pushkin House — Music: Sketches(?)
288. State Public Library, M. E. Saltykow-Schteschedrin (1975) — Music: K. 241, 263, 548 Letters

LIESTAL, SWITZERLAND
289. Mario Uzielli — Music: K. 553, 557

LILLE, FRANCE
290. Bibliothèque Municipale (1975)   Letters

LINKÖPING, SWEDEN
291. Stiftsbiblioteket (1975)   Letters

LINZ, AUSTRIA
292. Biblio-Landesmuseum   Music: K. 125d
                                           (149), 125f (151)
                                           Mozartiana

LISBON, PORTUGAL
293. Biblioteca de Ajuda (1987)   Letters

LIVERPOOL, ENGLAND
294. Heirs of A. George Kurtz (1888)   Mozartiana

LLANDUDNO, WALES, U.K.
295. William Barrow   Music: K. 386
                                           (partial)

LONDON, ONTARIO, CANADA
296. University of West. Ontario   Music: K. 386
     Library (1987)   (fragment)

LONDON, ENGLAND
297. Eva Albermann (1955)   Mozartiana
298. Heirs of Sterndale Bennett   Music: K. 386b
                                           (single leaf)
299. British Library (formerly British   Music: K. 20, etc.
     Museum), including Hirsch   Letters
     Collection, Zweig Collection, etc.)   Mozartiana
     (1987)
300. Heirs of S. L. Courtauld   Letters
     (formerly in Rhodesia)   Mozartiana
301. Clifford Curzon (1964)   Music: K. 516
                                           (partial)
302. W. J. M. Dennis (1975)   Letters

303.	Heinrich Eisemann Collection (1975)	Letters
304.	Heirs of John Ella	Mozartiana
305.	Heirs of Otto Goldschmidt (formerly in Berlin)	Portrait Mozartiana
306.	Heirs of Otto Haas (including former Leo Liepmannsohn Collection, Berlin)	Letters Mozartiana
307.	Peter Hatvany (1975)	Letters
308.	Mrs. Inge Henderson (1964)	Music: K. 353
309.	Leonard Hyman (1956)	Music: K. 555 (partial), 562
310.	Heirs of H. J. Laufer	Mozartiana
311.	Heirs of Lamson Locker	Mozartiana
312.	Dr. Max Mannheim (1964)	Music: K. 452c (Anh. 65)
313.	Heirs of W. Westley Manning (1964)	Music: K. 492 (No. 8) (sketch)
314.	Heirs of Jul. Marshall	Mozartiana
315.	E. W. H. Meyerstein	Mozartiana
316.	Neumann, W. (1964)	626a (partial)
317.	Novello & Company (1964)	Music: K. 562a Mozartiana
318.	Heirs of C. B. Oldman (1975)	Mozartiana
319.	Heirs of William Pole	Mozartiana
320.	Heirs of Harriet Plowden (probably all in British Library)	Mozartiana
321.	Heirs of Alberto Randegger	Mozartiana
322.	William Reeves (1955)	Music: K. 364 (cadenza)
323.	Albi Rosenthal (1986)	Music Letters
324.	Royal College of Music (1979)	Music: K. 491 Letters
325.	Royal College of Surgeons (1987)	Music: K. 386 (partial)

326. Jacques Samuel (1975)   Letters
327. Dr. Curt Sluzewski (1975)   Music: K. 300a
                                        (partial)
                                        Letters
328. Heirs of W. Barclay Squire   Mozartiana

LOS ANGELES, CALIFORNIA, U.S.A.
329. Heirs of Gregor Piatigorski   Music: K. 405

LUND, SWEDEN
330. University Library   Music

MAGDEBURG, GERMANY
331. Kaiser Friedrich Museum   Music: K. 574
                                        (lost)

MAINZ, GERMANY
332. Dr. H. Federhofer   Music: K. 459
                                        (cadenza?)
333. Heirs of Frau Emil Konig (1900)   Portrait
334. Municipal Library   Mozartiana

MANCHESTER, ENGLAND
335. Library   Mozartiana

MANNHEIM, GERMANY
336. Heirs of K. Ferd. Heckel   Mozartiana
337. Museum of the Castle   Mozartiana
338. Städtische Reiss Museum   Mozartiana
339. Town Archives   Mozartiana

MARBURG, GERMANY
340. Westdeutsche Bibliothek   Music: K. 386
                                        (partial)
                                        Mozartiana

341. In 1962 J. A. Stargardt auctioned a
     letter of Mozart, formerly in the

collection of Sophie Heckel-
Lichtenberger

MARIEMONT, BELGIUM
342. Museum (1975)   Letters

MELK, AUSTRIA
343. Bibliothek   Mozartiana

MILAN, ITALY
344. Civica Raccolta Stampe Bartarelli   Mozartiana
345. Conservatorio Giuseppe Verdi   Music: K. 246, etc.

MODENA, ITALY
346. Biblioteca Estense (1987)   Music: K. 492
                                             (sketches)
                                             Mozartiana

MUNICH, GERMANY
347. Bayerische Staatsbibliothek (1975)   Music: eight
                                             manuscripts
                                             Letters
348. Bayerische Verwaltung der   Mozartiana
      Schlösser, Garten und Seen
349. Heirs of T. von Dürnitz   Mozartiana
350. Heirs of Dr. Halm   Mozartiana
351. Staatliche Graphische Sammlung   Mozartiana
352. Stadtmuseum   Mozartiana
353. Theater Museum   Mozartiana
354. Professor Otto Winkler (1987)   Music: K. 560
                                             (see #430)

MÜNSTER, GERMANY
355. Bibliothek   Music:
                                             Instrumental
                                             Mozartiana

NANTES, FRANCE
356. Bibliothèque Municipale (1975)   Letters

NAPLES, ITALY
357. Biblioteca del Conservatorio   Mozartiana

NÄS, SWEDEN
358. Mrs. Silverstolpe (1975)   Letters
                                             Mozartiana

NEUBURG ON THE DANUBE, GERMANY
359. Count Hans Huyn (1964)   Music: K. 424a
                                             (430) (sketch)

NEUHAUS, CZECHOSLOVAKIA
360. Gräflich Czernisches Archiv (1975)   Music: K. 269b
                                             Letters

NEW YORK, NEW YORK, U.S.A.
361. Antonio Almeida, c/o Belwin   Music:
     Mills, publisher   K. 331
                                             (partial)
362. Ellery O. Anderson   Mozartiana
363. Pierre Baior (1973)   Music: K. 209
364. John Bass (1975)   Letters
365. Galerie St. Etienne   Music?
366. Mrs. Y. Geist   Music: Cadenzas,
                                             K. 595
367. Paul Gottschalk   Mozartiana
368. Yrsa Hein   Mozartiana
369. Mrs. Walter Hinrichson, c/o   Mozartiana
     C. F. Peters
370. Otto Kallir   Letters
371. Heirs of R. F. Kallir   Music: K. 417b,
     (Dr. Kallir, 1896–1987, discussed   etc.
     his adventures as a collector in
     Autographensammler

lebenslänglich, Zurich: Atlantis,
1977.)

372.	Robert O. Lehman	Music? Mozartiana
373.	Metropolitan Opera Guild, Lincoln Center (1987)	Letters
374.	Pierpont Morgan Library (includes prestigious Cary and Heinmann Collections) (1987)	Music: K. 385, 486, 467, 537, etc. Letters
375.	New York Public Library, Lincoln Center (1987)	Music: K. 296, 318, etc., many microfilms
376.	S. Orlinck	Music?
377.	O. H. Ranschberg	Music: K. 536
378.	Heirs of Felix Salzer-Wittgenstein	Letters
379.	Walter Schatzki, dealer	Music: K. 494, Mozartiana
380.	Heirs of Arturo Toscanini (1987)	Letters, Mozartiana
381.	Dr. Herman Vollmer	Music: K. 417 b (partial)
382.	E. Weyhe, dealer	Music: K. 125a, etc.
383.	Elisabeth Firestone Willis (1975)	Letters

NIEDERLINSBACH, SWITZERLAND

384.	Frau Maja von Arx (1964)	Music: K. 164, 530

NUREMBURG, GERMANY

385.	Library of the National Museum (1975)	Letters

OAKLAND, CALIFORNIA, U.S.A.

386.	Mills College Library (1987)	Music: K. 67 (41h), etc.

ODENSE, DENMARK

387.	Town Archive	Music: K. 452, etc.

OFFENBACH, GERMANY

388. André family and Frau F. André   Letters
     (1975)
389. Aug. André and family   Mozartiana
390. Stadtarkiv (1975)   Letters

OLMÜTZ, CZECHOSLOVAKIA
391. Bibliothek   Mozartiana

OXFORD, ENGLAND
392. Bodleian Library (1987)   Music: K. 312
                                              (590d)
393. Mrs. Margaret Deneke (1964)   Music: K. 590d

PARIS, FRANCE
394. Bibliothèque du Conservatoire   Music: K. 338
     de Musique (including Malherbe   (partial)
     and other collections) (1964)   Letters
395. Bibliothèque Nationale (1987)   Music: K. 527, etc.
                                              Letters
                                              Portraits
396. Bibliothèque de l'Opéra   Portraits, etc.
397. Carnavalet Museum   Portraits, etc.
398. Heirs of M. Charavay   Music: K. 626b/11
399. Heirs of Alfred Cortot   Music (?)
                                              Letters
                                              Portrait
400. Heirs of H. Darel   Music: K. 626b/
                                              21, 22, 41
401. Heirs of Alfred Dupont (1964)   Music: K. 73x
402. Roger de Garate (1975)   Letters
403. Heirs of François Habeneck   Mozartiana
404. Institut de France (1987)   Music: K. 141a
     (discussed in *Bulletin de la société*   (161), 189c (237),
     des études mozartienne, 1930)   213b (215), 214,
                                              239, 240b (188),
                                              248, 249, 250a,
                                              (101), 285e (315)

405.	Maurice Lehman (1975)	Letters
406.	Louvre Museum	Portraits
407.	André Meyer	Portrait
408.	Mickiewicz Museum (1987)	Music: K. 458
409.	Marc Pincherle	Music: K. 320 (364) (partial)
410.	Pleyel Collection (?)	Music: K. 516, Mozartiana (partial)
411.	Heirs of J. G. Prod'homme	Music: K. 626b/2
412.	Heirs of Henri Prunières	Mozartiana

PHILADELPHIA, PENNSYLVANIA, U.S.A.

413.	Curtis Institute of Music	Music: K. 73s (85)
414.	Mrs. Meyer Davis	Music: K. Anh. 17 (by Ligniville?)
415.	Historical Society (1975)	Music: K. 246 (sketch)

POUGHKEEPSIE, NEW YORK, U.S.A.

416.	Vassar College	Mozartiana

PRAGUE, CZECHOSLOVAKIA

417.	Betramka Museum	Mozartiana
418.	Bohemian Casanova Archives	Excerpt of K. 527?
419.	Clementinium Library (1975)	Music: K. 626b/38
420.	Heirs of Fritz Donebaur	Mozartiana, Portrait
421.	Hudební oddoleni Universitni (1975)	Letters
422.	Municipal Archives	Mozartiana
423.	National Museum (1975)	Letters
424.	National Central Archives	Mozartiana
425.	National Museum (1987)	Music: K. 572 (partial)
426.	National Theatre	Mozartiana

PRINCETON, NEW JERSEY, U.S.A.

427. William Scheide Collection (1987)   Music: K. 332
                                                    (partial)
                                                    Mozartiana

REGENSBURG, GERMANY

428. Bibliothek   Mozartiana
429. Frau Maria Vogel   Portrait
430. Otto Winkler (1964)   Music: K. 538
                                                    (partial)
                                                    (see #354)

REICHERSBERG, GERMANY

431. Bibliothek   Mozartiana

RHEINFELDEN, GERMANY

432. Frau Amalia Haas   Music: K. 492
                                                    (partial)

RIDGEHURST, ENGLAND

433. Heirs of Edward Speyer   Mozartiana?
                                                    (K. 469?)
                                                    (see #258)

ROCHESTER, NEW YORK, U.S.A.

434. Sibley Memorial Library (1987)   Music: K. 386
                                                    (partial)

SAINT GALL, SWITZERLAND

435. C. Buzzi (1975)   Letters

ST. LOUIS, MISSOURI, U.S.A.

436. Moldenauer Archive of Washington   Music
     University   Letters

SALZBURG, AUSTRIA

437. Alfred Heidl Collection   Mozartiana
438. Landesarchiv (1975)   Letters

439. Liedertafel (1975)	Letters
440. Internationale Stiftung Mozarteum (1987) Repository of unique collection and transmitter of living traditions. Its story has been profiled by Rudolph Angermüller and Geza Rech: *Hundert Jahre Internationale Stiftung Mozarteum,* 230 pp. illus. Kassel: Bärenreiter, 1980.	Music: K. 331, etc. Letters Mozartiana Portraits
441. Museum Carolino-Augusteum (1987)	Letters
442. Regierungsarchiv	Letters
443. Residenz	Mozartiana
444. Saint Peters Stift (1987)	Music
445. Städtische Museum	Letters
446. Musikwissenschaftliches Institut der Universität (including Deutsch Collection)	Mozartiana
447. Maria am Plain Cathedral	Mozartiana (?)

SCHLÄGL, AUSTRIA

448. Prämonstratenser Stift	Mozartiana

SEATTLE, WASHINGTON, U.S.A.

449. Dr. Eric Offenbacher (successors)	Mozartiana

SEITENSTEIN, AUSTRIA

450. Bibliothek	Mozartiana

SIGMARINGEN, GERMANY

451. Bibliothek	Mozartiana

SPEAN LODGE, ENGLAND

452. G. B. Davy	Portrait

SPOKANE, WASHINGTON, U.S.A.

453. Moldenauer Archive (See St. Louis, Missouri)	Portrait

STAMS, AUSTRIA
454. Zisterzienserschrift   Mozartiana

STANFORD, CALIFORNIA, U.S.A.
455. Stanford University Library (1987)   Music: K. 178
                                           (sketch), etc.

STOCKHOLM, SWEDEN
456. Freemason Archive   Music: K. 471
                                           (sketch?)
457. Royal Library (1987)   Music: K. 621,
                                           (sketches), etc.
458. Stiftelsen Musikkulturen   Music: K. 332
     (Rudolf Nydahl) (1975)   (partial), etc.

STUTTGART, GERMANY
459. E. Hörner   Mozartiana

TARTU, ESTONIA
460. University Library (1975)   Letters

THUN, SWITZERLAND
461. F. K. Hunziker (1964)   Music: K. 483, 484

TOKYO, JAPAN
462. Bin Ebisawa (1987)   Music: K. 386
                                           (partial), etc.
463. Mayeda Foundation   Music: K. 516
                                           (partial), etc.

TSCHENSTOCKAU, POLAND
464. Paulinenkloster   Music

TÜBINGEN, GERMANY
465. Robert Alexander Bohnke (1964)   Music: K. 46d, 46e
466. E. Kauffmann   Music: K. 295a
                                           (partial)

467. Universitätsbibliothek — Music: K. 384
(partial)

TUTZING, GERMANY

458. Hans Schneider (Antiquariat) (1975) — Letters
Mozartiana (First
Editions, etc.)

UPSALA, SWEDEN

469. University Library (1987)
Repository of many important
sketches (discussed in *Musical
Quarterly* 27 (1941): 343–355
by Richard Engländer, other
Engländer; other Swedish
collections are discussed by Alfred
Orel and Gösta Morin). — Music: K. 619, 620
621 (sketches)
Mozartiana

VERSAILLES, FRANCE

470. Museum of Versailles — Mozartiana

VIENNA, AUSTRIA

471. Bibliothek der Gesellschaft der
Musikfreunde — Music:
K. 550, etc.
Letters

472. Heirs of Oscar Bondy — Letters

473. Burgtheater — Mozartiana

474. Madame von Chavanne-Kantor — Mozartiana

475. Gesellschaft der Musikverein (1975) — Mozartiana

476. Gilhofer & Ranschburg (dealers) — Music: K.
626b/12, etc.

477. Heirs of J. Grafe — Letters

478. Graphische Sammlung, Albertina — Mozartiana

479. V. A. Heck (or successor) — Music: K.
626b/18, etc.
Mozartiana

480. H. Hinterberger — Mozartiana

481. Historische Museum der Stadt
(1975) — Letters
Portraits

482.	Antony van Hoboken (heirs)	Mozartiana
483.	Heirs of Otto Jahn	Letters Mozartiana
484.	Professor Hans Kahn	Mozartiana
485.	Kärntnertor Theater	Mozartiana
486.	Heirs of Viktor Keldorfer	Music: K. 621a
487.	Kunsthistorische Museum	Mozartiana
488.	George S. Michael	Letters
489.	Österreichische Nationalmuseum (Nationalbibliothek) (1987)	Music: K. 626, etc. Letters Mozartiana
491.	Heirs of Maestro Ludwig Rotter	Music: K. 356 (?)
492.	Heirs of Dr. K. R. (In 1987 Symphonies 22–30 were sold to an anonymous collector, through Sotheby.)	Mozartiana
493.	Heirs of Ludwig Schiedermair (see also #179)	Letters
494.	Madame Ilse Schmitzer-Burkhard	Mozartiana
495.	Michael George Schnitzler (1975)	Letters
496.	Schönbrunn Palace	Mozartiana
497.	Stadtbibliothek (1987)	Music: K. 442 (partial), etc. Letters
498.	Heirs of Emil Streicher (1937)	Music: K. 515 (?)
499.	Theater auf der Wieden	Mozartiana
500.	Waisenhauskirche	Mozartiana
501.	Heirs of Count Victor Wimpfen	Music: K. 579 (?)
502.	Winterreitschule	Mozartiana
503.	(Also many of Mozart's Viennese abodes have Mozartiana. See #660.)	

WALDBURG-ZEIL, AUSTRIA

504.	Bibliothek	Mozartiana

WARSAW, POLAND

505.	Chopin Gesellschaft	Music: K. 478, etc.

WASHINGTON, D.C., U.S.A.

506. Library of Congress (1987) Music: K. 370a
     (including former Henckel (361), 219, etc.
     Collection)

WEIMAR, GERMANY

507. Goethe Archiv (1964) Music: K. 385f
                           (396)

508. Landesbibliothek (1964) Music: K. 450
                              Mozartiana

WELS, AUSTRIA

509. Herr Drexler Music: K. 196?

WINDSOR, ENGLAND

510. Royal Collection (1964) Music: K. 35, etc.

WINTERTHUR, SWITZERLAND

511. Heirs of Dr. Werner Reinhart Music: K. 621b
                                   (partial)

ZURICH, SWITZERLAND

512. Max Reis (1975) Music: K. 271a
                      Letters

513. Dr. G. Walter (1964) Music: K. 384b
514. Zentralbibliothek Music: K. 33b, etc.

SWITZERLAND

515. Dr. Arthur Wilheim Music: K. 525

3.
MOZART'S WRITINGS

Letters

Beginning with Mozart's widow Constanze—and including his sister Nannerl (Marianne) and his two sons Carl Thomas and Franz Xavier (Wolfgang the Younger)—each person who has had anything to do with the remarkable letters of members of three generations of the Mozart family has had a particular and personal point of view. Today, the members of the family and persons who knew them have vanished, and our primary aim remains to understand Mozart and his music, along with his times, essentially apart from the generations of interpretations which lie between Mozart and ourselves. Thus, while much of the heroic work of Jahn and Köchel with regard to the world of Mozart and his works is still valid—as are contributions of Nohl, Wurzbach, and in this century Wyzewa and Saint-Foix, Deutsch, King, and Einstein—the beginning of a full understanding of the extraordinary character of the letters of the Mozart family came with the 1914 edition of 352 letters edited by Ludwig Schiedermair. The 1942 edition of 436 letters edited by Erich H. Müller von Asov was enriched by many facsimiles and by a number of amplifications and corrections. Although Henri de Curzon's corrected 1955 edition in French of 367 letters is useful, it does not print every letter completely, and this editorial decision inevitably forces the reader to use a German text which is complete (and sometimes more accurate), even when this means reading long passages which may be irrelevant to one's immediate needs in the exemplary Bauer/

Deutsch/ Eibl German edition. Our recommendation for readers whose native language is English is to turn first to Emily Anderson's practical edition of 616 letters (some unfortunately excerpted), in three successive editions, of 1938, 1966, 1985—with various editorial assistance: first Cecil Bernard Oldman; then Alexander Hyatt King and Monica Carolan; and finally Stanley Sadie and Fiona Smart. Footnotes in the Anderson editions are conveniently at the bottom of the page. While numerous other compilations of Mozart letters have been published, they are all superseded by Bauer/Deutsch/Eibl, to whose illuminating work in seven volumes all readers with German are directed. (Despite the fact that inevitably a few more letters are bound to be found, and a few more clarifications will be made, the unique Bauer/Deutsch/Eibl edition will remain definitive for some time.)

In addition to including 1450 letters by three generations of Mozarts written 1755–1857, the Bauer/Deutsch/Eibl edition (published 1962–1975) in four volumes of text and three volumes of notes and indexes, includes for convenience a concordance with the Anderson (second edition), and the Asov and Schiedermair editions. The 1985 Anderson edition courteously returns the compliment with a concordance of its own, but its general apparatus and completeness remains far less inclusive than that of the Bauer/Deutsch/Eibl.

Readers primarily interested in Constanze may consult Arthur Schurig's monograph. Those concentrating on Leopold Mozart (including Leopold's relationship with his daughter Nannerl) will find the Deutsch and Paumgartner volume contains valuable material on the period 1781–1787. A few letters have been discovered since 1975. They are reported in the journals listed in Appendix IV. In particular the *Mozart Jahrbuch* and *Mitteilungen der ISM* make every effort to keep up to date.

Documents

The documents of Mozart's life which are not letters include those concerned with various testamentary matters, discussed in Deutsch (#610). Others center around the teaching Mozart did apparently reluctantly (of theory and composition) of Barbara von Ployer, Thomas Attwood, Maximilian Stadler's niece Katherina (?), and others (and also Mozart's own lessons with his father, and Padre Martini). There are various manuscripts which are evidence, and there are various commentaries on the manuscripts.

Although we have the testimony of Grétry that Mozart's extraordinarily fluid sight-reading was not always accurate, and we have the evidence that in 1770 in Italy Mozart's memory of a composition was not always infallible, we also know of innumerable instances when he proved how unique his musicianship was. The information reviewed by Cecil Bernard Oldman certainly indicates Mozart was a good teacher of Thomas Attwood in 1786 (also see Attwood studies in NMA)—and the evidence with regard to his teaching of Barbara von Ployer also is very positive.

A document discussed by Robert Lach is basic to understanding Mozart's teaching. Apparently, about 1815 Tobias Haslinger and S. A. Steiner of Vienna printed a text ("Generalbassschule") attributed to Mozart which had been marketed by Heydenreich (in manuscript) as early as 1796 (at least tacitly with the approval of Constanze, and Abbé Maximilian Stadler, a good friend of the Mozarts who was her main musical advisor concerning remaining Mozart manuscripts). And in 1822 Schüppelsche of Berlin followed with another edition of the same material, the source of which is still open to discussion.

Somewhat later the Viennese version was translated into English by Samuel Goedbé (a member of the Thomas Attwood circle?); another English version of this "Generalbassschule" was made by Mary Sabilla Novello, and quite possibly this derives from one of the documents passing from Constanze to the Novellos during their brief but very warm visit to Salzburg in 1829. (At this time neither document is accepted as entirely by Mozart by a consensus of Mozart scholars.)

4.
BIBLIOGRAPHY

Section 4 presents publications in pertinent categories of subjects involving the person and music of Mozart; many of them provide additional bibliographies.

The first part lists works providing basic information for Mozart researchers. The initial entries are general works; the later entries list important specialized references, including those on writings (letters) and teaching. Noted particularly are the Keller, Schneider and Algatzy, and Angermüller volumes of bibliography, the Köchel catalogue, the Einstein biography, the Deutsch documentary biography, the King essays, and the Bauer/Deutsch/Eibl edition of letters. (The excellent RILM annotated bibliography is continuing, but entries could be expanded by appropriate notation where a publication has an index; Mozart entries in the New York Public Library catalogue are another useful source.)

The second part is devoted to important background—historic and cultural, and musical.

The third part is devoted to biography—general, and specialized, including colleagues and contemporaries, family and friends, followers, Freemasons, illnesses and death. Because of the problems inherent in separating biography from discussion of the composer's music, readers are advised to make full use of the Index as well as the Table of Contents.

The fourth part is concerned with the music of Mozart—first generally, then including commentary on works, editions, publishers, sources, performance practice, comparisons where useful with other composers, Mozart's methods and procedures of composition; next Mozart's various categories of vocal compositions; finally, Mozart's various categories of instrumental compositions. The fifth part is devoted to films and videos, lists and commentary.

General Publications

516. Adkins, Cecil, and Allis Dickinson. *Doctoral Dissertations in Musicology.* 7th ed. Philadelphia: American Musicological Society. 1984. 545 pp. ML 128. M 8A43.

Includes listing of thirty-nine dissertations relating to Mozart, and others on Mozart's contemporaries (the most relevant of which are included). Index.

517. d'Amico, Silvio, ed. *Enciclopedia dello spettacolo.* Rome: Le Maschere, 1954–1962. 9 vols. Index.

Pertinent illustrated articles on Mozart and his major operas, and many related subjects.

518. Bachmann, Alberto. *An Encyclopedia of the Violin.* Translated by Frederick H. Martens; edited by Albert E. Wier. New York: D. Appleton, 1925. 470 pp. Da Capo Reprint. 1966. ML 800. B 13.

This resource is dated, but like Eitner (#527) contains information collected from many sources, and is still convenient, particularly for its listing of composer-violinists of Mozart's time. Index.

519. Bauer, Anton. *Opern und Operetten in Wien, 1629–1955.* Graz: Böhlhaus Nachf., 1955. 156 pp.

Useful listing of about 5,000 works; valuable supplement to Loewenberg (#537). Indexes of musicians, librettists, and chronology. See also: A. J. Weltner. *Mozarts Werk und die Wiener Hof Theater.* Vienna: Verlag Künst, 1896. Also: Otto Michtner. *Das Alte Burgtheater als Operbühne, 1778–1792.* Vienna: Bühlhaus Nachf., 1970. 556 pp. illus. ISBN: 3-205-03204-7. PN 2610 T5. Also: Mary Sue Morrow. "Concert Life in Vienna, 1780–1810." Ph.D. dissertation, Indiana University. 1985. 538 pp.

520. Baumann, Thomas. *North German Opera in the Age of Goethe.* Cambridge: Cambridge University Press, 1985. 444 pp. ISBN: 0-521-26027-2. 782.1'0943. ML 1729.

An excellent volume—showing relations of the north with Vienna, and discussing Mozart opera productions, and singers (some of whom worked with Mozart). Notes; bibliography; appendix; index.

521. Blum, Fred. *Music Monographs in Series.* New York: Scarecrow, 1964. 197 pp. ML 113.B63.

Lists over 250 series from about 30 countries. Source of forty monographs on Mozart in many languages (some are translations). Of varying quality, but Czechoslovakian, Hungarian, and Polish entries are worth considering. Index.

522. Brook, Barry S. *Thematic Catalogues in Music: An Annotated Bibliography.* Hillsdale, New York: Pendragon Press, 1972. 347 pp. illus. ISBN: 0-918728-02-9. ML 113.B 86.

A vital tool for Mozart research—particularly sources and comparisons, including over 1444 listings. Index. (A new edition is reported in preparation.)

See also: Barry S. Brook. Book Review. *Journal of the American Musicological Society,* 32-3 (Fall 1979): 549–555. A perceptive review of three thematic catalogues which detail valuable information on Mozart manuscripts and early editions, as well as a wealth of information on his contemporaries. Published by G. Henle of Munich (1971, 1975, 1976), these catalogues are of Klosterkirchen Weygarn, Tegernsee und Benediktbeuren; Benediktinerinnenabtei Frauenwöth und der Pfarrkirchen Indersdorf, Wasserburg am Inn und Bad Tölz; Oettingen-Wallerstein'schen Bibliothek Schloss Harburg.

Another basic tool for research on Mozart's contemporaries is: *The Symphony, 1720–1780, The Reference Volume.* Preface by Barry S. Brook. 750 pp. New York: Garland, 1986. ISBN: 0-8240-380-6. ML 128.055. See also: Hill (#1006).

523. Brook, Barry S., ed. *The Breitkopf Thematic Catalogue (1762–1787)*. New York: Dover, 1966. 80 pp. plus 888 double columns.

Although Breitkopf (and later, Härtel) published only a few works by Mozart during the composer's lifetime, this impeccably edited and presented reprint edition of the catalogue of manuscript and other copies of compositions by 18th century composers handled by the firm is an invaluable tool for comparative research. Expansive index.

524. Burney, Charles. *A General History of Music from the Earliest Ages to the Present Period*. London: T. Becket, 1776–1789. 2nd reprint edition with notes by Frank Mercer, New York: Harcourt Brace, 1935. Vol. I: 816 pp.; Vol. II: 1096 pp. illus. ML 159 B96. 1957.

Although Mozart and Haydn are only mentioned in this comprehensive work, the discussions of their contemporaries are revealing. Indexes. More valuable than *A General History of Science and Practice of Music* by Sir John Hawkins (London: Payne & Son, 1776. 5 vols.) because Burney was himself a professional musician. See also: Burney's *The Present State of Music in Germany, the Netherlands and United Provinces* (a facsimile of the 1775 London edition, New York: Broude Brothers, 1969).

For a 19th-century view of music history, see William Rockstro. *General History of Music*. London: Scribner & Welford, 1886. 525 pp.

525. Cowden, Robert H., compiler. *Concert and Opera Singers: A Bibliography of Biographical Materials*. Westport, Connecticut: Greenwood Press, 1965. 278 pp. ISBN: 0-313-24828-1. ML 128 B3 C7.

More than 700 singers are listed, including over 200 not found in Grove. (More comprehensive than Andrew Farkas: *Opera and Concert Singers*. 388 pp. New York: Garland, 1986.) Appendix; bibliography; index.

526. Duckles, Vincent. *Music Reference and Research Materials*. 3rd ed. New York: Free Press, 1974. 526 pp. ISBN: 0-02-907700-1. ML 113. D83.

Although Mozart is barely mentioned, this carefully annotated listing of guides provides accurate information for Mozart researchers. 4th edition, coedited by Michael A. Keller. New York: Schirmer Books, 1988. ISBN: 0-02-870390-1. Index.

527. Eitner, Robert, ed. *Biographisch-Bibliographisches Quellen-Lexicon für Musiker and Musikgelehrten der Christlichen Zeitrechnung bis der Mitte des 19. Jahrhunderts.* Leipzig: Breitkopf & Härtel, 1900–1904. 10 vols. Z 6811. E 363.

Primarily a bibliography, Eitner also contains biographical data and source information which is useful, although dated. Mozart is treated in volume 7, pp. 91–100. As Duckles states: "Eitner remains the basic tool for locating primary sources of music before 1800," and its bibliography of about 160 items on Mozart is still useful, as many items are not mentioned elsewhere. (RISM is intended to supersede Eitner eventually.)

528. Gerboth, Walter. *An Index to Musical Festschriften.* New York: Norton, 1969. 185 pp. ISBN: 393-02134-3. ML 128. M8 G9.

Includes sixty-eight articles devoted to Mozart and his music. Indexes. The following six Festschriften are particularly worth checking: *Britten* (A. Gishford, ed.), with D. Mitchell's article on *Così; Buszin* (J. Riedel, ed.), with G. Crawford's article on Kierkegaard; *Deutsch* (W. Gerstenberg, J. LaRue, W. Rehm, eds.), with C. B. Oldman's articles on C. Potter; *W. Fischer* (Hans Zingerle, ed.) with articles on iconography, Mozart's reading, form, etc.; *Oldman* (*Music Review* 25 [May 1964]: 85–157, with an article by King on Mozart and Kreusser (see also King #768); *Scheurleer* (A. J. de Mare and W. N. F. Sibmacher-Zijner, eds.), with C. B. Oldman's article on Attwood's studies with Mozart.

529. *Grand Larousse Encyclopédique en Dix Volumes.* Paris: Larousse, 1960–1964. illus. 10 vols.

Particularly important source for native-born French musicians and artists.

530.   Green, Richard. *Index to Composer Bibliographies.* Detroit:
       Information Coordinators, 1985. 76 pp. ISBN: 0-899990-
       025-9.

       Lists 57 bibliographies of Mozart, issued chronologically
       1868–1982. Nine most important are included in this
       volume. Index.

531.   Gribenski, Jean, ed. *French Language Dissertations in Music.*
       New York: Pendragon Press, 1979. 270 pp. ISBN: 0-
       018728-09-6. ML 128 L3 O7.

       Inventory of 438 dissertations, 5 on Mozart. Index.

532.   *Grosse Brockhaus.* Wiesbaden, 1953. 12 vols. illus.

       Particularly useful for German-born musicians and
       artists.
       See also: *Brockhaus-Musik.*
       Also: E. Heinzel. *Lexikon Historischer Ereignisse und
       Personen in Kunst, Literatur und Musik.* Vienna: Holinek,
       1956. 782 pp. illus.
       Also: E. Heinzel, *Lexikon der Kulturgeschichte in Literatur,
       Kunst, und Musik.* Vienna: Holinek, 1962. 493 pp. illus.

533.   Grout, Donald J. *A Short History of Opera.* 2nd ed. New York:
       Columbia University Press, 1965. 862 pp. ML 1700. G83.

       Revised from 1947 edition, an outstanding reference
       work. Discusses Mozart and his master operas, pp. 274–298.
       Extensive bibliography; notes; index. (A new edition is in
       press.)
       See also: Renate Brockpähler. *Handbuch zur Geschichte
       der Barokoper in Deutschland.* Emsdetten: Verlag Lechte, 1964.
       394 pp.*

534.   Hixon, Don L., and Don Hennessee. *Women in Music.*
       Metuchen, N.J.: Scarecrow, 1975. 347 pp. ISBN: 0-8108-
       0869-2. ML 105. H6.

       Particularly useful for information on some singers who
       worked with Mozart. Index.

535.   Laborde, Jean Benjamin de. *Essai sur la musique ancienne et
       moderne.* Paris: Onfroy, 1780. 4 vols. illus.

       Laborde (1734–1794) wrote a wide-ranging history of
       theory and practice, somewhat parallel to Burney (see
       #524), with an expansive dictionary section useful for its

notes on many French composers of Mozart's time and before.

536. LaRue, Jan. "Symphony I." *The New Grove Dictionary of Music and Musicians* 18, 438–453. London: Macmillan, 1980. ISBN: 0-333-23111-2. ML 100. N48.

Important survey of 18th-century symphonies in various centers. Excellent bibliography of 120 items. Forthcoming by LaRue: *A Catalogue of 18th-Century Symphonies.* Indiana University Press.

537. Loewenberg, Alfred. *Annals of Opera, 1597–1940.* 3rd ed. Totowa, N. J.: Rowman & Littlefield, 1970. 1756 double columns. ISBN: 87471-007-3. ML 102. O6 L6.

An invaluable chronicle, with summaries of performance history (including details on many operas Mozart saw, as well as his own). In addition to chronological entries for operas, there are four indexes and an introduction. (When he died in 1987, Harold Rosenthal was preparing a new edition, bringing the work up to 1981.) See also: Surian (#912).

538. Marco, Guy A. *Opera: A Resource and Information Guide.* New York: Garland, 1984. 373 pp. ISBN: 0-8240-8999-5. ML 128.04M28.

Useful annotations of 13 titles on Mozart (all listed below), plus a number of publications dealing with 18th-century opera. Indexes.

539. ———. *Information on Music: A Handbook of Reference Sources in European Languages.* Littleton, Colorado: Libraries Unlimited, 1975–1984–et seq. Vol. I: 164 pp.; Vol. II: 296 pp.; Vol. III: 519 pp. ISBN: 0-87287-096-0; 0-87287-141-X; 0-87287-401-X.. ML 113.M33 016.78.

Contents: Vol. I: Basic and universal sources; Vol. II: The Americas; Vol. III: Europe. Each volume has its own index. Annotated list of useful books. Designed to extend Duckles.

540. Mooser, Robert. *Opéras, intermezzos, ballets, cantates, oratories joués en Russie durant le XVIIIe siècle.* Geneva: Kundig,

1945. 173 pp. 2nd ed. Geneva: R. M. Kister, 1955. 183 pp.

Useful alphabetical list of works performed in various theatres, with some production data. More than 500 works—by Cimarosa, Galuppi, Grétry, Mozart (2), Paisiello (among many other Russian and foreign composers)—are listed. Footnotes; bibliography; index.

541. Schaal, Richard. *Verzeichnis musikwissenschaftlicher Dissertationen.* Kassel: Bärenreiter, 1963. 91 pp. ML 128. M 853.

A few Mozart entries are included in this listing of 2819 German language dissertations to 1960; there is a supplement covering 1961–1970. Index.

542. Sheehy, Eugene. *Guide to Reference Books* (10th ed.). Chicago and London: American Library Association, 1986. 1560 pp. ISBN: 0-8389-0390-8. Z 1035. I. S43.

Valuable source book for researchers in many fields, including the humanities. Index.

543. Sonneck, Oscar G. T., compiler. *U.S. Library of Congress. Music Division. Catalogue of Opera Librettos Printed Before 1800.* Washington, D.C.: Government Printing Office, 1914. 2 vols. (Reprint New York: Burt Franklin, 1967; New York: Johnson Reprint, 1970.) IOM ML136 U55 C45.

Vol. I, title catalogue, with notes; Vol. II, author list, composer list, aria index. Including Mozart's major works, as well as many works by his contemporaries.

544. Stowell, Robin. *Violin Technique and Practice in the Late 18th and Early 19th Centuries.* London: Cambridge University Press, 1985. 411 pp. illus. ISBN: 0-521-232791. MT Z 62.

Includes valuable background on what string procedures were open to 18th-century composers. Index.

545. Tyrrell, John, and Rosemary Wise. *A Guide to International Congress Reports in Musicology, 1900–1975.* New York: Garland, 1979. 353 pp. ISBN: 0-8240-9839-0. ML 113 T95.

This valuable compilation of about 10,000 papers (the remarkable diversity of which makes representative selection and evaluation difficult) identifies place, title, series, sponsor, author, editor, and subject. Summary of the following congresses all note important articles on Mozart: G. Abraham, et al., eds. "Siebenten internationalen musikwissenschaftlichen Kongress," Cologne, 1958 (Kassel: Bärenreiter, 1959); P. Eckstein (for Union of Czechoslovak Composers, Prague), "Internationale Konferenz über des Leben und Werk Mozarts, 1956"; F. Giegling, ed. "Bericht über den neunten Internationale Kongress Salzburg, 1964" (Kassel: Bärenreiter, 1965–1966, 2 vols.); R. Pečman, ed. "Musica antiqua Brno, 1967"; G. Reichert and M. Just, eds. "Internationalen musikwissenschaftlichen Kongress Kassel, 1962" (Kassel: Bärenreiter, 1962); E. Schenk, ed. "Bericht über den Internationalen musikwissen-schaftlichen Kongress Wien, 1956" (Graz: Böhlhaus, 1958). Indexes. Also in preparation: Barry S. Brook and Sylvia Eversole, *Congress Reports in Music.*

Specialized References

546. Angermüller, Rudolph, and Otto Schneider. *Mozart-Bibliographie (bis 1970).* Kassel: Bärenreiter, 1976. 362 pp. ISBN: 3-7618-0516-0.

Because the Salzburg Mozarteum is a great center of Mozart studies, it is fitting that Professor Angermüller direct this important series of bibliographies, and although one could use more bibliographical facts per entry, there are many reasons to be grateful for this continuing series of listings: the person, subject, and work indexes (and the addenda and errata) make these volumes extremely useful. 6398 entries are alphabetical by author, listing title, publisher, year; not given for books are the number of pages, illustrations, appendixes, bibliography, notes, indexes. Contains many items in previous *Mozart Jahrbuch* bibliographies, in Schneider and Algatzy; subsequent volumes (#547, #548) add items listed in A. Mandelli and A. Zedda. "Bibliographica Mozartiana," Citta di Milano 72

(1955): 718–755, and Ottmar Wessely. "Ergänzungen zur Bibliographie des Mozart-Schriftums." *Studien zur Musikwissenschaft* 29 (1987): 37–68. 6398 entries.

547. ———. *Mozart-Bibliographie 1971–1975.* Kassel: Bärenreiter, 1978. 68 pp. ISBN: 3-7618-0603-5.
699 entries. See above.

548. ———. *Mozart-Bibliographie 1976–1980.* Kassel: Bärenreiter, 1982. 175 pp. ISBN: 3-7618-0678-7.
1276 entries. See above.

549. Angermüller, Rudolph. "Wissenschaftliche Beiträge in der Mozarteum, 1952–1972." *Mitteilungen der ISM* 23, 3–4 (August 1975): 56–61.
An index of contributions to Mozart research.

550. ———. "Mozart Research since 1970." *Current Musicology* 23 (1977): 12–19.
Covers much of the same ground as above, in English. Important survey.
See also: Alfred Mann. "The Present State of Mozart Research." *Current Musicology* 1 (1965): 92–94. Reading this article, one realizes that over two decades later we have not progressed very much.

551. Angermüller, Rudolph, and Geza Rech, eds. *100 Jahre Internationale Salzburg Mozarteum.* Salzburg: ISM, 1980. 229 pp. illus. ISBN: 3-7618-0626-4.
A useful general history of early Salzburg Mozart performances and studies, with emphasis on the Mozarteum since 1880. Bibliography; no index.
See also: C. Haushalter. *Geschichte des Mozart-Verein.* Enfurt: Körner, 1856. 54 pp.

552. *L'Année mozartienne.* Paris: *La Revue Musicale,* 1956. 302 pp. illus.
A special number devoted mostly to France's honoring Mozart's relations with France, but also discussing other influences and travels (Austria, Germany, Italy, Switzerland,

Holland, Belgium, England); includes four articles on Mozart's technique and aesthetic. No index.

553. Blume, Friedrich, ed. *Die Musik in Geschichte und Gegenwart. Allegemeine Enzyklopädie der Musik.* Kassel: Bärenreiter, 1949– . 14 vols. and 2 vols. supplement. illus. ML 100. M92.

Volume 9 contains the discussion of the Mozart family (columns 689–842, with columns 698–839 devoted to Wolfgang). The main article is very useful, although it cannot replace Jahn, Wyzewa and Saint-Foix, or Einstein. The bibliography lists over 650 items (c. 75% in German, with a sprinkling of other languages).

554. Keller, Otto. *Wolfgang Amadeus Mozart: Bibliographie und Ikonographie.* Berlin: Pestel, 1927. 274 pp.

Despite indispensable contributions by Nissen (#632) and Jahn (#622) and many others, the Keller bibliography— organized from material of the G. Fr. Hagen archive (Munich) and other sources—was the first comprehensive work. (It included important bibliographies up to 1927.) Although Keller is now out of print, it has 4280 entries, compared to Schneider's 3871. (Keller is better for bibliography than for iconography; for iconography see Deutsch and Zenger [#26].) Of course Schneider lists a number of more recent publications, and includes a fine chronology, but Keller's presentation and subdivision make his volume still very useful.

555. Sadie, Stanley, ed. *The New Grove Dictionary of Music and Musicians.* London: Macmillan, 1980. 20 vols. ISBN: 0-333-23111-2 ML100N.48

Volume 12, pp. 675-755, is devoted to the Mozart family, mostly to Wolfgang. The articles are easier to read, stylistically as well as typographically, than those in *Musik in Geschichte und Gegenwart* noted above (#553). The bibliography is about 400 items (55% in German).

See also: Stanley Sadie. *The New Grove Mozart.* New York: Norton, 1983. 247 pp. illus. ISBN: 0-393-01680-3. A brief monograph based on the Grove article on Wolfgang with a number of pertinent corrections, amplifications, and revisions bringing the selected bibliography up to 1982. Work list; index.

Also: Stanley Sadie. *Mozart Symphonies*. London: BBC, 1986. 101 pp. Discussion of forty-four accepted symphonies and four doubtful ones.

556.   Schneider, Otto, and Anton Algatzy. *Mozart-Handbuch: Chronik-Werk-Bibliographie*. Vienna: Brüder Hollinek, 1962. 508 pp.

As noted above (under Keller, #554), a very valuable chronology and bibliography. 3871 entries. Index.

Commentary

Letters (Editions)

557.   Anderson, Emily. *The Letters of Mozart and His Family*. 3rd ed. edited by Stanley Sadie and Fiona Smart. New York: Norton, 1985 (and London: Macmillan). 1038 pp. illus. Notes, bibliography, index. ISBN: 0-393-02248-X. ML 410. M9A402. 2nd ed. editors: A. H. King and M. Carolan.

558.   Asov, Erich H. Müller von. *Mozart Briefe*. Berlin: Metzner, 1942. 3 vols. 1163 pp. illus. Notes; index. (In 1942 Asov and Metzner also issued a deluxe facsimile edition of selected Mozart letters, 1779-1791.)

559.   Bauer, Wilhelm; Otto Erich Deutsch; and Joseph Heinz Eibl, eds. *Mozart Briefe und Aufzeichnungen*. Kassel: Bärenreiter, 1962–1975. 7 vols. I–IV: 2328 pp. ISBN: 3-7618-0401-6; V–VI: 1392 pp. ISBN: 3-7618-0144-0; VII: 671 pp. ISBN: 3-7618-0145-9.

Volume I (1756–1776) was published by Flammarion of Paris in 1986 (448 pp.), edited and translated into French by Geneviève Geffroy.

560. Curzon, Henri de. *Lettres de Mozart*. Paris: Plon, 1955. 2 vols. 659 pp. Notes, index.

561. Deutsch, Otto Erich, and Bernhard Paumgartner. *Leopold Mozarts Briefe an seiner Tochter*. Salzburg: Pustet, 1936. 592 pp. illus.

    After Mozart moved to Vienna and Nannerl moved to Saint Gilgen, Leopold kept in close touch with his daughter by letter, informing her about many public and private matters, including what he learned about Mozart's activity in Vienna. Notes, index.

562. Hitze, Wilhelm. "Die Briefe F. X. Niemetscheks und der Marianne Mozart (Nannerl) an Breitkopf & Härtel." *Jahrbuch (Der Bär)* [1928]: 101–116. [Leipzig: Breitkopf & Härtel.]

    A record of some attempts to keep Mozart's name before the public.

563. Ortheil, Hanns-Josef. *Mozart im Innern seiner Sprachen*. Frankfurt: Fischer, 1982. 222 pp.*

    Disscusses contents of Mozart's letters, 1777–1778, noting how he changed and matured.
    RILM: 1982—#541.

564. Rech, Geza. "Übersicht der seit 1956 neu aufgefunden Briefe." *Mitteilungen der ISM 15*, 3–4 (August 1967): 20–22.

    Discussion in tabular form of 24 newly found letters by Constanze Mozart Nissen, Carl Thomas Mozart, and Wolfgang Amadeus Mozart (the son), 1800–1858. For discussion of 25 letters Constanze wrote to J. J. André, 1800–1826, see *Mitteilungen der ISM 22*, 3–4 (August 1974). Other "new letters" are discussed in *Mozart Jahrbuch 16* (1968–1970): 211–241.

565. Schiedermair, Ludwig. *Die Briefe Wolfgang Amadeus Mozart und seiner Familie*. Munich: C. Müller, 1914. 5 vols. 1704 pp. illus. Notes; index.

566. Schurig, Arthur. *Konstanze Mozart. Briefe, Aufzeichnungen und Dokumente.* Dresden: Opal, 1922. 189 pp. illus.

At this writing, still the best single volume on Constanze. Index.
For a profile of Constanze in English, see Erna Schwerin. *Constanze Mozart.* New York: Friends of Mozart, 1981. 42 pp.

Teaching

567. Chesnut, John Head. "Mozart's Teaching of Intonation." *Journal of the American Musicological Society* 30 (Summer 1977): 254–271.

Concentrates on Mozart's teaching of Attwood. The Attwood manuscript in the British Library was published in NMA (Kassel: Bärenreiter, 1965). Chesnut's dissertation at the University of Chicago, 1976 (532 pp.) was entitled "Mozart as a Teacher of Elementary Music Theory."

568. Lach, Robert. *Mozart als Theoretiker.* Vienna: Holder, 1918. 100 pp. illus.

A comprehensive discussion of Mozart's teaching as practiced in the 1780s on Barbara von Ployer and others, central to which is a document I have seen in the Vienna National Library. However, in the light of recent research, Mozart's teaching materials and methods deserve further investigation. No index.

569. Lauer, Erich. *Mozart wie ihn niemand kennt.* Frankfurt: Hofmeister, 1958. 84 pp.

A summary of Mozart's own studies in counterpoint and fugue, with consideration as to how this applied to his teaching. Bibliography; no index.

570. Mozart, Wolfgang Amadeus. *Practical Elements of Thorough-Bass.* Trans. by Samuel Goedbé, with an introduction by Baird Hastings. New York: Patelson, 1976. 32 pp.

I was not able to compare the translation directly with the original which is at least partly by Mozart. In Goedbé's version, first issued in England about 1830, Mozart's ideas, and those of Kirnberger, Albrechtsberger, Marpurg, and others, may have been combined. Note that Mary Sabilla Novello published her translation of Albrechtsberger's *Generalbassschule* in 1835, and her translation of Mozart's *Generalbassschule* in 1854, with musical examples revised by Josiah Pittman.

571. Oldman, Cecil Bernard. "Two Minuets by Attwood, with Corrections by Mozart." *Music Review* 7, 4 (August 1946): 166–169.

Oldman's analysis supports the thesis that Mozart was a good teacher when he wanted to be. See also Oldman's contribution to the Scheurleer Gedenkboek, 1925 (#528).

571A. Senn, Walter. "Zur Mozarts Angeblichen 'Kurzgefasste Generalbass-Schule.'" *Mitteilungen der ISM* 29, 3-4 (September 1981): 28–33.

Discussing the Heydenreich-Steiner documents which probably were the basis for the Goedbé and Novello editions, Senn introduces evidence from which he concludes that, given Mozart's lack of enthusiasm for teaching, it is unlikely he prepared a manual for beginners. He also invokes various Mozart authorities who believe Heydenreich or a contemporary may have combined a few common practice notes of Mozart with precepts of Albrechtsberger, Kirnberger, and Rameau (and possibly Vogler).

Background

Historical and Cultural

There are some relationships which can be understoood only by investigating broader implications; important background is contained in the volumes cited below.

572. Babler, Otto F. "Mozart als Leser." *Philobiblon* (Vienna) 3, 2 (1930): 62 ff.*

     Discusses books Mozart read and their relation to his music. Cited in Schneider and Algatzy (#556). For discussion of Mozart's interest in poetry, see Erich Valentin. "Mozart und die Dichtung seiner Zeit." *Neues Mozart Jahrbuch* 1 (1941): 79–113.

573. Beales, Derek. *Joseph II, Volume I: In the Shadow of Maria Theresa, 1740–1780.* Cambridge: Cambridge University Press, 1987. 538 pp. ISBN: 0-521-24240-1.

     Probing history and biography of a true centrist who tried to help his subjects during changing times. Bibliography; index.

574. Beyle, Marie Henri (pseudonym originally Bombet, later Stendhal) (1783–1842). *Vies de Haydn, de Mozart et de Metastase.* Paris: Champion, 1814. 492 pp.

     A great writer's view of the arts, emphasizing Metastasio's librettos. Haydn's biography is adapted from G. Carpani's *La Haydine.* For Mozart, Stendhal relied mostly on Schlichtegroll (#643).

575. Crankshaw, Edward. *Maria Theresa.* New York: Atheneum, 1986. 366 pp. ISBN: 0-689-70708-8. DB 71.C7.

     Although popularly written, it is thoroughly researched—discussing politics, the Enlightenment, culture and personalities, 1706–1780, including Empress Maria Theresa's sons, Joseph II (reigned 1765–1790) and Leopold II (reigned 1790–1792). Bibliography; index.

See also: Ernst Wangermann. *The Austrian Achieve-ment 1700–1800*. London: Thames & Hudson, 1973. 216 pp. illus. ISBN: 0-500-32027-6. DB 69 7 W 35. Bibliography; index.

576. Durant, Will, and Ariel Durant. *Rousseau and Revolution*. New York: Simon & Schuster, 1967. 1091 pp. illus. ISBN: 671-63058-X.

Volume 10 in the authors' *Story of Civilization*, this book provides extensive information about the age into which Mozart was born. Rousseau's *Le Devin du village*, after Favart's adaptation as *Les Amours de Bastien et Bastienne*, became Mozart's *Bastien und Bastienne*—one link between the French writer-philosopher and the Austrian composer in the twilight of Absolutism and Enlightenment before the dawn of Revolution. Index.

See also: M.S. Anderson. *Europe in the 18th Century 1713–1783*. New York: Longmans, 1961. 2nd ed. 1976. 447 pp. ISBN: 0-582-4871-8. D 286 A5.

Also: Leo Gershoy. *From Despotism to Revolution, 1763–1789*. New York: Harper, 1944.

Also: Egon Bauer. "Mozart und die bildenden Kunst auf seiner Wege." *Acta Mozartiana* 28, 3 (1981): 55–57; brief discussion of church art Mozart appreciated.

577. Kennard, Joseph. *Goldoni and the Venice of his Times*. New York: Macmillan, 1920. Reprint edition, New York: Blom, 1967. 551 pp. illus.

A classic study of Goldoni, whose importance in the Mozart context is his influence on Coltellini's librettos for Mozart, *and* the fact that Mozart read and saw Goldoni's original plays. Index.

578. Metastasio, Pietro. *Tutte le opere*. Bruno Brunelli, ed. Verona: Mondadori, 1951–1965. 5 vols.

"The definitive edition of Metastasio's works." Mozart owned and read, and used several librettos by Metastasio (Trapassi) as bases for his works.

579. Pestelli, Giorgio. *Italian Music: The Age of Mozart and Beethoven*. Translated by Eric Cross. New York:

Cambridge University Press, 1984. 259 pp. illus. ML 240.3.

An introduction to the age, not the music. Index.

580. Ringer, Alexander. "Mozart and the Josephinian Era." *Current Musicology* 9 (Spring 1969): 158–165.

Ringer asserts that liberal Joseph II was generally more open to change in the Austrian Empire than his beloved, conservative mother Maria Theresa; actually each ruler fostered some progress under trying conditions. See Crankshaw (#575) above.

See also: Hans Wagner, "Der Josephinische Wien und Mozart." *Mozart Jahrbuch* 21 (1978–1979): 1–13.

Also: Franco Venturi. *Settecento riformatore.* Vol. 4, Part Two. Turin: Einaudi, 1986. (Detailed discussion of Joseph II's character.)

581. Rosenberg, Alfons. "Mozart und die Revolution." *Mitteilungen der ISM* 12, 1–2 (1964): 1–5; 3–4 (1964): 7–13.

Discussion of Mozart's reactions to various ideas and developments of the century.

582. Omitted.

583. Smith, Patrick J. *The Tenth Muse: A Historical Study of the Opera Libretto.* New York: Knopf, 1970. 458 pp. illus. ISBN: 0-394-44822-7. ML 401.1.

Survey includes many figures of Mozart's time: Da Ponte, Casti, Sedaine, Goldoni, Guillard, Marmontel, Bertati. Dates are sporadic. Notes; bibliography; index.

See also: Paul Nettl. "Da Ponte in Vienna." *Opera News* 17, 11 (February 3, 1952): 8–11. Brief discussion of Da Ponte's librettos for Martin, Salieri, Storace, Weigl.

Musical Influences

584. Angermüller, Rudolph, et al. *Mozart und seine Welt.* Kassel: Bärenreiter, 1979. 292 pp. illus.

   Based on one of the long series of significant conferences (dating from 1931) at the International Salzburg Mozarteum, with 21 excellent contributions. Virtually every chapter is important in this book, which includes biography, analysis, background. R. Angermüller discusses Mozart in Paris; H. Dennerlein considers the instruments Mozart played; D. Heartz compares *Idomeneo* with *Tito*; R. Kohlschütter considers seven composers of Salzburg before Mozart whose impress he must have felt; F. R. Noske explores psychological meanings of various orchestrations; K. Wagner describes conditions in Vienna affecting Mozart's finances. Index.

585. Angermüller, Rudolph. *W. A. Mozarts Musikalische Umwelt in Paris (1778).* Munich: Katzbichler, 1982. 351 pp. ISBN: 3-87397-116 X.

   Presenting contemporary documents to explain Mozart's problematic experiences in Paris, day by day, author discusses musical and social climate in Mozart's time. Index.

586. Autexier, Philippe A. "Giambattista Sammartini." *Revue musicale Suisse Romande* 4 (Winter 1975): 61–64. illus.

   Sammartini was an important (if often unacknowledged) influence on Gluck, Haydn, Monn, J.C. Bach, Johann Stamitz, Boccherini, Corrette, and Mozart, which Autexier makes clear by showing that Sammartini developed increased expressiveness in the orchestra, stressed nuances in symphonies, dramatized the overture, and used varied forms in orchestra music.

587. Bolongaro-Crevenna, Hubertus. *L'Arpa festante.* Munich: Callwey, 1963. 271 pp. illus.

   Although Mozart is featured only on pages 105–128, the year-by-year listing of repertoire gives details on many lyric works Mozart saw on his eight visits to Munich (1762–1790). Chronology; bibliography; indexes.

See also: Renate Schusky. *Das deutsche Singspiel im 18. Jahrhundert.* Heidelberg: University of Münster, 1981. 211 pp. Discussion of twenty works by Weisse, Hiller, etc., produced in various German theatres, 1730–1794.

588. Brook, Barry S. *La Symphonie française dans le seconde moitié du XVIIIe siècle.* Paris: L'Institut de Musicologie, 1962. 3 vols. illus.

Splendid discussion of some 1500 French symphonies by 150 composers, with pertinent comparisons to Mozart works. One vol. of scores; bibliography; appendixes; indexes.

589. Carse, Adam. *The History of Orchestration.* London: Kegan Paul, Trench, Trubner & Co., 1925. 348 pp. illus. (Reprint: New York, Dover, 1964; ISBN: 0-21258-0.) ML 455 C32. illus.

A splendid summary. Pages 167–199 concentrate on Mozart's period; the previous chapter discusses Gluck and the transition from the baroque. Notes; appendixes; indexes.

590. Charlton, David. *Grétry and the Growth of Opéra-comique.* Cambridge: Cambridge University Press, 1986. 371 pp. illus. ISBN: 0521-25129-X.

Good general background—as we know Mozart used Grétry as a model. Notes; bibliography; index.

See also: Christoph-Helmut Mahling. "Typus und Modell in Opern Mozarts." *Mozart Jahrbuch* 16 (1968–1970): 145–158, which considers Mozart's use of Grétry airs as a model.

591. Dean, Winton. *The New Grove Handel.* New York: Norton, 1983. 185 pp. illus. ISBN: 0-393-30086-2.

In summarizing Handel's impressive achievement, Professor Dean provides a fine background and an appropriate introduction to the influence of Handel on the world of Mozart. Bibliography; work list; index. (Drawn from author's article in Grove.)

See also: Fellerer (#837), and Siegmund-Schulze (#838).

592. Einstein, Alfred. *Gluck.* Translated by Eric Blom. London: Dent, 1936. 254 pp. ISBN: 0-374-93159-3. ML 410.G5E5.

Excellent survey of Gluck's life, but works need up-to-date treatment; refers to Mozart and his music more than any other musician. Chronology; catalogue of works; personalia; bibliography; index. See also: Herman Abert. "Mozart and Gluck." Translated by C. B. Oldman. *Music & Letters 10* (1929): 256–265.

593. Geiringer, Karl. *J. S. Bach.* New York: Oxford University Press, 1966. 282 pp. illus. ISBN: 0-19-500554-6.

An excellent one-volume standard discussion of Bach's life and works. Bibliography; notes; index.

594. Hickman, Roger. "The Nascent Viennese String Quartet." *Musical Quarterly* 67, 2 (April 1981): 193–212.

Although Mozart is not mentioned in this fine background article, the author considers works by Monn, Gassmann, and Haydn (incidentally noting that opera 1 and 2 of Haydn's quartets may be performed by string orchestra).

595. Howard, Patricia. *Christoph Willibald Gluck: A Guide to Research.* New York: Garland, 1987. 178 pp. illus. ISBN: 0-8240-8451-9. ML 134 G 56 H7.

Outstanding source for the period just prior to Mozart. Indexes.

596. Hutchings, A. J. B. *The Baroque Concerto.* London: Faber & Faber, 1956. 363 pp. illus. ML 1263 H85.

A pertinent survey—useful as background for Mozart's concertos. Bibliography; notes; index.

597. Jenkins, Newell, and Bathia Churgin. *Thematic Catalogue of the Works of Giovanni Battista Sammartini.* Cambridge, Massachusetts: Harvard University Press, 1976. 315 pp. illus. ISBN: 0-674-87735-7.

Authoritative presentation of the works of an important Italian instrumental and vocal composer Mozart knew, and whose influence he felt. Bibliography; notes; index.

598. Mozart, Leopold. *A Treatise of the Fundamental Principles of Violin Playing.* (Translated and edited by Editha Knocker, with a preface by Alfred Einstein.) London: Oxford University Press, 1951. 234 pp. MT 262. M 93.

An indispensable element in the formation of Mozart's style. Index.

On Leopold Mozart's music, see Max Seiffert, *Leopold Mozarts Werke* (20), selected, edited, and preceded by a catalogue, *Denkmäler der Tonkunst in Bayern* 9, volume 2, 1910.

See also: *Leopold Mozart* by Leopold Wegele (#708). Also: Cliff Eisen. "Leopold Mozart Discoveries." *Mitteilungen der ISM* 35, 1-4 (July 1987): 1-10. An up-to-date outline of informative sources on Leopold Mozart and a brief discussion of works.

599. Rainer, Werner. "Verzeichnis der Werke A.C. Adlgassers." *Mozart Jahrbuch* 13 (1964): 280–291.

Includes works Mozart heard in Salzburg which influenced his music.

600. Schmid, Manfred Hermann. *Mozart und die Salzburger Tradition.* Tutzing: Schneider, 1976. Vol. I: 306 pp.; Vol. II: 68 pp. music.

Analyzes a number of works, mostly after 1772, without fully relating them to Mozart. (Author, son of the late Mozart scholar, E. F. Schmid, compiled a catalogue of works of Leopold Mozart, Wolfgang Mozart, and Michael Haydn now in the Abbey of Saint Peter, Salzburg.)

See also: Alison Maitland. "The Development of Form and Style in 18th Century Salzburg Church Music." Ph.D. dissertation, Aberdeen University, 1972. 720 pp.*
RILM: 1972-1750dd.

601. Schneider, Constantin. "Die Oratorien und Schuldramen A. C. Adlgassers." *Studien zur Musikwissenschaft* 18 (1931): 36 ff.

Discussion of vocal music Mozart heard in Salzburg 1762-1777.

Cited in Schneider and Algatzy (#556).

602. Terry, Charles Sanford. *John Christian Bach.* (Rev. ed. by H. C. Robbins Landon.) London: Oxford University Press, 1967. 428 pp. illus. ISBN: 0-19-315211-8.

Splendid revision of the 1929 discussion of a composer Mozart liked, and whose works influenced him. Thematic catalogue; bibliography; notes; index.

603. Wellesz, Egon, and Frederick Sternfeld, eds. *The Age of Enlightenment.* London: Oxford University Press, 1973. 734 pp. ISBN: 0-19-316307-1. ML 160 N 44.

Volume 8 of The New Oxford History of Music, includes excellent accounts of various operas and other works by Mozart. Bibliography; index.

603A. Ziffer, Agnes. *Kleinmeister zur Zeit der Wiener Klassik.* Tutzing: Schneider, 1984. 178 pp. illus.*

Discussion of relationship between Haydn, Mozart, and lesser composers of the period; also discussion of Beethoven and Schubert.
Cited in Schneider Catalogue 293 (Tutzing, 1986).

Biography

There are occasions in the life of every creative person when the biographical activities and the intellectual activities are intertwined, and also at the same time independent. Mindful of the particular difficulties of separating logically and clearly these complementary and parallel aspects, the attempt has been made to concentrate the biographical entries in the Mozart Guide in this section, and to concentrate the musical entries in the next section. However, for a wide variety of reasons it is impossible and/or undesirable to separate some personal relationships and identities—Wolfgang–Leopold, Wolfgang–Constanze, Wolfgang–Aloysia, etc.—from their impact on Mozart's compositions. Readers will of course make full use of the index, and will, I hope, send in whatever comments they feel could help make a revised edition of this book more useful. Another thorny matter with

Mozart is that during much of the decade he lived in Vienna his finances were not in balance. Factors contributing to this include his own apparent indifference to adjusting the practical with the ideal, Constanze's frequent pregnancies, and the unstable state of the Austrian economy. This section lists the most valuable biographies—most of which contain important discussions of Mozart's music (just as many of the more technical books listed in the next section relate the music to biography), for elements of biography, including of course letters, illuminate compositional facts systematized by Köchel. Each of the following ten volumes is commended particularly (they range in publication date from 1798 to 1965)— five are in English, three are in German, two are in French): Blom (608), Deutsch (610), Einstein (612), Holmes (621), Jahn (622), Niemetschek (631), Nissen (632), Oulibischeff (634), Paumgartner (635), Wyzewa and Saint-Foix (647). The reader can choose from the varied manners of presentation those which are appropriate to his or her use.

General

604.   Abert, Hermann. *W. A. Mozart* (7th ed. of Jahn, see below #622). Leipzig: Breitkopf & Härtel, 1955–1956. 1584 pp. in 2 vols. illus. facs.

Newly reworked from Jahn's pioneer Mozart, this revision in German is useful but not indispensable if one studies Einstein, Jahn, and Wyzewa and Saint Foix, and the letters alongside the music. For discussion of the problems of revision, see King (#768). Notes. Index is a separate volume.

605.   Alberti, C. E. R. *Raphael und Mozart*. Stettin: Müller der Buchhandlung, 1856. 44 pp.

Issued for the celebration of Mozart's centennial, this comparison of two leading artists of their times is valuable if one wishes to understand the 19th-century approach to Mozart. No index.

606.   Baker, Richard. *Mozart*. London: Thames & Hudson, 1982. 144 pp. illus.

A well-illustrated up-to-date biography, with a chronology, map, bibliography, index.

607. Barrington, Daines. "Account of a Very Remarkable Young Musician." *Philosophical Transactions of the Royal Society,* 60 (1770): 54–64.

Valuable testimony, comparing Mozart to Handel, with a great future predicted.

608. Blom, Eric. *Mozart.* New York: Octagon, 1949. 348 pp. illus. ISBN: 0-374-95974-9. ML410 M9 B65.

First published in 1939 by Dent, London, this is one of the best short treatments of life and works. Catalogue of works; chronology; bibliography; personalia; notes; appendixes; index.

609. Burk, John N. *Mozart and his Music.* New York: Random House, 1959. 453 pp. ML 410 M9 B97.

Convenient, generally accurate summary of life and works. Appendix; index.

610. Deutsch, Otto Erich. *Mozart: A Documentary Biography,* 1756-1891. Stanford: Stanford University Press, 1965. 680 pp. ISBN: 6-8047-0233-0. ML 410 M9 D4782.

Translated by Eric Blom, Peter Branscombe, and Jeremy Noble from the German edition by a great musicologist, published by Bärenreiter in 1961, this is an indispensable work for Mozart research. Appendix; catalogue of works; bibliography; index.

Addenda und Corrigenda, prepared by Joseph Heinz Eibl, was published by Bärenreiter in 1978 in a German edition only. 134 pp. ISBN: 3-7618-0566-7.

See also: Cliff Eisen. "Contributions to a New Mozart Documentary Biography." *Journal of the American Musicological Society* 39, 3 (Fall 1986): 615–632; also: (#648).

611. Eibl, Joseph Heinz. *Wolfgang Amadeus Mozart—Chronik eines Lebens.* Kassel: Bärenreiter, 1966. 106 pp. illus.

Concise, accurate chronology. For expanded chronological treatment, see Deutsch (#610) or Schneider and Algatzy (#556).

612. Einstein, Alfred. *Mozart, His Character, His Work.* Translated
      by Arthur Mendel and Nathan Broder. New York:
      Oxford University Press, 1945. 482 pp. illus. Rev. ed.,
      1962. ISBN 0-19-500732-8. ML 410 M9 E4.

      A deep discussion of Mozart's life, with outspoken
      opinions of Leopold and Constanze, and penetrating
      observations on the music—by one of the greatest Mozart
      scholars. Catalogue of works; footnotes used for translations;
      index.

613. ————. *Essays in Music.* New York: Norton, 1956. 265 pp.
      ML60 E38.

      Includes nine significant critical and biographical
      articles on matters Mozartean. No index.

614. Fischer, Hans Conrad, and Lutz Besch. *The Life of Mozart.*
      London: Macmillan, 1969. 203 pp. illus.

      Text, prepared from the film premiered at London's
      Festival Hall in 1967 (see #1107), comments on the rare and
      evocative illustrations. No index.

615. Ghéon, Henri. *In Search of Mozart.* Translated from the
      French by Alexander Dru. New York: Sheed & Ward,
      1932. 484 pp. illus.

      This book, wonderfully evocative of the 18th century, is
      now out of print. Based on eye-witness accounts (as is *W. A.
      Mozart, Berichte der Zeitgenossen* by Albert Leitzmann, who
      concentrates on Mozart in Switzerland), the Ghéon is
      considerably superseded by Angermüller's recent *Mozarts
      Musikalische Umwelt*—see #585. Bibliography; index.

616. Giazotto, Remo. *Annali mozartiania.* (1930–.) Milan:
      Zerboni, 1956. 165 pp.

      Well-organized handbook with chronology, appendix,
      bibliography of over 200 titles. No index.
      See also: Alberta Albertini. *Mozart la vita, le opera.* Milan:
      Bocca, 1946. 434 pp. illus.

617. Gugitz, Gustav. *Gesammelte Aufsätze.* Vienna: Überreuter,
      1963. 93 pp.

Consideration of three important biographical areas: concerning Mozart's pupils, his finances, his death. Notes; no index.

618. Haas, Robert M. *Wolfgang Amadeus Mozart.* 2d ed. Potsdam: Athenion, 1950. 160 pp. illus.

A biography, first issued in 1933, to which German writers often refer, but the ten biographies mentioned above are all superior. Bibliography; index.

619. Hadamovsky, Franz, and Leopold Nowak. *Mozart: Werk und Zeit-Austellung.* Vienna: Österreichische National-bibliothek. 1956. 87 pp. illus.

A superb display, succinctly summarized, of the life and times, and work (682 compositions). By far the most important exhibition catalogue. No index.

620. Hildesheimer, Wolfgang. *Mozart.* Translated by Marian Faber. New York: Farrar, Straus & Giroux, 1982. 408 pp. illus. ISBN: 0-394-71591-8.

Author properly emphasizes that the key to Mozart is in his music, and by paring away some Mozartean myths he enables the reader to consider both the music and the man anew. However, the author's use of "psycho-history" is grossly exaggerated, and his assertion that words meant little to Mozart is untrue. Useful chronology; full index.

621. Holmes, Edward. *The Life of Mozart.* London: Dent, 1921. 303 pp.

First published in 1845 (revised in 1878 and 1912), this sound important early work by an Englishman is based partly on original work and partly on Nissen (#632) by a pupil of Vincent Novello. It is still well worth reading for its command of pertinent biographical facts and for its clear style. Chronological list of works; footnotes; no index.

Holmes is also the author of *Analytical and Thematic Index of Mozart's Piano Works.* London: Novello, 1852.

622. Jahn, Otto. *W. A. Mozart.* Leipzig: Breitkopf & Härtel, 1856. 4 vols.

The first edition of Jahn's indispensable biography included valuable features, many of which are still useful. The second edition was translated by Pauline D. Townsend under the supervision of Sir George Grove, and published in London in 1891—paperback reprint in 3 volumes issued by Kalmus, New York, 1972. Six successive revisions by Jahn, Dieters, and Abert have purported to keep it up-to-date, but the disconcerting problems of different points of view in the revisions have been surveyed by King (#768). Appendixes; index. (Professor Otto Jahn, an archaeologist and writer, 1813–1869, is the subject of an informative article by his nephew, A. Michaelis, in *Allgemeine deutsche Biographie*, 13, pp. 668–686.)

623. Kelly, Michael. *Reminiscences of the King's Theatre*. London: Henry Colburn, 1826. 2 vols. 716 pp. (Reprint, New York: Da Capo, 1965.) ML 420 K292.

This colorful memoir (perhaps partly written by Kelly's friend, Theodore Hook) includes unique material on Mozart in Vienna in the 1780s—although it was written many years later and thus is, like the memoirs of Da Ponte (#669) given more to generalizations than details. No index.

624. Keys, Ivor. *Mozart*. New York: Holmes & Meier, 1980. 248 pp. illus. facs. ISBN: 0-8419-0576-2. ML 410 M9 K4.

Useful biography, making use of the research of Plath and Tyson on manuscripts, and the Bauer-Deutsch-Eibl edition of the letters. Catalogue of works; notes; bibliography; index.

625. Köberle, Adolf. "Mozarts religiöse Heimat." *Acta Mozartiana* 21, 1 (1974): 1–10.

Excellent summary of influences on Mozart's underlying religious nature—the Enlightenment, enjoyment of life, preparation for death. As a Freemason he believed in their humanistic principles and hoped for financial support.

626. Kramer, Kurt. "Strittige Fragen in der Mozart-Biographie." *Acta Mozartiana* 28, 4 (1976): 75–84.

Although the biographical clues in this article are not fully developed, they provide trails which could be explored further—including the excellence of Mozart's teaching, and the inspirations and literary origins of *Così.*

627. Lichtenthal, Pietro. *Cenni biografici intorno al celebre Wolfgang Amadeus Mozart.* Milan: Silvestri, 1816. 40 pp.

This earliest serious work in Italian (by a German musician, 1780–1853), sketches the life of Mozart and discusses selected operas, chamber music, songs, keyboard works, concertos, dances, symphonies. It is of importance to realize that already in 1816 in Italy Mozart was recognized, and publicized. No index.

628. Marignano, N. Medici di, and Rosemary Hughes. *A Mozart Pilgrimage: Being the Travel Diaries of Vincent and Mary Novello in the Year 1829.* London: Eulenberg, 1955. 361 pp. illus. ISBN: 0-903873-10-9.

Although written 30 years after Mozart's death, an evocative biographical memoir, important because of interviews with Constanze and Nannerl. Bibliography; notes; index.

629. Massin, Jean, and Brigitte Massin. *Mozart.* Paris: Fayard, 1970. 1202 pp. illus.

Revised from the authors' earlier edition, this French biography includes commentary on virtually every composition. Its completeness gives it potential usefulness, but balance is lacking to a far greater extent than one finds in the classic books by Jahn and by Wyzewa and Saint-Foix. The Massins try too hard to be different, possibly thinking they are original, when I find them misguided—for example using Marxist, even Freudian arguments, and over-emphasizing the fairy tale, or being sensationalist without reasonable factual support. The appendixes include summary tabular analyses of works by time periods, maps, lists of works, chronology, bibliography. No index.

630. Münster, Robert. "Ich bin hier sehr geliebt." *Acta Mozartiana* 35, 1 (1978): 3–18.

Draws on letters and gives details of Mozart's stay in Munich in 1777; includes material on Consoli, Fiala, Myslivecek, Rossi, Woschita, etc.

631. Niemetschek, Franz Xaver [Neméček, František Petr].
     Lebensbeschreibung des K.K. Kapellmeister Wolfgang Amadeus
     Mozart. Prague: Herri, 1798. (English translation by
     Helen Mantner; published, London: Hynes, 1956. 87
     pp.)
     A very valuable prime source, as Professor Niemetschek
     (1766–1849) knew Mozart and his family.

632. Nissen, George Nikolaus von. *Biographie W. A. Mozarts.*
     Leipzig: G. Senf, Breitkopf & Härtel, 1828. 995 pp. illus.
     Written under the influence of Constanze, who had it
     completed and published after Nissen's death. A unique
     early source, although curiously the author devotes more
     space to years 1765–1781 than to final decade in Vienna. No
     index, but appendixes include bibliography, and list of
     subscribers.

633. Nohl, Ludwig. *Mozarts Leben.* Leopzig: E. J. Günter, 1877.
     481 pp. illus.
     Regarded by King as an important biography by a well-
     known scholar who also issued a collection of Mozart letters.
     Appendix; no index.

634. Oulibischeff, Alexandre Dimitrievich. *Nouvelle biographie de*
     Mozart. Moscow: Semon, 1843. 3 vols.
     An enthusiastic book, containing careful analyses of
     much material and many compositions. Volume I is devoted
     to Mozart's life. Volumes II and III discuss Mozart's
     keyboard playing, as well as his quartets and quintets, his
     symphonies, and the Requiem, *Idomeneo, Die Entführung,*
     Figaro, and *Don Giovanni.* No index.

635. Paumgartner, Bernhard. *Mozart.* Berlin: Wegweisen, 1927.
     493 pp. illus. Sixth edition. Zurich: Alantis Verlag, 1962.
     576 pp.
     Full of insights resulting from a lifetime of proximity to
     the Salzburg tradition, this book considers Mozart's times,
     his surroundings, his youth, and his years of mastery. One of
     the great interpreter-scholars of Mozart's music,
     Paumgartner considers Mozart's musical imagination, the

voices and instruments of his time, and how his tonal ideas may be projected. Bibliography; index.

636. Pohl, C. F. *Mozart und Haydn in London.* Vienna: C. Gerolds Sohn, 1867. (Reprint, New York: Da Capo, 1970.) 186 pp. plus 387 pp. (2 vols. printed as 1). ISBN: 306-70024-7.

Excellent documentation of the period; 186 pp. devoted to Mozart. (There is a third volume compiled by Hugo Botstiber.) Personalia; notes; bibliography; index.

637. Procházka, Rudolph von. *Mozart in Prag.* Prague: H. Dominicus, 1892. 236 pp. illus.

Important documentation of Mozart's four visits to Prague, including artistic and personal relationships. Appendix; index.

638. Prodhomme, Jacques Gabriel. *Mozart raconté par ceux qui l'ont vu.* Paris: Librairie Stock, 1928. 203 pp. illus.

Among the many "first hand" accounts are ones by Grimm, Salomon Gessner, Voltaire, L. Berger, Gyrowetz, Rochlitz (who includes Mozart's statement that Joseph Haydn's music was the only music which touched him and made him laugh), Lange, Suard, Griesinger, etc. For other "first hand" accounts, see also Ghéon (#615).

639. Rochlitz, Johann Friedrich. "Verbürgte Anekdoten aus Wolfgang Gottlieb Mozarts Leben: ein Beitrag zur richtigeren Kenntinis dieses Mannes, als Mensch und Kunstler." *Allgemeine musikalische Zeitung* 1 (1798–1799): 17, 49, 81, 113, 145, 177, 289, 480, 854; 3 (1800–1801): 450, 493, 590.

A contemporary of Mozart, Rochlitz collected "authentic" anecdotes and gossip for his series of articles (including Mozart's delight in Henriette Baranius' performance of Blonde in *Die Entführung,* Berlin 1789). In later issues Rochlitz discussed Mozart compositions.

640. Rolland, Romain. *Some Musicians of Former Days.* Translated by Mary Blaiklock. New York: Holt, 1915. Reprint as *Essays in Music,* David Ewen, ed., New York: Allen, Towne & Heath, 1948; Dover paperback, 1959. 371 pp.

This selection of rewarding essays is distilled from five different books by the French humanist Romain Rolland (1868–1944). The fine, brief chapter on Mozart presents the man through his letters. No bibliography or index.

641. Schenk, Erich. *Mozart and His Times*. Translated from the German by Richard and Clara Winston. New York: Knopf, 1959. 490 pp. illus.

One of the best standard biographies (by a former editor of Mozarteum publications). Chronology; notes; bibliography; index.

642. Scheurleer, Daniel. *Mozart's verblijf in Nederland*. The Hague: M. Nijhoff, 1883. 157 pp.

Sources of Mozart's education and documentation of his artistic development include his stay in the Netherlands in 1765, the facts of which were established by Scheurleer (1855–1927). Notes; bibliography.

643. Schlichtegroll, Friedrich. *Mozart's Leben*. Richard Schall, ed. Kassel: Bärenreiter, 1954. 124 pp.

First published in Gratz in 1791 as an obituary, and reprinted in 1793. The author includes recollections of Mozart's sister Nannerl, and of his long-time friend and occasional collaborator Andreas Schachtner. An important source.

644. Schurig, Arthur. *Wolfgang Amadeus Mozart*. Leipzig: Insel Verlag, 1923. 2 vols. 374 pp. illus.

Author's point of view presents Mozart without the "heroic" image. Index.

645. Torrefranco, Fausto. *Le origini italiane del romanticismo musicale*. Turin: Bocca, 1930. 779 pp. (Reprint, 1969.)

Includes a stimulating discussion of the influence of Italian music on Mozart's instrumental works. Wyzewa and Saint-Foix (below) has an excellent discussion of Italian influences on Mozart's operas.

646. Winckler, (K.) T.F. (1775–1856) *Notice sur Jean-Chrysostome Théophile Mozart*. Magazin Encyclopédique, 1801.*

Earliest known biography of Mozart published in France. Perhaps adapted in part from articles by Karl Friedrich Cramer. (See Section 5.) Cited in Bory (#25).

647. Wyzewa, Théodore, and Georges de Saint-Foix. *W. A. Mozart.* Paris: Desclée de Brouwer, 1946. 5 vols. (Reprint: New York: Da Capo, 1980, of the French edition of 1977, 5 vols. in 2. ISBN: 0-306-79561-2. ML 410. M9 W99.)

Authors have recognized the breadth of Mozart's music in meticulous discussion of virtually every composition, along with appropriate personal and artistic background. Although Théodore de Wyzewa (1862–1917) died when only the first two volumes were complete, his partner (1874–1954) carried the work to its conclusion. This complex and diverse publication is a monument of Mozart research, and with Jahn, Deutsch, Einstein, the Köchel catalogue, and the letters remains an indispensable guide to research. Appendixes; index.

Specialized Biographical Subjects, Including Travel and Miscellaneous Topics

648. Eisen, Cliff. "Mozart Apocrypha." *The Musical Times* 127, 1726 (December 1986): 683–685.

Discussion of several incidents in the life of Mozart of which biographers must be wary.

649. Engerth, Ruediger. *Hier hat Mozart gespielt.* Salzburg: SN Verlag, 1968. 128 pp.

Although Engerth's presentation is somewhat routine, his monograph with fifty-six pictures of places where Mozart made music is extremely valuable as a summary of where he actually performed. Notes; appendix; index.

650. Federhofer, Helmut. "Mozart als Schüler und Lehrer." *Mozart Jahrbuch* 17 (1971–1972): 89–106.

Federhofer states that although Leopold Mozart did not teach Wolfgang "Fux counterpoint," Wolfgang did teach his theory pupils "Fux counterpoint," and that he used elements of the Albrechtsberger "Generalbassschule" (which has parallels with the Steiner-published "Kurz . . . Generalbass" attributed to Mozart) rather than develop his own system. In his article in Angermüller, *Mozart und seine Welt* (#585), Federhofer discusses the Attwood manuscript and other related material.

651. ———. "Mozart in Steiermark." *Mozart Jahrbuch 8* (1957): 140–151.

Discusses Mozart's friends and colleagues who came from Steiermark, Austria to study or work with Mozart.

652. Ferrari, Virgilio. *Mozart in Italia. Catalogo mostra.* Milan: Commune di Milano, 1956.*

Cited in Schneider and Algatzy (#556).

653. Gottron, A. B. *Mozart und Mainz.* Mainz: Verlag für Kunst, 1951. 77 pp. illus.

Discussion of Mozart's visits to Mainz in 1763 and 1790. Notes; bibliography; appendix; no index.

654. Hummel, Walter. *Mozart in aller Welt.* Salzburg: ISM, 1956. 230 pp. illus.

A listing of major events of the Mozart Year, 1956, throughout the world. Index.

655. Lesure, François. *Mozart en France.* Paris: Bibliothèque Nationale, 1956.

An exhibition devoted to Mozart's visits to Paris.

656. Lippmann, Friedrich, ed. *Mozart und Italien.* Cologne: Arno Volk, 1970. 318 pp. illus.*

Proceedings of a colloquium held in Rome in 1974; nineteen essays (in German or Italian) by the editor, and A. A. Abert, Ludwig Finscher, Gerhard Croll, Carl Gustav Fellerer. Subjects include authenticity, Mozart and Rutini, etc.
RILM: 1979—#190.

657. Ostoja, Andrea. *Mozart e l'Italia.* Bologna: Luigi Parma, 1955. 45 pp. illus.

Concentrates on Mozart's visits to Bologna, including previously unpublished documents. No index.

658. Schmid, E. F. "Auf Mozarts Spuren in Italien." *Mozart Jahrbuch* 6 (1955): 17–48.

A thorough discussion of the places Mozart visited on his first Italian trip, noting the persons he met, organs he played on, etc.

659. ————. *Ein Schwäbisches Mozart Buch.* Lorch: Bürger, 1948. 500 pp. illus.

Detailed discussion of Augsburg connections of Leopold and Wolfgang Mozart by a noted authority. Bibliography; appendix; index.

660. Schönig, Heinz. "Mozarts Wiener Wohnungen." *Österreichische Musikzeitschrift* 11, 4 (1956): 137–143.

Precise information on Mozart's fourteen addresses in Vienna, 1781–1791. Notes; bibliography.
See also: Volkmann Braunbehrens. *Mozart in Wien.* Munich: Piper, 1986. 508 pp. ISBN: 3-492-02995-7.

661. Stahelin, Lucas E. *Die Reise der Familie Mozart durch die Schweiz.* Bern: Franke, 1968. 114 pp. illus.

Mozart' early, interesting exposure to French Switzerland. Bibliography; no index.

662. Strauss, H. "Mozart in Strasbourg." *Musica* (Paris) 27 (June 1957): 39–41.

Despite a short stay in 1778 on his way from Paris to Salzburg, Mozart gave several concerts in Strasbourg and made several friends.

663. Volkmann, H. "Mozart in Dresden." *Zeitschrift für Musikwissenschaft* 10 (1920): 201–207.

Concise, useful summary of friends and connections in Dresden.

664. Wendelin, Lidia F. *Mozart in Ungarn.* Budapest: Kõsivitár, 1958. 203 pp.

Recommended by O. E. Deutsch and Green, the text is in German and Hungarian. The focus is on Mozart in the music history of Hungary. Bibliography.

665. Würtz, Roland, ed. *Der Mannheimer Mozart-Buch.* Wilhelmshavn: Heinrichshofen, 1979. 368 pp.

Fourteen authors discuss significant creative and personal aspects of Mozart's relations with Mannheim.

Colleagues and Contemporaries

In the hope of reducing unnecessary cross-checking there follows a selective listing of personalities important in Mozart's life: Albrechtsberger, André, Da Ponte, De Jean, Dittersdorf, Eberl, Fischietti, Joseph Haydn, Michael Haydn, Kreusser, Koželuh Löschenkohl, Wenzel Müller, Naumann, Neefe, Piccinni, Rolla, Salieri, Schikaneder, Süssmayr, Swieten, Traeta, Varesco. These persons are all listed in Section 5. See also *New Grove.*

The following entries are alphabetized according to the major figure discussed (not according to author alphabetization.)

666. Omitted.

667. Albrechtsberger, Johann G. *Sämtliche Schriften.* Kassel: Bärenreiter, 1975. 693 pp.*

Collected writings and papers of the Viennese musician.

668. André, August Hermann. *Zur Geschichte der Familie André.* Garmisch: Selbstverlag, 1963.*

Story of the publishing-musical family. Noted in Angermüller and Schneider (#546).

669. Da Ponte, Lorenzo. *Memoirs.* Translated from the Italian by Elizabeth Abbott; edited and annotated by Arthur Livinston; preface by Thomas C. Bergin. New York: Orion Press, 1957. 298 pp. illus. ISBN: 0-8446-1945-0. ML 423 D15 A 22.

Although sparse in detailed references to Mozart, what there is contributes significantly to our understanding of the

Viennese years when Da Ponte wrote texts for about twenty operas—three of which were masterpieces by Mozart. Notes; index.

670. (Da Ponte) FitzLyon, April. *Lorenzo da Ponte.* New York: Riverrun, 1982. 268 pp. illus. ISBN: 0-7145-3783-7. ML 423 D15 F5.

Author (in a revised version of her *The Libertine Librettist,* London, 1975) fills in some details alluded to in the Da Ponte memoirs. Bibliography; indexes.

Other volumes on Da Ponte include Sheila Hodges' popular biography, and Jean François Labie's edition of Da Ponte's works, with commentary in French.

671. (DeJean) Lequin, Frank. "Mozarts . . . rarer Mann." *Mitteilungen der ISM* 29, 1-2 (February 1981): 3–19. illus.

Biography of Dr. DeJean (1731–1797), amateur Dutch flutist whom Mozart met in Mannheim in 1777, who commissioned several works from Mozart. DeJean knew three of Mozart's doctors: Johann N. Hunczowsky (1752–1798), Mathias von Sallaba (1764–1797), and Thomas F. Closett (1754–1813).

672. Ditters von Dittersdorf, Karl. *Autobiography.* Translated by A. D. Coolidge from the Leipzig German edition of 1801. London: Bentley, 1896. Reprint edition, New York: Da Capo, 1970. 316 pp. ISBN: 0-306-71864-2. ML 410. D6 A33 1970.

Comments on Mozart are brief, but valuable, because Dittersdorf knew Mozart personally, and understood his music, although he did not admire it without reservations. No index.

673. (Eberl) Ewens, Franz Joseph. *Anton Eberl.* Dresden: Wilhelm Limpert, 1927.*

Noted in Angermüller and Schneider (#546).

674. (Fischietti) Engländer, Richard. "Domenico Fischietti als Buffokomponist in Dresden." *Zeitschrift für Musikwissenshaft* 2 (1919–1920): 321–353; 399–442.

Apparently Fischietti's best compositions were for Dresden, while those he wrote for Salzburg or Italy were inferior.

675. (Joseph Haydn) Geiringer, Karl. *Haydn: A Creative Life in Music.* London: Allen & Unwin, 1947. 342 pp. ML 410 H4 G4.

This excellent volume (prepared in collaboration with Irene Geiringer) holds a place of honor in Haydn research somewhat comparable to that which Einstein's *Mozart* holds in Mozart research—just as the Robbins Landon volumes cited immediately below hold their place in Haydn research comparable to the multi-volume works on Mozart by Jahn, and by Wyzewa and Saint-Foix. Virtually any research on Haydn is bound to illuminate Mozart, and vice-versa. Notes; bibliography; index. A revised edition of the Geiringer volume was published by the University of California Press, 1982.

676. (Haydn) Landon, H. C. Robbins. *Haydn Chronicle and Works.* Bloomington: Indiana University Press, 1976 et seq. illus. 5 volumes.

   1. The early years, 1732–1765. 665 pp. ISBN: 0-253-37001-9. ML 410 H41.26.*
   2. Haydn at Esterhaza, 1766–1790. 799 pp. ISBN: 0-253-37002-7.
   3. Haydn in England, 1791–1795. 640 pp. ISBN: 0-253-37003-5.
   4. Haydn: the years of *The Creation,* 1796–1800. 656 pp. ISBN: 0-253-37004-3.
   5. Haydn: the late years, 1801–1809. 495. ISBN: 0-253-37005-1.

*ML listing remains the same for all volumes.

As in Geiringer volume above, many pertinent references to Mozart. Notes; bibliography, indexes.

677. (Haydn) Larsen, Jens Peter, Howard Serwer, and James Webster, eds. *Haydn Studies: Proceedings of the International Haydn Conference, Washington, D.C., 1975.* New York: Norton, 1981. 590 pp. ISBN: 0-393-01454-1. ML 36.159593.

Ninety authorities participated in this conference involving twenty-nine aspects of Haydn's music and times—one of which was "Haydn and Mozart." Particular elements of Mozart's music discussed include articulation, cantabile, church music, form and compositional techniques, dynamics, mutual influences, rhythm, scoring, and tempo, with examples from a variety of instrumental and vocal works. Index.
See also: Danckwardt (#839).
Also: Eva Badura-Skoda, ed. *Bericht . . . Haydn Kongress, Vienna, 1982.* Munich: Henle, 1986.

678. (Michael Haydn) Jancik, Hans. *Michael Haydn.* Vienna: Amalthea, 1952. 359 pp. illus.

This standard biography is still useful, but several scholars, including Charles Sherman and Harold Farbermann, are working on new publications and editions. Chronology; bibliography; index.
See also: Wolfgang Neuwirth. *Johann Michael Haydn.* Salzburg: Hochschulbibliothek Mozarteum, 1981. 128 pp. Concentrates on published works; helps trace relationship with Mozart. Bibliography; list of works; index.
Also: Lothar Herbert Perger. *Thematisches Verzeichnis der Instrumentalwerke von Michael Haydn.* Denkmäler der Tonkunst in Österreich, 14, 2. Vienna, 1907. Still useful.
Also: Anton Klafsky. *Thematische Katalog der Kirchen-musik von Michael Haydn.* Denkmäler der Tonkunst in Österreich, 62. Vienna: Universal, 1925.

679. (Koželuh) Postolka, Milan. "Leopold Koželuch." *Ber. über die Prager Mozartkonferenz, 1956.* Prague: 1958: 135 ff.*
Cited in Schneider and Algatzy (#556).

680. (Kreusser) King, Alexander Hyatt. "Mozart and Peter Anaton Kreusser." *Music Review* 25 (May 1964): 124–126.

A few facts on a Mainz composer appreciated by Joseph Haydn and the Mozart family.

681. (Löschenkohl) Glück, Franz. *Katalog der Ausstellung Hieronymus Löschenkohl.* Vienna: Stadt Historische Museum, Wien. 1959. illus.*

Löschenkohl was a well-known silhouette maker whose likenesses of Mozart and many of his contemporaries are important documents.

682. (Löschenkohl) Witzmann, R., and Vera Schwarz. *Musikalisches Kartenspiel des Löschenkohl.* Vienna: Platnik, 1981. 107 pp. illus.*

Facsimile of a deck of playing cards in the Vienna Historische Museum, and a booklet of Viennese music of the period. Several compositions illustrated on the playing cards are identified as being by Mozart. RILM: 1981—#581.

683. (Wenzel Müller) Haas, Robert. "Wenzel Müller." *Mozart Jahrbuch* 4 (1953): 81–84.

Discussion of the composer, and conditions under which Müller composed *Kaspar der Fagottist* (1791).

684. (J. G. Naumann) Engländer, Richard. *Johann Gottlieb Naumann als Opernkomponist.* Leipzig: Breitkopf & Härtel, 1922. 60 pp.

A Czechoslovakian composer who studied in Italy with Padre Martini and Tartini. Naumann was active in Sweden and Dresden (where Mozart met him). Bibliography in notes; no index.

685. (Naumann) Meissner, August Gottlieb. *Bruchstücke zur Biographie J. G. Naumanns.* Prague: K. Barth, 1803–1804. 2 vols.*

First-hand information on Bohemian composer active in Dresden, where Mozart knew him.

686. (Neefe) Leux, Irmgard. *Christian Gottlob Neefe.* Leipzig: Kistner & Siegel, 1925. 208 pp. illus.

German composer, conductor, organist in several courts, Neefe made piano-vocal scores of several of Mozart's operas. Index.

687. (Piccinni and Gluck) Fischer, Wilhelm. "Piccinni, Gluck and Mozart." *Mozart Jahrbuch* 5 (1954): 9–14.

Although more detail would be welcome, the author does discuss how Mozart combined buffo qualities of Piccinni and noble expression of Gluck.

688. (Rolla) Inzaghi, Luigi, and Luigi Bianchi. *Alessandro Rolla.* Milan: Nuove Edizioni, 1981. 298 pp.

Discussion of composer and conductor from Pavia who championed Mozart and Beethoven in Italy. Includes catalogue of 576 works. Bibliography; discography; no index.
RILM: 1981—#526.

689. (Salieri) Angermüller, Rudolph. *Antonio Salieri.* Munich: Katzbichler, 1972.*

Although I have seen only the excerpts which appeared in *Mitteilungen der ISM,* this book appears to provide balanced treatment of Salieri's works and his career; it is based on the author's doctoral dissertation. Index.

690. (Salieri) Heinzelmann, Josef. "Prima la musica, poi la parole—zu Salieri's Wiener Opernparodie." *Österreichische Musikzeitschrift* 28, 1 (January 1973): 19–28.*

Notes Salieri's use of French and German musical procedures, and progressive elements in Casti's libretto.
RILM: 1974—#389.

691. (Schikaneder) Honolka, Kurt. *Papageno: Emanuel Schikaneder.* Vienna: Residenz Verlag, 1984. 267 pp. ISBN: 3-7017-0373-6.

Covers more of Schikaneder's varied career and activities than we had known previously—more completely than publications by Walter Senn and Egon Komozynski. Notes; useful appendix; bibliography; index.

692. (Swieten) Schmid, Ernst Fritz. "Gottfried van Swieten als Komponist." *Mozart Jahrbuch* 4 (1953): 15–31.

Well known as a friend of Mozart, Haydn and Beethoven, Swieten was also an earnest minor composer who admired Bach, Handel, Graun, Monsigny.

693.   (Traeta) Sandberger, Adolf. "Tommaso Traeta." *Denkmäler der Tonkunst in Bayern* 14 (1913) 12–90.

       Works, notes.

694.   (Varesco) Kramer, Kurt. "F. B. Varesco." *Acta Mozartiana* 1 (1980): 2–15.

       A brief biography of the Salzburg poet whose text Mozart used for *Idomeneo.*

Family and Friends

695.   Belmonte, Carola Groag. *Die Frauen in Leben Mozarts.* 2d ed. Zurich: Amalthea, 1924. 158 pp.

       In the revised edition of a work first issued in 1905, the author (1859–1929) provides an admirable summary of relationships Mozart had with his mother, sister (Nannerl), Aloysia, Constanze, Sophie, Josepha (Weber), cousin Bäsle (Maria Anna Thekla), Empress Maria Theresia, Josepha Duček, Maria Theresia Paradies, Countess Thun, Baroness Waldstättin, Teresa Saporiti, Luisa Laschi, Dorotea Bussani, Celeste Coltellini, Catarina Cavalieri, Nancy Storace, Fräulein Stadler (a "niece"of Maxmilian Stadler, a pupil surmised to have used Mozart's *Generalbassschule*), and 15 others. Bibliography; notes, no index.

696.   Blümml, Emil Karl. *Aus Mozarts Freunden und Familien Kreis.* Vienna: Strache, 1923. 263 pp. illus.

       Complementary to the above, another important study of the lives and careers of relatives and colleagues— including children, mother-in-law, Joseph Lange and his first wife, Anna Maria Schindler, Josepha Weber and her first husband, Franz de Paula Hofer, Johann von Thorwart, K. L. Gieseke, Emanuel Schikaneder, Caroline Pichler, and others. Index.

697.   Carr, Francis. *Mozart and Constanze.* New York: F. Watts, 1984. (First published in the United Kingdom by John Murray, 1982.) 186 pp. ISBN: 0531-09820-6.

An inquiry into the cause of Mozart's death which focuses on certain happenings in Vienna during the last two years of his life. Although not indispensable for the study of Mozart's music, an intriguing view of the composer's last years and his relations with Magdalena Pokorny Hofdemel, and other pupils. Bibliography, index. See also: H. C. Robbins Landon. *1791.* New York: Schirmer, 1988. 240 pp. ISBN: 0-02-872592-1.

698. David, Ernest. "La veuve et la soeur de Mozart." *Chronique musicale* (Paris) 2 (1873): 18–24, and subsequent numbers.

An interesting memoir including information on Nannerl and Constanze, complementing Marignano (#628).

699. Fellerer, Karl Gustav. "Mozartstiftung und Mozart-verein." *Wiener Figaro* 44 (October 1977): 1–6.

Documentation of various ways family and friends acted to keep the memory of Mozart alive after 1791.

700. ———. "Mozarts Werk nach seinem Tode." *Wiener Figaro* 45 (December 1978): 11–18.

Documentation of how members of Mozart's circle promoted publication of his works in the years following his death.

701. Hummel, Walter. *Nannerl. W. A. Mozarts Schwester.* Zurich: Amalthea, 1952. 106 pp.

Convenient assemblage of pertinent facts. Appendix; notes; bibliography, no index.

702. ———. *W. A. Mozarts Söhne.* Kassel: Bärenreiter, 1956. 383 pp.

Biography of the two sons, beginning with discussion of Wolfgang as a husband and father. Author considers Carl Thomas and Franz Xaver (Wolfgang, Jr.) in detail. Notes; chronology; bibliography; indexes.

703. Komorzynski, Egon. *Pamina, Mozarts letze Liebe.* Berlin: Hesse, 1957. 121 pp.

Biography of Anna Gottlieb, who sang Barbarina in *Figaro* and Pamina in *Die Zauberflöte* premieres.

704. Marethe, Ursula. *Mozarts "Weberin."* Augsburg: Deutsche Mozartgesellschaft, 1980. 78 pp.

Using contemporary documents, author presents a biography of the singer Aloysia Weber, Mozart's pupil and great love, whose brother-in-law he became when he married Constanze. Index.

705. Schuler, Heinz. "Zur Familiengeschichte des Johann Joseph Lange." *Mitteilungen der ISM* 22, 1–2 (February 1974): 29–37.

Valuable background on Mozart's brother-in-law, the husband of Aloysia Weber.

706. Omitted.

707. Schurig, Arthur. *Leopold Mozart, Reise Aufzeichnungen, 1763–1771.* Dresden: Laube, 1920. 110 pp.

Leopold Mozart's assembled notes made during trips with his son to Munich, Vienna, London, Paris, Italy, etc.—including persons they met, organs on which Wolfgang played, etc. Index.

708. Wegele, Ludwig, ed. *Leopold Mozart.* Augsburg: Der Brigg, 1969. 141 pp. illus.

With contributions by Werner Egk, Adolf Leyer, Geza Rech, Hans Schurich, Erich Valentin, H. E. Valentin, and Wegele, this portrait of Leopold and his music provides a very good summary of the subject. Bibliography; index.

709. ———. *Der Lebenslauf der Marianne Thekla Mozart.* Augsburg: Der Brigg, 1967. 63 pp.

A charming sketch of Mozart's cousin, Der Bäsle (1758–1841); includes a letter Mozart sent her in May 1779. No index.

Followers

The timing and circumstances of the French Revolution in relation to the life of Mozart dictated that his musical followers were either composers like Beethoven, Cherubini, and Méhul (all near contemporaries who struck out in dramatic new directions), or lesser figures, such as Eybler, Gyrowetz, Hummel, Kelly, Pleyel, Schenk, Seyfried, Weigl—some of whom were Mozart's pupils, and whose work is discussed as appropriate—and of course Süssmayr, discussed last in this part. (They are all listed in Section 5; see also *New Grove.*) However, there have been a number of other "followers," including philosophers. Useful publications on a variety of followers are noted below, listed alphabetically.

710. (Eybler) Hausner, Henry. "Joseph Eybler." *Mitteilungen der ISM* 22, 3-4 (August 1964): 5–14.

Excellent summary discussion of Eybler, and the nature of his music.

711. Hermann, Hildegard. *Thematische Verzeichnis der Werke von Joseph Eybler.* Munich: Katzbichler, 1976. 176 pp.*

Cited in Angermüller (#546).

712. (Kierkegaard) Engel, Hans. "Mozart in der philosophischen und ästhetischen Literatur." *Mozart Jahrbuch* 4 (1953): 64–81.

Discussion of Mozart's reputation and influence as evidenced in the writings of Kierkegaard and others.

713. Görner, Rüdiger. "Zu Kierkegaards Verständnis der 'Zauberflöte.'" *Mitteilungen der ISM* 20, 3-4 (August 1980): 25–30.

Kierkegaard's view of truth and eroticism in *Don Giovanni, Figaro, Die Zauberflöte* is related to opinions of Momigny, Nägeli, Nietzsche, Schopenauer, and Wagner.

714. Kierkegaard, Søren. *Either—Or.* Translated by W. Lowrie. Vol. I. ISBN: 0-691-07177-2; Vol. II. ISBN: 0-691-07178-0. Princeton, New Jersey: Princeton University Press, 1971.

In the discussion of *Don Giovanni*, Kierkegaard notes how the seducer becomes a hero. Written in 1845, a psychological study which can be overemphasized. See also: Rolf Jacobs. "Kierkegaard und das Don Juan Thema." *Mitteilungen der ISM* 22, 3-4 (August 1974): 7–15. A summary of sensual and seduction themes Kierkegaard found in *Don Giovanni*. Also: T. H. Croxall. "Kierkegaard and Mozart." *Music and Letters* 26 (1945): 151–158, which is more general.

715. (Lyser) Valentin, Erich. "Johann Peter Lyser." *Mozart Jahrbuch* 4 (1953): 56–63.

A discussion of the process of matching Lyser's texts to music Mozart composed for other purposes.

716. (Mederitsch) Aigner, Theodor. "Johann Mederitsch (Gallus)." *Current Musicology* 20 (1975): 79–86.

Career of composer associated with Wagenseil as pupil, and Mozart and Schikaneder as copyist.

717. (Schopenauer) Schopenauer, Arthur. *World as Will and Representation*. Translated by E. F. J. Payne. Vol. I. ISBN: 0-486-21761-2; Vol. II. ISBN: 0-486-21762-0. New York: Dover Reprint, 1966.

As part of a study originally published in 1819, Schopenauer found *Don Giovanni* a sublime expression of the supernatural. Index.

718. (Stadler) Finscher, Ludwig. "Maximilian Stadler und Mozarts Nachlass." *Mozart Jahrbuch* 11 (1961): 168 ff.

Mozart's friend Stadler helped Constanze make the inventory of Mozart manuscripts after his death, and he advised concerning the publication, editing, and disposition of them.

719. Pisarowitz, K. M. "Beitragsversversuche zu einer Gebrüder Stadler Biographie." *Mitteilungen der ISM* 19, 1-2 (February 1971): 29–33.

Background on the Stadlers, longtime collaborators of the Mozarts. (See also monograph on Stadler published by ISM, 1972.*)

720. (Storace) Anderson, Judith. "The Viennese Opera of Steven Storace." Ph. D. dissertation, Catholic University, 1971.*

Discussion of *Gli sposi malcontenti* and *Gli equivoci*. Storace was a pupil of Mozart. Cited in Adkins (#516).

721. (Weigl) Hausner, Henry. "Joseph Weigl." *Mitteilungen der ISM* 14, 3-4 (August 1966): 9–17.

Excellent summary article on Weigl (a member of the Haydn-Mozart circle), and the nature of his music.

Miscellaneous

722. "1980 Mozart Colloquiem, Salzburg." *Mozart Jahrbuch* 22 (1980–1983). 430 pp.

A distinguished panel discusses various aspects of Mozart's music, as it was perceived in the 19th century. Included are papers on Nietzsche, Schlegel, Kierkegaard. One of a long series, now coordinated with NMA. (Dr. Angermüller at the Mozarteum can provide a complete list of colloquia and subjects.) The position of Franz Xaver Süssmayr in Mozart studies presents one of the many unsolved problems. Henry Hausner's short biography and summary treatment of Süssmayr's music offers a valuable introduction, but the diverse biographical and compositional aspects of the Mozart-Süssmayr relationship, 1789–1791, and later, are not susceptible to condensation.

Süssmayr (1766–1803) was a pupil of Salieri before he became associated with Mozart, as a pupil and assistant. After the death of Mozart, Süssmayr was a member of the Salieri circle for the remainder of his short life.

Although there is scant documentation of Süssmayr's personal life, during his period with Mozart, Süssmayr was a frequent companion of Constanze, but not later. There is also the possibility that Süssmayr, who never married, may have been involved with Constanze's sister, Sophie. It has been surmised that Franz Xaver Mozart, born in 1791, might have been the son of Süssmayr, rather than Mozart.

Constanze turned first to Mozart's former pupil Eybler rather than Süssmayr, Mozart's closest acolyte, asking him to complete the *Requiem* Mozart left unfinished at his death—

only returning to Süssmayr after Eybler had remitted Mozart's manuscript, still uncompleted, to Constanze.

Süssmayr's completed version of the Mozart *Requiem* was based on sketches by Mozart, but as the handwritings of Mozart and Süssmayr are similar, it is difficult to swear what parts are wholly by Mozart and what parts are not. Later, Constanze chose Maximilian Stadler, rather than Süssmayr, for advice and help with Mozart's remaining manuscripts. With the above comments in mind, readers are referred to the following specific titles on Süssmayr in which elucidation is attempted.

723. Angermüller, Rudolph. "Süssmayr, ein Schüler und Freund Salieris." *Mitteilungen der ISM* 21, 1-2 (February 1973): 19–21.

Review of facts, but ramifications are not fully considered.

724. Eibl, Joseph Heinz. "Süssmayr und Constanze." *Mozart Jahrbuch* 20 (1976–1977): 277–280.

A partial answer to Schickling (#729).

725. Hausner, Henry. *Franz Xaver Süssmayr*. Vienna: Berglund, 1964. 126 pp. illus.

A balanced introduction to the man and his music (with musical examples). Chronology; bibliography; no index.

726. Kecskeméti, István. "Beiträge zur Geschichte von Mozarts Requiem." *Studia musicologica* (Budapest) 1, fasc. 1-2 (1961): 147 ff.

Stylistic analysis attempting to separate the work of Mozart from that of Süssmayr. Discussion of Mozart's handwriting and consideration of a copy of the *Requiem* probably made by J. A. Hiller.

727. ———. "Süssmayr-Handschriften." *Mozart Jahrbuch* 10 (1959): 206 ff.

Examples of Süssmayr's handwriting in Hungary, with discussion.

728. Marguerre, Karl. "Mozart und Süssmayr." *Mozart Jahrbuch* 12 (1962–1963): 172 ff.

    Discusses Süssmayr's part in the Lacrimosa, Sanctus, Benedictus, and Agnus Dei of Mozart's *Requiem.*

729. Schickling, Dieter. "Einige ungeklärte Fragen zur Geschichte der Requiem Vollendung." *Mozart Jahrbuch* 20 (1976–1977): 265–276.

    Brief consideration of likelihood Süssmayr and Constanze were romantically involved and that they quarrelled after the death of Wolfgang. (Was Süssmayr also involved with Constanze's sister, Sophie?) Considers Süssmayr's use of Mozart's sketches for the Requiem and other compositions, and also the possibility that Maximillan Stadler orchestrated an Offertorium, with or without sketches.

    See also: Franz Beyer. "Mozarts Komposition zum Requiem." *Acta Mozartiana* 18 (1971): 27 ff.

730. Wlček, Walter. *F. X. Süssmayr als Kirchen Komponist.* Tutzing: Schneider, 1978. 242 pp.*

    Considers Süssmayr's participation in the completion of the Mozart Requiem, showing the relationship to twenty-two passages in Süssmayr's authentic compositions for the church.

    RILM: 1976—#2834.

Freemasons

Viennese Freemasons in the 1780s represented the cream of Austrian intellectuals—perhaps analagous to the Encyclopedists of the French Enlightenment, except that in Vienna the nobles were a part of the Freemasons, and in Paris the nobles generally were not part of the Enlightenment. Also, the Viennese Freemasons were not categorically anti-religious in the same way so many Parisian intellectuals were. Mozart's creative mind was far from being monopolized by music. He greatly enjoyed and profited from his association with Freemasons. Three writers have led the investigations of this significant aspect of Mozart biography: Otto

Erich Deutsch, Paul Nettl, and H. C. Robbins Landon (the only one of the three still alive); and many others have followed.

731. Deutsch, Otto Erich. *Mozart und der Wiener Loge.* Vienna, 1932. 35 pp. illus. ML 410 M 9 D 48.
Concise summary of Viennese Freemasons.

732. Landon, H. C. Robbins. *Mozart and the Masons: New Light on the Lodge "Crowned Hope."* New York: Thames & Hudson, Inc., 1985. 72 pp. illus.
Valuable discussion of Masons and Masonic activity in Mozart's Vienna, 1784-1791. Notes; bibliography; no index.

733. Nettl, Paul. *Musik und Freimaurerei: Mozart und die Königliche Kunst.* Esslingen: Bechtle Verlag, 1956. 190 pp. illus.
Paul Nettl wrote several books devoted to Mozart and Freemasonry in the 18th century, of which this is the clearest—although a definitive treatment of this complex subject remains to be produced. Excellent notes; index.
See also: Paul Nettl: *Mozart and Masonry.* New York: Philosophical Library, 1957, 150 pp. A reprint edition of this has been announced.

734. Thomson, Katherine. *The Masonic Thread in Mozart.* London: Laurence & Wishert, 1977. 207 pp. illus. ISBN: 85315-381-7.
Convenient summary, but above titles are more revealing. Notes; bibliography; index.

Illnesses and Death

735. Bär, Carl. *Mozart: Krankheit, Tod, Begräbnis.* Salzburg: ISM (Bärenreiter), 1966. 145 pp. illus.
Number 1 in the Mozarteum Schriftenreihe of important monographs—clearly written by a noted Swiss physician and musicologist. Covers illnesses, death, burial. Bibliography; index.

736. Dalchow, Johannes. *W. A. Mozarts Krankheiten, 1756–1763.* Berlin: Verlag Kurt Engber, 1955. 83 pp.

    Discussion of Mozart's childhood illnesses. Bibliography; no index.

737. Franken, Franz Hermann. "Mozarts Todeskrankheit." *Mitteilungen der ISM,* 28, 1-2 (February 1980): 23–24.

    Brief discussion of the infection and high fever which author believes led to Mozart's death (rather than a chronic condition).

Music

The first part of this section is devoted to *general* and *stylistic* matters in the works of Mozart, including commentary on *editions,* and *sources* of his music.

General

738. Albrecht, Otto E. *A Census of Autograph Music Manuscripts of European Composers in American Libraries.* Philadelphia: University of Pennsylvania Press, 1953. 331 pp. illus. ML 135. A2 A4.

    Author reports on seventeen collections in the U. S. A. having a total of about fifty Mozart manuscripts (now many more). Pages 197–204 are devoted to Mozart. Bibliography; index.

    See also: Hans Moldenauer. "Übersicht der Musikmanuskripte W. A. Mozarts in U. S. A." *Mozart Jahrbuch* 7 (1956): 88 ff..

    For discussion of Mozart's lost and fragmentary manuscripts, King (#768) offers a good introduction.

739. Angermüller, Rudolph. "Libraries, Archives, and Musicological Research in Salzburg." *Current Musicology* 16 (1973): 26–30.

Useful brief summary. For additional information, see *Fontes Artis* 107, 3-4 (July–December 1980): 174–177.

740. Arnold, Ignaz E. F. K. *Wolfgang Amadeus Mozart und Joseph Haydn.* Erfurt: Müller, 1810. 118 pp.

This early monograph (2/3 on Mozart and 1/3 on Haydn) contains anecdotes and musical comparisons which illustrate how seriously the music of Mozart and Haydn was taken. The author, who was not close to either composer, also compares Mozart with Raphael. Arnold's previous book on Mozart, *Mozart's Geist,* had been published in 1803. No index.

741. Asov, Erich H. Müller von. "Die Mozarthandschriften der Stadtbibliothek Leipzig." *Neue Mozart Jahrbuch* 2 (1942): 245–265.

Discussion of Mozart manuscripts in Leipzig.

742. ———. "Mozartiana." *Musikforschung* 8, 1 (1955): 74–83.

Discusses the whereabouts of some Mozart manuscripts.

743. Biancolli, Louis, ed. *The Mozart Handbook.* Cleveland: World Publishing Company, 1954. 629 pp. illus. (Reprint edition, Westport, Conn.: Greenwood Press, 1976. ISBN: 08371-8496-7.)

Although this useful volume on Mozart's life and works was intended as an introduction, its generous inclusiveness makes it a handy reference for biography and music. Chronology; bibliography; list of works; index.

744. Blaschitz, Mena. *Die Salzburger Fragmente.* Bonn: Diss. 1924. (Excerpt: Jahrbuch der Phil. Fakultät, 1924–1925.)*

Cited by King, Schneider and Algatzy, Tyson as a useful guide to manuscript fragments in Salzburg.

745. Blume, Friedrich. "Mozart's Style and Influence." See Landon-Mitchell (#774): 10–31.

In a revealing essay, author explores the phenomenon that led from almost indifference to Mozart's music on the part of the public to a passion for it; he discusses demarcation between youthful and mature works, as well as sources on style.

746. Bossarelli, Francesco. "Mozart alla Biblioteca del Conservatorio di Napoli." *Analecta musicologica* 5 (1968): 248–266; 7 (1969): 190–212.

Cited by Duckles (#526) for Mozart holdings.

747. Busoni, Ferruccio. "Aufzeichnungen und Tageblätter." (Translated anonymously into English from the German.) *The Sackbut* 11 (1921): 33–36.

Perceptive short comments on the perfection of mood setting, technical mastery, formal satisfaction, and fulfilling content in the music of Mozart, by a 20th century composer. Reprinted in King (#768).

748. Croll, Gerhard, ed. *Wolfgang Amadeus Mozart.* Darmstadt: Wissenschaftliche Buchgesellschaft, 1977. 505 pp.

Mozart scholarship 1850–1970, presented chronologically in twenty-three articles by O. Jahn, L. v. Köchel, H. Kretschmar, T. de Wyzewa, H. Abert, W. Fischer, L. Schrade, A. Einstein, B. Paumgartner, W. Gerstenberg, E. F. Schmid, H. Engel, E. Hess, F. Blume, W. Plath, A. A. Abert, O. E. Deutsch, J. P. Larsen, G. Allrogen. Index.

749. Deutsch, Otto Erich. "Mozarts Nachlass." *Mozart Jahrbuch* 4 (1953): 32–37.

Brief description of compositions in manuscript which Constanze inherited on Mozart's death. Using Constanze's correspondence, author discusses the sale of manuscripts to André and considers roles of Maximilian Stadler and Georg Nikolaus von Nissen as advisors/helpers/editors.

750. ———. "Sartis Streitschrift gegen Mozart." *Mozart Jahrbuch* 12 (1962–1963): 7–13.

Mozart's elder contemporary Sarti (1729–1802), originally a composer of opera seria, had little use for Mozart, and vice versa—an introduction to the subject.

751. Ebisawa (Bin E. Bisawa). "Mozart kenkyu noto." In *Mozart shosho* 1. Tokyo: Ongaku-no-tomo, 1973. 414 pp. (Notes on Japanese research, in Japanese.)*

Seventeen assembled articles on the Japanese relationship to Mozart.
RILM: 1973—#3435.
See also reports from Japan (and other countries) published frequently in *Mitteilungen der ISM* (Appendix IV).

752. Einstein, Alfred. "Two missing sonatas by Mozart." *Music & Letters* 31, 1 (January 1940): 1–17.

Discussion of autographs of organ sonatas K. 241, 264, in the Leningrad Public Library.

753. Eisen, Cliff. "Some Lost Mozart Editions of the 1780s." *Mitteilungen der ISM* 32, 1-4 (1984): 64–70.

Discussion of Mozart editions issued by Storck, Helmer, Martius.
See also: Cliff Eisen. "Some Contributions to a New Mozart Documentary Biography." *Journal of the American Musicological Society* 39, 3 (Fall 1986): 615–632. Discussion of Westphal and Rellstab (Bremen) editions of Mozart works, inter alia.

754. Emerson, John. "Materials for Mozart Research. An Inventory of the Mozart Nachlass of Alfred Einstein." Berkeley: Music Library, University of California, 1963. 28 pp. Typescript.

As Alfred Einstein was one of the outstanding Mozart scholars of this century, the careful catalogue of this corpus of notes and photostats is very valuable for the study of Mozart fragments, and works whose availability is limited.

755. Engländer, Richard. "The Sketches for 'The Magic Flute' at Upsala, Sweden." *Musical Quarterly* 27, 3 (July 1941): 343–355.

Revealing discussion of fragments acquired from Constanze by Count Silverstolpe (Swedish chargé d'affaires in Vienna, 1796–1802). These fragments were accompanied by similar sketches for *La Clemenza di Tito*, as well as Mozart's last *Masonic Music*, K. 619, a facsimile of which is noted

(#127). Revealing background concerning Mozart's methods of composition.

756. Farmer, Henry George, and Herbert Smith. *New Mozartiana: the Mozart Relics in the Collection of the University of Glasgow.* Revised. Glasgow: University, 1976. 157 pp.

Originally printed in 1935, a catalogue of Mozartiana of V. H. Zavertal, who had inherited the material from Carl Thomas Mozart. Includes Leopold Mozart's long petition to Emperor Joseph II concerning Count Affligio's refusal to produce *La finta semplice* (in which Leopold listed the compositions of Wolfgang up to 1767). Index.

757. Floros, Constantin. *Mozart Studien.* Wiesbaden: Breitkopf & Härtel, 1979. 172 pp. illus.* ISBN: 3-7651-0167-2.

Excellent discussion of Mozart's last symphonies; the structures of opera overtures; Mozart's synthesis of opera buffa and opera seria; Mozart's place in Austrian church music. Notes; bibliography; no index.

758. Graf, Max. "Mozart in Musical Criticism." In *Composer and Critic.* New York: Norton, 1946, pp. 130–140. ISBN: 393 00497.

An introduction to critics' opinions of Mozart and his music, during his lifetime and shortly thereafter, placed in the context of "200 years of music criticism."

759. Haberkamp, Gertraut. *Die Erstdrucke von Wolfgang Amadeus Mozart.* Tutzing: Schneider, 1986. 2 vols. 494 pp. and 387 pp. illus.*

Original and early editions of Mozart's music. Excerpts have appeared in Schneider's catalogues (see #810). Indexes.

760. Hafner, Otfried. "Mozart in steirischen Musikalienhandel von 1800." *Mitteilungen der ISM* 29, 1-2 (February 1981): 29–33.

Discussion of dissemination of Mozart's music around Graz, Austria.

761.   Hammer, Karl. *W. A. Mozart—eine theologische Deutung.* Zurich: EVZ Verlag, 1974. 443 pp.

The fact that no musical examples are included presupposes the reader already has considerable knowledge at his finger tips. The author discusses the expansive variety of Mozart's music from a theological and cultural point of view—exploring the broad range of his achievements: style and development, compositional techniques, relation to Gluck, relation to Beethoven, relation to humanity, to God, and to such themes as freedom, and to such other themes as death and reconciliation. Bibliography; indexes.

762.   Hopkinson, Cecil. *A Dictionary of Parisian Publishers, 1700–1950.* London: Hopkinson, 1954. 131 pp. illus. map.

Useful alphabetical descriptive listing and history of over 500 Parisian publishers, some of whom published early editions of works of Mozart. Bibliography.

763.   Hrabussay, Zoltán. "Mozart Dokumente." *Bericht . . . Mozart Konferenz.* Prague, 1956.*

Describes documents in Czechoslovakian collections. Cited in Tyrrell (#545).

764.   Johansson, Carl. *French Music Publishers' Catalogues in the Second Half of the Eighteenth Century.* Upsala: Almquist & Wiksell, 1955. 2 vols. Vol. 1: Text, 228 pp.; Vol. 2: Plates, 145 facsimiles. Index.

More specialized than Hopkinson, above.
See also: Anik Devries and François Lesure. *Dictionnaire des éditeurs de musique française.* 2 vols. Geneva: Minkoff Editions, 1979. ISBN: 2-8266-0460-0.
Also: Georges de Saint-Foix. "Les éditions françaises de Mozart, 1765–1801." Pp. 247–248 in *Mélanges de musicologie offerts à M. Lionel de la Laurencie.* Paris: Société française de musicologie. 294 pp.
Also: François Lesure. *Catalogue de la musique imprimée avant 1800 conservée dans les bibliothèques publiques de Paris.* Paris: Bibliothèque Nationale, 1981. 708 pp. ML 125 P 27 L 5. Arranged alphabetically by author.

765. Kaut, Josef. *Festspiele in Salzburg: Eine Dokumentation.* Munich: Deutsche Taschen Verlag, 1981. 500 pp. illus. (First edition, 1970. 291 pp.)

An excellent chronology of Salzburg Festivals, 1920–1963. Index.

766. King, Alexander Hyatt. *Mozart: A Biography with a Survey of Books, Editions & Recordings.* London: Bingley, 1970. 114 pp. ISBN: 85157-091-7.

An excellent brief life, plus a splendid bibliographical essay, plus a unique profile of editions of the music of Mozart. (The recordings, reviewed by Brian Redfern, do not receive the same informed treatment.) Index.

767. ————. "Some Aspects of Recent Mozart Research." *Proceedings of the Royal Musical Association* 100 (1973–1974): 1–18.

Discusses the Bauer, Deutsch and Eibl seven-volume edition of Mozart letters (above), as well as important elements in the research of Einstein, Oldman, Plath.
Cited in Angermüller and Schneider (#546).

768. ————. *Mozart in Retrospect.* London: Oxford University Press, 1955; revised, 1970. (Reprinted, Westport, Conn.: Greenwoood Press, 1976. 279 pp. illus. ISBN: 0-8371-8760-5.) ML 410 M9 K55.

The latest edition includes a new introduction, plus sixteen remarkable essays, and three appendixes, dealing with the history of Mozart's reputation, the publication of his works, Mozart and the organ, certain compositional techniques, the fate of some manuscripts, and other historical subjects partly reprinted from articles previously published. Notes; bibliography; indexes.

769. ————. *A Mozart Legacy; Aspects of the British Library Collection.* London: British Library, 1984. 110 pp. illus. ISBN: 0-7123-0044-9.

Reproducing important Mozartiana in various categories, the author continues his wide-ranging series of pertinent inquiries into the significant British relationship to Mozart on several levels. Bibliography; index.

770. Köhler, Karl-Heinz. "Die Ewerbungen der Mozart-Autographen der Berliner Staatsbibliothek." *Mozart Jahrbuch* 12 (1962–1963): 55–68.

Brief discussion of Mozart treasures in Berlin, and how they got there. In 1982 Hans Günter Klein edited the most recent listing of Mozart holdings.

771. ————. "*Mozartiana '81: zum Handschriften Nachlass und Vermächtnis des Komponisten.*" *Musik und Gesellschaft* (DDR) 31, 1 (1981): 13–17. illus.*

Author asserts documents in Mozart's will and estate are sources of information on Mozart's orchestration and editorial practices in composition.
RILM: 1981—#530.

772. Kolbin, Dmitri. "Autographs Mozart und seiner Familie in der UdSSR." *Mozart Jahrbuch* 16 (1968–1970): 281–303.

Discussion of sixteen letters and manuscripts of Mozart and his family, including K. 456, their whereabouts in Russian libraries and museums, and how they got there; facsimiles and music.
See also Tyson (#818).

773. Krummel, D. W. *Guide for Dating Early Published Music.* 263 pp. illus. Hackensack, New Jersey: Boonin, 1974. ISBN: 0-913574-25-Z.

Issued under the auspices of the International Association of Music Libraries, this is a valuable introductory tool for persons interested in eighteenth century publishers and early Mozart editions. Bibliography; skimpy index.

774. Landon, H. C. Robbins, and Donald Mitchell, eds. *The Mozart Companion.* New York: Norton, 1956. 397 pp. illus. mus exx. ISBN: 0393-00499-6.

Twelve essays: "Mozart Portraits" by Otto Erich Deutsch; "Mozart's Style and Influence" by Friedrich Blume; "The Keyboard Music" by Arthur Hutchings; "The Serenades for Wind Bands" by Donald Mitchell; "The Chamber Works" by Hans Keller; "The Smaller Orchestral Works" by Hans Engel; "The Symphonies" by Jens Peter Larsen; "The Concertos, Their Sources" by Friedrich Blume; "The

Concertos, Their Musical Origin and Development" by H. C. Robbins Landon; "The Operas" by Gerald Abraham; "The Concert Arias" by Paul Hamburger; "The Church Music" by Karl Geiringer. The Larsen, Deutsch, Hutchings, Blume/Landon chapters all provide brilliant summaries of their respective subjects. Notes; bibliographies; index.

Readers of German are referred to a parallel volume in which many of the same subjects are discussed by different writers: *Mozart Aspekte.* Paul Schaller and Hans Kühner, eds. Olsten: Walter, 1956. 300 pp. (Contributions by Kühne, Paumgartner, etc.)

775. ———. "Two Works Falsely Attributed to Mozart." *Music Review* 17 (February 1956): 29–34.

Robbins Landon is one of the important scholars providing reports on chronology, authenticity, and other important research areas, in between editions of the Köchel catalogue.

776. ———. *Essays on the Viennese Classical Style.* New York: Macmillan, 1970. 187 pp. illus. ML60 L225 E9.

Twelve collected essays considering aspects of Mozart's *Requiem,* and contemporary compositions of Joseph Haydn, Michael Haydn Gluck, Beethoven. Occasional notes and references. Index.

777. Lang, Paul Henry, ed. *The Creative World of Mozart.* New York: Norton, 1963. 149 pp. illus.

Introduction by Paul Henry Lang; "Mozart's Creative Process" by Erich Hertzmann; "On Mozart's Rhythm" by Edward Lowinsky; "Mozart and the Clavier" by Nathan Broder (revealing analysis, although inconclusive as to when Mozart finally preferred the piano); "Mozart and Haydn" by E. F. Schmid; Requiem but no Peace" by Friedrich Blume (thoughtful essay); "The Melodic Sources of Mozart's Most Popular Lied" by F. W. Sternfeld; "The First Guide to Mozart" by Nathan Broder; "Some Fallacies in Mozart Biography" by O. E. Deutsch. Reprinted from *Musical Quarterly,* valuable insights, but often not as probing as Landon-Mitchell above. No index.

778. Lewicki, Rudolph. "Die Mozartsammlung des A. Fuchs." *Mitteilungen der ISM* 1, 2 (February 1920): 36 ff.

Although the research of Fuchs was early, it was serious, and clues concerning Mozart music which has since disappeared may prove useful.
See also: Richard Schaal. "Quellen zur Sammlung Fuchs." *Musikforschung* 16 (1963): 67–72.

779. Luoma, Robert G. "The Function of Dynamics in the Music of Haydn, Mozart, and Beethoven." *College Music Symposium* 16 (Spring 1976): 32–41.

Author notes dynamic climaxes are either departures or returns, depending on what the composer emphasizes for structural balance. Keys and forms used by classical composers govern dynamic markings and can guide interpreters as to which "ff" is the loudest, etc., and also give guidance in other questions of dynamics.

780. Major, Ervin. *Mozart und Ungarn.* Budapest: Franklin Nymoda, 1956.*

Discussion of Mozart manuscripts in Hungary—written in German and Hungarian. Cited in Schneider and Algatzy (#556).

781. Milligan, Thomas. "Zu einer frühen französischen Ausgabe von Mozarts Kalavierwerken." *Mitteilungen der ISM* 29, 1-2 (February 1981): 34–35.

Clarification of relationships and chronology of some early Paris editions of Mozart works published by Carli, Launer, Pleyel.

782. *Mozart, Klassik für die Gegenwart.* Oldenburg: Stalling-Druck, 1978. 156 pp. illus. ISBN: 3-922154-00-X.

Articles by nine authorities, including Constantin Floros on Mozart's last symphonies, Siegfried Goslick on Mozart's operas, with emphasis on Hamburg, a place Mozart never visited; chronology by Gisela Jaacks. No index.

783. *Mozart Memorials in Salzburg.* ISM. Salzburg, 1946. 60 pp. illus.

Useful as an introduction to Salzburg collections. See also Angermüller and Rech. *100 Jahre ISM,* Salzburg (#551).

784. *Wolfgang Amadeus Mozart: Autograph Manuscript of Nine Symphonies.* Stephen Roe, ed. London: Sotheby's 1987. 16 pp. illus.

This attractive publication reproduces full size facsimile pages from Mozart Symphonies K. 162, 162b, 161b, 186a, 173dA, as well as brief discussions of these symphonies and also K. 173dB, 161a, 189k, 186b. The text by Dr. Roe summarizes the origin of the bound collection of symphonies, and its importance. Sold at Sotheby's May 22, 1987. (Autograph owner might be reached through Sotheby's or through the Pierpont Morgan Library, New York City.)

785. Münster, Robert. "Eine Salzburger Handschrift der Sinfonia Concertante K. V. 364." *Mitteilungen der ISM* 15, 1-2 (February 1967): 3–6.

The Bavarian Staatsbibliothek has a set of parts of K. 364 by a copyist who worked for Mozart, and Münster considers these parts very probably the most accurate available (and regrets they were not used in the preparation of NMA).

786. Musiol, Karl. "Mozartiana in Paulinenkloster zu Tschenstockau." *Mitteilungen der ISM* 15, 3-4 (August 1967): 5–10.

Eighteen (?) works of Mozart, with incipits, in Poland are discussed.

787. ———. "Mozartiana in schlesischen Archiven und Bibliotheken." *Mozart Jahrbuch* 14 (1965–1966): 142–151.

Bibliographical research and listings of Mozart material in north Germany.

788. ———. "Mozartiana in einem unbekannten periodischen Verkaufskatalog der Firma F. E. C. Leuckart aus dem Jahren 1812–1819." *Mitteilungen der ISM* 20, 1-2 (February 1972): 5–10.

Discussion of Leuckart's dissemination of various early editions of Mozart's works, and music criticism of the composer from 1785.

789. *Nachtrag zu Köchel.* Leipzig: Breitkopf & Härtel, 1889. List of known owners of Mozart autographs, as of 1889.

790. *Neue Mozart Ausgabe* (NMA). Kassel: Bärenreiter, 1955– .

Planned as a replacement for the original Breitkopf & Härtel complete edition of the nineteenth century, the excellent notes of the individual volumes of this improved ongoing series include the whereabouts of the original manuscript, if it is known.

791. Nielsen, Carl. "Mozart og vor tid." (Mozart and our Time.) *Orfeus* 4 (1927). (Translated from Danish into English by Reginald Spink and printed in *Living Music,* Copenhagen: Wilhelm Hansen, c. 1950, pp. 13–23.)

An attractive essay on the importance of Mozart as a model for composers.

792. Nottebohm, Martin Gustav. *Mozartiana.* Leipzig: Breitkopf & Härtel, 1880. 139 pp.

Letters and documents concerning Mozart which had not been previously printed, including communications to and from Constanze and Nannerl. Notes; no index.

793. Nowak, Leopold. "Die Wiener Mozart-Autographen." *Österreichische Musikzeitschrift* 11 (1956): 180 ff.

Authoritative brief discussion of Mozart manuscripts in Vienna.

794. Oldman, Cecil Bernard. "Cipriani Potter's Edition of Mozart's Piano Works." In *Festschrift Otto Erich Deutsch zum 80. Geburtstag am 5. September 1963,* Walter Gerstenberg, et al., eds. Kassel: Bärenreiter, 1963. 392 pp. Bibliography; index.

Oldman's article, on pages 120–127, discusses Coventry's "complete" English edition (1836–), later taken over by Novello, and provides informed historical background.

795. Orel, Alfred. "Mozartiana in Sweden." *Acta Mozartiana* 1 (1959): 3–8.

Discussion of Mozart manuscripts in various Swedish collections.

See also: Gösta Morin. "Mozart und Schweden." In *Bericht über den Internationalen musikwissenschaftlichen Kongress Wien, 1956:* 416 ff. Cited in Tyrrell (#545).

796. Pesková, Jitrenka, and Jiri Zaloba. *Katalog Mozartiana* (Schwarzenberg) Praha, 1981.*

Seventy-five first editions of Mozart compositions are listed in this collection in Krumlov, along with miscellaneous Mozartiana.

RILM: 1981—4141.

797. Pfannhauser, Karl. "Unechter Mozart." *Mitteilungen der ISM* 7, 3-4 (1958): 9 ff.

Discusses confusion of Mozart's handwriting with that of his father, Leopold.

798. Pierpont Morgan Library. *The Mary Flagler Cary Music Collection.* New York: Pierpont Morgan Library, 1970. 101 pp. illus.

Discusses several autographs, including K. 467. Other Morgan Library publications discuss other Mozart autographs; for example, the Heinemann Collection catalogue discusses K. 537 and other Mozart compositions.

799. Plath, Wolfgang. "Beiträge zur Mozart-Autographie I. Die Handschrift Leopold Mozarts." *Mozart Jahrbuch* 11 (1960–1961): 82–117.

Thorough study of Leopold's handwriting establishes he copied or composed more of Wolfgang's early music than had been realized previously.

See also: *Mozart Jahrbuch* 17 (1971–1972): 19–36, and *Mozart Jahrbuch* 20 (1976–1977): 131–173, for further outstanding articles in which Plath discusses authenticity, use of the name Mozart, Wolfgang's handwriting (with examples), Mozart's estate, manuscript fragments, various arrangements (by Mozart, and by others), Michael Haydn's personal and professional relationship with the Mozarts.

800. ————. "Mozartiana in Fulda und Frankfurt." *Mozart Jahrbuch* 16 (1968–1970): 333–386.

Discussion of the collection of Heinrich Henkel (1822–1899), particularly of K. 390, autograph of #30 of *Così*, and K^6 Ann. C.23.01; Henkel was a student of J. A. André.

801. ————. "Gefälschte Mozart-Autographe II: Der Fall Jelinek." *Acta Mozartiana* 26, 5 (1979): 72–80.

Plath considers evidence accusing F. X. Jelinek (1818–1880), archivist of Salzburger Dom Musikverein und Mozarteum and cathedral choir director, of forging Mozart documents.

802. Racek, J. *Neznámá Mozartova autografní torsa.* Ostrava: Hudební, 1959.*

A Czech discussion of Mozart autograph fragments. Cited in Schneider and Algatzy (#556), and Blum (#521).

803. Raeburn, Michael, and Christopher Raeburn. "Mozart Manuscripts in Florence." *Music & Letters* 40, 4 (October 1959): 334–336.

Summary discussion of invaluable early, authoritative copies of Mozart operas: *Die Entführung, Figaro, Don Giovanni, Così, Tito, Idomeneo, Die Zauberflöte.*
See also: A. Holschneider. "Neue Mozartiana in Italien." *Die Musikforschung* 15 (1962): 227 ff.

804. Reich, Nancy B. "The Rudorff Collection." *Notes* 31, 2 (December 1974): 247–261.

List of Mozart compositions (15 manuscripts, 100 printed editions) and other music in the private Berlin collection of Ernest Rudorff (1840–1916).

805. Reijen, Paul W. van. "Corrections and Supplements to Köchel." *Mozart Jahrbuch,* 17 (1971–1972): 342–401.

Again, corrections, which will find their way into the next edition of Köchel.

See also: Reijen. "Die Literaturangaben im Köchel-Verzeichnis." *Mitteilungen der ISM Salzburg*, 30, 1-2 (February 1982): 12–27. Reijen exhorts researchers to aim for careful observation and diligent transcription, even in small matters.

806. Schaal, Richard. "Zur Musiksammlung von Richard Wagner." *Mozart Jahrbuch* 16 (1968–1970): 387–390.

Discusses Mozart autographs and other manuscripts of Wagner given to the Berlin Staatsbibliothek in 1874.

807. Scharnagel, August. "Freiherr Thaddäus von Dürnitz und seine Musikaliensammlung." *Mitteilungen der Ges. für Bayerische Musikgeschichte* 7 (1973): 144–150.*

Dürnitz's name was linked with Mozart in connection with Mozart's keyboard sonata in D, K. 284 and other works. Housed in Munich, the Dürnitz collection, of 997 works by 220 composers, disappeared after 1861.
RILM: 1974—#586.

808. Schlosser, Joh. Aloys. *W. A. Mozarts Biographie.* 3rd ed. Augsburg: J. A. Schlosser Buch und Kunsthandlung. 1844. 192 pp. illus.

Based largely on Schlichtegroll, with some other facts and anecdotes which ring true. Includes list of Mozart works by category, with publishers. Also reprints Mozart's own list of works, originally published by André. No index.

809. Schmieder, Wolfgang. "Mozart-Dokumente in Arkiv von Breitkopf & Härtel." *Jahrbuch der deutschen Musik* (Leipzig) 1943: 187–191.

Identifies persons involved in some Breitkopf early editions of Mozart music: Franz Leitl, H. Schnorr von Carolsfeld (1764–1831), Julius Rietz (1812–1877), and discusses Breitkopf relations with Constanze and with Niemetschek.

810. Schneider, Hans. *Mozart und Zeitgenossen.* Katalog 293. Tutzing: Musikantiquariat, 1986. 115 pp. illus.

One of a long series of distinguished publications, thoroughly researched for previously forgotten facts.

811. Shaw, Bernard. *London Music in 1888–1889*. New York: Dodd Mead & Co., 1937. 439 pp.

Among Shaw's sparkling journalistic reviews are several articles on Mozart concerned with his operas, the *Requiem*, songs, symphonies, quartets, and his "thorough bass tutor." Index.

See also Shaw's *Collected Works*.

812. Sommer, Susan T., and Richard Koprowski. "The Toscanini Memorial Archives at The New York Public Library." *College Music Symposium* 17, 2 (Fall 1977): 103–123.

Lists forty-nine Mozart scores on microfilm available for study—a splendid resource, growing regularly.

813. Squire, W. Barclay. *Catalogue of Printed Music Published Between 1487 and 1800 Now in the British Museum*. Vol. II (L–Z). Nendeln, Liechtenstein: Kraus Reprint, 1980. 720 pp. + supplement of 85 pp.

Includes Mozart.

814. Steinpress, Boris. "Neues über Mozarts Beziehungen zu Russland." *Sovetskaya muzyka* 12 (1956): 40 ff.*

Discussion of manner in which Mozart's influence in Russia was felt long before his advocacy by Pushkin, Dargomysky, and Rimsky-Korsakov. Cited in Schneider and Algatzy (#556).

815. ———. "Russische Ausgaben der Mozart-Werke in 18. Jahrhundert." *Mozart Jahrbuch* 13 (1964): 292–298.

Steinpress notes B. Klostermann published three keyboard sonatas in 1788, and that the following Russian firms had all published works by Mozart by 1796: K. Gerstenberg, Lissner, Logan, and Rospini.

816. Szabolcsi, Bence. "Mozart et la comédie populaire." *Studie musicologica* 1 (1961): 65–91.*

Article published under the auspices of the Budapest Hungarian Academy of Sciences discusses the influence of popular works Mozart saw on the music he composed. Cited in Schneider and Algatzy (#556).

817. Tovey, Donald Francis. *Essays in Musical Analysis.* London: Oxford University Press, 1935. 7 vols.

    Seven Mozart symphonies, fourteen concertos, and ten other works are discussed here by Tovey. While some readers may find Tovey's classic essays too general, others will welcome their breadth and clarity. Index.

818. Tyson, Alan. *Mozart. Studies of the Autograph Scores.* Cambridge, Mass.: Harvard University Press, 1987. 381 pp. ISBN: 0-674-58830-4. ML 410. M 9 T 95

    In eighteen carefully reasoned chapters (all but one revised from various sources), Dr. Tyson addresses a number of the perplexing problems in Mozart research. His answers help date Mozart manuscripts, separate his autographs from Süssmayr's, clarify questions on horn concertos. operas, and piano concertos. Notes; appendix; indexes.

    See also: *Festschrift Albi Rosenthal.* Rudolf Elvers, ed. Tutzing: Schneider, 1984. 319 pp. illus.

    Five among twenty-seven contributors discuss Mozart and his music. Particularly interesting is Tyson's discussion indicating that one can date works as before or after 1781 on the evidence that Mozart composed on 10 stave paper up to 1781, and that in Vienna he used 12 stave paper.

819. Vetter, Walther. "Deutschland und das Formgefühl Italien." *Deutsches Jahrbuch des Musikwissenschaft* 4 (1959): 7–37.

    Discussion of how Mozart, Gluck, and Wagenseil used forms of Vinci, Jommelli, Caldara, and Paisiello.

820. Waters, Edward N. "Musical Vienna in the Library of Congress." *Festschrift Josef Stummvoll.* Josef Mayerhofer and Walter Ritzer, eds. Vienna: Hollinek, 1970, pp. 593–615.

    Mozart compositions discussed include K. 361, 515.

821. Weinmann, Alexander. *Beiträge zur Geschichte des alt-Weiner Musikverlages.* Vienna, 1948–.

    An important open-ended series on early Viennese publishers.

See also: Otto Erich Deutsch. "Mozarts Verleger." *Mozart Jahrbuch* 6 (1955): 45–55.

Also: Otfried Hafner (#760).

Also: Erich Valentin. *Mozart und seine Verleger*, Katalog 51. Tutzing: Schneider, c. 1970.

822. ———. *Wolfgang Amadeus Mozart Verzeichnis von Erst und Frühdrucken bis etwa 1800.* Kassel: Bärenreiter, 1978. 217 pp. ISBN: 3-7618-0596-9.

823. Wolf, Eugene K. "Communication." *Journal of the American Musicological Society* 25, 1 (Spring 1972): 122–123.

Relating aspects of Mozart style to Stamitz and Mannheim, based on author's work with Henkel material (now owned by the Library of Congress) and on Wolfgang Plath's excellent article on Mozartiana in *Mozart Jahrbuch* 16 (1968–1970), cited above (#799).

824. Wurzbach, Constantin von. *Mozart Buch.* Vienna: Wallishaufer, 1869. 295 pp. illus.

Although inevitably Wurzbach repeats some of Nissen (#632), he provides a very useful summary of Mozart musical and biographical studies up to 1869. Biography; index.

Performance Practice

(Readers are reminded that in this field *interpretation* of facts is subject to change.)

825. Albrecht, Hans, ed. *Die Bedeutung der Zeichen Keil, Strich und Punkt bei Mozart.* Musikwissenschaftliche Arbeiten 10. Kassel: Bärenreiter, 1957. 110 pp.

Herman Keller, Hubert Unferricht, Oswald Jones, Alfred Kreutz, and Ewald Zimmermann discuss the meaning and interpretation of three signs (wedge, stroke, dot) in the music of Mozart, including solo, chamber, orchestra, vocal works, with nearly 200 musical examples. Bibliography; notes, no index.

826. Babitz, Sol. "Some Errors in Mozart Performance." *Mozart Jahrbuch* 16 (1968–1970): 62 ff.

   Observations of ways not to be true to Mozart's works, in spirit and in letter.
   See also Paumgartner (#635).

827. *Current Musicology* 8 (1969): 1–96. "Bibliography of Performance Practice."

   1131 titles, plus index. An extremely useful bibliography. This was issued in an expanded, corrected version as *Performance Practice: A Bibliography*. Mary Vinquist and Neal Zaslaw, eds. New York: Norton, 1970. 114 pp.

828. Engel, Hans, et al. "Interpretation und Aufführungspraxix." *Mozart Jahrbuch* 16 (1968–1970): 5–46.

   Engel reports a Salzburg colloquium on 18th-century performance practice—leading the orchestra, ornaments, pitch, wind instruments technique, and other related subjects.

829. Göhler, Georg. "C und ₵ bei Mozart." *Schweizerische Musikzeitung* 76, 23 (1936): 667 ff.; 77, 1 (1937): 22–23.

   An indispensable consideration toward achieving appropriate tempo in performance. In instrumental as in vocal works, Mozart's tempo indications by Italian terms and by figures in the clef generally were idiomatic for his time. However, as Göhler notes with examples, Mozart was not invariably consistent; as a rule he wanted the fast movements to be brilliant without the notes becoming imprecise or the words garbled. Sections in moderate tempo could be accelerated in their conclusions with the change from C to ₵, or 4/4 to 6/8.

830. Keller, Hermann. *Phrasing and Articulation*. New York: Norton, 1973. 117 pp. ISBN: 0-393-00881-6.

   Specific aspects in relation to performances of works by J. S. Bach, Mozart, and Beethoven are considered. Bibliography; index.

831. Mackerras, Charles. "Sense about the Appoggiatura." *Opera* 14, 10 (October 1963): 669–678.

Alert to the expression and elegance obtained by approproate use of ornaments, the conductor-musicologist offers a judicious, useful, brief guide for performers. Seven of the musical examples are from compositions of Mozart.

See also: Charles Mackerras: "A Search for Style," with John W. Freeman in *Opera News* 51, 5 (November 1986): 20–23.

Also: Kenneth Stern. "In Defense of Embellishment." *Opera News* 51, 11 (February 14, 1987): 18–21.

Also: F. Neumann (#833).

832. Mies, Paul. "The Meanings of the Corona in Mozart." *Monthly Music Record* 90 (July–August 1960): 132–138.

A corona is Italian for pause. Mozart used it in three ways for dramatic effect: lengthening a note or rest, or preparing for a cadenza; a division mark between sections of movements; an indication of the end of a movement. The last two usages do not necessitate lengthening of notes.

833. Neumann, Frederick. *Ornamentation and Improvisation in Mozart.* Princeton: Princeton University Press, 1986. 301 pp. ISBN: 0-691-9123-4. MT 80 N48.

Admirably researched data on the main elements of vocal and instrumental ornamentation in Mozart's time (with examples) and how they applied to improvisation. The fine publications of the Badura-Skodas (#1031) give performers valuable practical suggestions (which Neumann usually finds appropriate), but Neumann's work also reports contemporary theory. The Badura-Skodas and Neumann both note Mozart opposed over-embellishment, that he did follow certain rules, but that as an artist he approached each composition on a fresh basis (however often one can trace his personal solutions to particular sources—his father, J. C. and C. P. E. Bach, Grétry, Padre Martini, etc.). Mozart was convinced that proper expression demanded flexible procedures. However, Neumann sometimes approves performing Mozart's blunt endings as written. Excellent notes, bibliography, index.

834. Patzak, Julius. "Richard Strauss als Mozart-Dirigent." *Österreichische Musikzeitschrift* 11 (July–August 1954): 274–275.

Personal memories of performances the tenor sang under the direction of Strauss.

See also: Strauss (#935), and Del Mar (#960).

Also: Roland Tenschert. "Richard Strauss und Mozart." *Mozart Jahrbuch* 5 (1954): 195–205. Consideration of how Strauss used Mozart music.

835. Paumgartner, Bernhard. "Zur Aufführungspraxis Mozartscher Werke." *Schweizerische Musikzeitung* 81, 12 (1 December 1941): 321–328.

Practical discussion by an acknowledged authority, who charges interpreters to study facsimiles, to realize instruments were weaker in the 18th century, but seek balance. Noting it is difficult to reproduce 18th-century sound, he advises on problems of remaining true to the essence of a work, and its gaiety, its true message as it was at the time.

MOZART AND OTHER COMPOSERS

This section emphasizes technical or stylistic matters, but see also section devoted to Mozart's contemporaries and colleagues (#666–694).

836. (Beethoven) Singer, I. *Mozart and Beethoven.* Baltimore: Johns Hopkins, 1977. 155 pp.

Central discussion is the comparison of the concept of love as found in the operas of Mozart and Beethoven; also discusses Beethoven's idealism. Sources cited in footnotes; index.

837. (Handel) Fellerer, Karl. "Mozart und Handel. *Mozart Jahrbuch* 4 (1953): 47–55.

Discusses Handel's influence on Mozart's vocal works as early as 1767. Also treats other aspects of their musical relationship, but ignores fact that Mozart heard Handel's music when in England.

838. Siegmund-Schulze, Walther. "Wolfgang Amadeus Mozart unter dem Einfluss Georg Friedrich Händels." *Händel Jahrbuch* 8 (1956): 21–55. [Leipzig: Deutscher Verlag für Musik.]

More comprehensive discussion of the relationship of
the music of Mozart to that of Handel than above, yet both
are instructive.

839. (Joseph Haydn) Danckwardt, Marianne. *Die langsame
Einleitung, ihre Herkunft, ihr Bau bei Haydn und Mozart.*
Tutzing: Schneider, 1977. 435 pp.

Author links Haydn and Mozart's slow introductions to
opening fanfares of 17th-century operas and to the initial
movement of the sonata da chiesa. Bibliography; index.
See also: Walter Gerstenberg, in *Festschrift Wilhelm
Fischer.* H. Zingerle, ed. Innsbruck, 1956, 177 pp. Listed in
Gerboth (#528).

840. (Jommelli and Majo and Traeta) Ballola Carli, Giovanni.
"Mozart e l'opera seria di Jommelli, de Majo e Traeta."
Analecta Musicologica 18 (1978): 138–147.

A useful discussion of the influence the works of these
three composers had on the compositions of young Mozart.

841. (Lang) Davis, Shelley. "J. C. Lang and the Early Classical
Keyboard Concerto." *Musical Quarterly* 66 (January
1980): 21–52.

A prolific (40 symphonies, 31 concertos) elder German
contemporary of Haydn and Mozart, Lang (1722–1798) was
active in instrumental music in Augsburg, Coblenz,
Dresden, Trier—as composer and conductor.

842. (Monsigny) Schmid, Ernst Fritz. "Mozart und Monsigny."
Mozart Jahrbuch 8 (1957): 57–62.

Discusses relationship of Mozart to French style, and
Monsigny (1729–1812) in particular.

843. (Mysliveček) Očadlík, Mirko. "Myslivečekuv Oratorium
Abrama e Isaaco a Mozartuv Idomeneus." *Národní
divadlo* 9, 11 (1931).*

Discussion of Mozart's debt to Mysliveček, in particular
a source for *Idomeneo.* Cited in Schneider and Algatzy
(#556).
See also: J. Celada. *Josef Mysliveček.* Prague: Tvurce
Prazskeho Nareci Hudebniho Rokoka Terezianskeho, 1946.

See also: Pfannhauser (#858).

844.   (Paisiello) Abert, Hermann. "Paisiello's Buffokunst und ihre Beziegungen zu Mozart." *Archiv für Musikwissenschaft* 1 (1919): 402–421.

An interesting article in a stimulating publication: Mozart is shown to have used many of Paisiello's procedures—was it common practice (which he improved upon), or was it imitation, witting or unwitting?

845.   (Schobert) Schünemann, Kurt. "Mozart und Schobert." *Allgemeine Musikzeitung* 39, 20 (13 March 1910): 463 ff.*

An important relationship, dating from Mozart's first visit to Paris—it is also discussed carefully in Wyzewa and Saint-Foix (#647).

846.   (Various) Verchaly, A., ed. *Les influences étrangères dans l'oeuvre de Mozart.* Paris: Editions du Centre National de la Recherche Scientifique, 1958. 273 pp. illus.

Report of a Paris conference, 1956. Contents: S. Walin, "Sur des conditions générales de l'internationalisme de Mozart"; E. Schenk, "Mozart incarnation de l'âme autrichiènne"; H. C. Robbins Landon, "La crise romantique dans la musique autrichiènne vers 1770, Quelques precurseurs inconnus de la symphonie en sol mineur (K. 173dB)"; H. Wirth, "Mozart et Haydn"; E. F. Schmid, "L'Héritage souabe de Mozart"; K. G. Fellerer, "Mozart et l'Ecole de Mannheim"; l'abbé Carl de Nys, "Mozart et les fils de J. S. Bach"; C. Valbrega, "Mozart et le goût Italien"; L. F. Tagliavini, "L'Opéra Italien du jeune Mozart"; D. Bartha, "Mozart et le folklore musical de l'Europe centrale"; V. Dobias, "Mozart et la musique tcheque"; P. Fortassier, "Le récitatif dans l'écriture instrumentale de Mozart"; E. Hess, "Remarques sur l'authenticité de l'Ouverture K. 311a." Index.

See also: Françoise Lesure. *Mozart en France.* Paris: Bibliothèque Nationale, 1956. Exhibition catalogue (#655).

MOZART'S COMPOSITIONAL
PROCEDURES AND TECHNIQUES

847. Brown, Maurice J. E. "Mozart's Recapitulations: A Point of Style." *Music and Letters* 30 (1949): 109–117.

An analysis of how small melodic changes in his chamber music and other pieces make Mozart's style unique through harmonic and structural changes.

848. Broyles, Michael. "Organic Form and the Binary Repeat." *Musical Quarterly* 66, 3 (July 1980): 339–360.

Author examined 347 first movements of instrumental works by ten classic composers (including Mozart and Haydn). Ninety-eight percent of symphonies composed before 1780 observed the second half repeat; by 1810 only twelve percent observed the second half repeat. Sonatas and quartets were slower to abandon the second half repeat than symphonies.

849. Chantavoine, Jean. *Mozart dans Mozart.* Paris: Desclée de Brouwer, 1948. 370 pp.

Author (1877–1952) deals primarily with vocal music in his survey of sources Mozart used—which ones are identifiable in the works of other composers, and which ones Mozart used on more than one occasion in his own works.

See also: K. G. Fellerer. "Mozarts Bearbeitung eigener Werke." *Mozart Jahrbuch* 4 (1953): 70 ff.

Also: M. Flothuis, *Mozarts Bearbeitungen eigener und fremder Werke.* Kassel: Bärenreiter, 1969. 104 pp.; King (#768).

850. Clapham, John. "Chromaticism in the Music of Mozart." *Music Review* 17 (February 1956): 7–18.

A thoughtful survey of Mozart's use of chromatics in several compositional procedures, and in different vocal and instrumental forms.

851. Gerstenberg, Walter. "Über Mozarts Klangwelt." *Mozart Jahrbuch* 14 (1965-1966): 50–60.

Gerstenberg is reliable in his discussion of Mozart's tonal world, but as yet no authority has dealt fully with Mozart's use of tonality (along with form, rhythm, dynamics, and texture) to create mood—in the way Neumann attempted to deal comprehensively with ornamentation (#833).

See also: Luethy (#857); Massin (#629); Steglich, in *Acta Mozartiana* 3, 1 (1956): 9–21.

852. Hastings, Baird. "Vergleich der konzertanten Techniken in der Sinfonien der Mozarts und Haydns." *Mitteilungen der ISM* 16, 3–4 (August 1968): 6–10.

A comparison of concertant techniques used by Mozart and Haydn.

853. Heuss, Alfred. "Das dämonische Element in Mozarts Werken. *Zeitschrift der internationalen Musikgesellschaft* 7 (1906): 175–186.*

This article was praised by King (#768), but we have not yet seen a comprehensive treatment of Mozart's portrayal of the demonic passion through tonality, orchestration, form, etc.

See also: Geoffrey Clive. "The Demonic in Mozart." *Music and Letters* 37, 1 (January 1944): 1–13.

854. Kecskeméti, István. "Opernelemente in die Klavierkonzerte Mozarts." *Mozart Jahrbuch* 16 (1968-1970): 111–118.

Themes from *Die Zauberflöte, Così, Don Giovanni, Figaro* found in piano concertos K. 414, 415, 456, 459, 466, 482, 491, 365.

855. Kelterborn, Rudolf. *Zum Beispiel Mozart.* Kassel: Bärenreiter, 1981. 248 pp. 2 vols. ISBN: 3-7618-0651-5.

A significant selective analysis of the forms and procedures used by Mozart. No index.

856. Korisheli, Wachtung. "Die Entstehung und Geschichte der vierhändigen Klavierliteratur bis zum Schubert und seinen Zeitgenossen." Breisgau: University of Freiburg dissertation, 1975. 106 pp.*

Discusses Mozart's pioneering place in four-hand keyboard music.

RILM: 1975—#959.

857. Luethy, Walter. *Mozart und die Tonarten-charakteristik.* Strasburg: Heitz & Co., 1931. 90 pp.

Discusses 15 tonalities Mozart used in scenes from 7 operas, considering how Mozart used tonality to enhance mood and action in solos and ensembles. Good as far as it goes. Bibliography; no index.

858. Pfannhauser, Karl. "Mozart hat kopiert." *Acta Mozartiana* 3 (1954): 38–41.

On occasion as he was pressed for time, Mozart appropriated a theme or structure from one of his own works, or adapted something that was in common usage. There are a few cases where he employed a particular theme or procedure by a composer he knew, e.g. Mysliveček.
See also: Chantavoine (#849).

859. Rosen, Charles. *The Classical Style: Haydn, Mozart, Beethoven.* New York: Norton, 1972 (rev. 1977). 467 pp. ISBN: 0-670-22510-X. ML 195 R68.

Pages 185–328 discuss Mozart's use of tonalities and compositional techniques. Covers mainly concertos, string quintets, *Le nozze di Figaro, Die Zauberflöte.* Notes; index.

860. Shamgar, Beth. "Elusive Borders: Haydn or Mozart. A Reappraisal of Mozart's Piano Sonatas." *Mitteilungen der ISM* 32, 1-4 (1984): 71–80.

Comparison and interpretation of different ways Haydn and Mozart made use of sonata form and structure to achieve the message of a given work.

861. Siegmund-Schulze, Walther. *Mozarts Melodik und Stil.* Leipzig: Deutscher Verlag für Musik, 1957. 185 pp.

Although it is not indexed, this is a serious, important monograph, discussing melodic formulas with over 100 musical examples. Notes.

862. Taling-Hajnali, Maria. *Der fugierte Stil bei Mozart.* Bern: P. Haupt, 1959. 130 pp.

Careful consideration of Mozart's contrapuntal studies at various stages: Salzburg; under Italian influence; under influence of Michael Haydn; under influence of Handel;

under influence of J. S. Bach—also discussed in Landon-
Mitchell (#774).

863. Tobin, J. Raymond. *Mozart and the Sonata Form.* London: W.
      Reeves, 1916. 156 pp. ISBN: 70027-1; Da Capo reprint
      edition.

      The form of each movement of each piano sonata is
      analyzed in this pioneering study; still useful. Index.
      See also: J. M. Hartunian. Ph.D. dissertation, University
      of California, Los Angeles.

864. Ujfalusay, J. "Intonation Charakterbildung und
      Typengestaltung in Mozarts Werken." *Studia Musicolgia.*
      Budapest: Hungarian Academy of Sciences, 1961, pp.
      93–145.*

      Cited in Schneider and Algatzy (#556).

865. Wolff, Christian, ed. *The String Quartets of Haydn, Mozart and
      Beethoven.* Cambridge, Mass.: Harvard University Press.
      357 pp. ISBN: 0-674-84331-2.

      Contributors discussing Mozart quartets are: L. Fischer,
      "Mozart's Compositional Process"; M. Flothuis, "A Close
      Reading of the Late Quartets"; A. Tyson, "Paper Studies"; C.
      Wolff, "Quartet Fragments." Notes; bibliography; index.

Vocal Music

GENERAL

Often it has been said that Mozart was a "vocal" composer,
and numerous commentators have attempted to define this
statement. This section presents the best available thinking of
perceptive commentators on various aspects of this
characterization.

865A. Flothuis, Marius. "Mozart and the Human Voice." *American
      Choral Review* 24, 2-3 (April-June 1982): 61–66.

      Taking K. 275 and 345 as his main examples, author
      notes Mozart generally avoids long phrases, he uses
      homophonic and polyphonic procedures together, he is
      careful which vowels are used on high notes.

866. Klein, Herbert. *The Bel Canto, with Particular Reference to the Singing of Mozart.* London: Oxford University Press, 1923. 53 pp. mus. exx.

Dedicating his book to Sir Thomas Beecham—whose Mozart was always stimulating and stylish, if not invariably as authentic as possible—the author considers succinctly lines of Mozart tradition, vocal demands of Mozart's music, language and diction, recitative, appogiatura, marks of expression *and* the technique of bel canto (with pertinent remarks on breathing, resonance, vowels, sostenuto, legato, portamento, messa da voce, agility), along with vital principles of Manuel Garcia's teaching. No bibliography or index.

867. Kunze, Stefan. "Aufführungspraxis im Rezitativ des späteren 18. Jahrhunderts." *Mozart Jahrbuch* 16 (1968–1970): 132–144.

A presentation of rules leading to theatrical naturalness, without imposing a straight jacket. Other discussions of recitative in Mozart operas include: Heinrich Franke. "Zu den Secco-Rezitativen in Mozarts Opern." *Die Musik* 29, 8 (May 1937): 561 ff.; Otto Nicolai. Über die Instrumentierung der Rezitative in den Mozart'schen Opern." *Wiener Allgemeine Musik-Zeitung* 7, 33 (18 March 1847): 133 ff., 55 (8 May 1847): 221 ff., 58 (15 May 1847): 232 ff.; see also Neumann (#833).

RELIGIOUS WORKS

There is no one source on the religious music which covers all important points. Perhaps this is because of a diversity of opinion on the purpose of religious music, and therefore its content, form, and style. All publications listed below have something to contribute. Readers are also referred to Hammer (#761), and to #723–730.

868. Fellerer, Karl Gustav. *Mozarts Kirchenmusik.* Salzburg: Schäffer, 1955. 151 pp.

A general introduction. Index, but no bibliography.

869. Kerner, Dieter. "Das Requiem-Problem." *Neue Zeitschrift für Musik* 130, 8 (1974): 475–479.

Summary of documentary evidence of chronology involved in the composition of the Requiem.

870. Komorzynski, Egon. "Mozart und Kirchen in Wien." *Musikerziehung* 9, 4 (1956): 249–251. illus.

Brief description of the churches in Vienna Mozart is known to have been in.

871. Lunde, Alfred Everett. *A Conductor's Analysis of Glorias by Michael Haydn, Joseph Haydn, and Mozart.* DMA dissertation, Southwestern Baptist Theological Seminary: 1981. 176 pp. illus.

Analyzes one Gloria by Michael Haydn, two by Joseph Haydn, and two by Mozart.
RILM: 1981—#540.

872. MacIntyre, Bruce C. *The Viennese Concerted Mass of the Early Classic Period.* Ann Arbor, Mich.: UMI Research Press, 1986. 764 pp. illus. ISBN: 0-8357-1673-2. ML 3088. M24 783.2'1'0943613.

Comprehensive, splendid discussion of 18th-century church music and its composers, including Mozart. Revealing detail. Appendix; notes; bibliography; index.

873. Plath, Wolfgang. "Requiem Briefe aus der Korrespondenz J. A. Andrés, 1825–1831." *Mozart Jahrbuch* 20 (1976–1977): 174–203.

Includes discussion of letters André received from Constanze and from Süssmayr about the Requiem.
See also: W. Plath. "Noch ein Requiem Brief." *Acta Mozartiana* 28, 4 (1981): 96–101, with consideration of handwriting of Mozart and of Süssmayr.

874. Rosenthal, Karl. "The Salzburg Church Music of Mozart and his Predecessors." *Musical Quarterly* 18, 4 (October 1932): 559–577.

Essential background to understanding the joyous religious music of Mozart—including discussion of works by Andreas Hofer, Matthias Biechteler v. Greiffenthal, Carl Heinrich Biber, Ernst Eberlin, A.C. Adlgasser, Michael Haydn.

875. Stadler, Maximilian. *Vertheidigung der Mozart'schen Requeim.* Vienna: Tendler, 1826. 30 pp.

    One of several pamphlets by Stadler, who was an informed witness of the creation of the Mozart *Requiem*, replying to various misinformed pamphleteers. (Also, Stadler "completed" several of Mozart's works for publication.) No index.

876. Tangeman, Robert S. "Mozart's 17 Epistle Sonatas." *Musical Quarterly* 32, 4 (October 1946): 588–601.

    An historical and critical discussion of Mozart's works for organ composed for religious services in Salzburg. See also: Hans Dennerlein (#1032).

SECULAR VOCAL MUSIC

877. Ballin, Ernst August. *Das Ton-Wort Verhältnis in der Klavierbegleiten Liedern Mozarts.* Kassel: Bärenreiter, 1984. 153 pp. ISBN: 3-7618-0721-X.

    Discussion of the meaning and relation of words and sound, with musical examples from songs and operas. Notes; bibliography; appendix; no index.

878. Brown, Maurice J. E. "Mozart's Songs for Voice and Piano." *Music Review* 17, 1 (February 1956): 19–28.

    Interesting survey of the publishing history of the songs by a well-known authority.

879. Hamburger, Paul. "The Concert Arias." See: Landon-Mitchell (#774): 324–360.

    An excellent summary of the aesthetic and technical aspects involved. Readers of German may also consult Stefan Kunze. "Mozarts Konzertarien." *Mozartgemeinde Wien* 39 (May 1971): 1–15.

880. Mila, Massimo. "I Canoni di Mozart." *Nuova revista musicale italiana* 15, 1 (January–March 1981): 7–33.*

    After presenting a brief history and evolution of the canon before Mozart, the author discusses origins and form of Mozart's canons, with pertinent citations from the composer's letters.
    RILM: 1981—#544.

881. Werba, Erik. "Das Mozart Lied in der Aufführungspraxis der Gegenwart." *Österreichische Musikzeitschrift* 11 (Special number, 1967): 12–16.

   For anyone intersted in the songs, this excellent article in German illuminates and expands horizons by the use of evocative comparisons. In his concise descriptions Werba characterizes the dramatic contents by citing particular protagonists in Mozart operas who parallel the text and mood of the songs: Zerlina (K. 596), Donna Elvira (K. 520), Countess Almaviva (K. 523), Susanna (K. 518 and 531), Barbarina (K. 530), Constanze (K. 473), Fiordiligi (K. 597), Cherubino (K. 524), Guglielmo (K. 517 and 587), Belmonte (K. 519), and various songs for the temperaments of Tamino, Osmin, Pamina, Blondchen.

OPERAS/DRAMATIC WORKS

General

882. Abert, Anna Amalie. "Mozart's italianità in 'Idomeneo' and 'Titus.'" *Analecta Musicologica* 18 (1978): 205–216.

   Despite narrow title, considers procedures Mozart used in many of his Italian operas; also discussed in Wyzewa and Saint-Foix (#647).

883. Allanbrook, Wye Jamison. *Rhythmic Gesture in Mozart's "Le nozze di Figaro" and "Don Giovanni."* Chicago: University of Chicago Press, 1984. 396 pp. mus. exx. ISBN: 0-226-01403-7.

   Penetrating analysis of two master operas, emphasizing Mozart's frequent use of dance forms and procedures (revised from Stanford thesis). Index.
   See also: "Mozart's Gagliarda." Pp. 382–387 in H. C. Robbins Landon, ed. *Studies in 18th Century Music.* New York: Oxford University Press, 1970.

884. Ballantine, Christopher. "Social and Philosophical Outlook in Mozart's Operas." *Musical Quarterly* 68, 4 (January 1981): 507–526.

   Discusses Mozart's development of three themes within the framework of the later 18th century: first, how Mozart stripped away the mask (which is exactly what dancers and actors were doing during this period in ballet and drama);

second, how Mozart reacted against the maintenance of the social and political status quo; third, how Mozart believed in the value of forgiveness and reconciliation. Isolation of particular themes can lead to pertinent generalizations or to over-simplification.

885.   Breydert, Frédéric. *Le genie créateur de Wolfgang Amadeus Mozart.* Paris: Alsatia, 1956. 186 pp.

A discussion of the music of important characters in *Figaro, Don Giovanni,* and *Die Zauberflöte.* Author is convincing on *Figaro.* His presentation of *Don Giovanni* and *Die Zauberflöte* forces the reader to think, but not necessarily to agree. No bibliography or index.

Decorators of Mozart Operas, 1768–1791

See Section 5: Bellotto, Bibiena, Diesbach, Galli, Nessthaler, Quaglio, Platzer, etc. These and other designers of the period are discussed briefly in *Baroque and Romantic Stage Design,* Janos Scholz, ed., with an introduction by A. Hyatt Mayor. New York: Dutton, 1962. 22 pp., plus 121 plates; bibliography; no index.

886.   Dent, Edward Joseph. *Mozart's Operas: A Critical Study.* (2nd ed.) London: Oxford University Press, 1947. 276 pp. illus. ISBN: 0-19-28001-0.

First edition of this important book was 1913. Broader than Mann (#899), although not as systematic. Selective discussions are penetrating. Emphasis on late operas. Rare footnotes; no bibliography. Index.

887.   Engel, Hans. "Die Finali der Mozartschen Opera." *Mozart Jahrbuch* 5 (1954): 113–134.

A valuable summary of keys, characters, mood, structure in finales of 20 operas.
    See also: Alfred Ottokar Lorenz. "Das Finale in Mozarts Meisteropern." *Die Musik* 19 (June 1927): 621–632.
    Also: Georges Horst. *Das Klangsymbol des Todes im Dramatischen Werk Mozarts.* Wolfenbüttel: Kallmeyer, 1937, with bibliography. 236 pp.
    Also: John Platoff. "Music and Drama in the Opera Buffa Finale: Mozart and his Contemporaries in Vienna, 1781–1790." Ph.D. dissertation, University of Pennsylvania, 1984. 462 pp.*

Also: Luethy (#857).

888. Goldovsky, Boris. *Bringing Opera to Life.* New York: Appleton-
      Century-Crofts, 1968. 436 pp. Diagrams.

      Goldovsky is one of the most rounded persons in opera
      today, for staging opera to Goldovsky means making the
      meaning of the work logically clear to the audience. In this
      important book he discusses staging 12 scenes—4 of which
      are from Mozart operas. Bibliography; appendixes; index.

889. Granturco, Carolyn. *Mozart's Early Operas.* London: Batsford,
      1981. 216 pp. illus.

      Brief survey of operas up to *Idomeneo* as music, text,
      theatre. Includes contemporary opinion, and discusses
      other contemporary music. Index.
      See also: S. Kunze (#894).

890. Heartz, Daniel. "Che mi sembre di morir: Donna Elvira and
      the Sextet." *Musical Times* 122, 1661 (July 1981): 448–
      451.

      In a brief, charged article, Heartz finds the sextet
      originally concluding Act III of *Don Giovanni* (before the
      four acts were made into two) draws together various
      dramatic strands; Donna Elvira and Leporello and Don
      Ottavio are characterized by motives from Act I in a
      sequence of tonalities from the overture—d, d sharp, e, g, f
      sharp. Heartz observes that Donna Elvira's sexual passion is
      represented by rising chromatics in crescendo; he notes that
      suffering and death are brought out by descending
      chromatics.

891.———. "Three Schools for Lovers: the Mozart Da Ponte
      Trilogy." *About the House* (Covent Garden) (Spring
      1981): 18–21.

      Traces how *Figaro* led to *Don Giovanni* —both operas
      taking a theme of French literature, nobility's abuse of
      privilege; then turns to how the Vienna revival of *Figaro* led
      to the commission of *Così*, showing how both operas were in
      debt to the wit of Marivaux; illustrations.

892. Kaiser, Joachim. *Who's Who in Mozart's Operas.* Translated by Charles Kessler. London: Weidenfield & Nicholson, 1986. 212 pp. ISBN: 0-297-788612.

Fifty-six characters from seven major operas are considered; there is some insight, but too much is on the surface. Author is unduly impressed by what he calls J. P. Ponnelle's "analysis." Author states he had professionals in mind, but much of subject is trivialized (as translated) and thus is of limited value. Footnotes; index.

See also: Appendix IV, where 150 characters are listed.

893. Killer, Hermann. *Die Tenorpartien in Mozarts Opern.* Kassel: Bärenreiter, 1929. 292 pp.

A useful survey of the place of the tenor in Mozart's operas, from *La finta semplice* to *Idomeneo,* with more detailed treatment of the tenors in *Die Entführung, Don Giovanni, Così, Die Zauberflöte.* Bibliography; mus. exx.; no index.

894. Kunze, Stefan. *Mozarts Opern.* Stuttgart: Reclam, 1984. 685 pp. illus. ISBN: 3-15-00326-6.

Early Mozart operas have 111 pages; the 7 later operas have nearly 90 pages each. Very pertinent and fair discussion—probably the best general Mozart opera book to date. Chronology; bibliography; notes; index.

895. Lert, Ernst. *Mozart auf dem Theater.* Berlin: Schuster & Löffler, 1918. 491 pp. illus.

A standard book, cited by all subsequent authorities as understanding the basic character of Mozart operas. Bibliography; index.

896. Liebner, Janos. *Mozart on the Stage.* New York: Praeger, 1972. 254 pp.

Discusses music, drama, and also social conditions and theatrical conventions of the period; an excellent antidote to oversimplification. Imaginative use of intuition may assist resolution of imponderables regarding *Così.* Appendix; bibliography; no index.

897. Loft, Adam. "The Comic Servant in Mozart's Operas." *Musical Quarterly* 32, 3 (July 1946): 376–389.

After profiling the background (from the Greeks to commedia dell'arte), the author considers protagonists in *La finta giardiniera, Die Entführung, Figaro, Don Giovanni, Così, Die Zauberflöte.*

898. Mainka, Jürgen. "Der Opernkomponist Mozart." *Musik und Gesellschaft* 31 (1981): 28–33.

Discusses Mozart's use of Enlightenment themes with examples from *Idomeneo* through *Die Zauberflöte.*

899. Mann, William. *The Operas of Mozart.* London: Cassell; New York: Oxford University Press, 1977. 675 pp. ISBN: 0-304-29381-4 (London); ISBN: 0-195198-913 (New York).

Excellent background discussion of all Mozart's dramatic works. Somewhat more comprehensive than Dent or Newman, although not superior in clarity. Rare footnotes; bibliography; index.

900. Meyer, Reinhart. "Der Anteil des Singspiel und Oper am Repertoire der deutschen Bühnen in der 2. Hälfte des 18. Jahrhunderts." (Pp. 21–76 in Renate Schusky. *Das deutsche Singspiel im 18. Jahrhundert.* Heidelberg: University of Münster, 1981. 281 pp.*)

Meyer presents the repertoire of 150 travelling troupes and resident theatres in different locations and milieus. RILM : 1981—#543.

901. Moberly, Robert B. *Three Mozart Operas: Figaro, Don Giovanni, The Magic Flute.* New York: Dodd, Mead, 1968. 303 pp.

Comprehensive scene-by-scene analysis of three operas. Discusses appropriateness of scene order changes in *Figaro.* Author's value judgements must be weighed carefully. Bibliography; index.

See also: Andrew Steptoe. *The Mozart-Da Ponte Operas.* New York: Oxford University Press, 1988. 288 pp. ISBN: 313215-X.

902. Mooser, Aloys R. "L'apparition des oeuvres de Mozart en Russie." *Mozart Jahrbuch* 15 (1967): 226 ff.

The first two operas of Mozart to be presented in Russia (St. Petersburg) were *Die Zauberflöte* (1794) and *La clemenza di Tito* (1797).

903. "Mozart und die Oper seiner Zeit. Opernsymposium 1978 in Hamburg." *Hamburger Jahrbuch für Musikwissenschaft* 5: Laaber, 1981. 264 pp.*

Articles by R. Angermüller, C. Floros, G. Gruber, D. Heartz, S. Kunze, F. Lippmann, H. Lühning, C. H. Mahling, W. Rehm, M. Ruhnke, on Mozart's genres, forms, and style. RILM: 1981—#4344.

904. Muraro, Maria Teresa, ed. *Venezia e il melodramma nel settecento*. Florence: Olschki, 1978. 462 pp. illus.

The chapters are all based on conference papers. Perhaps the most pertinent is "The Italian opera in Vienna in the 18th century" by Wolfgang Greisenegger, although most contributors provide interesting background.

905. Newman, Ernest. *Stories of the Great Operas*. Garden City, New York: Garden City Publishing Co., 1936. 3 vols. in one.

Includes life of Mozart, and excellent descriptions of *Figaro, Don Giovanni, Die Zauberflöte* by a splendid writer.

906. Noske, Frits. *The Signifier and the Signified*. The Hague: Nijhof, 1977. 425 pp.

These studies of *Figaro, Don Giovanni,* and *Così* force the reader to think. However, we note Noske is unnecessarily harsh on some pioneering colleagues. (More than half the book is devoted to Verdi.) Footnotes; index.

907. Osborne, Charles. *The Complete Operas of Mozart*. London: Gollancz, 1978. 349 pp. illus. ISBN: 0-575-02221-3.

Clear, forthrightly written, somewhat less inclusive than Mann (above). Osborne's discussion of *Die Zauberflöte* is one of the best I know. He considers the elements of good and evil, man versus woman, as well as Masonic influences. Osborne and Mann agree that however one may interpret certain "Masonic elements," *Die Zauberflöte* is above all a "magic opera"—which Mozart saw as a farce *and* a solemn, spiritual piece. Notes; bibliography; index.

908. Pirrotta, Nino. "The Tradition of the Don Juan Plays and Comic Operas." *Proceedings of the Royal Music Society* 107 (1981): 60–70.

Tracing the Don Juan theme from *L'Empio punito* (1669), author states Mozart and Da Ponte made Don Giovanni a character of everyday comedy, a negative hero whose character implied social criticism (one of the elements of success in *Figaro*).

909. Robinson, Michael. *Opera before Mozart*. London: Hutchinson, 1966. 168 pp. ISBN: 0-09-080421-X. ML1700 R56.

An excellent brief summary, with pertinent background and with numerous musical examples. Author discusses how Mozart combined both seria and comic elements in his operas. Notes; bibliography; index.

910. Rosenthal, Karl. "Über Vokalformen bei Mozart." *Studien zur Musikwissenschaft* 14 (1927): 5–32.*

Cited in Schneider and Algatzy (#556).

911. Rudolf, Max. "Ein Beitrag zur Geschichte der Temponahme bei Mozart." *Mozart Jahrbuch* 20 (1976–1977): 204–224.

Discusses how to be faithful to Mozart in matters of tempo. States that listed metronome figures in piano-vocal opera scores published by Schlesinger (1822) are not to be trusted unquestioningly.

912. Surian, E. *A Checklist of Writings on 18th Century French and Italian Opera (excluding Mozart)*. Hackensack, New Jersey: Boonin, 1970. 121 pp. ML 128 04 S9.

Fifteen hundred and one selections divided into 10 categories. Useful coverage of contemporaries—composers, librettists, etc.

913. Szabolcsi, Bence, and Dénes Bartha. *In Memory of Mozart*. Budapest: Hungarian Academy of Sciences, 1956. 500 pp.*

Discusses dramaturgy of Mozart's operas, Mozart and the popular stage, forms in Mozart. In Hungarian, with a summary in English. Recommended by *Mitteilungen der ISM*.

914. Tondorf, Franz Josef. "Die Solovokalensembles in Wolfgang
      Amadeus Mozarts Opern." Ph.D. dissertation, Marburg
      University, 1980. 1065 pp.*

      Discusses melody, form, and style in solo vocal
      ensembles, and their place in Mozart's operas and aesthetic.
      Bibliography; tables; index.
      RILM: 1980—#4640.

915. Zingerle, Hans. "Musik-und Text-form in Opernarien
      Mozarts." *Mozart Jahrbuch* 4 (1953): 112–115.

      Considers Mozart's use of da capo form in arias in
      Idomeneo and *La clemenza di Tito.*

Alphabetical by Title

      (All NMA editions of opera scores have valuable
      introductions.)

916. *(Ascanio)* Engel, Hans. "Hasse's 'Ruggiero' und Mozarts
      Festspiel 'Ascanio.'" *Mozart Jahrbuch* 11 (1960–1961): 29
      ff.

      Discussion of two 1771 Milan premieres.

917. *(Bastien)* Angermüller, Rudolph. "Mozart und Rousseau."
      Mitteilungen der ISM 23, 1-2 (February 1975): 22–37.

      A revealing discussion, with musical examples, in which
      the author asserts that the translation from the French by
      F. W. Weiskern and J. F. Müller does not reflect properly the
      peasant and lower class characters of the original.

918. *(La clemenza di Tito)* Giegling, Franz. "Metastasios Oper 'La
      clemenza di Tito' in der Bearbeitung durch Mazzola."
      Mozart Jahrbuch 16 (1968–1970): 88–94.

      Considers how Mazzola's modifications of Metastasio's
      original helped Mozart make a poetic "vera opera." By
      eliminating much of Metastasio's Act II, Mazzola reduced
      the length of the libretto by one-third; however, he left most
      of the secco recitatives, and he added ensembles.

919. Heartz, Daniel. "Mozart and his Italian Contemporaries: 'La
      clemenza di Tito.'" *Mozart Jahrbuch* 21 (1978–1979):
      275–293.

Comparison of different versions of Metastasio's libretto used by various composers.

920. Lühning, Helga. "Zur Entstehungsgeschichte von Mozarts 'Titus.'" *Die Musikforschung* 27, 3 (July–September 1974): 300–318.*

After considering the nature of the sources, author concludes that although Mozart may have composed several parts early, he completed most of the opera just before the premiere.

RILM: 1974—#2336.

921. Moberly, R. B. "The Influence of French Classical Drama on Mozart's 'La clemenza di Tito.'" *Music and Letters* 55, 3 (July 1974): 286–298.

Metastasio's libretto was based on dramatic models of Corneille and Racine. Beginning with *Mitridate,* Mozart was stimulated by French dramatic procedures, both in the composition of his opera seria and in the way he combined opera seria and opera buffa.

922. Neville, Don J. "La clemenza di Tito." *Studi Musicali* (1975): 124–148.

Consideration and comparison of the reworkings by Mazzola and the contributions by Mozart to the revised drama.

923. Tyson, Alan. "'La clemenza di Tito' and its Chronology." *The Musical Times* 116 (March 1975): 221–227.

Discussion of the order of composition of the musical numbers. Includes paper and watermark analysis.

924. Wandruszka, Adam. "Die Clementia austrica und der aufgeklärte Absolutismus." *Österreichische Musikzeitschrift* 31, 4-5 (April–May 1976): 186–193.

Pertinent political background related to *La clemenza di Tito,* with illustrations.

925. *(Così fan tutte) L'Avant-Scène Opéra,* 16–17. Paris, 1978. 178 pp.

Contains fourteen perceptive essays by S. Bouvier-Lapierre, Alain Lombard, Pierre Brunel, Jean-Louis Dutronc, Jacques Gheusi, Roger Le Winter, Marie-Françoise Vieuille, Elisabeth Bouillon, Alain Guellette, J. V. Hocquard, Marie-Armelle Dussour, Sylvia Murr, Jean-Louis Martinoty, Monique Disault, Pierre Malbos. Musical and dramatic interpretation are well covered; deeper exploration of historical relationships is absent. Includes libretto. Poorly designed, and as a result very difficult to read. Bibliography; no index.

926. Brandstetter, Gabriele. "So machens alle." *Die Musikforschung* 35, 1 (1982): 27–44.

Discusses several early translations of *Così* and how they wrought changes on the singspiel.

927. Gloede, Wilhelm. "Die Overture zu 'Così fan tutte.'" *Mitteilungen der ISM* 32, 1–4 (July 1984): 35–50.

A penetrating discussion of form and content, including tracing one of Mozart's formulas to Paisiello's *Il barbiere di Siviglia* (1782).

928. Goldovsky, Boris. "Accents on 'Così fan tutte.'" *Opera News* 17, 14 (1953): 29–30.

Incisive, revealing comments on motivations of characters by distinguished Mozart conductor and stage director.

929. Gombrich, E. H. "Così fan tutte." *Journal of the Warburg and Courtauld Institutes* 17 (1954): 372 ff.

Art historian discusses the way Da Ponte used the story of Cephale and Procris. Cited in Schneider and Algatzy (#556).

930. Hocquard, Jean-Victor. *Così fan tutte.* Paris: Aubier, 1978. 220 pp. illus.

Hocquard's writings on Mozart are often useful as general introductions, but here as elsewhere his treatment is superficial. No index. (The present author hopes to complete a comprehensive treatment of *Così*.)

931. John, Nicholas. *Così fan tutte.* London: Calder; New York, Riverrun, 1983. 128 pp. ISBN: 0-7145-3882-5. ML 410 M9.

    A good brief survey of background, plot, and music. Includes Italian libretto, plus inaccurate English translation. Bibliography; discography; no index. (Series includes monographs on *Figaro, Don Giovanni, The Magic Flute.*)

932. Kramer, Kurt. *Da Ponte's Così fan tutte.* Göttingen: Vanderhoeck & Ruprecht, 1973.*

    Discussion of "parody and irony." Cited by Angermüller and Schneider (#546).

933. Nef, Albert. "Das Orchester in Mozarts 'Così.'" *Schweizerische Musikzeitung* 73, 24 (1933): 787 ff.

    Excellent discussion of the part played by the orchestra in *Così.* (The author has written a series of articles in *Schweizerische Musikzeitung* on the orchestra in *Die Entführung, Figaro, Don Giovanni, Die Zauberflöte.*)

934. Steptoe, Andrew. "The Sources of Così." *Music and Letters* 62 (July–October 1981): 281–294.

    An intriguing discussion of Da Ponte and Mozart's attempt to please Viennese audiences with *Così.*

935. Strauss, Richard. "Mozart's Così fan tutte." Translated by Maurice Magnus. *Monthly Music Record* (June 1912): 141–143.

    Strauss was esteemed as a conductor of *Così,* and other Mozart operas—in spite of which fact, he seemed to agree with Wagner's mistaken opinion that *Così* was not up to Mozart's own standard. In any event Strauss applauded Hermann Levi's model 1897 production of *Così* (which cleared away almost a century of interpretations, including Eduard Devrient's misguided adaptation of *Così,* in which Despina tells her mistresses of their sweethearts' wager with Don Alfonso).

936. Tyson, Alan. "Notes on the Composition of Mozart's 'Così fan tutte.'" *Journal of the American Musicological Society* 37, 2 (Summer 1984): 356–401.

Excellent discussion of Mozart's procedure of composition of *Così*, and the order in which the numbers were composed.

937. Vill, Susanne, et al. *Così fan tutte.* Bayreuth: Werner Fehr, 1978. 319 pp.

   Ten chapters devoted to Mozart's artistic philosophy and the performance history of *Così*, by Susanne Vill, M. Dietrich, Ludwig Finscher, Gisela Glagla, Götz Friedrich, H. P. Glöckner, K. Hortschansky, Christa Jost, Karin Werner, Nikolaus Westphal.

   On *Così* exhibition in Salzburg, see also: Susanne Vill, *Mitteilungen der ISM* 27, 3–4 (September 1979): 20–24.

938. (Don Giovanni) Abert, Hermann. *Mozart's 'Don Giovanni.'* Translated by Peter Gelhorn. London: Eulenberg, 1976. 138 pp. ISBN: 0903873-117.

   Following an introduction on Mozart and Prague, Abert details the drama of the opera, with musical examples. Notes, but no index.

939. Bleiler, Ellen, ed. *"Don Giovanni" by Mozart.* New York: Dover, 1964. 209 pp. illus.

   A very useful introduction to the revised Vienna version. Contains Da Ponte's Italian libretto with English translation, as well as six pertinent essays. Bibliography; no index.

940. Csampai, Attila, and Dietmar Holland, eds. *W. A. Mozart: 'Don Giovanni.'* Hamburg: Rororo, 1981. 281 pp. illus.

   Includes libretto in Italian and German, and several uneven essays. Chronology; bibliography; discography; no index.

941. *Don Giovanni. L'Avant-Scène Opéra,* 24 (November-December 1979). Paris. 218 pp.

   Useful volume in continuing series. Essays. Libretto in Italian and French. Bibliography; no index.

942. Gerstenberg, Walter. "Authentische Tempi für Mozarts 'Don Giovanni.'" *Mozart Jahrbuch* 11 (1960–1961): 58 ff.

Based partly on memories of Jan Václaw Tomášek (1774–1850). Corresponds generally to Hummel statements on Mozart symphonies reported by Robert Münster (#1024)—fast means very fast but not scrambled; slow means moderate.

943. Gounod, Charles. *Mozart's "Don Giovanni": a Commentary.* Translated from the third French edition by Windeyer Clark and J. T. Hutchinson. London: Cocks and Co., 1895. Reprint New York: Da Capo, 1970. 144 pp.

An excellent, non-technical introduction (number by number) of the original Prague version of the opera, by the French composer. No index.

944. Heartz, Daniel. "Goldoni, 'Don Giovanni' and dramma giocoso." *Musical Times* 120, 1642 (1979): 993–998.

Important to understand Mozart's unique approach in combining buffa and seria, which was inspired by Goldoni's own characterizations in collaborations with Galuppi. See also: Heartz (#890)

945. Hoffman, E. T. A. "A Tale of Don Juan." Translated from the German, this tale is available in several collections, including Jacques Barzun's *Pleasures of Music,* New York: Viking, 1951.

Intense, romantic notions about Don Juan and Mozart's opera were developed in the 19th century. *Musikalische Zeitung* (Leipzig) of March 31, 1813, this atmospheric tale helps show us the power of the story to arouse the emotions.

946. Kristek, Jan, ed. *Mozart's 'Don Giovanni' in Prague.* Prague: Theatre Institute, 1987. 191 pp. illus.

Revealing survey of *Don Giovanni* productions, beginning with the world premiere with sets created or supervised by Josef Platzer. Cited by A. H. King in *The Musical Times* 128, 1738 (December 1987).

947. Kunze, Stefan. *Don Giovanni vor Mozart.* Munich: Wilhem Fisk, 1972.*

A noted German expert discusses many 18th-century opera-buffas on the theme.

Cited in Angermüller and Schneider (#546).

948. Rosenberg, Alfons. *Don Giovanni.* Munich: Prestel, 1968. 342 pp. illus.

Excellent discussion, although not as unusual as Rosenberg's book on *Die Zauberflöte.* Bibliography; index.

949. Rushton, Julian, compiler. *W. A. Mozart: "Don Giovanni."* Cambridge: Cambridge University Press, 1981. 165 pp. illus. ISBN: 0-521-22828-3.

An excellent volume to consult first in serious research. Clarifies difference between original (Prague) and revised (Vienna) versions. Thoughtful handbook for serious opera-goer and scholar, one of a series. Bibliography; index.

See also: Christof Bitter. *Wandlungen in den Inszenierungsformen des 'Don Giovanni' von 1787 bis 1928.* Regensburg: 1961. An often cited survey of 140 years of staging.

950. Russell, Charles C. "The First Don Giovanni Opera, 'La pravità castigata' of E. Bambini, 1734." *Mozart Jahrbuch* 22 (1980–1983): 385–391.

Brief summary of the opera.

951. Stefan, Paul. *Don Giovanni.* Vienna: Reichner Verlag, 1938. 127 pp. illus.

Excellent survey of music and dramatic background and details of stagings. Index.

952. Valentin, Erich. "Variationen zum Don-Juan Thema." *Acta Mozartiana* 19, 2 (1972): 29–35.

Comparing Faust and Don Juan traditions, author states that Mozart's treatment of confrontation with death is more sensitive than earlier artistic treatments.

953. *(Die Entführung aus dem Serail)* Balk, Howard Wesley. "The Mozart Operas and the Director." Ph. D. dissertation, Yale University, 1965.*

A directional analysis of *Die Entführung* as an example of the dramatic meaning in Mozart's operatic music.

954. Croll, Gerhard. "Ein Janitscharen-Marsch zur 'Entführung.'" *Mitteilungen der ISM* 28, 1-2 (February 1980): 2-5.

Discussion of March in C, alla breve, which Mozart composed to begin the sixth scene of Act I. Elsewhere, Gabriel Banat reminds us that Dénes Bartha has identified some so-called "Turkish" themes as actually Hungarian; see Banat (#103).

955. Csampai, Attila. *W. A. Mozart: "Die Entführung aus dem Serail."* Hamburg: Rororo, 1983.

Includes libretto in German. Useful volume. No index.

956. Nef, Albert. "Das Orchester in Mozarts 'Entführung aus dem Serail.'" *Schweizerische Musikzeitung* 63, 30 (December 22, 1923): 413 ff.

Consideration of "Turkish," concertante, and other unusual, characteristic elements of Mozart style in opera.

957. Protz, Albert. *Die Entführung aus dem Serail.* Berlin: Robert Lienau, 1959. 52 pp.

Good as an introduction, but much needs to be investigated, described, analyzed. No index.
See also: Roland Würtz. "Das Turkische im Singspiel des 18. Jahrhunderts bis zu Mozarts 'Entführung aus dem Serail.'" *Wiener Figaro* 47 (June 1980): 8-14.
Also: Thomas Baumann. *W. A. Mozart: Die Entführung aus dem Serail.* Cambridge: Cambridge University Press, 1988. 160 pp. ISBN: 0-521-32545-5.

958. Schweizer, Hans Jörg. "Bassa Selim." *Soldalitas Florhofrana,* Festgabe für Prof. H. Haffter zum 65. Geburtstag. Zurich: Juris, 1970, pp. 140-149.*

Relations between Menander and *Die Entführung* in plot, chracterization, ensembles, contrasts, and humanitarian ideas.
RILM: 1974—#4506.

959. *(La finta giardiniera)* Angermüller, Rudolph. "Wer war der Librettist von 'La finta giardiniera?'" *Mozart Jahrbuch* 20 (1976-1977): 1-21.

Asserts that Giuseppe Petrosellini, rather than Raniero Calzabigi, was the librettist. It is now believed that Petrosellini wrote the libretto for Anfossi's *Finta* (1774), and that Mozart used Anfossi's text.

960. *(Idomeneo)* Del Mar, Norman. *Richard Strauss.* New York: Chilton Books, 1962–1972. Three volumes.

On pages 381–384 Del Mar discusses carefully the differences effected in the Strauss version of Mozart's *Idomeneo.* Notes; bibliography; list of works; appendix; index.

961. Heartz, Daniel, et al. "Idomeneo." *Mozart Jahrbuch* 18 (1973– 1974). 297 pp.

Important articles on tonal design and other stylistic and formal procedures by Heartz, H. Federhofer, László Somfai, Janos Liebner, Frederick Neumann, Georg Feder, and Gernot Gruber.

962. Heartz, Daniel. "Raaff's Last Aria." *Musical Quarterly* 60, 4 (October 1974): 517–543. illus.

Author shows Mozart's art and courtesy toward tenor Anton Raaff (1714–1797), as he referred librettist Varesco to verses of Metastasio which would improve the text Varesco had prepared in his reworking of the French model of *Idomeneo* by Danchet and Campra.

See also: Daniel Heartz. *Musical Quarterly* 64, 1 (1978): 29–49.

Also: Hans Freiberger. *Anton Raaff.* Cologne: Pilgrim, 1929. 83 pp. illus.*

Also: Baird Hastings. "Aida of Troy." *Opera News* 27, 6 (1962): 6.

963. Heuss, Alfred. "Mozarts 'Idomeneo' als Quelle für 'Don Giovanni' und 'Die Zauberflöte.'" *Zeitschrift für Musikwissenschaft* 13 (1931): 177–199; 328–329.

Careful consideration of Mozart's self-borrowing.

964. Hirschberg, Jehoash. "Formal and Dramatic Aspects of Sonata Form in Mozart's 'Idomeneo.'" *Music Review* 38 (1977): 192–210.

In formal analysis of arias and ensembles, author shows Mozart was changing from da capo to sonata form.
See also: Mirko Očadik (#843).

965. *(Mitridate)* Mitridate. *L'Avant-Scène Opéra* 25 (1983). 146 pp. illus.

Libretto. Interesting articles. Bibliography; no index.

966. *(Le nozze di Figaro)* Allanbrook, Wye Jamison. "Pro Marcellina: the Shape of 'Figaro' Act IV." *Music and Letters* 63, 1-2 (January-April 1982): 69-82.

Correctly emphasizes how Marcellina's and Basilio's arias change the form, complete the action, and round out personalities as they prepare for Figaro's "Aprite," and Susanna's "Deh vieni."

967. Angermüller, Rudolph. *Das Buch zur Austellung und zum Figaro Jahr 1986*. Salzburg: Mozarteum, 1986. 160 pp. illus.*

Discussion of the creation and history of Mozart's opera. Bibliography; index.
Cited in *Mitteilungen ISM*, 1986.

968. Beaumarchais, Pierre Augustin Caron de. *Oeuvres complètes*. Saint-Marc Girardin, ed. Paris, 1872.

Includes texts of *Le barbier de Seville*, *Le mariage de Figaro*, and *La mère coupable*—texts which both Mozart and Da Ponte knew in German translation and in French. Beaumarchais' own notes to his trilogy provide invaluable character studies of the protagonists.

969. Blom, Eric. "Literary Ancestry of 'Figaro.'" *Musical Quarterly* 13 (1927): 528 ff.

Traces characters in opera back to Beaumarchais, and through Molière to commedia dell'arte.

970. Csampai, Attila, and Dietmar Holland. *Die Hochzeit des Figaro*. Hamburg: Rororo, 1981.

Libretto and essays, no index.

971. Köhler, Karl-Heinz. "Figaro Miscellen." *Mozart Jahrbuch* 16
      (1968–1970): 119–131.

      Noting divergences of Berlin *Figaro* autograph with
      Prague *Figaro* autograph, author discusses scribal errors,
      considers "impersonation" of Susanna and Countess, asserts
      Figaro's masterful "Aprite" in Act IV was transformed from a
      recitative.

972. Einstein, Alfred. "Eine unbekannte Arie der Marcellina."
      Zeitschrift für Musikwissenschaft 13 (1930–1931): 200 ff.

      Discussion of aria for Marcellina as an alternative for
      Marcellina-Susanna duet in the first act of the Prague
      production. Although Einstein once thought it was by
      Mozart, he later changed his mind.
      See also: Siegfried Anheisser. "Urfassung von Mozart's
      'Figaro.'" *Zeitschrift für Musikwissenschaft* 15 (1932–1933): 301
      ff. For further discussion of Figaro, including speculation on
      the unused Siciliano interlude at measure 134 of the
      overture (also discussed in NMA *Figaro*).

973. Levarie, Siegmund. *Mozart's Le nozze di Figaro. A Critical
      Analysis.* Chicago: University of Chicago Press, 1952.
      (Reprint ed. New York: Da Capo, 1969. 268 pp. ISBN: 0-
      70897-3.)

      An important book, with structural analysis. Unifies
      dramatic and musical elements. Footnotes, but no
      bibliography, no index.
      See also: Erich Schenk. "Zur Tonsymbolik in Mozarts
      'Figaro.'" *Neues Mozart Jahrbuch* 1 (1941): 114-134.

974. *Le nozze di Figaro (Le mariage de Figaro).* L'Avant-Scène Opéra 21
      (1979). 170 pp. illus.

      Libretto. Several good articles. (Perhaps French
      understanding of this opera is superior because the play is
      originally French—so very French! Next to Austrian
      performances, French productions stand out in my memory
      as by far the best I have experienced.) Bibliography; no
      index.
      See also: Tim Carter. *Le Nozze di Figaro.* New York:
      Cambridge University Press, 1988. 192pp.

975. Merkling, Frank, ed. *The Opera News Book of Figaro.* New York: Dodd, Mead & Co., 1967. 146 pp. illus.

Introductory handbook with informed essays by Edward Downes, Lloyd Harris, Baird Hastings, Tibor Kozma, Paul Nettl, William Weaver, and 13 others. Index.

976. Ollivier-Smith, Martine. "Beaumarchais et Mozart." Ph. D. dissertation, Université de Paris, 1974.

Comparative study of *Le mariage de Figaro* (5 acts) as a play and *Le nozze di Figaro* (4 acts) as an opera.

977. Ruf, Wolfgang. *Die Rezeption von Mozarts 'Le nozze di Figaro' bei die Zeitgenossen.* Wiesbaden: Steiner, 1977. 148 pp. ISBN: 3-515-02408-5.

Discussion of the Vienna premiere, and comparison with the success of Paisiello's *Il re Tedoro.* Bibliography; no index.

978. Tyson, Alan. "'Le nozze di Figaro.'" *Musical Times* 122, 1661 (July 1981): 456–461.

Careful analysis, collating extant manuscript versions.
In May 1985 Dr. Tyson gave a lecture at the New York Public Library, "Figaro: Sources, Corrections, and Revisions." His discussion of several variants demonstrated the difficulty of presenting the definitive version.

979. *(Les petits riens)* Angermüller, Rudolph. "'Le finte gemelle' und 'Les petits riens' auf der Bühne der Pariser Académie royale de musique." *Wiener Figaro* 48 (June 1981): 3–14.

As our information on the successful double bill of Piccinni and Mozart in 1778 is meager, this article along with Harald Heckmann's notes to NMA of *Les petits riens* is welcome.

980. Sandt, Alfred. "Les Petits riens." *Mozart Jahrbuch* 3 (1929): 95–100.

Discussion of three versions, all with choreography by Noverre: 1768 (Vienna, Franz Asplmayr); 1778 (Paris, Mozart, etc.); 1781 (London, François Barthélemon).

981. *(Thamos)* Orel, Alfred. "Mozarts Beitrag zum Deutsche
      Sprechtheater, 'Thamos.'" *Acta Mozartiana* 4 (1957): 2–
      4.

      Not a great play, Gebler's *Thamos*, appearing during the
      Enlightenment, had a place in German literature,
      particularly with Mozart's fine music (which foreshadowed
      Die Zauberflöte). Outstanding brief discussion.

982. *(Die Zauberflöte)* Armitage-Smith, J. N. A. "The Plot of 'The
      Magic Flute.'" *Music and Letters* 35 (1954): 36-39.

      Contrasts Einstein's opinion that the plot of *The Magic
      Flute* was basically agreed on by Mozart and Schikaneder
      before Mozart began composition with that of Dent that the
      plot underwent many changes *while* Mozart was composing
      Act I. Concludes with Einstein.
      See also: Lowes Dickinson. *The Magic Flute.* London: G.
      Allen and Unwin, 1920. A fantasy quoted by King.

983. Batley, A. M. *A Preface to The Magic Flute.* London: Dobson,
      1969. 175 pp. illus. ISBN: 234-77205-0.

      Discussion of the plot, with careful relation of the
      narrative to the music. Uses many early sources. Notes;
      bibliography; index.

984. Blümml, Emil Karl. "Ausdeutingen der 'Zauberflöte.'" *Neues
      Mozart Jahrbuch* 1 (1923): 109-146.

      Comparison of interpretations by an important Mozart
      authority.

985. Brukner, Fritz. *Die Zauberflöte.* Vienna: Gilhofen &
      Rauschburg, 1934. 214 pp. illus.

      Discussion of productions and early parodies. Notes;
      index.

986. Chailley, Jacques. *La flûte enchantée, opéra maçonnique.* Paris:
      Robert Laffont, 1968. 342 pp. (Reprint Paris: Editions
      d'Aujourd'hui, 1975.) In English: *The Magic Flute;
      Masonic Opera.* Translated by Herbert Weinstock. New
      York: Knopf, 1971. 348 pp. ISBN: 0-394-4345-8. ML 410
      M8 C 432.

Although it is better to begin with the writings of Dent, Mann, Newman, or Osborne (above), and (if one has a knowledge of German) Kunze or Rosenberg, this book does consider Masonic points not fully covered elsewhere. Bibliography; index.

See also: Edgar Istel. "Mozart's 'Magic Flute' in Freemasonry." *Musical Quarterly* 13/4 (1927): 510–527. Discussion of idealism in the music of Mozart.

Also: Joachim Kaiser. *Mein Name ist Sarastro.* Munich: Piper, 1985. 299 pp.*

987. Csampi, Attila, and Dietmar Holland. *W. A. Mozart: Die Zauberflöte.* Munich: Ricordi, 1982. 281 pp. illus.

Includes German libretto, and essays on genesis, symbolism, productions. Chronology; discography; bibliography; no index.

988. Cole, Malcolm S. "The Magic Flute and the Quatrain." *The Journal of Musicology* 3, 2 (Spring 1984): 157–176.

Author shows that Mozart changed from frequent use of sonata form in *Die Entführung* and earlier operas to use of four-line quatrain, infinitely varied, in most numbers of *Die Zauberflöte.*

989. Eckelmeyer, Judith A. "Structure as Hermeneutic Guide to 'The Magic Flute.'" *Musical Quarterly* 72, 1 (Spring 1986): 51–73.

Analyzes structure (notes opening and closing tonality is E flat) to interpret how Mozart produced a unified work musically out of what might appear as unrelated elements.

See also: Judith A. Eckelmeyer. "Two Complexes of Recurrent Melodies Related to 'Die Zauberflöte.'" *Music Review* 41, 1 (February 1980): 11–25. This is further work along the lines of Chantavoine (#849). "Ach ich fühls" and the Final Chorus are related to works composed in Salzburg, through a series of similar themes. The author, who has made a complete translation of the original libretto, is at Cleveland State University, Ohio.

990. Omitted.

991. *La Flûte Enchantée. L'Avant-Scène Opèra* (1976). 130 pp.

Libretto in French. Twelve interpretive articles on background; casts, bibliography, filmography. Bibliography; no index.

992. Freyhan, Michael. "Towards the Original Text of Mozart's 'Die Zauberflöte.'" *Journal of the American Musicological Society* 39, 2 (Summer (1986): 355–380.

Stimulating discussion of autograph and first edition text, with exploration of reasons for variations.

993. Grasberger, Franz. "Zum Inhaltsproblem der Zauberflöte." Vienna: Verlag der Österreichisches Akademie der Wissenschaft, 1981. 12 pp.*

Discusses the spiritual opposition between the world of Sarastro and the world of the Queen of the Night.
RILM: 1981—#520.

994. Gruber, Gernot. "Das Autograph der 'Zauberflöte.'" *Mozart Jahrbuch* 16 (1968–1970): 99–110.

The editor of *Die Zauberflöte* for NMA describes the autograph, and compares corrections by Mozart with those of others.
See also: K. H. Köhler (#128).

995. Hausner, Henry H. "Zur Wiederaufführung von 'Kaspar der Fagottist.'" *Mitteilungen der ISM*, 18, 3–4 (August 1970): 18–20.

Wenzel Müller's *Kaspar* and Mozart's *Die Zauberflöte* are both based on tales from Wieland's *Lulu, oder die Zauberflöte*—different tales.
See also: A. H. King (#768).
Also: Marilyn Kielbasa. "Paul Wranitzky's 'Oberon' and its Influence on Mozart's 'Die Zauberflöte.'" Ph.D. dissertation, University of Southern California, 1975.*
Noted in C. Atkins (#516).

996. John, Nicholas, ed. *Die Zauberflöte.* London: Calder; New York: Riverrun, 1983. 128 pp. illus. ISBN: 0-7145-3768-3.

Like other informative, well-designed English National Opera Guides, this has the original language libretto and

English translation (more or less accurate), essays, musical themes, bibliography, discography. No index.

997. Orel, Alfred. "Die Bühneninstrumente der 'Zauberflöte.'" *Acta Mozartiana* 6, 3 (1959): 45–52.

Information for producers: Pan flute (fife), transverse flute, glockenspiel, large black horns with gold decorations.

998. Rosenberg, Alfons. *Die Zauberflöte.* Munich: Prestel Verlag, 1964. 344 pp. illus.

One of the most balanced and comprehensive presentations of this multi-faceted comic opera, treating allegory, satire, fairy tale, magic. Notes; documents; bibliography; index.

999. Schneider, Otto. "'Die Zauberflöte' in der Literatur. Ein bibliographischer Überblick." *Österreischische Musikzeitschrift* 22, 8 (August 1967): 458–464.

In spite of its musical transparency, *Die Zauberflöte* is one of the most difficult Mozart operas to understand—dramatically, philosophically. The issue as to whether it is a serious opera or a comic one may never be decided—nor may it be decided how much weight should be attached to the Masonic elements, given Mozart's broad humanism and his deep religiousness. Author provides a useful bibliographical survey of the diverse elements, treatments, and opinions, beginning with Johann Eybel in a Linz weekly of 1794, and continuing down to important commentaries by Egon Komorzynski, Bruno Walter, Alfons Rosenberg. To this list one should add H. C. Robbins Landon, whose latest book is *Mozart's Last Year.* London: Thames & Hudson, 1988. 240 pp. ISBN: 0-500-01411-6.

1000. Tanimura, Ko. "The Relationship Between Music and Theater in Mozart's 'Die Zauberflöte.'" *Ongaku* 20, 4 (March 1974): 217–227.

Believes *Die Zauberflöte* is a comic opera, disagreeing with Brigid Brophy and such authorities as Bruno Walter.

1001. Vaughan, Denis. "A Question of Magic." *Opera News* 37, 8 (December 23, 1972): 20–21.

Describes aspects of Sir Thomas Beecham's very convincing interpretation.

1002. Walter, Bruno. *Vom Mozart der 'Zauberflöte.'* Frankfurt: S. Fisher Verlag, 1955. 24 pp.

Pertinent essay about the nobility of themes, by one of the great Mozart conductors (also translated into English).

1003. Wyzewa, Théodore de. "Mozart's Operas by Edward Dent." Review. *Revue des Deux Mondes* (February 1913): 12 pp.

The score of *Die Zauberflöte* presents us with a pot-pourri, which Wyzewa feels audiences should savor as such, rather than through preconceptions of writers, producers, and performers. (Wyzewa uses "pot-pourri" in a favorable connotation.)

TEXTS

1004. Moberly, Robert B. "Mozart and his Librettists." *Music and Letters* 54, 2 (April 1973): 161–169.

An interesting comparison of collaborations with Varesco, Stephanie, Da Ponte, Mazzola, Schikaneder.
See also: P. Smith (#583).

Instrumental Music

GENERAL

1005. Hickman, Roger. "Leopold Koželuh and the Viennese Concertant." *College Music Symposium* 26 (1986): 42–52.

Revealing discussion of relationship of Koželuh to Haydn, Mozart, and Pleyel.

1006. Hill, George R. *A Preliminary Checklist of Research on the Classic Symphony and Concerto to the Time of Beethoven* (excluding Haydn and Mozart). Hackensack, New Jersey: Boonin, 1970. 58 pp.

Over 400 composers from England France, Italy, Mannheim, North Germany, Vienna are surveyed. Valuable for contemporaries. Bibliography; indexes.

1007. King, Alexander Hyatt. *Mozart's Wind and String Concertos.* London: BBC, 1978. 76 pp. ISBN: 0-295-95478-7.

An excellent brief survey. Index.

1008. Kirkendale, Warren. "Ein unveröffentliches Mozart Autograph." *Mozart Jahrbuch* 12 (1962–1963): 140–155.

Study of Mozart's transcriptions of J. S. Bach—K. 405.

1009. Zaslaw, Neal. "Mozart, Haydn, and the Sinfonia da Chiesa." *Journal of Musicology* 1, 1 (1982): 95–124.

Revealing discussion of the form of the sinfonia da chiesa, and its place in later eighteenth century instrumental music. With examples of the music—Mozart, Haydn, and others.

See also: Friedrich Blume. "The Concertos: Their Sources," and H. C. Robbins Landon, "The Concertos: Musical Origin and Development." Both of the above (in #774) are important articles on Mozart's concerto style.

1010. Zingel, H. J. "Mozart und die Harfe." *Neue Zeitschrift für Musik* 117, 1 (January 1956): 18–20.

Discussion of K. 299 and a piece for harp solo (listed in Köchel Anhang) which is dubious.

CHAMBER MUSIC (PRIMARILY STRINGS)

1011. Cobbett, Walter William. *Cyclopedic Survey of Chamber Music.* London: Oxford University Press, 1929. 3 vols. ML 1100 C 7.

Hermann Abert's article on Mozart, Volume II, pp. 150–183, is a solid resource for program notes.

1012. Einstein, Alfred. *Preface and Critical Report to W. A. Mozart: Ten Celebrated Quartets.* Volume 12 of the Publications of the Paul Hirsch Music Library, Cambridge, 1945. (Reprinted in Lea Pocket Scores, New York, 1979.)

This searching analysis is a fine introduction for anyone embarking on Mozart research, as many points in K. 387, 417b (421), 421b (428), 458, 460, 465, 499, 575, 589, 590 have wide application in the study of Mozart's music.

1013. Hümmeke, Werner. *Versuch einer strukturwissenschaftliche Darstellung der ersten und vierten Sätze der zehn letzen Streichquartteten von Wolfgang Amadeus Mozart.* Kassel: Bärenreiter, 1970. Ph.D dissertation. Münster, 273 pp.*

Author finds Mozart's late quartets twice as "integrated" as earlier quartets, based on Mozart's use of specified procedures.
RILM: 1973—#2594.

1014. King, Alexander Hyatt. *Mozart Chamber Music.* London: BBC, 1978. 68 pp.

An excellent introduction. Index.
See also: Eric Blom. "Mozart," in *Chamber Music*, Alec Robertson, ed. Baltimore: Penguin, 1957, pp. 60–93. (Excellent survey.)
Also: Karl Maguerre. "Mozarts Klaviertrios." *Mozart Jahrbuch* 11 (1968–1961): 282 ff.

1015. Leeson, Daniel N., and David Whitwell. "Concerning Mozart's Serenade in B flat for Thirteen Instruments." *Mozart Jahrbuch* 20 (1976–1977): 97–130.

An interesting discussion of Mozart's compositional procedure, and of authenticity.

1016. Marguerre, Karl. "Die beiden Sonaten-Reihe für Klavier und Geige." *Mozart Jahrbuch* 16 (1968–1970): 327–332.

Informative discussion of K. 301, 306, 296, and K. 376, 377, 378, 379, 380.

ORCHESTRA MUSIC (EXCEPT CONCERTOS)

1017. Allrogen, Gerhard. "Mozarts Lambacher Sinfonie." In *Festschrift für Georg von Dadelson.* Thomas Kohlhase and Volker Scherliess, eds. Stuttgart: Hänsler, 1978. 384 pp.*

Discusses three works: K. 45 (with tonalities of D, G, D [G], D in four movements); 45a (with tonalities of G, C, G in three movements); 45b (with tonalities of B flat, E flat, B flat [F], B flat in four movements). Questions reasoning that 45a is by Leopold Mozart and that 45 is by Wolfgang Mozart.
RILM: 1978—#2705.

See also: Gerhard Allrogen. "Mozarts erste Sinfonien." In *Festschrift Heinz Becker*, J. Schlader and R. Quendt, eds. Laaber: Laaber Verlag, 1982. 482 pp.* Allrogen discusses K. 45a, 19a, 16, pages 392–404.

1018. Angermüller, Rudolph. "Wer spielte die Uraufführung von Mozarts 'Pariser Symphonie', K. 297." *Mitteilungen der ISM* 26, 3-4 (August 1978): 12–20.

In addition to providing important background on players and repertoire at the time of the first performance of K. 297 by the Concert Spirituel in 1778, the author sheds some light on Anhang 14 C.01 (297b), as well as other aspects of Mozart's activity (musical and personal) in Paris in 1778.

1019. Dearling, Robert. *The Music of Wolfgang Amadeus Mozart. The Symphonies.* East Brunswick, New Jersey: Associated University Presses, 1982. 224 pp. ISBN: 0-8386-2335-2.

Useful discussion of sixty-six symphonies plus four spurious works, plus related works by Leopold Mozart. Approach resembles that of Robbins Landon on Haydn symphonies. Appendix; index.

See also: Cliff Eisen. "The Symphonies of Leopold Mozart and Their Relationship to the Early Symphonies of Wolfgang Amadeus Mozart: A Bibliographical and Stylistic Study." Cornell University, Ph.D. dissertation, 1986.*

(In preparation: Neal Zaslaw: *Mozart's Symphonies*. To include careful discussion of the Lambach catalogue, comprising many symphonies by Wolfgang, Leopold, and their contemporaries. Also forthcoming: Jan LaRue's volume on 18th-century symphonies [Indiana University].)

1020. Della Croce, Luigi. *Le 75 Sinfonie di Mozart. Guida e analisa critica.* Turin: Eda, 1977. 315 pp. illus.

After profiling Mozart's life, this book considers chronologically sixty-five symphonies (some identical with opera overtures), including some questionable and lost works, and also K. 136, 137, 138, the sinfonie concertante, and sinfonie dramatica from *Thamos*. It is both useful and provocative. Tables; discography generally sober. No index.

1021. Engel, Hans. "The Smaller Orchestral Works." In Landon-Mitchell (#774), pp. 138–155.

An excellent summary.

1022. ———. "Der Tanz in Mozarts Kompositionen." *Mozart Jahrbuch* 4 (1953): 29 ff.

An excellent summary (excluding dance in keyboard works).
See also: W. J. Allanbrook (#883) for Mozart's use of dance forms, particularly in opera.

1023. Flothuis, Marius. "Neue Erkenntnisse in Bezug auf Mozarts Tanzmusik." *Mitteilungen der ISM* 28, 3-4 (August 1980): 12–15.

Various details on Mozart's dance music, including his method of composing piano and orchestral versions. Early editions in Mozart's lifetime also show variations in the instrumentation. Author indicates K. 448b/462 was a forerunner of the ballroom scene in *Don Giovanni.* Also the order of sequences in Mozart's dance music is discussed, showing differences between autograph order and published order.

1024. Münster, Robert. "Authentische Tempi zu den Sechs Letzten Sinfonien Mozarts?" *Mozart Jahrbuch* 12 (1962–1963): 185 ff.

Münster considers metronome markings left by J. N. Hummel (a Mozart pupil) who heard many early performances, and also played the Mozart concertos. Although the accuracy of Hummel's statements cannot be corroborated by any of Mozart's own performances, it is interesting that among numerous recorded versions checked by Münster, only those conducted by Richard Strauss and Erich Kleiber even came close to Mozart's apparent indications of generally rapid tempos, particularly in the finales.
See also: Max Rudolf (#911).

1025. ———. "Neue Funde zu Mozarts symphonische Jugendwerke." *Mitteilungen der ISM* 30, 1-2 (February 1982): 2-11.

Meticulous discussion of K. 16, 19, 19a, 22, 45a, and eight other works; perceptive comments on chronology and style.

See also: Clemens von Gluck. "Die frühesten Quellen zur Temponahme bei Mozart." *Mitteilungen der ISM* 35, 1-4 (July 1987): 106–114.

1026. Saint-Foix, Georges de. *The Symphonies of Mozart*. Translated by Leslie Orrey from the French edition of 1932. London: Dobson, 1947. 217 pp.

Convenient, important, generally accurate survey. Notes; bibliography; appendix; index. For excellent summary, see Jens Peter Larsen, "The Symphonies," in Landon-Mitchell (#774).

1027. Sechter, Simon. *Das Finale von W. A. Mozarts Jupiter Symphonie*. Vienna: Philharmonische Verlag, 1923.*

Widely quoted treatment of one of Mozart's immortals. Cited in Schneider and Algatzy (#556).

1028. Smith, Erik. *Mozart Serenades, Divertimentos, and Dances*. London: BBC, 1982. 68 pp. ISBN: 0-563-12862-3.

Survey of Mozart's compositions specifically for enjoyment, including strings, winds, ensembles. Index.

See also: Gunter Hausswald. *Mozarts Serenaden*. Leipzig: Breitkopf & Härtel, 1951. 209 pp. (Rev. ed. 1975.) Discusses serenade style, and the place of serenades in the 18th century. Index.

1029. Thieme, Carl. *Der Klangstil des Mozartsorchestra.*. Leipzig: Noske, 1936. 88 pp.

Survey of instruments and sound of Mozart's orchestra; usefulness would have been increased by more examples. Notes; index.

1030. Tyson, Alan. "The Two Slow Movements of Mozart's Paris Symphony." *Musical Times* 122, 1655 (January 1981): 17–21.

The standard opinion—that the 3/4 version of the slow movement was composed prior to the 6/8 meter version—

questioned recently, is here supported by Tyson, with convincing evidence.

PIANO AND KEYBOARD MUSIC
(INCLUDING CONCERTOS)

1031. Badura-Skoda, Eva, and Paul Badura-Skoda. *Interpreting Mozart on the Keyboard*. New York: St. Martin's Press, 1962. Translated from the German by Leo Black. 310 pp.

An excellent introduction for anyone performing the works of Mozart. Indispensable to keyboard players. (Generally supersedes Hans Dennerlein: *Der unbekannte Mozart*, and is more practical than F. John Adams: *The Place of the Piano Concerto in the Career of Mozart*.) Appendixes; notes; bibliography; index.

See also: A. H. King (#768), whose discussion includes Cramer's early favorable reviews.

Also: Geoffrey Crankshaw. "Clementi and the Piano Sonata." *Musical Opinion* 80, 900 (September 1957): 725 ff.

1032. Dennerlein, Hans. "Zur Problematik von Mozarts Kirchensonaten." *Mozart Jahrbuch* 4 (1953): 95–111.

Careful discussion of the characteristics of Mozart's church sonatas—minor, but interesting pieces.

See also: Robert S. Tangeman. (#876).

1033. Eisley, Irving. "Mozart's Concertato Orchestra." *Mozart Jahrbuch* 20 (1976–1978): 9–20.

Useful discussion of instrumentation in Mozart keyboard concertos, 1784–1786.

1034. Fairleigh, James P. "Transition and Retransition in Mozart's Sonata-Type Movements." *College Music Symposium* 26 (1986): 14–26.

Analysis of K. 332, 283, 201, 550, 590, 442.

1035. Ferguson, Linda. "'Col Bass' and 'General Bass' in Mozart's Keyboard Concertos: Notation, Performance Theory, and Practice." Ph. D. dissertation, Princeton University, 1983. 430 pp. illus.*

Cited in Adkins (#516). Appendixes; bibliography; indexes.

1036. Flotzinger, Rudolf. "Die Klaviervariationen W. A. Mozarts in der Tradition dem 18 Jahrhunderts." *Mitteilungen der ISM* 23, 3-4 (August 1975): 13–27.

Useful survey of Mozart's interest in keyboard variations, illustrated with music.

1037. Forman, Denis. *Mozart's Concerto Form: The First Movements of the Piano Concertos.* New York: Praeger, 1971. 303 pp. ISBN: 0-246-64008-1.

States first movements are closely related to extended aria types used by J. S., C. P. E., and J. C. Bach: Galant—K. 482; Melodic—K. 595; Symphonic—K. 491. Quite theoretical. Index.

1038. Gallini, Natale. "Mozart e sua spinetta." *La Scala Milano* no. 36 (November 1952): 19–21.

Describes characteristics of harpsichord Antonio Scotti of Milan built in 1753, which Mozart used for *Mitridate* (1770).

1039. Gieseking, Walter. "Mozart auf dem Klavier—Mit oder ohne Pedal?" *Das Musikleben* 1, 1 (February 1948): 11 ff.

Cites examples with pedal, and examples without.

1040. Girdlestone, Cuthbert. *Mozart and His Piano Concertos.* New York: Dover, 1964. (Reprint edition of author's English version, London, 1948 of work originally published in French in Paris, 1939.) 509 pp. ISBN: 0-486-21271-8. MT 130 M8 G62.

Although too general at times, it is an indispensable survey, also useful for reference. Notes; appendixes; index.

1041. Gottron, Adam. "Wie spielte Mozart die Adagios seiner Klavierkonzerte?" *Musikforschung* 73 (1960): 334 ff.

A discussion of comments by contemporaries, noting Mozart did practice ornamentation and improvisation in differing manners, depending on his own mood.

1042. Haggin, B. H. "Three Mozart Andantes." *Sewanee Review*
       (Summer 1965): 622–629.

       Author's observations on the operatic elements Mozart
       used in the middle movements of K. 482, 453, and 467 are
       cogent and pertinent. Haggin (1900–1987) was, with Shaw
       and Tovey, an outstanding critic writing in English.
       See also: István Kecskeméti (#854).

1043. Hutchings, Arthur. *A Companion to Mozart's Piano Concertos.*
       London: Oxford University Press, 1948. 208 pp. MT 180
       M8 H8.

       A broad survey, briefer but in the manner of
       Girdlestone (#1040). Notes; bibliography; no index.

1044. ———. "The Keyboard Music." in Landon-Mitchell (#774):
       32–65.

       A splendid summary of all Mozart's solo keyboard
       music, except the concertos.

1044A. Irmer, Otto von. Preface and Appendix to *Mozart Klavier
       Sonaten.* Cologne: Henle, 1955.

       Discussion of when Mozart trills start on main note, and
       when on upper note.

1045. Jonas, Oswald. "Eine Skizze von Mozart (K. 503)." *Acta
       Mozartiana* 2, 3-4 (1955): 54–58.

       Interesting documentation of Mozart's use of
       preliminary sketches, in this case a piano concerto.

1046. King, Alexander Hyatt. "Mozart and the Organ." In King
       (#768): 228–241.

       Informative treatment of Mozart's ability and attitude,
       noting he called the organ the king of instruments, but
       looked for a position as conductor-composer.

1047. Lorenz, Franz. *Mozart als Klavier Componist.* Breslau:
       Leuckart, 1866. 63 pp.

       After introducing the cultural ambiance in Mozart's
       Vienna, Dr. Lorenz discusses Mozart's instrument, and how
       he used it in solos, chamber music, and concertos. Notes; no
       index.

1048. Mishkin, Henry G. "Incomplete Notation in Mozart's Piano Concertos." *Musical Quarterly* 61, 2 (July 1975): 345–359.

Interesting analysis of K. 491, noting that generally solo plays whenever the bass plays, and that solo never plays in a woodwind *a cappella* passage. (However, beware an author who concludes Shakespeare is better in modern dress than as a museum piece! Granted that "museums" can be deadly—often they are inspiring. Moreover, most modernization inevitably entails loss of true character.)

1049. Müller, August Eberhard. *Anweisung zum genauen Vortrage der Mozartschen Clavier Concerte hauptsächlich in Absicht richtiger Applicatur.* Leipzig: Schmiedt & Rau, 1796.*

An introduction to performing Mozart piano concertos by one who probably heard Mozart perform, and who edited scores of several works including *Don Giovanni*. Recommended by A. H. King and F. Neumann.

1050. Neumann, Friedrich. "Der Typus des Stufenganges der Mozartschen Sonaten Durchführung." *Mozart Jahrbuch* 10 (1959): 247–261.

A useful style study of Mozart's practice in modulation in piano sonatas and selected other compositions.

1051. Newman, William S. "The Pianism of Haydn, Mozart, Beethoven, and Schubert Compared." *Piano Quarterly* 105 (Spring 1979): 14–30.

Exploring respective techniques and resources of keyboard treatment of these composers, author notes Mozart and Beethoven wrote more idiomatically for the keyboard—Mozart was more natural, Beethoven was more demanding, both were more challenging than Haydn or Schubert. Bibliography.

1052. Richner, Thomas. *Orientation for Interpreting Mozart's Piano Sonatas.* New York: Teacher's College, 1953. 96 pp.

Brief discussion of keyboard influences: Leopold Mozart, Eckhardt, Schobert, J. C. Bach, J. S. Bach, Michael Haydn, Joseph Haydn; pianos in Mozart's time; tonalities and harmonies; ornamentation; Mozart's ideas; hands and wrists, speed and inaccuracies, body weight, taste and restraint, ease of execution, freedom from affectation, rhythm, rubato, tone; interpretation; analysis. Bibliography; no index.

1053. Rosenberg, Richard. *Die Klaviersonaten Mozarts.* Hofheim bei Taunus: Hofmeister, 1972. 148 pp.*

Analyzes sonatas chronologically, giving suggestions for interpretation based on themes and structure. Biographical facts included.
RILM: 1975—#1013.

1054. Stevens, Jane R. "Theme, Harmony, and Texture in Classic-Romantic Descriptions of Concerto First-Movement Form." *Journal of the American Musicological Society* 27, 1 (Spring 1974): 25–60.

Excellent background description of form at time Mozart was composing.

1055. Tischler, Hans. *A Structural Analysis of Mozart's Piano Concertos.* Brooklyn: Institute of Medieval Music, 1966. 140 pp.

Critical of Girdlestone and Hutchings (above); attempts to analyze selected concertos in depth. No index.

STRING MUSIC (INCLUDING CONCERTOS)

1056. Felinski, Zenon. *Über die Interpretation der Violinwerke Mozarts.* Cracow: Polskie Wydawnictwo Muzycne, 1956.*

Cited in Angermüller and Schneider (#546).

1057. Kaperl, Otto. "Mozart als Geiger." *Anbruch* 18, 3 (November 1936): 226 ff.*

Cited in Schneider and Algatzy (#556).

1058. Kolbin, Dmitrij. *The Violin Concertos of Mozart.* Moscow: Institute of Music, 1974. 180 pp.*

"Analysis" of the violin concertos, discussion of interpretation, and their role in the evolution of the genre. Bibliography.
RILM: 1976—#5564dd.
See also: G. Banat (#103).

1059. Lebermann, Walter. "Mozart-Eck-André." *Music and Letters* 22, 1 (January 1941): 41–53.

Presents evidence that J. F. Eck (1767–1838) was the composer of K. 268.

1060. Melkus, Eduard. "Die Kadenzen in Mozart Violinconzerten." *Musica* 36 (1982): 24–30.

Discusses transfering cadenza patterns from piano concertos to violin concertos and/or recasting existing violin cadenzas to structural and modulation schemes which fit.

1061. "Mozart and the Violin." *Violin and Violinists* 17, 3 (May 1956): 105, 106, 139.

General introduction.

WIND MUSIC (INCLUDING CONCERTOS)

1062. Birsak, Kurt. "Salzburg, Mozart und das Klarinette." *Mitteilungen der ISM* 33 (July 1985): 40–49.

A discussion of Mozart and the clarinet, noting influences of works by Michael Haydn and Franz Xaver Pokorny. Because of Mozart's avowed interest in the clarinet, and his mastery of its possibilities, a number of writers have explored the compositions in which he used it; Mozart's first important use of the clarinet was in K. 113.

1063. Dazeley, G. "The Original Text of Mozart's Clarinet Concerto." *Music Review* 9 (1948): 166–172.

A good discussion of ways to deal with passages below the range of an A clarinet.

1064. Etheridge, David. *Mozart's Clarinet Concerto.* Gretna: Pelican, 1983. 192 pp. ISBN: 0-88289-372-6.

Author's practical point of view is useful. Perhaps even more valuable are the quoted comments made on the conerto by eight leading clarinet players from various countries. Index.

1065. Jeurisson, Herman. "An Unknown Horn Concerto by Mozart." *The Horn Call* 10, 2 (April 1980): 12–14.

A good general discussion of the Mozart horn music.
(Peter Damm adds pertinent complementary comments.)
See also: Pizka (#111).

1066. Kingdon-Ward, Martha. "Mozart and the Clarinet." *Music
and Letters* 28, 2 (April 1947).

Martha Kingdon-Ward's outstanding article on the
clarinet is valuable to all woodwind players, as are her
discussions of "Mozart and the Bassoon." *Music and Letters*
30, 1 (January 1949).
See also: "Mozart and the Horn." *Music and Letters* 31, 4
(October 1950); "Mozart and the Flute." *Music and Letters*
35, 4 (October 1954).

1067. Komorzynski, Egon. "Die Posaunen bei Mozart." *Neue
Musik Zeitung* 27, 24 (25 September 1906): 526 ff.

Rather general.
See also: Felix Weingartner. "Die Posaunen in Mozarts
Requiem." *Musik* 5, 7 (January 1906): 41–43.*
A much debated subject, perhaps insoluble.

1068. Leeson, Daniel N., and Robert D. Levin. "On the
Authenticity of K. Anh. C 14.01 (297b), a Symphonie
Concertante for four Winds and Orchestra." *Mozart
Jahrbuch* 20 (1976–1977): 70–96.

A careful discussion of how the concertante for solo
flute, oboe, horn, and bassoon (as described in Mozart's
letters), may have been changed by Mozart and/or others
to solo oboe, clarinet, horn, bassoon. Authenticity is in
question, in part because of the length of the first
movement—longer than any other concerto first
movement by Mozart.
See also: Robert Levin. *Who Wrote the Mozart Four Wind
Concertante.* Stuyvesant, New York: Pendragon, 1987.*
ISBN: 0-918728-33-9.

1069. Marguerre, Karl. "Das Finale von Mozarts 'Erste
Hornkonzert.'" *Acta Mozartiana* 26, 2 (1979): 34–36.

Mozart's first version (1782) is believed authentic, but
the revised version (1797) is labeled an adaptation.

1070. Spitzer, John. "Musical Attribution and Critical Judgement: The Rise and Fall of the Sinfonia Concertante for Winds, K. 297b." *The Journal of Musicology* 5, 3 (Summer 1987): 319–356.

Author considers 168 "opinions of the work"—the composite of which seems to be that the work is doubtful at best.

1071. Steibel, Harold. "Stammt die heute gebräuchliche Fassung der 'Sinfonia concertante' KV 297b (Anh. C 14.01) doch von der Hand Mozarts?" *Mitteilungen der ISM* 34, 1-4 (July 1986): 41–49.

Presents effective arguments in favor of Mozart's authorship. Concurs with Einstein whose opinion was cited by Brody in *Notes* 37, 4 (June 1981): 823–826. (On the basis of evidence available, the present writer believes this masterpiece is basically authentic, even if "edited" by another hand.)

Films and Videos

The following listing of visual material has been divided into three parts: Operas, Other Films, and Commentary. The arrangement is alphabetical. Information for these selections has been compiled from the International Music Centre's Music in Film and Television: an international selective catalogue 1964–1974, Central Opera Service Bulletin, 19, 2; the Video Source Book, film reviews from the New York Public Library's Theatre Collection, and reviews from the cultural and entertainment media through March 1988.

Operas

1072. *Così fan tutte.*
Producer: Vaclav Kaslik, ORF/Neue Thalia/ UNITEL. Distributor: Neue Thalia. Technical data: TV film 35 mm/color/156 min. Date: 1969. Language: Italian.
Cast: Gundula Janowitz (Fiordiligi), Christa Ludwig (Dorabella), Olivera Miljakovic (Despina), Luigi Alva (Ferrando), Hermann Prey (Guglielmo), Walter Berry (Don Alfonso); Karl Böhm conducts the Vienna Philharmonic in a studio performance. VCR available for purchase.

1073. ———.
Glyndebourne Festival Opera Production. Distributor: Video Arts International. Technical data: Beta; VHS/150 min. (cut). Date: 1975. Language: Italian/English subtitles.
Cast: Helene Döse (Fiordiligi), Sylvia Lindenstrand (Dorabella), Daniele Perries (Despina), Anson Austin (Ferrando), Thomas Allen (Guglielmo), Franz Petri (Don Alfonso); John Pritchard conducts the London Philharmonic. VCR available for purchase.

1074. ———.
Drottningholm, Sweden Production. Director: Willy Decker. Technical data: TV film/141 min. Date: 1985. Thorn EMI/HBO Video.
Cast includes: Magnus Linden, Lars Tibell, Maria Hoeglind, Anne Biel (Fiordiligi), Ulla Severin; Arnold Ostman conducts orchestra of original instruments.

1075. ———.
BBC Production. Producer: Jonathan Miller. Technical data: TV film/210 min. Date: 1985. Language: English.
Cast includes: Ashley Putnam (Fiordiligi), Jean Rigby (Dorabella), Anthony Rolfe Johnson (Ferrando), Thomas Hampson (Guglielmo); Peter Robinson conducts the London Sinfonietta.

1076. *Don Giovanni.*

Glyndebourne Festival Opera Production. Director: Peter Hall, Southern Television. Technical data: Beta, VHS/color/173 min. Date: 1977. Language: Italian/English subtitles.

Cast includes: Benjamin Luxon (Don Giovanni), Stafford Dean (Leporello), Leo Goeke (Don Ottavio), Horiana Branisteanu (Donna Anna), Rachel Yakar (Donna Elvira), Elizabeth Gale (Zerlina); Bernard Haitink conducts the London Philharmonic. VCR is available from Video Arts International.

1077. ———.

Salzburg Festival Production. Producer: Dr. Paul Czinner, Harmony Films Productions. Distributor: I. R. Maxwell. Technical data: photographed duplications/color/150 min. Date: 1956.

Cast: Cesare Siepi (Don Giovanni), Otto Edelmann (Leporello), Deszo Ernster (Commendatore), Anton Dermota (Don Ottavio), Walter Berry (Masetto), Elisabeth Grummer (Donna Anna), Lisa della Casa (Donna Elvira), Erna Berger (Zerlina); Wilhelm Furtwängler conducts the Vienna Philharmonic and the Stae Opera Chorus. (Very fine performance—BH.) Available for purchase.

1078. ——— *(Don Juan).*

Director: H. H. Kolm-Veltee, Akkord Film of Vienna; Times Films. Adaptation: Kolm-Veltee, Alfred Uhl, Ernest Henthaler. Technical data: film. Date: 1956. Language: German.

An abbreviated version of the opera—singing voices have been dubbed in for the actors, and dialogue often is spoken rather than sung. The Vienna Symphony performs and the Ballet of the Vienna State Opera dances.

1079. ———.

Film directed by Joseph Losey. Producers: M. Seydoux, R. Nador. Technical data: 177 min. Date: 1979. Language: Italian.

Cast: Ruggero Raimondi (Don Giovanni), José van Dam (Leporello), Kenneth Riegel (Don Ottavio), John

Macurdy (Commendatore), Malcolm King (Masetto), Edda Moser (Donna Anna), Kiri Te Kanawa (Donna Elvira), Teresa Berganza (Zerlina); Loren Maazel conducts the orchestra and chorus of the Paris Opéra. VCR available for purchase from Kultur.

1080. *Die Entführung aus dem Serail.*

Glyndebourne Festival Opera Production. Director: Peter Wood. Producer: Dave Heather. Sets: William Dudley. Video Arts International. Technical data: 145 min. Date: 1980. Language: German/English subtitles.

Cast includes: Valerie Masterson (Constanze), Lillian Watson (Blonde), Ryland Davies (Belmonte), James Hoback (Pedrillo), Willard White (Osmin); Gustav Kuhn conducts the London Philharmonic. VCR and Beta available from Fine Arts International.

1081. ———.

Distributor: Historical Recording Enterprises. Technical data: Beta, VHS/color/120 min. Date: 1980. Language: German.

Cast includes: Reri Grist (Constanze), Martti Talvela (Osmin); Karl Böhm conducts a performance originating in Munich. Videocassette available for purchase.

1082. ———.

Dresden Opera Production. Technical data: 130 min. Date: 1980? Language: German.

Cast includes: Carolyn Smith-Meyer (Constanze), Barbara Sternberger (Blonde). VCR available from Video Revolution, Concord, Massachusetts.

1083. ———.

Directed by Harry Kupfer. V. I. E. W. Video. Technical data: 129 min. Date: 1985? Language: German.

Cast includes: Armin Uhde, Rolf Tomaszewski, Uwe Peper, Carolyn Smith-Meyer; Peter Gulke conducts the Dresden State Opera.

1084. *Idomeneo.*

Metropolitan Opera Production. Producer: Jean-Pierre Ponnelle. Technical data: 184 min. Date: 1983. Language: Italian, English subtitles.

Cast: Luciano Pavarotti (Idomeneo), Hildegard Behrens (Electra), Ileana Cotrubas (Ilia) Frederica von Stade (Idamante), John Alexander (Arbace); James Levine conducts the Metropolitan Opera and Chorus. VHS—RV 80; Beta—RV 81. Available for purchase.

1085. ———.

Glyndebourne Festival Opera Production. Technical data: 184 min. Date: 1984. Language: Italian., English subtitles.

Cast includes: Richard Lewis (Idomeneo), Josephine Barstow (Electra), Leo Goeke (Idamante), Bozena Betley (Ilia), Alexander Oliver (Arbace); John Pritchard conducts the London Philharmonic. VA1.

1086. ———.

Glyndebourne Festival Opera Production. Director: Trevor Nunn. Technical data: HBO/Cannon Video/181 min. Date: 1986. Language: Italian.

Cast includes: Philip Langridge (Idomeneo), Carol Vaness (Electra), Jerry Hadley (Idamante), Yvonne Kenny (Ilia); Bernard Haitink conducts the London Philharmonic. Available for purchase.

1087. ———.

Drottningholm, Sweden Production. Director: Michael Hampe. Date: 1986.

Cast: Joseph Protschka (Idomeneo), Anita Soldh (Electra), Ingrid Tobiasson (Idamante), Christine Biel (Ilia), Lars Magnuson (Arbace); Arnold Ostman conducts.

1088. *Le nozze di Figaro.*

Glyndebourne Festival Opera Production. Director: Peter Hall/Southern Television. Technical data: Beta/VHS/color/168 min. Date: 1973. Language: Italian/English subtitles.

Cast includes: Kiri Te Kanawa (Countess), Ileana Cotrubas (Susanna), Frederica von Stade (Cherubino), Bejamin Luxon (Count), Knut Skram (Figaro); John Pritchard conducts the London Philharmonic. VCR available from Video Arts International.

1088A.———.

Deutsche Grammophon Video. Director: Pierre Ponnelle. Technical data: 184 min.

Cast includes: Te Kanawa, Freni, Ewing, Begg, Prey, Fischer-Diskau, Montarsolo. Karl Böhm conducts the Vienna Philharmonic. Available for purchase.

1089. ———.

Producer: Pierre Gerin, Productions Cinématiques Film. Director: J. Meyer. Distributor: Contemporary/McGraw Hill Films; Union Films. Technical data: 16 mm and 35 mm/color/105 min. Date: 1963. Language: French/English subtitles.

A filmed version of Beaumarchais' play (abbreviated), acted by members of the Comédie Française, with Mozart's music as background.

1090. ——— (Marriage of Figaro).

Writer/director: Georg Wildhagen, Deutsche Film A. G. of Berlin. Distributor: Central Cinema Corporation. Technical data: film/ 90 min. Date: 1950.

A German-made film of the opera (abbreviated). The voices have been dubbed in; Arthur Rother conducts the Berlin State Orchestra.

1091. ——— (scenes).

Distributors: Opera Productions, Inc. A. V. Center, University of Michigan; Select Films; Willoughby Peerless. Technical data: 16 mm/black and white/25 min. Date: 1948. Language: Italian/English narration.

Cast: Members of the Rome Opera, with the Rome Opera Orchestra.

1092. ——— (scenes).

Distributor: Budget Films. Technical data: 16 mm/black and white/ 14 min. Date: 1930s. Rehearsal and performance excerpts.

1093. *Die Zauberflöte.*

Glyndebourne Festival Opera Production. Technical data: 164 min. Date: 1978. Sets: David Hockney. Language: German/English subtitles.

Cast includes: Leo Goeke (Tamino), Felicity Lott (Pamina), Benjamin Luxon (Papageno), May Sandoz (Queen of the Night), Thomas Thomaschke (Sarastro); Bernard Haitink conducts the London Philharmonic. Videocassette available from Video Arts International.

1094. ———.

Leipzig Gewandhaus Production. V. I. E. W. Video. Technical data: 156 min. Language: German.

Cast includes: Horst Gebhardt (Tamino), Magdalena Falewicz (Pamina), Inge Uibel (Queen of the Night), Hermann Poster (Sarastro), Deiter Schloz (Papageno); Heidrun Haik; Gert Bahner conducts the Leipzig Gewandhaus Orchestra. VCR available from Video Revolution, Concord, Massachusetts.

1095. ———.

Producer/Director: Ingmar Bergman. Distributor: Surrogate Releasing Corporation; Paramount Home Video. Technical data: 35mm/videocassette/ color/134 min. Date: 1973. Language: Swedish/ English subtitles.

Cast includes: Haakon Hagegård (Papageno), Ulrik Cold (Sarastro), Irma Urrila (Pamina), Josef Kostlinger (Tamino), Bergit Nordin (Queen of the Night), Radnar Ulfung (Monostatos); Eric Ericson conducts the Swedish Broadcasting Symphony. The camera moves from the performance to the audience, and also backstage, during a presentation at the Drottningholm Court Theatre. One reviewer said: "Mr. Bergman hasn't set out to interpret 'The Magic Flute' but rather to present it as it originally was, bursting with the life of an exquisite stage production as it would look within the physical limitations of an 18th century court theater." Many others were less enthusiastic, despite the ingenious camera work. Available for purchase.

1095A. ———.

Canadian National Arts Centre (CBC). Home Vision.

198   *Bibliography*

Cast includes: Rita Shane, Patricia Wells, David Holloway, Nancy Hermiston; Mario Bernardi conducts.

1096. ——— (*Papageno*).
Distributor: Audio-Visual Services, University of Pennsylvania. Technical data: 16mm/black and white/10 min. Date: 1961.
A Lotte Reiniger silhouette/film, suitable for children.

1097. *Mozart* (Two films of opera scenes).
Producer: NET. Distributor: NET Film Service, Audio Visual Center, Indiana University. Technical Data: 16 mm./black and white/29 min. each. Date: 1958. Language: English.
Produced for NET as part of the "Spotlight on Opera" series, it provides analysis of operatic characters and includes excerpts from various operas with piano accompaniment. Jan Popper is the narrator.

Other Films

1098. *The Mozart Miracle: Symphony in A minor, K. 16a.*
Producer: Arts & Entertainment, Hearst/ABC/RCTV (New York). Technical data: 60 min. Date: 1985. Language: English.
With Tom Hulce as host. After interviews with several Mozart authorities, The Odense Orchestra of Demnark performs this four-movement work very well. The problem is that although the symphony uses an authenticated theme, it has been at the least edited, and is not pure Mozart. Still it is recommended for its serious approach to musical considerations.

1099. *Elvira Madigan.*
Director/writer: Bo Wilderberg. Janco Film/Europa film. Distributor: Cinema V Distribution. Technical data: film/90 min. Date: 1967. Language: English.
Film primarily known for its use of Mozart's *Piano Concerto in C major*, No. 21, K. 467.

1100. *The Great Composers: W. A. Mozart.*

Producer: John Seabourne. Distributor: Visual Aides Service, University of Illinois. Technical data: 16mm, Beta, VHS/color/26 min. Date: 1973. Language: English narration.

Performers are the London Mozart Players with Nina Milkina, piano. Videocassette available for purchase from the International Film Bureau.

1101. *Mozart.*

Technical data: videocassette/55 min.

Photographed at a castle in the Rhone Valley, France. Alain Marion, flutist, Jeremy Menuhin, pianist, and the Polish Chamber Orchestra conducted by Jerzy Maksymiuk perform the *Flute Concerto* in D (K. 314), the *Andante in C for Flute and Orchestra* (K. 285e.), and the *Piano Concerto* in E flat, No. 9, K. 271. Videocasette available for purchase from Sony Video.

1102. *Mozart and his Music.*

Distributor: Modern Talking Picture Service; University of Connecticut; Southern Illinois University, et al. Technical data: 16 mm/black and white or color/ 13 and one-half min. Date: 1954. Language: English.

Includes selections of Mozart's music performed against the visual sights of Salzburg and Vienna. Study guide is available. Videocassette available for purchase from Coronet Films.

1103. *Mozart, the Clarinet and Keith Purdy.*

Producer: Thames Television. Technical data: Beta, VHS/³/₄" u-matic color/26 min. Date: 1975.

Purdy and the Gabrieli Quartet perform. Videocassette available for purchase from the Media Guild.

1104. *The Ageless Mozart.*

Producer: Robert Saudek Associates. Distributor: I. Q. Films. Technical data: 16mm kinescope/black and white/60 min. Date: 1965. Language: English.

Originally produced as a television documentary.

1105. *Amadeus.*

Director: Milos Forman. Executive producers: Michael Haussman, Bertil Ohlsson. Producer: Saul Zaentz, Orion Pictures. Screenplay: Peter Shaffer. Technical data: film/color/158 min. Date: 1984. Language: English.

Cast includes: F. Murray Abraham (Salieri), Tom Hulce (Mozart), Elizabeth Berridge (Constanze); Neville Marriner conducts the Academy of St. Martins in the Fields. One reviewer wrote: "'Amadeus' has done for the late 18th century Viennese court musician Antonio Salieri what 'Mutiny on the Bounty' did for Captain Bligh: i.e., seized on a few dubious bits of historical evidence to make him a byword for malignity among people who had not previously been aware of his existence." Attractive scenery, but very distorted history. Videocassette available for purchase.

1106. *The Life and Loves of Mozart.*

Writer/director: Karl Hartl, Cosmopol. Distributor: Bakros International Films. Technical data: film/color/87 min. Date: 1959. Language: German/English subtitles.

A reviewer wrote that the picture is threaded with melodic excerpts, primarily operatic, beautifully rendered by Hilde Gueden, Erich Kunz, Anton Dermota, Erika Koeth, Gottlob Frick and the Vienna Philharmonic. Oskar Werner plays Mozart.

1107. *The Life of Mozart.* (Austria/West Germany.)

Producer: Hans Conrad Fischer, Fischer Film- und Fernsehproducktion. Distributor: FFF (& Connoisseur Films). Technical data: film 35 and 16mm/COMMAG/M in 3 parts/48 min./38 min./56 min. Date: 1967. Language: German and English.

Excerpts from record, films, magnetic recordings of Karl Böhm, Carlo Felice Cillario, Jörg Demus, Ferenc Fricsay, Wilhelm Furtwängler, Ernst Hinreiner, Eugen Jochum, Herbert von Karajan, Franz Konwitschny, Fritz Lehmann, Franz Litschauer, Jean-François Paillard, Kurt Redel, Karl Richter, Vaclav Smetaček, Gerhard Wimberger, Berlin Philharmonic, Camerata Academica of the Mozarteum, Munich Bach Orchestra, Praha Czech Philharmonic, Pro Arte Chamber Orchestra, Dresden

Staatskapelle, Vienna Symphony; Hugh Burden, narrator. "Deeply impressive" (BBC, London).

1108. *Mozart.*

Producer: Roland Gritti, TFI & Telecip. Director: Marcel Bluwal. Technical data: TV/color/six 90 min episodes. Date: 1982. Language: French or English.

Expensive series with cast headed by Christoph Bantzer (Mozart), Michel Bouquet (Leopold)—filmed in Italy, Austria, Hungary, France. Music selected by Bruno Monsaigeon and recorded by the Hungarian Symphony and Chamber Orchestras.

1109. *Mozart.*

Producer/director: Basil Dean, Mozart Film, Inc. Writer: Margaret Kennedy. Technical data: film/ 60 min. Date: C. 1929?

Produced in England with Stephen Haggard (Mozart), and the London Philharmonic Orchestra conducted by Sir Thomas Beecham.

1110. *Mozart: a Childhood Chronicle.*

Writer/director: Klaus Kirschner, Bayerische Rundfunk Artfilm Pitt Koch. Technical data: film/black and white/224 min. Date: 1976. Language: German/English subtitles.

Documentary based on the Mozart letters up to the composer's 21st year. A reviewer write: "A wonderfully big, complex and moving film that should not be missed by anyone who has even a passing interest in the work of Wolfgang Amadeus Mozart and in the lives and relationships that were a part of his work." Available from Facets, Chicago, Illinois.

1111. *Mozart in Love.*

Technical data: film/100 min. Date: 1975.

A narrated love story using music from Mozart's operas.

1112. *The Mozart Story.*

Director: Carl Hartl. Distributor: Patrician Pictures. Technical data: 16 mm, Beta VHS/91 min. (Subsequently twenty-two additional minutes were produced by Abrasha Haimson, directed by Frank Wisbar/black and white.) Language: English, dubbed.

Originally produced in Vienna in 1939, the later edition was released in 1948. Traces Mozart's life in Mannheim, Prague, Vienna. Cast includes Hans Holt (Mozart). Brief instrumental and operatic passages are played by the Vienna Philharmonic. A reviewer wrote: "sketchy and episodic." Videocassette available for purchase from Video Yesteryear.

1113. *Mozart's Last Requiem.*

Producer: George Kleine, The Moving Picture World Production Co. Technical data: film/940 feet.

A melodramatic account of Mozart's last days.

1114. *Noi tre.*

Director: Pupi Avati. Technical data: film. Date: 1986.

Film portrays 14-year-old Mozart's visit with his father to an Italian estate where, studying for his examination at the Bolognese Academy he plans to fail the test in order to stay with his new friends, but is forced to be "Mozart." A reviewer wrote: "delicate narrative unfolded in a wry and tender manner and filmed with exquisite attention to detail and nuance."

1115. *Requiem for Mozart* (USSR).

Director: Vladimir Gorikker, Riga Film Studio. Distributor: Artkino Pictures, Brandon Films. Technical data: 35 mm/black and white/47 min. Date: 1967.

Music: Nikolai Rimsky-Korsakov. Conductor: S. Samosud. Acting cast: I. Smoktunovskiy (Mozart), P. Glebov (Salieri) A. Milbret (blind musician); singers: S. Lemeshev (Mozart), A. Pirogov (Salieri). Sources: Puskin: *Motzart i. Salyeri*; Rimsky-Korsakov: *Motzart i Salyeri.*

1116. *Vergesst Mozart.*

> Director: Slavo Luther. Distributor: Oko Film Karel Dirka production, Munich. Executive producer: Harald Kügler. Technical data: film/color/93 min. Date: 1985.
>
> Filmed in Prague, and "taking up where *Amadeus* left off," hearings are held to determine responsibility for Mozart's death.

1117. *Der Liebling.*

> (A Mozart film by Bela Balaza.) 1937?* Reference from New York Public Library Catalogue of the Music Collection.

Commentary

1118. Green, H. "Celluloid Mozart." *Opera News* 23 (9 February 1959): 31.

> A brief review of several films.

1119. Kunz, Otto. "Mozart in Film." *Allegemeine Musikzeitung* 70 (1943).*

> A survey of early films.

1120. Simpson, Alexander Thomas. "Opera on Film." Dissertation in Musicology in preparation, University of Louisville, Kentucky.*

> Title cited by C. Atkins (#516)—"a study of the history and the aesthetic, conflicts of a hybrid genre."

5.
ALPHABETICAL DICTIONARY OF MOZART'S CONTEMPORARIES (AND OTHERS IN HIS WORLD)

Names are spelled according to autograph, Bauer/ Deutsch/Eibl *Mozart Briefe,* Grove, or such other sources of information as Deutsch (#610), Loewenberg (#537), *Musik in Geschichte und Gegenwart,* etc.

In preparing this dictionary of more than 1400 figures in Mozart's world, I have included a number of persons, whose depth of association with Mozart is undefined because further research probably will turn up new facts that will enrich our understanding of the man and his music. This is particularly true in the case of figures who were not professional musicians.

Abel, Carl Friedrich 1723–1787

German composer who settled in London in 1759. Student and colleague of J. C. Bach and J. A. Hasse. Mozart admired his music; see K. 18 for Abel's influence.

Abos, Geronimo 1708–1786

Italian composer whose operas also were heard in Vienna and Munich. Teacher of Giuseppe Aprile, whose tenor voice pleased both Mozart and his father, Leopold.

Accorimboni, Agostino c. 1740–1818

Italian composer whose work Mozart heard in 1778 in Paris (sung by the castrato M. Amantini, a favorite singer of Queen Marie Antoinette).

Adam, Jacob   1748–1811

Artist, engraver, in the circle of Grassi and Posch (Vienna).

Adam, Johann Baptist   c. 1740–1800?

A Salzburg widower who courted Mozart's sister, Nannerl, but failed to receive Leopold's consent (although he was the personal valet of Archbishop Colloredo).

Adamberger, Johann Valentin   1743–1803

Bavarian tenor active in Italy, England, Vienna (from 1780) where he sang in the premieres of Mozart's *Die Entführung* and *Der Schauspieldirecktor*. Fellow Freemason. His wife, Maria Anna (1752-1804), acted in *Der Schauspieldirektor*.

Adelaide, Madame Marie de Bourbon   1732–1808

Daughter of Louis XV of France, after whom Mozart's so-called "Adelaide" violin concerto was named.

Adelheit, Fräulein von   c. 1760–1810?

Singer-actress who performed "Warum, o Liebe" (K. 365a) in an early collaboration of Mozart and Schikaneder: Gozzi's play *Le due notti affanose* (translated as *Die zwei schlaflosen Nächte* by F. A. C. Werther), produced in Munich, December 1, 1780.

Adlgasser, Anton Cajetan   1729–1777

Bavarian composer; Salzburg court organist from 1762. Married: Maria Eberlin (c. 1730–1755); Maria Schwab (1735–1766); Maria Fesemayer (1740–1780?), who sang in Mozart's *La finta semplice* and *Die Schuldigkeit*.

Affligio, Giuseppe   1722–1788

Viennese court theatre director whose intrigue prevented the Viennese premiere of *La finta semplice* in 1769.

Agrell, Johann   1701–1765

Nuremberg instrumental composer whose music was known to Leopold.

Agujari, Lucrezia 1743–1783

Italian coloratura who made her debut in Florence. Mozart met her in 1770, noting her impressive range and ability, probably the highest voice he heard.

Albanese, Antoine 1730–1800

Neapolitan tenor and composer, collaborator of S. Champein in Paris, whose song "Hélas, j'ai perdu mon amant" Mozart used for his variations, K. 374a (360).

Albert, Franz 1728–1789

Munich friend, manager of hotel where Mozart stayed.

Albertarelli, Francesco 1760–1820?

Baritone active in Vienna in 1780s and London in 1790s. Sang *Don Giovanni* in Vienna premiere, also "Un bacio di mano," K. 541.

Alberti, Ignaz c. 1750–1794

Vienna artist, printer, publisher of K. 586, 587, 598, etc. and libretto of *Die Zauberflöte*. Fellow Freemason, friend of Schikaneder.

Albertini, Gioacchino 1751–1812

Italian opera composer of *Don Juan* (1783), also active in Germany and Poland.

Albrechtsberger, Johann Georg 1736–1809

Respected, friendly Viennese composer, organist, teacher.

Alessandri, Felice 1742–1790

Roman composer, also active in Vienna, London, Berlin, Paris, St. Petersburg. Married to soprano Maria Guadagni (c. 1740–1790?), sister of Italian singer-composer, Gaetano Guadagni (c. 1730–1790).

Allard, Marie 1742–1802

Paris Opéra dancer in *Les petits riens* (1778), etc.

Allegranti, Maddalena c. 1750–1802

Leading singer in Mannheim and Dresden in 1780s and 1790s. Pupil of Holzbauer.

Alphen, Eusebius Johann   1741–1772

Portrait painter active in Vienna, Paris Milan. Probable painter of ivory miniature of Mozart and his sister Nannerl (1765), now in the Mozarteum.

Altomonte, Katharina von   c. 1765–1810?

Amateur soprano in Vienna, 1780s and 1790s, who sang in Mozart's arrangement of *Messiah* presented by Baron van Swieten. Friend of the Jacquins.

Alxinger, Johann Baptist von   1755–1797

Vienna poet, translator of Gluck; member of Swieten circle, fellow Freemason, friend of Mozart from 1781.

Amann, Basil   1756–1785

Salzburg friend of Mozart; fellow Freemason.

Ambreville, Leonora   c. 1745–1800?

Soprano active in 1770s in Italy, where she sang with Mozart in Mantua.

Amon, Johann   1763–1825

German instrumental composer, also active in Paris; related to Heilbronn publisher of K. 246?

Anderson, Emily   1891–1962

Distinguished British musicologist who specialized in Mozart and Beethoven.

André, Johann   1741–1799

Offenbach composer, member of a musical family. Founder of publishing house in 1774 which was continued by his son Anton (editor of Mozart works), and other family members.
Anfossi, Pasquale   1727–1797

Successful composer of Neapolitan operas in several centers, for whose works Mozart wrote (several) insert arias.

Angiolini, Gaspare   1731–1803

Important Italian choreographer (and composer); unfriendly with Noverre, Angiolini was active in Vienna 1758–1766 and 1774–1776.

Anseaume, Louis 1741–1784
Important French librettist for Grétry, Gluck, Duni, etc.

Antoine (Anton Dionys Crux) 1743–1810
Ballet master and dancer in Munich premiere of *Idomeneo* and other works.

Antonini, Sra. c. 1770–1820?
Sang Servilia in Prague premiere of *La clemenza di Tito*, 1791.

Apponyi, Count Anton 1751–1817
Viennese noble patron of Mozart; accomplished violinist; member of Swieten circle.

Aprile, Giuseppe 1738–1814
Italian male contralto active in 1760s and 1770s. Sang with Mozart in Bologna.

Arbauer, Joseph Felix c. 1740–1800?
Paris acquaintance, 1778.

Arbesser, Ferdinand 1719–1794
Viennese church composer.

Arco, Count Karl 1743–1830
Austrian administrator in Milan, favorable to Mozart at first; later unfavorable.

Arne, Thomas 1710–1778
English composer whose music Mozart heard in London (1765).

Arnold, Ferdinand c. 1760–1830?
Singer at Vienna's Italian opera in 1780s. Married Thérèse Teiber (1787).

Arnold, Ignaz Ernst Ferdinand Karl 1774–1812
Author of two books on Mozart, and other biographies.

Arnould, Sophie   1740–1802

Famous French soprano, active when Mozart was in Paris (1778).

Arnstein, Benedikt   c. 1740–1810?

Dramatist and librettist active in Austria in 1780s; his works were seen by the Mozart family.

Artaria, Carlo   1747–1808

Vienna music publisher from 1778, originally from Como, then Mainz. Beginning as a publisher of art reproductions, the expanding family firm published many works of Mozart. Other members of the family included Francesco, Domenico, Pasquale, Giovanni, Matthias, and August; several were Freemasons.

Arth, Eleonore   17561–1821

Actress-singer who married E. Schikaneder.

Aspelmeyer, Franz   1728–1786

Viennese composer of symphonies, operas, and ballets, including the original version of Noverre's *Les petits riens* (Vienna, 1768). See also Barthélemon, composer of third version of *Les petits riens*.

Asselin, Mlle.   c. 1748–1795?

Paris Opéra dancer in Mozart's *Les petit riens* (1778). Also active in Italy, Germany, Vienna, London, with members of her family.

Astarita, Gennaro   1745–1803

Neapolitan opera composer whose works were also produced in Vienna, and elswhere in Europe.

Attwood, Thomas   1765–1838

English composer and organist who studied in Naples, and in Vienna with Mozart. Fellow Freemason.

Aubert, Louis   1720–1784

French instrumental and vocal composer active in Paris.

Auenbrugger, Dr. Joseph Leopold von   1722–1809

German dramatist and librettist for Salieri. Friend of Mozart.

Auernhammer, Josepha 1758–1820
Vienna keyboard pupil from 1781; often played Mozart's concertos.

Auersperg, Prince Adam 1721–1795
Patron of Mozart. A private performance of *Idomeneo* was produced in his Viennese palace in 1786.

Auffmann, Johann Anton c. 1720–1780?
Augsburg organist and composer.

Aumann, Franz Joseph 1728–1797
Austrian sacred ("cloister") composer at St. Florian, whose style resembles that of Michael Haydn and Mozart; Aumann is probably the author of a mass listed in K. [6], Anh. C.1.15.

Ayrenhoff, Cornelius c. 1740–1800.
Austrian writer whose works were adapted as opera librettos.

Bach, Carl Philipp Emanuel 1714–1788
Berlin composer admired by Leopold and Wolfgang Mozart, and Baron van Swieten, for his formal and creative style.

Bach, Johann Christian 1735–1782
After studying in Italy with Padre Martini, Bach settled in England; his Italian operas and galant music were important influences on Mozart, with whom he was very friendly.

Bach, Johann Sebastian 1685–1750
Mozart's admiration for the music of J. S. Bach increased after he joined the Swieten circle in 1781.

Bach, Wilhelm Friedemann 1710–1784
Mozart's interest in the music of Friedemann was enhanced by the enthusiasm of Baron van Swieten.

Bachmann, Sixtus 1754–1818
German organist and composer whom Mozart met as a youth.

Bader, Philipp Georg (also Baader) c. 1740–1790?
German librettist for Haydn, etc.

Badini, Francesco 1740–1800?

Italian librettist and translator for Blaise, Grétry, Linley, Haydn.

Bagge, Baron Charles-Ernest de 1722–1791

A composer and melomane whose acquaintance Mozart made in France (1778).

Baglioni, Antonio c. 1760–1820?

Tenor active in Vienna, Venice, Prague, and other centers. Sang in Prague premieres of *Don Giovanni* and *La clemenza di Tito.*

Baglioni, Clementine c. 1735–1790

Soprano active in Vienna and other centers. Perhaps related to above.

Bähr, Joseph 1770–1819

Admired clarinettist and composer, sometimes confused with Joseph Beer (1744–1811). Mozart played K. 595 at Bähr's Vienna concert, March 4, 1791.

Bailleux, Antoine 1720–1798

Composer, publisher; active in Paris when Mozart was there (1778).

Baillot, Pierre 1771–1842

French composer, violinist (inspired by Viotti, Nardini) who studied K. 271a (271c)—perhaps the "Sauzay copy" traced to Habeneck Estate (1837).

Ballo, Franziska c. 1750–1800?

Soprano active in Salzburg in 1770s. Later married Johann Marschauer, an actor, and toured in Böhm's company.

Bambini, Eustacio 1697–1770?

Composer of *La pravita castigata* (an early "Don Giovanni" opera), heard in Brno in 1734. Perhaps related to Felice Bambini (1742–1794), Bolognese opera and symphony composer active in France, whose work Mozart knew.

Bantin, Brigida 1756–1806

Leading singer in Paris, London, Germany (1778–1802).

Baranius, Henriette   1768–1853

Soprano who sang Blonde in Berlin premiere of *Die Entführung*. Mozart is said to have found her delightful. Later she sang Zerlina in *Don Giovanni* and Susanna in *Figaro*.

Barba, Danielle   1712–1801

Mantuan conductor and instrumental composer whom Mozart met in 1770, whose works were later performed in Vienna.

Barbella, Emanuele   1704–1773

Neapolitan violinist and composer whose work Mozart knew.

Barisani, Dr. Sigmund   1758–1787

Salzburg neighbor, friendly to Mozart family, also Mozart's doctor.

Baroni-Cavalcabò, Julie von   1820–1887

Friend and pupil of Mozart's younger son, Wolfgang, Jr.

Barrière, Etienne   1748–1816

French violinist and instrumental composer of works performed at the Concert Spirituel.

Barrington, Daines   1727–1800

Prominent English jurist who wrote a glowing report on the remarkable faculties of young Mozart when he met with him in London.

Barsanti, Francesco   1690–1772

Italian instrumental composer also active in London.

Barta, Joseph   1746–1787

Vienna composer of symphonies and singspiels, and fellow Freemason. Barta's librettist was another Freemason, Paul Weidmann, who also collaborated with Umlauf, Winter, Schenk.

Bartolozzi, Francesco   1727–1815

Italian artist, engraver of Haydn, active in Vienna and London.

Barthélemon, François Hippolyte   1741–1808

French composer, violinist who settled in London. Among his stage works was the London revival of Noverre's *Les petits riens*.

Bartsch, Konrad   c. 1750–1810?

Secretary of Mozart's Masonic Lodge, "The Crowned Hope," Vienna.

Bassano, Gaspare   c. 1735–1790?

Tenor, sang Marzio in Milan premiere of *Mitridate,* K. 74a (87), 1770.

Bassi, Luigi   1766–1825

Italian baritone, sang Almaviva (*Figaro*) in Vienna and the title role of *Don Giovanni* in the Prague premiere (1787), later touring Europe with Bondini's company.

Batthyány, Count Anton   c. 1720–1799

Tutor of young Emperor Joseph II; patron of Mozart's concerts, and of the Swieten circle.

Baudelaire, Charles   1821–1867

French poet who admired the music of Mozart.

Baudron, Antoine Laurent   1743–1834

French violinist, conductor, composer who worked with J. J. Rousseau, and composed "Je suis Lindor" for Beaumarchais' *Le barbier de Seville.* Mozart's K. 299a is a set of keyboard variations on "Je suis Lindor."

Baumann, Friedrich   1763–1841

Bass at Vienna court opera in 1780s and 1790s, for whom Mozart composed K. 539 in 1788. Also an important comic actor.

Baumberg, Gabriele von   1766–1839

Text author for K. 520, 530 (1787). Friend of Haydn.

Bauernfeld, Joseph von   c. 1760–1820?

Viennese friend, fellow Freemason; financier who backed Schikaneder at the Freihaus Theater.

Baumgarten, Countess Maria (also spelled Paumgarten)   1762–1839

Favorite of Elector Karl Theodor, who commissioned Mozart to compose *Idomeneo* in Munich (1781).

Beck, Franz Ignaz   1734–1809

German instrumental composer active in France, where Mozart heard his music.

Beck, Josepha   c. 1770–1827

Singer in such Mozart operas as *Die Zauberflöte* (Pamina) and *Die Entführung* (Constanze), mostly active in Mannheim, Munich and Weimar.

Becké, Johann Baptist   1743–1817

Composer, flutist active in Munich and Salzburg (1775).

Becker, Wilhelm G.   c. 1760–1820?

Singspiel composer of works produced in Vienna in 1780s.

Bedini, Domenico   c. 1760–1810?

Castrato, sang Sesto in Prague premiere of *La clemenza di Tito* (1791). Related to Bedini in *Idomeneo*?

Beecke, Ignaz Franz von   1733–1809

Vocal and instrumental composer active in Vienna from 1780s.

Beethoven, Ludwig van   1770–1827

Piano pupil (1788).

Bellantani, Gasparo   1770–1830?

Bass active at Vienna court opera from 1790s.

Bellevite, Innocente   c. 1715–1775

Predecessor of Galliari Brothers as Milan theatre designer; collaborator of Gluck.

Bellotto, Bernardo   720–1780

Important Italian artist and stage designer active in Vienna and Germany.

Benda, Christian   c. 1750–1810?

Bass active in Vienna and Germany in 1770s and 1780s; sang Osmin in *Die Entführung* in Berlin (1788).

Benda, Georg   1722–1795

Bohemian composer, keyboard, and oboe player. Member of a family of musicians active in Berlin and Italy.

Benedetti, Pietro (called Il Sartorio) 1745–1800

Castrato who sang Farnace in the Milan premiere of *Mitridate* (1770).

Benedikt, Prince Joseph V. Donaueschingen c. 1740–1800?

Melomane admirer of Mozart who had contemporary manuscript copies of the scores of *Don Giovanni*, and Acts I and II of *Le nozze di Figaro*. The *Figaro* manuscript includes an aria for Marcellina in Act I which may have been sung in some early productions in place of the Susanna-Marcellina duet. Although Alfred Einstein first thought the aria was by Mozart, later he decided it was not.

Bengraf, Joseph 1745–1791

Composer and violinist active in Pest from 1780s.

Bennett, Sterndale 1816–1875

English composer, Mozart collector, whose heirs have (1987) part of K. 386 manuscript (which had been "completed" by C. Potter, A. Einstein, P. Badura-Skoda and C. Mackerras).

Benucci, Francesco 1745–1825

One of Mozart's favorite singers, a bass active in Vienna and elsewhere over a long career. Sang title role in *Figaro* premiere. Married to Anna Cabazza (c. 1760–1810?).

Bérault, Jean-Baptiste c. 1725–1780?

Oboist at the Concert Spirituel and minor French composer whose widow published his music, along with music by others such as Cambini (an intriguer against Mozart) until her stock was taken over by Sieber (c. 1784).

Berchtold zu Sonnenberg, Johann Baptist von 1736–1801

Widower who became the husband of Mozart's sister, Nannerl.

Berg, Georg 1730–1790

German composer and organist who settled in London.

Berger, Daniel 1744–1824

Engraver active in Vienna, member of Mozart circle.

Berger, Fräulein c. 1760–1810?

Soprano who sang in Vienna 1782 concert with Mozart and Josepha Auernhammer.

Berger, F. G. 1730–1806
Munich composer and organist.

Berger, Karl Gottlieb c. 1760–1810?
Leipzig violinist who played with Mozart in 1789.

Berks, Johann 1758–1816
Prague musician and music copier.

Bergopzoomer, Johann Baptist 1742–1804
Actor-manager, translator in Vienna, married the singer Katherina Leithner-Schindler (1755–1788), active for a decade, also text poet for Süssmayr.

Berhandsky, J. A. Placidus 1735–1815
Salzburg friend of Mozart family.

Bernasconi-Andrea 1706–1784
Italian composer active in Rome, Vienna, Munich.

Bernasconi-Wagerle, Antonia 1741–1803
Italian soprano, daughter of above, active more than two decades; sang Gluck's *Alceste* in Vienna, and Aspasia in Mozart's *Mitridate* in Milan, also active in London.

Berntgen, Johann Gottlieb 1703–1759
Composer whose works Leopold taught young Mozart.

Bertati, Isidore 1752–1802
Prominent librettist, active in Vienna, of Gazzaniga's *Don Giovanni*, Cimarosa's *Il matrimonio segreto*, Süssmayr's *L'incanto superato*, etc.

Bertheaume, Isidore 1752–1802
French composer and violinist active when Mozart was in Paris; also toured Russia.

Bertoni, Ferdinando 1725–1813
Venetian opera and instrumental composer and organist, pupil of Padre Martini.

Bertuch, Friedrich Justin Johann   1747–1822

Co-editor (with Georg Melchior Kraus, c. 1750–1810?) of *Journal des Luxus der Moden,* publishing articles praising the music of Mozart (1786–1788).

Besozzi, Antonio   1736–1790?

Touring Italian composer and oboist, in Salzburg in 1770s.

Bett, Johann Sebastian   c. 1750–1800?

Violinist at Salzburg court in the 1770s.

Beyle, Henri (Stendhal)   1783–1842

Distinguished French novelist and writer on Mozart, Haydn, Rossini, etc. (Early pseudonym was Bombet.)

Bianchi, Francesco   1752–1810

Italian opera composer also active in London, whose music interested Joseph Haydn. Mozart composed additional numbers for the Vienna 1785 production of Bianchi's *La villanella rapita,* with text by Bertati.

Bianchi, Giovanni Batista   c. 1740–1800?

Milan printer of programs for *Ascanio, Lucio Silla.* (Related to instrumental composer of same name?)

Bianchi, Marianna   c. 1745–1800?

Soprano, active in London and Milan from 1770s, married to Francesco Bianchi.

Biber, Heinrich Ignaz Franz von   1644–1704

Salzburg composer, whose influence may have touched Mozart.

Bibiena

Family of distinguished 17th- and 18th-century stage designers and artists (one of whose members probably was involved in the stage designs for *Mitridate* in Milan).

Biechteler von Greiffenthal, Sigismund   1670–1744

Salzburg composer, whose influence may have touched Mozart.

Biedermann, ——— c. 1760–1810?

Collaborator of Schikaneder.

Billington, Elizabeth 1765–1818

Noted English soprano, sang "La ci darem la mano" from *Don Giovanni* with John Bannister, interpolated in a London performance of William Shield's comic opera *The Czar Peter* (1790).

Binder, Christlieb 1723–1789

Important Dresden instrumental composer.

Binder von Kriegelstein, Baron Joseph 1758–1790

Translator/librettist for the German comic opera version of Goldoni's *Servitore di due padrone* (K. 416a), which Mozart began in 1783 but did not complete. Fellow Freemason.

Binetti, Anna c. 1745–1790?

Dancer in Milan premiere of *Lucio Silla*, K. 135 (1772), also active in London; wife of Charles LePicq.

Birck, Wenzel (or Pirck) 1717–1763

Church and instrumental composer and organist active in Vienna. Music teacher of Joseph II.

Blache, Mimi c. 1750–1800?

Dancer in Milan premiere of *Ascanio* (1772). (Related to dancer Jean-Baptiste Blache, 1765–1834?).

Blainhoffer, ———— c. 1750–1800?

Munich opera composer.

Blaise, Benôit 1700–1772

French composer of popular opera, *Annette et Lubin* (1762).

Blek, Riccardo c. 1745–1800

Important dancer in Milan premiere of *Ascanio* (1771) and *Lucio Silla* (1773).

Blois, Charles 1737–1785

French composer, conductor, violinst whose music was performed when Mozart was in Paris (1778).

Blumauer, Aloys 1755–1798

Text poet of K. 506, friend, and fellow Freemason.

Boccherini, Luigi 1743–1805

Italian composer, also active in Madrid, Paris, London. Mozart's violin concertos show affinity with Boccherini's style. Boccherini's brother, Gastone, was a librettist in Vienna.

Bode, Johann Joachim 1730–1793

Instrumental composer, translator, printer mainly active in Hamburg and Weimar.

Bohdanowicz, Basilius 1740–1817

Polish instrumental composer active in Vienna, whose works (published by Trattner) Mozart knew.

Böhm, Amadeus Wenzel 1770–1823

Engraver, friend of Haydn; worked for Breitkopf & Härtel.

Böhm, Johann 1740–1792

German theatre director and producer of touring versions of *Thamos* and *La finta giardiniera*, as well as his own works. Friend of Mozart.

Bolt, J. Friedrich 1769–1836

German engraver also active in Vienna who worked on early Mozart editions (for Breitkopf).

Bondini, Catarina c. 1760–1800?

Soprano active in Prague, etc., performing Susanna (*Figaro*), and creating Zerlina (*Don Giovanni*) in 1787.

Bondini, Pasquale 1737–1789

Successful bass singer and producer: *Die Entführung, Figaro, Don Giovanni,* etc. Married to above.

Bonno, Joseph 1710–1788

Austrian instrumental and vocal composer at the Vienna court; not favorably disposed toward Mozart.

Boog, Johann Nepomuk 1724–1784

Viennese church composer.

Borghi, Giovanni Battista 1713–1796

Italian opera composer, conductor, and violinist pupil of Pugnani whose music the Mozarts knew. Also active in Vienna and London.

Born, Baron Ignaz von 1742–1791

Viennese friend, fellow Freemason, and patron of Mozart.

Boroni, Antonio 1738–1797

Italian composer active in Stuttgart, Dresden, Prague, Venice (where Mozart saw his *La contadine furlane*, 1771).

Bossler, Heinrich Philipp 1744–1812

Artistic German publisher of prints and music in Speyer.

Bouin, J. F. c. 1720–1798

Parisian publisher of early editions of Mozart's music.

Boyer, Pascal 1743–1794

French publisher of first editions of Mozart's music.

Boyce, William 1710–1779

Esteemed English composer whose music Mozart heard in London.

Braganza, Duke Johann 1719–1806

Portuguese noble friendly to Mozart in Vienna.

Brahms, Johannes 1833–1898

Member of editorial board of Mozart Collected Edition of Breitkopf & Härtel; collector of Mozart manuscripts.

Branca, Maria Theodora von c. 1760–1810?

Munich piano pupil of Mozart (1777).

Brander, J. C. 1735–1799

Czechoslovakian playwright and librettist active in Germany during the Sturm und Drang period, collaborating with Georg Benda, Johann Friedrich Reichardt, and others.

Brandl, Christian c. 1760–1820?

Bass singer in Austria in 1780s and Germany in 1790s, performing such Mozartean roles as Osmin (*Die Entführung*) and Masetto (*Don Giovanni*).

Brandstetter, Karl   c. 1750–1800?
Viennese ballmaster, fellow Freemason.

Brasaglia, Marianne Bettinelli   c. 1740–1790?
Friend of Mozart in Mantua (1770).

Braun, Heinrich   c. 1740–1800?
German author whose works Mozart read.

Braun, Johann von   c. 1735–1788
Melomane, Viennese patron of Mozart; father of Peter von Braun (1758–1819), pianist, composer, merchant.

Braunhofer, Maria Anna   1748–1819
Salzburg soprano who sang in the premieres of *Die Schuldigkeit* and *La finta semplice*.

Breitinger, Friedrich   c. 1900–1970?
Authority on many Salzburg contemporaries of Mozart.

Breitkopf, Johann Gottlieb Immanuel   1719–1794
Leipzig publisher, founder of the firm of Breitkopf & Härtel which handled manuscript and printed copies of music by Leopold and Wolfgang Mozart (and hundreds of others), and first began a "complete" edition of Wolfgang's works in 1798.

Bretfeld zu Cronenburg, Baron Joseph   1729–1809
Prague professor, and host to Mozart.

Bretzner, Christoph Friedrich   1748–1807
Leipzig merchant, poet, and popular librettist who complained that Stephanie der Junger had plagiarized his plot in the libretto for Mozart's *Die Entführung*.

Bréval, Jean-Baptiste   1753–1823
French instrumental composer and violoncellist of the Concert Spirituel in 1770s.

Breymann, Anton   1762–1841
Violinist in Salzburg Court orchestra in 1780s, later in Vienna.

Bridi, Giuseppe   c. 1760–1810

Milanese singer, active in Vienna in 1787 with Mozart. Member of a musical family.

Brixi, Franz Xaver   1732–1771

Prague instrumental and religious composer, organist, and conductor at cathedral. Mozart knew his works and improvised at the organ on themes from them when in Prague in 1787.

Brochard, Magdalena (?)   1746–1794

Member of Salzburg family friendly with the Mozarts. Her daughter Maria and son Joseph were pupils of Leopold.

Brockmann, Franz   1745–1812

Actor in *Der Schauspieldirektor.*

Bruendl, Josephus   c. 1750–1810?

Sang in Salzburg premiere of *Apollo et Hyacinthus.*

Brunati, Gaetano   c. 1750–1805

Vienna translator, and librettist for Storace (1785), Dittersdorf (1787), Dalayrac, Philidor.

Brunetti, Antonio   1744–1798

Italian violinist, long active in Salzburg, for whom Mozart composed a new middle movement to the *Violin Concerto* in A, K. 219.

Brunetti, Gaetano   1753–1808

Italian violinist and composer of many symphonies, also active in Spain.

Bullinger, Abbé Joseph, and family   1744–1810

Close Salzburg friends of the Mozarts.

Bürger, Gottfried August   1748–1794

Viennese librettist and poet for Haydn, Kauer, Sterkel, Mozart (K. 384, 530).

Bussani, Dorotea Sardi   1763–1810

Soprano active at Vienna court opera, singing in *Figaro* premiere (1786) and *Così* premiere (1790). Married to Francesco Bussani.

Bussani, Francesco   1743–1807

Baritone long active in Vienna, sang Don Alfonso in *Così* premiere (1790).

Cabalati, Regina (or Gabalati)   c. 1740–1790?

Dancer in the Milan premiere of *Lucio Silla*, K. 135 (1772).

Cafaro, Pasquale   1706–1787

Active Neapolitan composer whose music Mozart heard (1770).

Caldara, Antonio   1670–1736

Important Italian composer of vocal and instrumental works.

Callegari, Giuseppe   c. 1740–1812

Italian composer of *Il convitato di Pietra* (1777), etc.

Calvesi, Vincenzo   1760–1810?

Italian tenor, active in Venice, Naples, Vienna. Sang Ferrando in *Così* premiere (1790), and other works of Mozart.

Calzabigi, Raniero de   1715–1795

Important librettist for Gluck, and possibly Mozart.

Camasina, Joseph   c. 1750–1800?

Mozart's landlord in 1784.

Cambini, Giovanni Giuseppe   1746–1825

Italian vocal and instrumental composer successful in Paris, where he intrigued against Mozart in 1778.

Camerloher, Placidus von   1718–1782

German instrumental composer active in Munich.

Campagnoli, Bartolomeo   1751–1827

Italian violinist and instrumental composer active in Dresden, etc.

Campe, Joachim Heinrich   1746–1818

Text author of K. 523, etc.

Campi, Antonie (Miklasewicz) de 1773–1822

Prague singer of Mozart roles, including the premiere of *La clemenza di Tito* (1791); later active in Vienna and Germany.

Campi, Gaetano 1765–1810?

Sang Publio in Prague premiere of *La clemenza*. Married to above.

Campioni, Carlo 1720–1790

Composer, conductor at Tuscan court where Mozart heard his music (1770).

Canal, Count Joseph 1745–1826

Prague botanist, horn player (in his own private orchestra), fellow Freemason, friend of Mozart.

Candeille, Pierre Joseph 1744–1827

French opera composer whose works Mozart heard; father of Amélie Candeille (1767–1834), composer, singer, actress.

Canarisi, Marquis Vincenz 1751–1800?

Fellow Freemason in Prague; came to Vienna on visits.

Canitz, Baron Friedrich Rudolph Ludwig von 1654–1699

Mozart used his text for K. 125f (151).

Cannabich, Christian 1731–1798

Composer, conductor, violinist at Mannheim and Munich courts. Good friend of Mozart. Daughter, Rosa, was a piano pupil of Mozart (1778).

Cappi, Johann 1765–1815

Viennese publisher active from 1780s.

Cardon, Jean-Guillain 1732–1788

Maître de violon to Louis XVI.

Cardonne, Jean-Baptiste 1730–1792

French composer whose music was played at the Concert Spirituel.

Carl, Anton 1717–1784

Viennese church composer.

Carlotti, Marquis Alessandro   1740–1828
Noble melomane who welcomed Mozart in Verona.

Carmontelle, Louis Carrogis de   1717–1806
Popular portraitist and writer of Paris, who painted the Mozarts.

Carolsfeld, H. Schnorr von   1764–1831
Editor of Mozart compositions for Breitkopf & Härtel.

Cartelleri, Antonio   1772–1807
Composer, conductor for Prince Lobkowitz, etc.

Cartoli, Francis   1705–1772
Bass singer at Vienna court opera, cast as Cassandro in *La finta semplice,* which was cancelled after the dress rehearsal because of Affligio's intrigue.

Casacci, Francesco   c. 1730–1790?
Dancer, ballet master active in Milan in 1770s, whose wife Maria danced in Milan premiere of *Lucio Silla* (1772).

Casanova, Giacomo   1725–1798
Venetian adventurer, writer, and friend of Da Ponte, who was in Prague at the time of the premiere of *Don Giovanni*; although the scene Casanova "rewrote" was found by Paul Nettl, there is no evidence it was staged in Mozart's time.

Casparo, S.   c. 1750–1800?
Touring tenor for whom Mozart composed K. 209 in 1775.

Cassell, Joseph Thomas (Castel?)   c. 1750–1788
Violinist, flutist, double bass player, active in Salzburg in 1770s and 1780s.

Casti, Giovanni Battista   1724–1803
Esteemed poet and librettist, active in Vienna in 1780s.

Caselli, Francesco   c. 1745–1800?
Italian composer of the ballets for the Milan premiere of Mozart's *Mitridate.* (Related to castrato, Vincenzo Caselli?)

Cavalieri, Caterina 1755–1801

Soprano favored by Salieri, sang at Vienna court in 1780s and 1790s, where she sang the Countess in the revival of *Figaro*. Mozart composed concert arias for her.

Ceccarelli, Francesco 1752–1814

Castrato, sang a number of Mozart's compositions while in service in Salzburg.

Celioniat[ti?], Ignazio c. 1740–1790?

Touring instrumental and opera composer active in 1760s and 1770s.

Champein, Stanislas 1753–1830

French operetta composer active in Paris from 1770s.

Charlotte, Queen of England 1744–1818

Gracious dedicatée of six early keyboard and violin sonatas.

Chartrain, Nicolas 1740–1793

Violinist, composer from Liège whose works Mozart heard at the Concert Spirituel.

Chiarini, Pietro 1717–1770

Italian opera and keyboard composer whose music Leopold taught to young Mozart.

Chiesa, Melchior c. 1740–1800?

Milanese instrumental composer Mozart met in 1771.

Chodowiecki, Daniel 1726–1801

Eminent German artist, friend of F. H. Ziegenhagen, and other Freemasons.

Chotek, Count Johann Rudolf 1748–1800?

Viennese patron of Mozart.

Christa, Bartolomeus 1714–1778

Munich abbé to whom Mozart gave his Mass, K. 196b (composed in Munich, 1775).

Chudy, Joseph   c. 1750–1810?

Conductor for Count Ladislas Erdödy in Pressburg, where he directed *Die Entführung* (1785).

Cicognani, Giuseppe   1735–1785

Bolognese male alto, sang Farnace in the Milan premiere of *Mitridate* (1770).

Cigna–Santi, Vittorio Amadeo   1725–1785

Poet who adapted Racine's play for Mozart's *Mitridate,* and later collaborated with Mysliveček and Zingarelli.

Cimadoro, Giambattista   1761–1805

Italian composer whose operas were produced in Vienna, London, etc. Pupil of Haydn(?).

Cimarosa, Domenico   1749–1801

Important Italian composer known throughout Europe. See K. 578, etc., for arias Mozart composed to be inserted in his operas.

Ciprandi, Ercole   1738–1790

Tenor, sang K. 19c in a London pasticcio of Metastasio's *Ezio.*

Cirri, Giovanni Battista   1724–1808

Italian composer Mozart knew in London.

Clam-Gallas, Count Christian   c. 1760–1805?

Musical patron in Prague, protector of Josepha Duček.

Claudius, Matthias   1752–1832

Text poet of two songs: Anh. C.8.01-02 ("Die Nase") and Anh. C.8.28 ("Mai Lied")—according to K^6 probably spurious.

Clement XIV   1705–1774

Pope, 1769–1774, who awarded the Knight of the Golden Spur to Mozart.

Clementi, Muzio   1752–1832

Composer, pianist based in England, where he also founded a publishing house and a piano factory. Although a piano rival of

Mozart (with whom he competed December 24, 1781, in Vienna in front of Emperor Joseph II), after Mozart's death he praised K. 550 and other works.

Clerico, Francesco   c. 1755–1833

Milan choreographer and dancer in premiere of *Lucio Silla*, (1772). Also active in Venice and Vienna.

Closset, Dr. Thomas Franz   1754–1813

Mozart's last physician.

Cobenzl, Count Ludwig   1765–1810?

Vienna piano pupil (1782), member of noble musical family; fellow Freemason.

Cocchi, Giacchino   1715–1804

Neapolitan opera composer, active in Venice and London, where Mozart saw him.

Cochet, Thomas   c. 1760–1813

Paris publisher of early editions of the music of Mozart.

Coignet, Horace   1736–1821

French composer, collaborator of Rousseau on *Pygmalion.*

Colla, Giuseppe   1731–1806

Italian composer, also active in England. Husband of famous soprano, Lucrezia Agujari.

Colloredo, Archbishop Hieronymous   1732–1812

Reigning authority in Salzburg following the death of the more liberal Sigismund von Schrattenbach (1771). Relative of Rudolf von Colloredo, one of Empress Maria Theresia's most trusted noble ministers. An amateur violinist.

Colombazzo, Vittorio   c. 1750–1800

Viennese musician; fellow Freemason.

Coltellini, Anna   1764–1817

Soprano, active in Vienna in 1780s, daughter of Marco Coltellini.

Coltellini, Celeste   1760–1829

Soprano, active in Vienna in 1780s, daughter of Marco Coltellini. Mozart composed K. 479, 480 for her. In 1791 she married Mozart's friend Johann Georg Meurikofer from Lyon.

Coltellini, Marco   1719–1777

Poet and librettist-collaborator of Gluck and nine composers in Vienna and Germany, including Mozart—*La finta semplice*, and *La finta giardiniera.*

Consoli, Tommaso   1753–1812

Castrato, active in Salzburg and Munich in 1770s, sang in premieres of *Il re pastore* and *La finta giardiniera.*

Conti, Francesco B.   1681–1732

Italian composer active in Vienna whose music Mozart knew.

Conti, Prince Louis François de   1717–1776

Patron of Beaumarchais who invited Mozart to play at his salon, attended by Madame Tessé and other members of Parisian society. His daughter played harp.

Cook, Thomas   1744–1818

English engraver of the Carmontelle painting of the Mozarts.

Coratoli, Francesco   c. 1740–1800?

Bass singer active at Vienna court in 1760s and 1770s. Chosen to perform in the scheduled Vienna premiere of *La finta semplice* which was prevented by intrigue.

Cornetti, Alesandro   c. 1750–1800?

"Composer" active in Vienna in 1780s (perhaps a pseudonym).

Corticelli, Luigi   c. 1750–1800?

Dancer in the ballet of *Lucio Silla*, premiere Milan (1772).

Cousineau, Georges   1733–1800

Parisian publisher of early editions of Mozart works, succeeded by son, Jacques-Georges (1760–1836); Pierre Cousineau was a harpist.

Cramer, Johann Baptist 1777–1758
German composer, also active in London, where he published K. 588b.

Cramer, Karl Friedrich 1752–1807
German composer, pianist, and publisher of Magazin der Musik (Hamburg, 1783–1789) which gave Mozart favorable reviews.

Cranz, August 1789–1870
Hamburg publisher and Mozart collector, later in Leipzig.

Cremonini, Clementina c. 1730–1780?
Soprano active in London in 1760s, where she sang with J. C. Bach, and with Mozart.

Crespi, Madame Prospero c. 1760–1810?
Sang such Mozartean roles as Donna Anna (*Don Giovanni*), in Leipzig premiere, 1788.

Crispi, Giovanni Pietro 1737–1797
Roman composer of many symphonies, 18 in D major!

Crux, Marianne 1774–1820
Pianist, member of a large family of Mannheim and Munich musicians and dancers who were friends of the Mozarts. Her father, Peter Crux, was ballet master at the Vienna court opera.

Czernin, Count Johann von 1757–1845
Patron of Mozart and admirer of his music. Member of a musical family; brother of Countess Lützow.

Czerwenka, Franz Joseph c. 1750–1810?
Organist, oboist, and bassonist in Prince Esterházy's orchestra in 1780s. Performed with Mozart.

Dalberg, Baron Johann Friedrich Hugo 1752–1812
German instrumental composer, patron of Mozart.

Dalberg, Baron Wolfgang 1750–1806
Mannheim theatre director, poet, librettist, friend of Schiller. Brother of above.

Dalla Rosa, Saverio 1745–1821
Italian painter, probably the artist of the Verona portrait of Mozart.

Damilaville, Etienne Noel 1723–1768
French Encyclopedist friendly with Mozart in 1764.

Danner, Christian 1745–1803
Composer, conductor, violinst, who studied with Mozart in 1777–1778.
(Two other Danners were painters.)

Danzi, Franz 1763–1826
Munich composer and violoncello player.

Da Ponte, Lorenzo (originally Emmanuele Conegliano) 1749–1838
Important Italian librettist and poet, active in Vienna, London, New
York. Fellow Freemason.

Daube, Johann Friedrich 1733–1797
Viennese instrumental composer and theorist.

D'Auberval, Jean (Bercher) 1742–1806
Important French dancer and choreographer. Ballet master for *Ascanio*
premiere, Milan (1771). Appeared in *Les petits riens* (Noverre–Mozart,
Paris, 1778).

Daubrawaik, Johann von 1731–1810
Prominent Salzburg councilor, friend of Mozart family.

Dauer, Johann Ernst 1746–1812
Esteemed tenor at Vienna court opera; sang Pedrillo in the premiere of
Die Entführung (1782).

Daun, General Leopold Joseph 1705–1766
Viennese Minister of State. Members of his family were from Salzburg
and knew the Mozarts.

Davaux, Jean-Baptiste 1742–1822
French instrumental composer active in Paris from 1770s.

Dauvergne, Antoine 1713–1797
Successful French composer of such operas as *Les Troquers* (1753), text
by Jean Joseph Vadé.

David, Anton   c. 1760–1810?
Clarinettist and basset horn player in Vienna from 1780s.

David, Hans T.   1902–1967
Music teacher, and editor of Breitkopf reprint of the works of Mozart, 1956.

De Amicis-Buonsolazzi, Anna Lucia   1733–1816
Esteemed Italian soprano in 1760s and 1770s. Sang Giunia in premiere of Mozart's *Lucio Silla,* Milan (1772).

Debucourt, Philibert   1755–1832
Parisian artist active in 1770s.

Degenfeld, Count F. C.   1722–1781
Dutch ambassador in Vienna, backer of Wolfgang, but unable to force Vienna production of *La finta semplice.*

Deglé, Franz Joseph   1724–1812
Portraitist active in Salzburg, who may have painted the Mozarts in the 1770s.

Deibl, Franz   c. 1698–1783
Wind and string player in Salzburg court orchestra.

Deiner, Joseph   c. 1740–1800?
Leopold Mozart's valet in 1760s, who later was a musician under Wenzel Nordlinger at the Donaueschingen court.

Deiters, Hermann   1833–1910
Editor of the first revision of Jahn's biography of Mozart.

De Jean, Dr. Ferdinand   1731–1797
Dutch physician and flutist, who knew many members of Mozart's circle, in Mannheim, and Vienna, including Dr. Matthias von Sallaba (1764–1797), Dr. J. M. Hunczovsky (1752–1798), Dr. Thomas Franz Closset (1754–1813), Franz von Baader (1765–1841), Joseph von Quarin (1733–1814), Michael Steinhauser (1753–1818), and the Jacquin family.

Delafosse, Jean-Baptiste   1721–1775
Parisian artist, illustrator, engraver of the Carmontelle portrait.

Deller, Florian 1729–1773

Viennese composer of ballets (for Noverre), operas and instrumental works.

Demmler, Johann Michael 1748–1783

Augsburg composer, organist, keyboard player friendly with Mozart.

Denis, Johann Nepomuk Michael Cosmos 1729–1800

Friend and fellow Freemason. Author of an ode, "Gibralter," which Mozart began composing but never finished (1782).

Desaugiers, Marc-Antoine 1742–1793

French composer active when Mozart was in Paris (1778).

Desprez, L. J. 1743–1804

Active French artist, stage designer, also worked in Sweden.

Dessler, Anton c. 1740–1800?

Merchant friend of Mozart family who moved to Wels, Austria, where he directed an amateur theatre, and planned to produce *La finta giardiniera* after its Munich premiere (1775).

Destouches, Franz Seraph von 1772–1844

Munich pupil of Mozart, who later composed operas, etc.

Deyerkauf, Franz c. 1760–1820?

Freemason, Graz admirer of the music of Mozart who erected a monument to Mozart in his garden in 1792.

Deym von Stritetz, Count Joseph (alias Müller) 1752–1804

Owner of a collection of antiques and curiosities, including Mozart's death mask, which has disappeared.

Dezède, Nicolas 1740–1792

Mozart composed two sets of keyboard variations on themes by this popular French composer of operas, etc.

Diderot, Denis 1713–1784

Important French dramatist, Encyclopedist, and man of letters, whose works the Mozarts knew.

Diesbach, Joseph Emmanuel c. 1750–1810?

Prague artist and printer of *Figaro* libretto.

Dieter, Christian Ludwig 1757–1822

German singspiel composer whose *Belmont* (1784) used the same plot as Mozart's *Die Entführung*.

Dietrichstein, Count Joseph c. 1740–1810?

Vienna patron of Mozart's concerts in 1780s. (Protector of Antonia Bernasconi?)

Dimmler, Franz 1753–1815

Member of Mannheim musical family, horn player, and instrumental composer known to Leopold Mozart.

Distler, Elisabeth 1769–1789?

Sang second soprano (Jonathas) in *Davidde Penitente* premiere in Vienna (1785); sister of Haydn's pupil J. G. Distler (Stuttgart chapel conductor), and actor Joseph Anton Thomas Distler.

Ditta, Franz c. 1760–1810?

Minor lyric composer whose works were played in Vienna from 1790.

Dittersdorf, Karl Ditters von 1739–1799

Respected Austrian composer and violinist. Friend of Mozart and Haydn.

Doblhoff-Dier, Baron Karl 1762–1836

Pupil of Albrechtsberger, composer who at one point was in possession of the Mozart *Requiem* manuscript completed by Süssmayr.

Doisy, Charles c. 1750–1807

Parisian publisher of early editions of Mozart works.

Doles, Johann Friedrich 1715–1797

Composer, pupil of J. S. Bach, who marveled at Mozart's organ playing in Dresden in 1789.

Dolfin, Andrea   c. 1730–1790?

Friend from Venice who became Venetian envoy to Austria, and at whose residence Mozart performed in February 1788.

Donberger, Georg Joseph   1709–1768

Austrian sacred composer whose church music may have influenced Mozart.

d'Hosson, Marie von   1757–1779

Munich patron of Mozart in 1778; member of Hepp family.

Dragonetti, Domenico   1763–1846

Composer, double bassist. Friend of Haydn and Beethoven. Collector of Mozart manuscripts.

Drasil, Franz   c. 1720–1790?

Bohemian horn player, violoncellist, sometimes active in Salzburg.

Dreyer, Johann Melchior   1746–1824

Viennese organist, composer; also active in Germany.

Druschetzky, Jiri   1745–1819

Successful Hungarian opera and instrumental composer.

Duček, Franz Xaver   1731–1799

Czechoslovakian instrumental composer, and friend. Member of a large family of musicians. Husband of Josepha.

Duček, Josepha (née Hambacher) 1754–1790

Soprano who often sang with Mozart, and performed his music in many concerts. Married to above.

Duhan, Jeanne Elisabeth   1760–1823

Parisian publisher of early editions of Mozart works.

Duni, Egidio Romaldo   1709–1775

Italian opera and instrumental composer successful in Paris.

Duport, Jean-Pierre 1741–1818

French composer and violoncellist also active in Berlin. Mozart composed *Nine Variations for Clavier* on a theme by Duport, K. 573. Jean-Pierre's brother, Jean-Louis (1749–1819) was a French composer and violoncellist mostly active in Paris.

Dupreille, Charles Albert 1728–1796

Munich court musician, pupil of Tartini. Performed in Munich concert with Mozart.

Durante, Francesco 1684–1755

Important Neapolitan composer whose works Mozart studied.

Durazzo, Count Jacobo 1717–1794

Austrian ambassador in Italy, friendly to Mozart.

Dürnitz, Baron Thaddeus von c. 1750–1803

Munich patron and pianist who commissioned and collected musical works, but infrequently paid the composer.

Dutilleu, Pierre 1754–1798

French lyric composer active in Italy, Russia, and Vienna, beginning in 1790.

Dyk, Johann Gottfried c. 1750–1800?

German playwright and translator whose works Mozart read, and used in his K. 365a.

Ebeling, Christoph Daniel 1741–1817

Translator of Handel's *Messiah* for Mozart's version for van Swieten. (Also a geographer.)

Eberhardi, Teresa c. 1745–1800?

Contralto at Vienna court opera cast as Giacinta for *La finta semplice* performances, cancelled because of intrigue.

Eberl, Anton Franz 1765–1807

Viennese composer and pianist. Pupil and friend of Mozart, and of Constanze.

Eberl, Ferdinand   c. 1760–1820?

Viennese author, librettist for Dittersdorf and Müller, and translator for Soler and Sarti, in 1780s. Brother of above.

Eberl, Leopold (no relation to above)   1737–1799

Viennese musician and copyist.

Eberlin, Johann Ernst   1702–1762

Salzburg church composer whose music influenced Mozart's sacred works. Related to Adlgasser's first wife, Maria Eberlin.

Ebers, Carl Friedrich   1770–1836

Mecklenburg composer; fellow Freemason.

Ebert, Johann Jakob   1723–1792

German writer Mozart read; translator of Edward Young's *Night Thoughts*.

Eck, Johann Friedrich   1767–1838

Munich violinst and composer. Performed in Vienna in 1780s with Mozart. Attested to authenticity of K. 365b (288), although some authorities are doubtful. Eck's connection with Mozart merits further exploration.

Ecker von Eckhoffen, Baron H. H.   1750–1790

Viennese, fellow Freemason.

Eckhard, Johann Gottfried   1735–1809

Augsburg composer, also active in Paris. In composing his K. 37 and 40, Mozart adapted works by Eckhard, Honauer, and C. P. E. Bach.

Edelmann, Johann   1749–1794

Strasbourg harpsichordist and composer active in Paris, known by Mozart.

Eder, Joseph   1760–1835

Viennese publisher of arrangements of Mozart works (from 1789), first with Ignaz Sauer, then Joseph Berman.

Edling, Anselm von   1741–1794

Writer, author of three-act German libretto, *Der lustige Tag*, found in Mozart's estate but not composed.

Ehrenstein, Dr.   c. 1740–1800?
Fellow Freemason in Vienna.

Eichler, G.   1677–1759
Augsburg painter of Leopold Mozart.

Eichner, Ernst   1740–1777
Mannheim woodwind player and instrumental composer, one of whose concertos Mozart played in Munich.

Eisen, Jacob   1756–1796
Viennese horn player, friend of Mozart.

Elisabeth, Princess of Mannheim   c. 1750–1800?
Dedicatée of K. 293a (301), etc.

Elsner, Joseph   1769–1854
Polish conductor and opera composer also active in Vienna (friend of Gyrowetz).

Engel, Johann Jakob   1741–1802
Berlin writer and librettist for Neefe's *Die Apotheke* (1771) based on Goldoni's *Lo Speziale*, also composed by Joseph Haydn. Author of text for Anhang C.8.18.

Engel, Karl Immanuel   c. 1740–1795
Organist in Leipzig for whom Mozart composed a gigue in 1789 (K. 574).

Engeström, Baron Lars   c. 1740–1800?
Swedish chargé d'affaires in Vienna. Mozart patron and fellow Freemason.

Englemann, Wenzel   1748–1803
Viennese music printer.

Enzenberg, Baron Franz Joseph von   c. 1740–1800?
Innsbruck dignitary who received Mozart.

Enzinger, Christian   c. 1750–1810?

Performed Hyacinthus in Salzburg premiere of *Apollo et Hyacinthus*.

d'Epinay, Louise   1726–1783

French writer in the circle of Jean Jacques Rousseau; mistress of Baron Grimm; friend of Diderot, and Mozart.

Epp, Friedrich   1747–1802

Mannheim tenor who sang Tamino in *Die Zauberflöte* and other Mozart roles.

Eppinger, Heinrich   1766–1810

Viennese composer, violinist, also active in Paris.

Epstein, Wendel Tobias   1758–1824

Fellow Freemason and friend of Mozart in Vienna.

Erard, Marie   1777–1851

With her sister Catherine (1779–1815), an early Parisian publisher of Mozart's music.

Erdödy, Count Ladislas   c. 1750–1810?

Melomane member of distinguished Hungarian family. Patron of Mozart. Freemason.

Erlach, Fischer von   1656–1723

Outstanding Austrian architect largely responsible for style of Viennese churches and palaces (with follower, C. von Hohenberg).

Ernst, Anton   1745–1805

Bohemian composer and violinist, active in Dresden, who attested to authenticity of K. 365b (268).

Ernst, Johann   c. 1750–1810?

Performed Apollo in Salzburg premiere of *Apollo et Hyacinthus*.

Eschenburg, Johann Joachim   1745–1820

German friend of Lessing; librettist and translator from French and Italian of works by Gluck, Lully, Grétry, etc., produced in Vienna and elsewhere in 1770s and 1780s.

d'Espagne, Franz 1828–1878

Berlin court librarian and member editorial board of Breitkopf & Härtel Mozart Edition.

Esser, Michael K. von 1736–1795

German composer friendly with Mozart in Munich, praised by Leopold; also active in Vienna, London, Paris, Italy. Mozart heard him play the violin in Mainz, and said he "overornamented."

Esterházy, Count Johann 1747–1796

Vienna patron who invited Mozart to give concerts in his palace.

Estlinger, Joseph Richard 1720–1791

Salzburg court bassoonist and copyist.

d'Ettore, Guglielmo c. 1745–1800?

Tenor in Milan premiere of *Mitridate*, also active in Munich.

Eunike, Friedrich c. 1760–1810?

Cologne musician and arranger of piano-vocal score for K. 620 (1793).

Ewelart, ———— c. 1750–1810?

Minor German composer of works in Mozart style, and flutist in Concert Spirituel when Mozart was in Paris.

Eybel, Johann 1741–1810

Austrian author of an important article on *Die Zauberflöte*, published in Linz in 1794.

Eybl, Franz c. 1750–1810?

Austrian artist, lithographer of portrait of Michael Haydn.

Eybler, Joseph 1765–1846

Austrian composer who became court conductor in Vienna. Pupil of Mozart (1790) and Albrechtsberger.

Faber, Johann Heinrich c. 1740–1800?

Mainz librettist for Seydelmann, and translator of operas by Gluck, Duni, Gossec, Grétry, Monsigny, Philidor, etc.; active in 1770s and 1780s. His work was known to the Mozarts.

Fabrizi, Vincenzo   1764–1812
Italian opera composer of *Il nuovo convitato di Pietra* (1787), etc.

Falchini, Geltrude   c. 1750–1800?
Soprano in Milan premiere of *Ascanio in Alba* K. 111.

Falgera, Mad.   1760–1800?
Dancer in Munich premiere of *Idomeneo*, K. 366. Wife of Sigmund Falgera (1752–1790), violinist in Mannheim and Munich orchestras who was a Freemason.

Faller, ——— c. 1750–1800?
Director of touring company performing *Die Entführung* and *Figaro* in numerous German towns.

Falter, Markarius   1762–1843
Munich publisher Mozart knew.

Faltis, J.
Harpsichordist, composer active in Vienna.

Fantozzi, Maria Marchetti   1767–1807
Sang Vitellia in Prague premiere of *La clemenza di Tito*. Married Angelo Fantozzi (tenor) in 1788.

Fasch, Johann Friedrich   1688–1758
Influential German instrumental and vocal composer.

Favart, Marie Justine Benedicte Duronçeray   1727–1772
French actress and author, who with Harny de Guerville and her husband Charles Simon Favart (1710–1792) adapted Rousseau's *Le Devin du village* into *Bastien et Bastienne*, which in turn provided the basis for Mozart's early one-act opera, *Bastien und Bastienne*.

Favier, Jean   c. 1750–1810
Ballet master for Milan premiere of *Ascanio* (1771).

Federico, Gennaro Antonio   c. 1710–1780?
Italian librettist for Pergolesi, Leo, Cocchi, Paisiello.

Fedi, Antonio   c. 1750–1800?
Portraitist of Adriana Ferrarese del Bene (c. 1786).

Feiner, Ludwig   c. 1750–1800?
Oboist in Salzburg court orchestra.

Fendl, P.   c. 1750–1810?
Portraitist, member of Swieten circle.

Ferlendis, Giuseppe   1755–1802
Salzburg oboist, for whom Mozart may have composed K. 313 before transforming it into a flute concerto.

Ferrand, Antoine   1678–1719
Text poet for K. 307.

Ferrandini, Giovanni   1715–1793
Italian opera composer and oboist whom Mozart met in 1771, also active in Germany.

Ferrarese del Bene, Adriana (Francesca Gabrieli)   1755–1795
Soprano trained in Venice, also active in London, and Vienna, where she sang Fiordiligi in *Così* premiere (1790), and in many other operas.

Ferrari, Gian Carlo   1759–1842
Italian composer also active in England, who appreciated many Viennese instrumental works of Mozart (particularly piano concertos and quartets). (Related to Antonio Ferrari, Salzburg violinist 1766–1789?)

Fesemayer, Maria Anna   1742–1782
Soprano performing in Salzburg premieres of *Die Schuldigkeit des ersten Gebotes* and *La finta semplice* (later married Anton Adlgasser).

Feuerstein, Johann Heinrich   c. 1790–1850
Completed Nissen's historic biography of Mozart under the direction of Constanze when Nissen died before his biography was published.

Fiala, Joseph   1748–1816
Salzburg oboist, composer in 1770s, friend of Mozart family.

Fichtl, Johann Baptist von   c. 1720–1790
Viennese patron and friend of Mozart.

Filtz, Anton   1730–1760?
Important Mannheim composer.

Fink, G. W.   c. 1750–1800?
Organist active in Salzburg in 1780s, friend of the Mozarts.

Fioroni, Giovanni Andrea   1704–1778
Conductor, Milan Cathedral, 1747–1778, friend of the Mozarts.

Firmian, Count Carl Joseph   1716–1774
Austrian governor in Milan who appreciated Mozart. Mozart composed several arias in his honor.

Fischer, Barbara (Strasser)   1758–1800
Accomplished singer at Vienna Court in 1780s. Previously in Mannheim (?).

Fischer, Carl Ludwig   1745–1825
German bass active in Munich, Berlin, Paris, Italy, Vienna, where he sang Osmin in the Vienna premiere of *Die Entführung* (1782).

Fischof, Joseph   c. 1790–1857
German collector of Mozartiana now housed in the Berlin Library.

Fischietti, Domenico   1725–1810
Opera composer active in Venice, Dresden, Prague, and Salzburg.

Fisher, John Abraham   1744–1806
English composer and violinist, also active in Vienna where he married Nancy Storace, but their union did not last.

Fixlmillner, Abbe Placidus   1721–1791
Kremsmünster Cloister friend of Mozart family.

Flamm, Antonie   c. 1764–1795?
Singer, daughter of F. X. Flamm, friend of Mozart.

Fleischmann, Johann 1766–1798

German opera composer of *Geisterinsel,* libretto by F. W. Gotter.

Fleury, Mademoiselle c. 1755–1800?

French pianist who performed K. 271 and 238, two concertos she acquired through Madame Heina (?).

Flies, Dr. Bernard c. 1760–1820?

Minor Berlin composer of "Schlafe mein Prinzchen" (text by F. W. Gotter), once thought to be by Mozart (K. 350).

Fodor, George(?) 1752–1828

Touring German violinist and composer of concertos and instrumental music.

Forster, Georg 1754–1794

Writer from Mainz who met Mozart through Countess Thun.

Förster, Emanuel Aloys 1748–1843

Viennese conductor and pianist, friendly with Mozart.

Fortini, Francesco c. 1750–1810?

Castrato member of Pietro Rosa's touring company of singers in 1770s, for whom Mozart probably composed K. 255 in 1776.

Fossati, Domenico 1743–1784

Eminent Italian stage designer active in Venice, Verona, Milan.

Franchi, Carlo c. 1730–1772

Opera composer heard in Vienna in 1770s.

Frank, Dr. Joseph c. 1765–1810?

Amateur composer, pupil of Mozart in 1790. Married Christine Gerardi (1798), who sang in the Vienna premiere of Joseph Haydn's *The Creation (Die Schöpfung).*

Frankenberg, Franz 1759–1789

Bass, sang Osmin in *Die Entführung* during Mozart's 1789 visit to Berlin.

Fränzl, Ferdinand   1770–1835

German composer, conductor, violinist active in Munich, Vienna, etc. Instrumental in Dalberg's Mannheim productions of Mozart operas: *Die Entführung* (1784), *Don Giovanni* (1789), *Figaro* (1790), *Die Zauberflöte* (1794).

Fränzl, Ignaz   1736–1811

Mannheim composer, conductor, violinist, friend of the Mozarts.

Frasel, Wilhelm   c. 1770–1830?

Singer in Vienna premiere of *Die Zauberflöte* (1791).

French, ——— c. 1750–1800

Viennese engraver of scene with Mozart and Josepha Hofer (c. 1791).

Freyhold, Johann Philipp   c. 1750–1810?

Mainz flutist, friend of Mozart, who toured in 1770s and 1780s.

Freysinger, Josepha   c. 1760–1810?

Munich keyboard pupil of Mozart in 1777. Daughter of Franziskus Freysinger, schoolmate of Leopold Mozart.

Freysinger, Juliana   1755–1810?

Munich keyboard pupil of Mozart. Sister of above.

Freystädtler, Franz Jakob   1768–1841

Viennese composition pupil of Mozart (1787), later lyric composer.

Friberth, Karl   1736–1816

Austrian composer, conductor, tenor, friend of Haydn and Mozart.

Fridzeri, Alessandro   1741–1825

Opera composer of *Les Souliers*, etc. heard in Paris, Munich, etc.

Frieberth, Joseph von   1736–1816

Austrian composer of *Das Serail* premiered in Bozen (1779), where K. J. Weiss published the libretto (by Sebastiani). May have inspired Mozart's *Zaide*.

Friedel, Johann   1751–1789

Viennese theatre manager in 1780s.

Friedrich II (der Grosse) [Frederick the Great] 1712–1786
Powerful, musical Prussian monarch.

Friedrich Wilhelm II 1744–1797
Prussian monarch (successor to above), who commissioned K. 575, etc.

Friedrich, Gottfried c. 1760–1810?
Viennese publisher fron 1780s.

Friedrich, Jacob André c. 1730–1820?
Augsburg engraver of Leopold Mozart portrait.

Frischmuth, Johann Christian 1741–1790
Berlin violinist and opera composer active from 1760s.

Fuchs, Aloys 1799–1853
Important Mozart collector, whose catalogue was a useful tool for Köchel, and most of whose collection went to the Deutsche Staatsbibliothek in Berlin.

Fuchs, Felix 1752–1800?
Sang Melia in Mozart's *Apollo et Hyacinthus*, and later taught voice at the Salzburg court.

Füger, Friedrich Heinrich 1751–1818
Artist member of Lange circle, active in Vienna from 1780s.

Fux, ——— c. 1750–1810?
Bass at Vienna court opera in 1780s.

Fux, Johann Joseph 1660–1741
Famous Austrian composer, conductor, theorist.

Gabler, Christopher August c. 1750–1805?
German composer active in Leipzig (related to organ builder?).

Gabrielli, Caterina 1730–1796
Touring Italian soprano who sang "Ombra felice" in London—either the version of J. C. Bach, or Mozart's K. 255. Sister of soprano Francesca Gabrielli (1735–1795).

Gaelle, P. Meingosus c. 1740–1790?

Musician friend who composed "Der Arme" in 1777 in Salzburg.

Gall, Ludwig (see also Mederitsch) 1752–1835

Vienna singer and keyboard pupil of Mozart in 1785. Sang at Swieten concerts.

Galliani, Angiola c. 1740–1790?

Sang with Mozart in Mantua (1770).

Galliari, Giuseppe 1709–1790

Milan co-designer of decors for *Mitridate* premiere, with his brother Bernardino (1707–1794). Other members of this Italian artistic family also active in Germany include: Giovanni, Gaspare, and Fabrizio.

Galuppi, Baldasare 1706–1785

Popular Venetian opera and instrumental composer whose works Mozart knew.

Gamerra, Giovanni di 1743–1803

Librettist for Mozart's *Lucio Silla*, K. 135, and translator into Italian of *Die Zauberflöte* (a widely performed version first seen in Prague in 1794). Also librettist for Sarti, Paisiello, Salieri, Weigl, Paer, etc.

Gardi, Francesco 1760–1810

Italian opera composer of *Il nuovo convitato di Pietra* (1787), etc.

Garibaldi, Giaocchino 1743–1783

Tenor of Vienna court opera, cast for the Vienna premiere of *La finta semplice* which was cancelled because of intrigue.

Gaspari, Gaetano c. 1820–1880?

Italian scholar who published an article in the *Gazetta musicale di Milano* (May 9, 1858) identifying Mozart's K. 86, composed October 9, 1770 in Bologna (where it is in the G. B. Martini collection at the Liceo musicale).

Gasparini, Quirico 1725–1778

Mozart knew several works of this Turin opera composer before composing his *Mitridate*, K. 74a (87).

Gassmann, Florian Leopold 1729–1774

Bohemian opera and instrumental composer and conductor active in Vienna.

Gatti, Luigi 1740–1817

Composer from Mantua, first conductor in Salzburg from 1783.

Gatti, ——— c. 1760–181-

Singer who performed in *Die Entführung* in Vienna in 1780s.

Gaviniès, Pierre 1726–1800

Paris composer and violinist whose playing impressed Mozart and influenced his style.

Gayl, Johann c. 1760–1830?

Frankfurt music dealer who sold piano-vocal score of K. 620.

Gayl, Joseph c. 1760–1830

Austrian stage designer, collaborator with Nessthaler on the decors for the Vienna premiere of *Die Zauberflöte* (1791).

Gazzaniga, Giuseppe 1743–1818

Italian composer also active in Vienna (later writing only religious music). Mozart knew some of Gazzaniga's operas; Da Ponte knew the Bertati libretto for Gazzaniga's *Don Giovanni*. The story was set to music a number of times, by Righini, Callegari, Tritto, Albertini, Gardi, etc., in the decade before 1787.

Gebler, Baron Tobias Philipp von 1726–1786

Author of *Thamos, König in Ägypten*, a five act drama for which Mozart composed incidental music, K. 345 (later also used for K. M. Plümicke's play, *Lanassa*). Fellow Freemason.

Geissenhof, Franz 1754–1821

String instrument maker in Vienna.

Geissler, Georg Daniel c. 1720–1790?

German poet (?) acquaintance of Mozart family in 1760s.

Gelinek, Joseph 1758–1825

Minor composer active in Vienna, friend of Mozart.

Gellert, Joseph 1715–1769

Important Austrian poet Mozart read whose verses were affixed to the music of Mozart after the death of both artists.

Geminiani, Francesco 1680–1762

Famed Italian composer, violinist esteemed by Leopold Mozart.

Gemmingen-Homberg, Baron Otto Heinrich von 1753–1836

Mannheim official, composer, and dramatist who moved to Vienna, where he was an active music patron, fellow Freemason, and friend.

Genée, Rudolph c. 1850–1925

Mozart authority, editor of Berlin Mozart Mitteilungen (1895–1925); relative of Berlin composer.

Genzinger, Peter Leopold von c. 1740–1800?

Mozart performed several times in the 1780s at the Genzinger home in Vienna. Frau von Genzinger (1755–1793) was a good friend of Joseph Haydn.

Gerber, Ernst Ludwig 1746–1819

German musician, organist for Prince Schwarzenburg–Sondershausen. In his *Historische-Biographisches Lexikon der Tonkunstler* (Leipzig, 1790) there are notices on both Leopold and Wolfgang Mozart.

Gerl, Barbara (née Reisinger) 1770–1806

Soprano, sang Papagena in premiere of *Die Zauberflöte*. Married to below.

Gerl, Franz 1764–1827

Minor Viennese composer and bass singer who performed Sarastro in the premiere of *Die Zauberflöte* (1791). Mozart also composed K. 612 and 613 for him.

Gerl, Johann Georg 1757–1813

Mannheim bass singer whose Mozart roles included Sarastro in *Die Zauberflöte* (1794).

Gerstner, Dr. Franz 1756–1832
Viennese fellow Freemason.

Gessner, Solomon 1730–1788
Important German writer Mozart knew, and whose books he read.

Gestewitz, Friedrich Christoph 1753–1805
German composer active in Leipzig and Dresden from 1770s.

Gewey, Franz Carl 1774–1819
Collaborator of E. Schikaneder.

Ghelen, Ignaz Rudolph von c. 1720–1785?
Viennese publisher of Gluck, Metastasio, Freemason texts.

Ghelen, Jakob Anton von c. 1740–1800?
Minor composer of singspiels enjoyed by Mozart family. (Related to Vienna publisher?)

Giardini, Felice de 1716–1796
Italian composer friendly to the Mozarts in London.

Giarnovichi, Giovanni 1745–1804
Polish composer, publisher, and excellent traveling violinist whom Mozart knew in Vienna in the 1780s.

Gieseke, Johann Georg Karl Ludwig 1761–1833
Poet, translator, librettist, fellow Freemason, and scholar. Sang First Slave in *Die Zauberflöte* premiere (and may have helped fashion the libretto).

Gignoux, Anton Christoph 1721–1795
Augsburg musician, and friend of the Mozart family.

Gilowsky von Urazowa 1757–1816
Salzburg family (several were Freemasons) well known by the Mozarts: Katharina (1705–1805), close friend of Nannerl; Franz Wenzel (1757–1816), surgeon in Vienna, best man at Mozart's wedding.

Giorgetti, Silvio c. 1750–1800?
Mannheim-Munich male soprano in 1770s and 1780s.

Girelli, Maria Antonia Aguilar   c. 1735–1780?

Italian soprano, sang in *Ascanio* premiere in Milan (1771); later appeared in works by Gluck and Vento in London; also a dancer.

Girzik, F. X.   c. 1750–1810?

Active librettist and translator into German for a dozen successful composers, including Mozart, Haydn, Cimarosa, Paisiello, Paneck, Salieri.

Gitschin, Bauer von   1748–1800?

Prague violinist Mozart met in 1787.

Giulini, Count Georgio   1717–1780

Milanese poet and composer of symphonies and other works. Perhaps related to Andreas Giulini (1723–1772), Augsburg composer Leopold Mozart knew.

Giustinelli, Giuseppe   c. 1730–1790?

Italian castrato active in London when Mozart was there.

Giustinini, N. A.   1712–1796

Verona host to Mozart in 1771.

Gleim, Johann Wilhelm Ludwig   1719–1803

Popular lyricist in Vienna, text poet for K. 539 (1788). Haydn also used his work.

Gleissner, Franz Johann   1759–1818

Viennese horn player and church composer, also active in Munich, who knew Mozart. Editor for first André editions of Mozart's works.

Glöggl, Franz Xaver   1764–1839

Linz cathedral music director; friendly with Süssmayr.

Gluck, Chevalier Christoph Willibald von   1714–1787

Major opera composer active in Vienna and Paris. Admired *Die Entführung,* but did not really help Mozart.

Goedbé, Samuel   c. 1800–1850?

Editor-translator of English version of Mozart's "Generalbassschule." Pupil of Attwood? (Related to English engraver, Godby?)

Goepfert, Karl Andreas   1768–1818

Keyboard pupil of Mozart, later active as composer, clarinettist, violinist.

Goethe, Johann Wilhelm von   1749–1832

Distinguished German writer and poet, whose librettos were popular, and whose *Das Veilchen* was set as a song by Mozart (and many others). Goethe attempted a sequel to *Die Zauberflöte*.

Goldoni, Carlo   1707–1793

Outstanding Italian playwright whose works Mozart appreciated, and used several times.

Goldschmidt, Otto   1829–1907

Hamburg-born composer, owner of Mozart instrumental manuscripts, editor of Breitkopf Mozart Edition, also active in London.

Golicyn, Prince Demetrius (Galitsin)   1720–1794

Russian ambassador to Vienna who invited Mozart to give concerts in his palace in 1780s.

Gonard, François   1756–1819

Artist active in Vienna in 1780s. Silhouettist of many in Mozart's circle, particularly Freemasons.

Gontard, J. S. von   1739–1819

Vienna financier, patron, fellow Freemason.

Görner, Karl Friedrich   c. 1735–1790?

Leipzig organist who heard Mozart play organ in 1789, son of J. G. Görner.

Gossec, François   1734–1829

French composer who was cordial to Mozart in 1778.

Gotter, Friedrich Wilhelm 1746–1797

German poet, librettist, and translator providing texts for melodramas by Benda, Schweitzer, Zumsteeg, 1775–1795. Gotter's *Der Geisterinsel* (based on Shakespeare's *The Tempest*) planned for Mozart was later set by Reichardt. Gotter's text for the song originally listed as K. 350 was actually composed by Dr. Bernhard Flies of Berlin.

Gottlieb, Anna 1774–1856

Viennese soprano who sang Barbarina in *Figaro,* and Pamina in *Die Zauberflöte* at the Viennese premieres.

Gottsched, J. C. c. 1700–1766?

Important liberal writer-educator active in Vienna as a colleague of Baron van Swieten, J. T. von Trattner, etc.; his daughter Louise Gottsched was also important in literary circles.

Götz, Johann Friedrich von c. 1750–1810?

German librettist of Winter's *Lenardo und Blandine* (1799), mostly active in Munich and Vienna (related to Mannheim publisher Michael Götz?)

Gozzi, Count Carlo 1720–1806

Distinguished Italian dramatist whose works Mozart appreciated.

Graefe, Johann Friedrich 1711–1787

Brunswick vocal and instrumental composer whose songs Leopold taught young Mozart.

Graf, Christian Ernst 1723–1804

German composer, conductor active in The Hague in 1760s, whose music Mozart appreciated, and used (K. 25).

Graf, Friedrich Hartmann (brother of above) 1727–1795

Composer, conductor, and flutist active in Augsburg; a third brother lived in Zurich.

Gräffer, Rudolf c. 1740–1800

Viennese publisher active with brother, August, from 1760s; fellow Freemason.

Grams, Anton 1752–1823

Prague violinist, music copyist.

Grandi, Tommaso c. 1740–1790?

Librettist for Sarti's *Le gelosie villane,* for which Mozart composed a new final chorus in 1791 (K. 615).

Grassalkovics, Prince Anton 1733–1794

Son of Hungarian Count who helped arrange the coronation of Empress Maria Theresia as Queen of Hungary in 1741. Grassalkovics' musical establishment at Pressburg included Mozart's good friend, the violinist Joseph Zistler.

Grassel, Laurenz c. 1740–1800

Member of Viennese musical family; composer, horn player.

Grassi, Joseph 1758–1838

Viennese painter active in 1780s (miniature of 1785?). Participated in Mozart's "Masquerade" (K. 446), in which Aloysia and Joseph Lange and other friends and relations were rehearsed by Louis Mergery (?). Brother of Anton Grassi, painter.

Grassi, Martin c. 1740–1790?

Salzburg horn player in 1760s.

Grassnick, F. c. 1840–1900

Berlin musician and Mozart collector. Editor for Breitkopf Mozart Edition.

Graun, Karl Heinrich 1704–1759

Berlin vocal composer and singer; brother of Johann Gottlieb Graun (1703–1771); primarily an instrumental composer. Works of both were performed at Baron van Swieten's Sunday concerts in Vienna.

Graziani, Carlo c. 1730–1787

Italian composer and violoncellist active in Berlin, Paris, and London, where Mozart may have played at one of his concerts.

Greibe, Ferdinand Ernst c. 1760–1810?

Tenor in Berlin, whose Mozart roles included Pedrillo in *Die Entführung* (1789) and Basilio in *Figaro.*

Greiner, Franz Sales von   1731–1798

Vienna councilman, fellow Freemason and patron of Mozart, friend of Joseph Haydn (related to Fräulein von Greiner).

Greipel, Johann   1720–1798

Vienna court painter who also depicted operatic scenes.

Grenser, Johann Friedrich   1758–1795

Dresden instrumental composer, oboist and oboe maker also active in Sweden.

Grétry, André   1741–1813

Belgian opera composer active in Paris after 1767. Agreed to Mozart's remarkable keyboard facility, but questioned his sight-reading accuracy. Mozart owned several scores by Grétry, and utilized a number of his compositional procedures.

Greuze, Jean-Baptiste   1725–1805

French painter esteemed by Diderot, whose portrait of Mozart has not been authenticated by scholars.

Grillparzer, Franz   1791–1872

Important Austrian dramatist who admired Mozart's music.

Grimm, Baron Friedrich Melchior von   1723–1807

German man of letters erratically supportive of the Mozart family, long active in Parisian arts and music, Piccinnist (anti-Gluck); friendly with Carmontelle, Diderot, Greuze, and many influential patrons; secretary to the Duc d'Orléans.

Grosheim, Georg Christoph   1764–1830?

German composer from Kassel: editor, arranger of Mozart piano-vocal scores for Simrock.

Grossman, Frederica   c. 1760–1810?

Soprano applauded as Blonde (*Die Entführung*) in Kassel and Hanover.

Grossman, Gustav Friedrich Wilhelm 1742–1796

German theatre manager, translator, librettist for Neefe's *Adelheit von Veltheim*. Husband of above.

Grua, Francesco de Paula 1754–1833?

Italian composer, principally of sacred music, also active in Mannheim and Munich.

Gruner, Nathaniel 1732–1792

Important North German sacred and instrumental composer.

Grünwald, J. J. c. 1750–1800?

Viennese song composer active in 1780s.

Gspan, Ignatius 1750–1800?

Singspiel composer active in Vienna in 1770s and 1780s.

Gsur, Tobias 1725–1794

Bass singer and composer at Vienna court chapel. Performed in Mozart's arrangement of Handel's *Acis and Galathea* at Baron van Swieten's in 1788.

Guadagni, Gaetano 1725–1797

Celebrated Italian castrato and composer who knew Mozart. Also active in Vienna and London, where he sang with Handel.

Guardasoni, Domenico 1731–1806

Italian singer and musician friendly to Mozart, who took over Bondini's company after his death and produced operas in Prague and elsewhere.

Guardasoni, Tommaso c. 1740–1790

Italian castrato who sang with Mozart in Florence (1770).

Guénin, Marie-Alexandre 1744–1835

Paris instrumental composer and concertmaster of the Concert Spirituel in 1778. Publisher of early Mozart editions.

Gugl, Matthias 1683–1721

Salzburg composer and organist whose music may have influenced Mozart, along with that of Muffat, Biber, Eberlin.

Guglielmi, Pietro 1727–1804

Italian operatic and instrumental composer, also active in Vienna and Berlin, whose works Mozart saw.

Guillard, François 1752–1814

Famous French librettist for Grétry, Sacchini, Gluck, and others.

Guimard, Madeleine 1743–1816

Famous Parisian dancer who appeared in Mozart's *Les petits riens.*

Guines, Count Adrien-Louis de Souastre de 1735–1806

French amateur flutist for whom Mozart composed the *Flute and Harp Concerto* (K. 299). His daughter, Mozart's keyboard and composition pupil in 1778, also played the harp.

Günther, Friedrich c. 1750–1810?

Popular German bass singer, active in Vienna from 1780, where he was a successful Osmin (*Die Entführung*). his singer-actress wife, Sophie, was also applauded in *Die Entführung,* in Dresden.

Günther, Johann Christian 1695–1723

Mozart used his texts for songs: K. 125d, 125e.

Günther, Johann Valentin 1746–1800?

Viennese Freemason, friend.

Gürrlich, Joseph Augustin 1761–1817

Berlin composer and touring conductor Mozart encountered on his 1789 trip to Berlin.

Gusetti, Giovanni Battista 1744–1789

Salzburg merchant, violinist, friend of the Mozart family.

Gyrowetz, Adalbert 1763–1850

Bohemian composer, conductor active in Vienna. Pupil of Mozart (1784).

Haasy, Pater Johannes von c. 1740–1790

Austrian priest for whom Mozart composed K. 74f.

Habbegger, Johann c. 1740–1795
Viennese composer of sacred music.

Habermann, Franz Johann 1706–1783
Bohemian composer, chiefly of sacred music.

Hackel, Johann Christoph c. 1750–1800?
Viennese song composer active in 1780s.

Hacker, Benedikt 1769–1829
German composer, pupil of Michael Haydn. Fellow Freemason, and later a friend of Constanze.

Hadik, Count Andreas 1710–1790
Viennese patron and friend of Mozart, as was his son.

Hafeneder, Joseph c. 1750–1800?
Salzburg composer, violinist, friend of the Mozart family.

Haffner, Johann Ulrich 1711–1767
Nuremberg composer, lutenist, publisher whose works were appreciated by Leopold Mozart.

Haffner, Sigmund 1699–1772
Salzburg merchant and mayor, whose family was friendly with the Mozarts, for whom Mozart composed K. 250, 385. Daughter Elisabeth married F. X. Späth (1714–1790).

Hafner, Philipp 1731–1764
Austrian playwright, whose writings Mozart knew; his *Megära* may have been one of the sources of the plot of *Die Zauberflöte*.

Hagedorn, Friedrich von 1708–1754
Hamburg poet, whose text Mozart used for K. 517.

Hagenauer, Dominique 1744–1811
Abbot of St. Peter monastery, Salzburg, who kept a diary often mentioning Mozart, who composed K. 69 for the first mass Hagenauer celebrated. The entire family were friends of the Mozarts. Cousin Johann Hagenauer (1732–1810) was an important sculptor, married to portrait painter, Rosa Barducci.

Haibl, Petrus Jakob 1761–1826

Viennese composer, conductor, singer who married Mozart's sister-in-law, Sophie Weber.

Haina, Franz 1729–1790?

Traveling horn player Mozart knew.

Hamm, Maria Anna von 1765–1810?

Munich "pianist" who took several lessons from Mozart (1777).

Hampel, Franz 1766–1811

Violinist, member of musical family in Mannheim and Munich. Son of Johann Hampel, violist, and clarinettist; Freemason.

Handel, George Frideric 1685–1759

Distinguished composer, whose influence on Mozart can be observed in many pieces, including K. 10, 394, 399, 566, 572, 592 (some were Handel compositions arranged by Mozart for presentation to the Swieten circle).

Handelgruber, ——— c. 1770–1820?

Viennese singer who performed in *Die Zauberflöte* premiere.

Hanke, Karl 1750–1803

German singspiel composer, singer, and conductor, whose works were performed in Vienna and Germany in 1780s. His librettists included K. M. Plümicke and Sophie Seyler.

Hansen, Hans 1769–1828

Danish portraitist, of Constanze (1802), Carl Thomas and Wolfgang, Jr. (1798), and F. S. Silverstolpe (c. 1800), etc. Friend of Haydn.

Hänsler, Joseph c. 1760–1820?

Prague harpist, friend.

Häring, Johann Baptist von 1761–1818

Viennese banker, violinist, friend, and patron of Mozart.

Harny de Guérville c. 1720–1780?

French literary figure who collaborated with the Favarts in the adaptation of Rousseau's *Le Devin du Village* into *Les Amours de Bastien et Bastienne*, the source of Mozart's K. 50/46b.

Harold, Joseph Georg c. 1750–1800?

Viennese music copyist.

Härtel, Gottfried 1763–1827

Important Leipzig publisher, successor of Johann Breitkopf.

Hartig, Franz Christian 1750–1819

Tenor who sang Belmonte in Munich premiere of *Die Entführung*, also active in Mannheim. His wife danced in the world premiere of *Idomeneo* (Munich, 1781).

Hartmann, Friedrich Ludwig von 1773–1820?

Friend of Mozart family.

Haschka, Lorenz Leopold 1749–1827

Text poet for K. 468a, a fellow Freemason, but a disloyal one.

Haschka, Simon c. 1740–1800?

Viennese collaborator of Mozart, Haydn, etc. Freemason.

Haselbeck, Joseph Anton c. 1760–1820?

Collaborator in Schikaneder's company; one of several who contributed to the libretto of *Die Zauberflöte*.

Hasse, Johann Adolph 1699–1783

Important composer of Italian operas, active in Dresden, etc. Married to soprano Faustina Bordoni (1693–1781). An influence on Mozart, and a friend.

Hässler, Johann Wilhelm 1747–1822

German composer and organist who "competed" with Mozart in Dresden on April 15, 1789. Later Hässler performed Mozart piano concertos on tour in London, etc.

Hatzfeld, Count August von 1756–1787

Patron, close friend, and pupil of Mozart. Amateur violinist who played in the 1786 Vienna performance of *Idomeneo*. Fellow Freemason.

Hatzfeld, Countess Hortense von   c. 1760–1800?

Good friend of Mozart, sister-in-law of above; accomplished soprano who sang Electra in the Vienna performance of *Idomeneo* (1786).

Haydinger, Franz   c. 1745–1800?

Viennese friend from the 1760s.

Haydn, Franz Joseph   1732–1809

Great contemporary composer, influence, friend, fellow Freemason.

Haydn, Johann   1743–1805

Mediocre tenor, brother of above.

Haydn (Johann) Michael   1737–1806

Austrian composer in Salzburg service 1762–1806; a friend and influence on young Mozart, particularly in church music; brother of above.

Haydn, Magdalena Lipp   1745–1827

Soprano who sang in many of Mozart's works, including *Die Schuldigkeit* and *La finta semplice*; wife of Michael Haydn.

Hayn, Griedrich Gottlob   c. 1760–1820

Minor German composer who published variations on works of Mozart (related to Austrian playwright Juliane Hayn?).

Hebelt, Wenzel   c. 1740–1800?

Salzburg violinist, and assistant to Leopold Mozart.

Heeger, Wenzel   1740–1807

Viennese schoolmaster Mozart knew in 1780s.

Heerman, Gottlob Ephraim   1727–1815

German writer, translator, librettist collaborating with J. A. Hiller, E. W. Wolf, and J. L. Schubaur in 1770s and 1780s, in works seen in Weimar, Berlin, and Vienna.

Hefner, Heinrich Wilhelm von   1720–1774

Salzburg friend of Mozart family.

Heina, Madame Gertrude Brockmüller 1729–1790

German-born publisher active in Paris. She and her husband helped Mozart at the time of his mother's death.

Hek, F. VI. 1769–1847

Czechoslavakian composer whose sacred music resembles that of Mozart.

Helbling, Thadäus c. 1740–1800?

Painter whose portrait of Mozart (c. 1767–1770) is doubted.

Heller, Gaudenz 1750–1784

Munich violoncello player whom Mozart knew.

Hellmuth, Friedrich c. 1750–1810?

Composer and singer active in Weimar and other German towns.

Hellmuth, Josepha c. 1750–1800?

Soprano active in Weimar from 1770s; married to above. Sang Donna Elvira (*Don Giovanni*) in various towns.

Hellmuth, Marianne c. 1760–1810?

German soprano active in Berlin whose Mozartean roles from 1790 included Cherubino (*Figaro*), Donna Elvira (*Don Giovanni*). (Related to above?)

Henikstein, Marianne c. 1770–1820?

Keyboard pupil of J. A. André; collected Mozart manuscripts that are now in the Library of Congress, Washington, D. C.

Henneberg, Johann 1768–1822

Viennese composer, member of Schikaneder circle from late 1780s. Also collaborator of P. Winter.

Hennig, C. F. 1759–1825

German composer who wrote minor key symphonies in 1770s.

Hensler, Karl Friedrich c. 1760–1810?

Popular librettist of singspiels for Müller, Kauer, etc.; theatre manager. Fellow Freemason.

Hepp, Ignaz c. 1750–1790?

Member of Munich musical family; friend of the Mozarts. Fellow Freemason.

Herder, Johann Gottfried 1744–1803

Follower of Rousseau. German writer and librettist active in Weimar. Important "romantic" influence on Goethe. Fellow Freemason.

(K) Herffert, ——*Franz*—— c. 1740–1800?
German symphonist. *and composer of concertos*

Hergen, ——— c. 1750–1800?
German symphonist.

Herklotz, Karl Alexander c. 1760–1820?

Viennese librettist, translator, and poet for several composers, including Mozart.

Hermes, Johann Timotheus 1738–1821

Text poet for Mozart's K. 340c, etc.

Hertel, Johann Wilhelm 1727–1784

German instrumental and vocal composer active in several centers.

Hess, Carl Ernst Christoph 1755–1828

German engraver active in Munich.

Heufeld, Franz von 1731–1795

Viennese dramatist, official, translator, and friend of the Mozarts.

Heydenreich, Joseph 1753–1821

Viennese composer, publisher, friend.

Hickel, Joseph 1736–1807

Viennese friend, and court painter and engraver (in a circle of artists including Herzesryn, Schuster).

Hieber, Wilhelm c. 1750–1800?

Oboist active in Mannheim and Munich from 1770s.

Hiller, Johann Adam   1728–1804

Important early German singspiel composer whose works Mozart knew.

Himmel, Friedrich Heinrich   1765–1814

German vocal and instrumental composer whose works were known in Vienna and elsewhere.

Hirsch, Paul   1881–1951

German Mozart authority and collector who moved to England and transferred his large collection of Mozartiana to the British Library.

Hochbrucker, Christian   1733–1792

German composer who specialized in the harp, active in Paris, where he was friendly with the Mozart family.

Hoeck, Karl   1707–1772

North German instrumental composer and brilliant violinist.

Hofdemel, Franz   1755–1791

Vienna official, friend, and fellow Freemason.

Hofdemel, Magdalena Pokorny   1766–1810?

Wife of above; pupil of Mozart, and possibly his mistress.

Hofer, Andreas   1629–1684

Salzburg composer, whose music may have influenced Mozart.

Hofer, Franz de Paula   1755–1796

Vienna court violinist who performed with Mozart. First husband of Josepha Weber.

Hoffman, A. Johann   c. 1750–1810?

Vienna court choirmaster, composer, violinist 1780s.

Hoffman, Heinrich   c. 1750–1810?

Vienna song composer, active in 1780s.

Hoffman, E. T. A.   1776–1823

Imaginative poet and composer. He admired *Don Giovanni,* and wrote his tale "Don Juan" for the *Allgemeine Musikalische Zeitung,* March 31, 1813.

Hoffman, H. Anton 1770–1842

Violinist Mozart met in Mainz in 1790, where they performed together, along with his brother Karl Hoffmann (1760–1842).

Hoffman, Joseph 1765–1843

Composer and violinist at Esterháza and the Vienna court chapel.

Hoffmann, Dr. Joseph 1760–1806

Vienna fellow Freemason.

Hoffman, Philipp Karl 1769–1842

Vienna pupil of Mozart in 1790.

Hofmann, Elisabeth c. 1760–1797

Performed Second Lady in Vienna premiere of *Die Zauberflöte* (1791).

Hoffmeister, Franz Anton 1754–1812

Viennese instrumental composer, friend of Mozart. Publishing partner of organist Ambrosius Kühnel (1770–1813).

Hofman, Isabella 1766–1820?

Salzburg friend of Mozart family.

Hofmann, Leopold 1738–1793

Viennese church and instrumental composer.

Hofstetter, Felix 1744–1814

Composer, violinist, and copyist in Vienna whose works were published in Paris; known to Mozart and Joseph Haydn.

Holi, ——— c. 1750–1800?

Munich vocal composer active in 1780s.

Holly, Franz Andreas 1747–1787

Bohemian composer and conductor of singspiels in Berlin and elsewhere; he helped popularize "Turkish" instrumentation.

Holty, Ludwig 1748–1776
Mozart used his text in K. 520.

Holzbauer, Ignaz 1711–1783
Mannheim composer and conductor praised by Mozart, on whom he was an influence, particularly 1777–1778.

Holzer, Johann 1753–1818
Viennese pianist, song composer to texts by Leon Gottlieb, etc., fellow Freemason, and friend of Mozart.

Holzmann, Joseph Aloys 1762–1815
Austrian cloister composer of symphonies, at Stams.

Holzschneider, Andreas c. 1750–1810?
Hamburg musician and copyist; source of rare copies of Mozart compositions.

Homilius, Godefroi Augustus 1714–1785
Bohemian composer, organist, fellow Freemason, active in Dresden.

Honauer, Leontzi 1717–1809
German composer of instrumental music active in Paris from 1760. Mozart adapted Honauer's keyboard sonata in G in composing his Concerto K. 41, first movement.

Horeischy, Thérèse 1751–1809
Soprano for whom Mozart composed K. 125g (147).

Hörmann, Johann 1748–1816
Prominent Viennese horn player.

Hornung, Joseph c. 1740–1790?
Austrian baritone. Sang Cassandro in the Salzburg premiere of *La finta semplice.* Later collaborated on opera texts and stage design. Married to Anne Wittman, Salzburg singer and actress (c. 1760–1800?).

Houdart de la Motte, Antoine 1672–1731
French writer whose verses Mozart set in K. 307, 308.

Hraschansky, Joseph   1752–1806
Vienna friend, Freemason, and publisher of first edition of K. 623.

Huber, Antonie   1780–1857
Austrian soprano (sister-in-law of Anton Stoll) Mozart heard sing in Baden (1791).

Huber, Franz Xaver   c. 1760–1820?
Austrian writer active in Salzburg, Vienna, and Munich, who published favorable articles on Mozart, and probably wrote librettos for Winter, Gyrowetz, and Süssmayr. Loewenberg states that there were two Hubers who wrote, and it is not clear which one knew Mozart and his music.

Huber, Pancrazio   c. 1740–1790?
Viennese court ballet master, violinist, and church composer, whose works were published in Paris. (Related to Viennese symphonist, Thaddäus Huber, c. 1750–1798?)

Huber, Sophie   c. 1750–1800?
Soprano active in Berlin, Leipzig, Dresden in the 1770s and 1780s.

Huberty, Anton   1722–1791
Viennese music copier.

Hübner, Lorenz   1753–1807
Writer, editor friendly to the Mozarts. Fellow Freemason.

Hüllmandel, Nikolaus Joseph   1751–1823
Strasbourg composer, pupil of C. P. E. Bach, active in Paris and London. Mozart appreciated his music.

Hulover, Joseph   c. 1750–1800?
Violinist at Salzburg court in the 1770s.

Hummel, Johann Julius   1728–1798
Publisher Leopold Mozart knew in Amsterdam who later moved to Berlin.

Hummel, Johann Nepomuk   1778–1837
Austrian composer and conductor who was Mozart's pupil, 1786–1787.

Hunczowsky, Johann Nepomuk 1752–1798
Viennese friend, fellow Freemason, and physician.

Hupfeld, Bernard 1717–1780?
German composer, flutist, active in Vienna, Italy, etc.

Hurka, Franz 1762–1805
Composer, also active from 1780s as a tenor in Dresden and Prague
(e.g., Belmonte in *Die Entführung*).

Hurlebusch, Konrad Friedrich 1696–1765
Brunswick composer of vocal and instrumental works (also active in
Sweden, Holland) which Leopold taught to young Mozart.

Iffland, August Wilhelm 1759–1814
Austrian poet, playwright, translator whose works the Mozarts knew.

Ihlee, Johann Jakob c. 1770–1825
Translator of Mozart's *La clemenza di Tito* into German; author of
various translations for Salieri, Méhul, etc.; also librettist for Kunzen,
Spohr, and others.

Imbault, Jean 1753–1832
Active Paris publisher and violinist.

Jacobé, Johann 1733–1797
Important Viennese engraver, teacher of Wrenk, Pichler, Kininger, etc.

Jacobi, Johann Georg 1740–1814
Member of the literary circle including Goethe, Herder, and
Klopstock, he was the author of the text for K. 524.

Jacobi, Baron Klöst von 1745–1816
Patron of Mozart and Prussian Ambassador to Vienna, he purchased
eight of Mozart's compositions from his widow Constanze for King
Friedrich Wilhelm II in 1792. Brother of above.

Jacquin, Franziska (Lagusius) von 1769–1853
Pupil of Mozart in 1787, for whom he composed K. 436. Sister of his
good friend, Gottfried von Jacquin.

Jacquin, Baron Gottfried von 1767–1792

Pupil of Mozart in 1787, minor Austrian composer who later published some of Mozart's songs as his own.

Jäger, Daniel 1762–1802

Text poet for two strophes of K. 531, also a translator.

Jahn, Ignaz von 1744–1810

Patron of Mozart, music-loving Vienna merchant who lent out concert space in the 1780s and 1790s.

Jähndl, Anton 1783–1861

Choral conductor who assisted Nissen in his biography of Mozart.

Janitsch, Anton 1753–1812

Composer, violinist Mozart met in Mannheim.

Jantz, Dominik 1732–1806

Actor who portrayed Pasha Selim in Vienna premiere of *Die Entführung* (1782).

Jelinek, Franz Xaver 1818–1880

Archivist at Salzburg Mozarteum, and cathedral choir director.

Jélyotte, Pierre de 1713–1787

Minor composer, guitarist, prominent tenor at the Paris Opéra (1733–1779), friend of Mozart.

Jeunehomme, Mademoiselle c. 1760–1800?

French concert pianist Mozart knew in 1777 and 1778, for whom he composed K. 271 (no more information traceable).

Joachim, Joseph 1831–1907

Berlin composer, violinist, editor of Breitkopf Mozart Edition, and owner of instrumental manuscripts of Mozart's music.

John, Friedrich 1769–1843

Viennese artist in Lange circle.

Joly, Maria Anna Rosalia 1726–1788

Salzburg friend of the Mozart family. In service of Count Arco.

Jommelli, Niccolò 1714–1774

Important Italian opera composer, active in Austria and Germany, whose music influenced Mozart.

Joseph II 1741–1790

Austrian Holy Roman Emperor (1765–1790), son of Empress Maria Theresia (with whom he was at first co-ruler). Conscientious, liberal monarch whose interest in Mozart was benevolent, but rather passive.

Jouve, Pierre c. 1770–1830

Parisian publisher of early editions of Mozart.

Jünger, Johann Friedrich 1759–1797

Popular Viennese writer and librettist for Dittersdorf and J. C. Kaffka (1754–1814), touring composer whose works were popular in Vienna.

Kaffka, J. C. 1754–1814

Touring composer, singer, member of a musical family from Regensburg.

Kainz, Joseph 1738–1810

Viennese church composer.

Kaiser, Philipp Chr. c. 1745–1800?

German song composer.

Kaiser, Mademoiselle Margarethe (?) c. 1760–1810?

Munich soprano (active in Vienna after 1784), in whom Mozart was interested, in 1781.

Kalkbrenner, Christian 1755–1806

German composer and music theorist mostly active in Berlin and Paris.

Kammel, Antonin 1730–1787

Violinist and instrumental composer from Hungary who also toured.

Karl Theodor, Elector Palatinate, Mannheim (later Bavaria) 1724–1799

Commissioned Mozart to compose *Idomeneo* for Munich (see also Countess Baumgarten).

Kaselitz, ——— c. 1760–1810?

Bass who performed Commendatore at Berlin premiere of *Don Giovanni* (1790).

Kauer, Ferdinand 1751–1831

Prolific Viennese composer, conductor of singspiels and instrumental works (librettos by Hensler, etc.) in 1780s and 1790s.

Kaunitz, Prince Wenzel 1711–1794

Longtime chief minister of state of Empress Maria Theresia. Prince Dominik and other members of his family were patrons and friends of Mozart.

Kayser, Philipp Christoph 1755–1823

German composer, piano virtuoso, friend of Goethe.

Kazinsky, Franz 1759–1831

Hungarian poet, protegé of Baron van Swieten, who admired Mozart's music.

Kees, Franz Bernard von 1720–1795

Viennese court councilman, patron of Mozart and Haydn, who produced concerts of their music.

Keglevich, Count Joseph Busin von 1729–1800

Music-loving patron of Mozart's concerts in Vienna, and theatre director.

Keller, Maximilian 1770–1855

Organist, editorial assistant to Nissen in the preparation of his Mozart biography.

Keller, Otto c. 1850–1930?

Important Munich Mozart scholar.

Kellner, J. C. 1736–1803

German organist, instrumental composer, and theorist active in Kassel, Mannheim, etc.

Kelly, Michael (also known as O'Kelly) 1762–1826

Irish composer, tenor, author, pupil and good friend of Mozart who sang in the Vienna premiere of *Figaro* (1786), etc.

Kerl, Vitus c. 1750–1800?

German opera composer active in Munich.

Kerpen, Baron Franz von c. 1740–1800?

Salzburg friend of Mozart family, instrumental composer.

Khevenhüller-Metsch, Count Johann Joseph von 1709–1784

Friend and fellow Freemason; husband of Countess Zichy, also a friend and patron of Mozart.

Kierkegaard, Sören 1813–1855

Danish philosopher who wrote persuasively on Mozart works he admired, particularly *Don Giovanni* and *Die Zauberflöte*.

Kimmerling, P. Robert 1737–1799

Austrian instrumental composer and choir director at Melk known to Mozart.

Kininger, Vincenz G. 1767–1851

Viennese engraver of Haydn portrait and of title pages of Mozart works; friend of Haydn.

Kinsky, Countess Maria Theresia 1715–1778

Viennese hostess to Mozart family.

Kircher, Athanasius 1601–1680

Musician and teacher whose canons were among those which interested Mozart. K.Anh. 284d is by Kircher.

Kirchgässner, Marianne 1769–1808

Brilliant harmonica player, for whom Mozart in 1791 composed K. 617, 616a, 617a.

Kirchoff, Johann Gottfried 1685–1746

Hallé instrumental composer whose works Leopold used to teach young Mozart.

Kirmair, Friedrich Joseph   c. 1740–1814

German instrumental and vocal composer active in Munich, Berlin, Kassel. (Related to Wolfgang Kyrmair, Munich composer, 1727–1795?)

Kirnberger, Johann Philipp   1721–1783

Esteemed Berlin composer, conductor, theorist.

Kistler, Johann Michael   c. 1770–1820?

Singer who performed Second Priest in Vienna premiere of *Die Zauberflöte* (1791).

Klass, Karl Christian   c. 1740–1800?

German artist active in Italy where he met (and sketched) Mozart in Milan.

Klein, Professor Anton   1758–1810

Librettist of Holzbauer's *Günther von Schwarzenburg* (1777), which Mozart appreciated. However, apparently Mozart never began composition of *Kaiser Rudolf von Hapsburg*, which Klein sent Mozart in 1785.

Kleinhardt, Johann Thomas   c. 1760–1810?

Prague artist who admired Josepha Duček's singing, and Mozart's accompaniment, at the Vienna court in 1786.

Kleinknecht, Jakob Friedrich   1722–1794

German instrumental composer, conductor, violinist at several courts.

Kleinmayr, Johann Franz Thaddäus   1735–1805

Secretary to Salzburg court council who settled the partition of Leopold Mozart's estate between Mozart and Baron Berchtold zu Sonnenburg (husband of Mozart's sister, Nannerl).

Kloeffler, Johann Friedrich   1725–1790

German flutist and instrumental composer active in several towns.

Klopfer, Fräulein   c. 1770–1820?

Singer who performed First Lady in *Die Zauberflöte* premiere (1791).

Klopstock, Friedrich Gottlieb   1724–1803

Famous German poet whose works Mozart knew.

Klug, ——— c. 1750–1800?
German instrumental composer of symphonies.

Knecht, Justin Heinrich 1752–1817
German opera and instrumental composer and theorist active in several towns.

Knigge, Baron Adolf 1752–1796
German translator, and writer on Mozart in the 1780s. Friend and fellow Freemason.

Kniter, ——— c. 176—1810?
Sang Priest in *Die Zauberflöte* premiere.

Knoller, Martin 1725–1804
German portraitist who may have painted Mozart in Italy (1773).

Kobell, Wilhelm von 1766–1855
German painter in the circle of Cannabich.

Kobrich, Johann Anton 1714–1791
Bavarian composer and organist active in Augsburg and Nuremberg.

Koch, Heinrich Christoph 1748–1802
German violinist and theorist who also toured.

Koch, Franziska c. 1750–1800?
German soprano active in Weimar from the 1770s.

Koch, Johann c. 1740–1790?
Berlin opera composer and violinist active from 1770s.

Köchel, Ludwig von 1800–1877
Great Mozart scholar and cataloguer, and editor of the 19th century.

Kohaut, Karl von 1726–1784
Vienna court secretary, minor instrumental composer, attended Baron van Swieten's Sunday concerts. Brother of composer Joseph Kohaut, 1736–1793.

Kohl, Clemens 1754–1807

Prague-born artist-engraver active in Vienna; friend of Joseph Haydn.

Kolb, Andrä 1705–1785

Salzburg violinist, composer, friend who played Mozart's music and directed it.

Königsberger, Marianus c. 1710–1780

Bavarian church and instrumental composer whose works may have influenced Mozart.

Körzel, Franz c. 1740–1790?

Viennese symphonist and instrumental composer.

Kospoth, Baron Otto von 1753–1817

Opera and instrumental composer, active in Munich and Berlin from 1780.

Kosta, ——— c. 1760–1810?

Sang Don Giovanni at Leipzig premiere (1780).

Kotzbue, August von 1761–1819

Important German writer and librettist.

Koželuh, Leopold Anton 1747–1818

Austrian composer, publisher, teacher, rival of Mozart and Haydn.

Kotzwara, Franz 1750–1791

Prague instrumental composer, active in several towns, who died in London.

Krafft, Barbara 1764–1825

Painter whose copy of a Mozart portrait is regarded as one of the most accurate extant.

Krafft, François 1721–1795

Composer whose music Leopold used to teach young Mozart.

Kraft, Anton 1749–1820

Composer and violoncellist from Eisenstadt who played quartets with Mozart in Dresden (1789).

Kraus, Joseph Martin 1756–1792

North German opera and instrumental composer mostly active in Sweden; fellow Freemason.

Krause, C. G. c. 1710–1770?

German composer whose works Leopold taught young Mozart. Krause set verses of K. W. Ramler (1725–1798).

Kreibich, Franz 1728–1797

German composer, director of chamber music and first violinist for Emperor Joseph II. Unfriendly to Mozart.

Kreusser, Georg Anton 1746–1810

Mainz composer and violinist friendly to Mozart family, highly regarded by Leopold whose music was heard in Vienna.

Krommer, Franz 1759–1831

Czechoslovakian composer and violinist.

Kronauer, Johann Georg c. 1750–1810?

Viennese language teacher; Freemason and friend of Mozart.

Krottendorfer, Joseph 1741–1798

Viennese singer and church composer.

Krüger, Ephraim Gottlieb 1756–1834

Dresden engraver who worked for Breitkopf & Härtel.

Krumpholz, Johann Baptist 1745–1790

German harpsichordist and composer active in Paris, where Mozart met him.

Kuchař, Jan 1751–1815

Prague pupil of Sager, opera and instrumental composer, conductor, organist, and editor of Mozart opera scores.

Kuefstein, Count Johann von 1752–1818

Noble Viennese violinist and conductor, patron of Mozart.

Küffel, Ignaz c. 1740–1800?

Salzburg violoncellist who also played at Esterháza. Friend of the Mozarts.

Küffner, Johann Jacob Paul 1727–1786
German organist, harpsichordist, and instrumental composer.

Kuntz, A. K. 1750–1810?
German composer of symphonies.

Kunz, Thomas Anton c. 1760–1810?
Czechoslovakian composer also active in Vienna; fellow Freemason.

Kunzen, Friedrich Ludwig Aemilius 1761–1817
Son of composer Adolf Kunzen, he composed instrumental works and operas popular in Frankfurt, Prague, Copenhagen.

Kürtzinger, Paul c. 1760–1820
German opera composer active in Vienna and Munich from 1780s.

Kurz, Joseph, Felix 1717–1784
Bernardon was the real name of this famous and popular Hanswurst (clown) who used the music of Joseph Haydn in his comedies.

Kurzböck, Joseph von c. 1740–1800?
Viennese publisher of librettos for *Der Schauspieldirektor* and *Figaro*; active from 1770s on.

Lacépède, Count Bernard 1756–1825
Composer and critic active in Paris when Mozart was there (1778).

Lachner, Franz 1803–1895
Austrian conductor, composer, who performed many Mozart works.

Lachnith, Ludwig 1746–1820
Prague composer of symphonies and arrangements of Mozart operas.

Lackenbacher, Heinrich c. 1760–1820?
Viennese friend, 1790.

Lackner, Joseph   c. 1750–1800?
Violinist at Salzburg court in 1770s.

La Houssaye, Pierre   1735–1818
French composer, violinist who played Mozart's works in Paris in 1778, also active in England.

Lamotte, Franz   1751–1781
Viennese violinist who toured, and whose staccato playing Mozart praised.

Lampugnani, Giovanni Battista   1708–1788
Italian opera and instrumental composer also active in England, who, like Hasse, encouraged young Mozart.

Lang, Johann Georg   1722–1798
German instrumental composer whose works Leopold knew.

Lang, Martin   c. 1740–1800?
Munich horn player, for whose actress wife, Marianne Boudet, Mozart composed K. 367a (349), and both of whom he later saw in Vienna. (Related to J. G. Lang, above?)

Lange, Joseph   1751–1830
Important Viennese actor whose first wife was the singer Anna Maria Schindler, and whose second wife was Aloysia Weber. In 1780s, Lange painted an unfinished portrait of Mozart. Fellow Freemason.

Lange, Anna Maria Elisabeth Schindler   1757–1779
Singer at Vienna court opera; married to above before Aloysia Weber.

Langenmantel, Jakob Alois Karl von   1719–1790
Mayor of Augsburg, friend of Mozart family.

La Noche, Sophie   c. 1750–1800?
Singer active in Mannheim from 1770s.

Laroche, Johann   1745–1806
Famous actor as "Kasperl" in Vienna.

Laschi, Luisa   1766–1830

Daughter of Viennese court tenor scheduled to perform in performance of *La finta semplice* which was cancelled, Luisa sang in both *Figaro* and *Don Giovanni* in Vienna, and also appeared in Italy. Married to Domenic Francesco Mombelli (1775–1838) in 1787.

Lasser, Johann   1751–1805

German tenor and successful singspiel conductor, theorist, and composer whose works were performed in Mannheim, Munich, and Vienna from 1770s, whose music Mozart knew.

Latilla, Gaetano   1711–1788

Roman opera and instrumental composer who appreciated Mozart's instrumental works.

Laube, Antonin   1718–1784

Instrumental and opera composer whose works were produced in Hungary, Prague, and Berlin.

Lauchéry, Etienne   1732–1820

Mannheim ballet master for Holzbauer's opera *Günther von Schwarzenburg* (1777), also active in England, etc.

Laudon, Baron Ernst Gideon von   1717–1790

Austrian general who battled valiantly for Empress Maria Theresia, and was admired by Joseph Haydn and the Mozart family.

Lausch, Laurent   c. 1750–1810?

Vienna composer, copyist of *Figaro*, etc., publisher known to Mozart, Haydn, etc.

LeBrun, Franziska Danzi   1759–1791

Singer and musician active throughout Europe. Daughter of Mannheim violoncello player, and wife of oboist Ludwig August LeBrun.

LeBrun, Ludwig August   1752–1790

Composer and oboist who performed several times with Mozart, with whom he was a fellow Freemason. Active in Munich, Mannheim, England, Vienna, Russia.

LeChantre, Mademoiselle c. 1740–1790?

French composer, organist, keyboard player who composed several piano concertos around 1770. Probably performed Mozart's works.

LeDuc, Simon 1742–1777

Paris composer, violinist, brother of Pierre LeDuc (1755–1816), violinist and publisher, active also in England.

LeGrand, Jean-Pierre 1734–1809

Ballet master and dancer in Munich premiere of *Idomeneo* (1781).

LeGros, Joseph 1739–1793

Conductor and tenor, director of the Paris Concert Spirituel, where works of Mozart were performed in 1778, etc.

Lehmann, Lilli 1848–1929

World famous Mozart singer and guiding spirit of many Salzburg Festivals, as well as prima donna in works by Bellini, Wagner, Beethoven, Weber, etc.

Leisewitz, Anton c. 1750–1800?

German playwright whose works the Mozarts knew.

Leitgeb, Franz Anton 1744–1812

Estate manager for Count Walsegg, the pretentious musical dilletante who sent Leitgeb to commission the *Requiem* from Mozart.

Leitl, ——— c. 1750–1800?

Prague composer, flutist.

LeMenu, Christophe c. 1710–1774

Paris music publisher whose widow, Roze (1720–1800), published early works by Mozart.

Lenz, Ludwig Friedrich 1717–1780

Text poet of *Freimaurerlied*, K. 125h; fellow Freemason. Friend of Goethe.

Leo, Leonardo 1694–1744

Italian instrumental and opera composer; teacher of Jomelli and Piccinni.

Leon, Gottlieb   c. 1750–1800?

Viennese poet, fellow Freemason; collaborator with Mozart on two lost songs.

Leopold II   1747–1792

Austrian Emperor, 1790–1792; second son of Empress Maria Theresia.

Le Picq, Charles   1744–1806

Touring French dancer for whom Mozart wrote K. 73a, who worked with Noverre on dances for *Lucio Silla* in Milan (1772), and whose ability Mozart admired, mentioning him in K. 584.

Lerchenfeld, Baron Hermann von   1723–1800

Father of melomane Countess Baumgarten. He and his wife (1732–1819) were supportive of Mozart while he was composing *Idomeneo* in Munich (1780).

LeRoy, François   c. 1730–1790?

Parisian publisher of early editions of Mozart's music.

Lessing, Gotthold Ephraim   1729–1781

A major 18th century German writer whose works Mozart and Haydn read.

Leuckart, F. E. C.   1748–1817

Important Breslau publisher whose firm was founded in 1782; published early editions of Mozart.

Leutgeb, Joseph Ignaz   1745–1811

Austrian horn player, pupil, friend of Mozart, for whom he composed horn concertos.

Levy, Hermann   1839–1900

Distinguished Mozart conductor; translator of *Figaro, Don Giovanni, Così fan tutte.*

Lichnowsky, Prince Karl   1755–1814

Viennese friend, fellow Freemason, and pupil of Mozart. Son-in-law of Countess Thun.

Lichtenberg, Karl Friedrich   c. 1750–1810?
Librettist for Georg Joseph Vogler, German opera composer, active in Mannheim.

Lickl, Johann Georg   1769–1843
Austrian church, instrumental, and theatre composer active in Vienna.

Liebeskind, August Jakob   c. 1740–1800?
Author of tale, "Lulu oder die Zauberflöte," published in Wieland's collection *Dschinnisten.*

Liechtenstein, Prince Alois   1759–1805
Son of one of Empress Maria Theresia's favorite generals, a patron of Mozart.

Lierzer, Jakob von   c. 1750–1800?
Viennese friend of Mozart.

Ligniville, Marquis Eugenio   1730–1778
Italian composer and director of music at the Tuscan court where Mozart met him.

Lindemayer, Abbé Maurus   1723–1783
Lambach conductor and literary man.

Linka, Jiri   1725–1791
Czechoslovakian composer of symphonies and choral works.

Linley, Thomas   1756–1781
English composer and violinist who performed with Mozart in Italy, brother of soprano Elizabeth Linley (1754–1792), wife of Richard Brinsley Sheridan.

Lipp, Franz Ignaz   1734–1790
Salzburg second court organist, whose playing Mozart did not like. Father of singer Magdalena Lipp Haydn.

Lippert, Friedrich Karl   c. 1755–1805
Viennese tenor, also active in Berlin, who sang leading roles in *Die*

Entführung, Figaro, and *Don Giovanni,* (which he later translated); also translated librettos for Süssmayr, Gassmann, Guglielmi, Leseur.

Liste, Anton 1774–1832
Vienna piano pupil of Mozart (1788).

Livigni, Filippo c. 1750–1800?
Italian librettist for Paisiello, Anfossi, Cherubini, Cimarosa, etc.

Livraghi, Luigi c. 1740–1790?
Italian oboist who performed with Mozart in Mantua (1770).

Locatelli, Pietro 1693–1764
Important Italian composer Mozart met in Amsterdam on his European tour.

Lodron, Countess Antonia (née Arco) 1738–1780
Member of noble Salzburg family, patron of the Mozarts, for whom Mozart composed K. 242, etc.

Logenmeister, ——— c. 1750–1800?
Viennese publisher of libretto to *Die Entführung.*

Löhlein, Georg 1725–1781
German composer, violinist, and theorist.

Loehmann, Norbert 1750–1820?
Organist at Prague Strahof Church who heard Mozart play the organ (1787). Admirer of Mozart and Haydn. His superior at Strahof was Johann Lohelius Oelschlagel (1724–1788).

Loibl, Johann Maria c. 1760–1810?
Viennese friend, neighbor, notary, music lover, fellow Freemason, wine merchant.

Lolli, Antonio 1730–1802
Touring Italian composer, violinist; his sister, the singer Brigida, was married to the dancer Giuseppe Anelli—connections of Mozart in 1770.

Lolli, Giuseppe 1767–1826

Italian singer who performed the Commendatore and Masetto in *Don Giovanni*, Prague (1787) and Leipzig (1788), etc.

Lolli, Giuseppe Francesco 1701–1778

Italian violinist, conductor, active in Salzburg (1763–1778).

Lorenzi, Giovanni Battista 1719–1805

Italian librettist for Haydn, Cimarosa, Tritto, Paisiello, Palma, etc.

Lorenziti, Joseph–Antoine 1730–1802

Italian instrumental composer and violinist active in Paris, whose work was not appreciated by Leopold Mozart.

Lorenzoni, Pietro Antonio 1721–1786

Italian painter, also active in Austria. Probable painter of the Mozarts.

Löschenkohl, Hieronymous 1753–1807

Successful engraver, artist, publisher of silhouettes, and music in Vienna. In 1807 the business was taken over by H. F. Müller.

Lotter, Johann Jacob c. 1726–1804

Augsburg publisher, son of founder of family business (1720–1844), family friend of Leopold Mozart. Published Wolfgang Mozart works in 1793.

Lotz, Theodor c. 1750–1810?

Czechoslovakian composer and performer on the viola, clarinet, bassoon, active in Vienna. Played Mozart's Masonic music.

Luchesi, Andrea 1741–1801

Venetian opera and instrumental composer whose works were known to Leopold Mozart.

Lugiati, Pietro 1730–1802

Verona host to Leopold and Wolfgang Mozart in 1770. Patron who commissioned portrait by Saverio dalla Rosa.

Lützow, Countess Antonia Czernin 1738–1780

Salzburg patron and keyboard pupil of Mozart. Wife of Count Johann Lützow (1742–1822).

Lyser, Johann Peter 1803–1870

German poet whose verses were set to Mozart's music, posthumously.

Mahaut, Antoine 1720–1785

French instrumental composer whose works were known to Leopold.

Mahlmann, August 1771–1821

Member of Schikaneder circle who collaborated on *Die Zauberflöte*.

Mainzer, Joseph 1801–1851

Instrumental composer, friend of Constanze and Nannerl, author of articles on Mozart, etc.

Majo, Gian Francesco 1732–1770

Pupil of Martini. Successful opera composer from 1758 in Naples, Rome, Vienna, whose work Mozart knew.

Maldère, Pierre van 1724–1768

Brussels court composer of operas and instrumental music, whose works Leopold knew.

Malherbe, Charles-Théodore 1853–1911

Librarian, Paris; collector of Mozartiana, including Leopold's *Verzeichnis* of Wolfgang's early works.

Malzat, Ignaz 1723–1797

Czechoslovakian instrumental composer, also active in Vienna (brother, Johann Michael, also a composer).

Mandini, Maria c. 1760–1800?

Sang Marcellina in Vienna premiere of *Figaro*, and other works of Mozart. Wife of Stefano Mandini.

Mandini, Paolo 1757–1842

Sang at Vienna Burg Theater in 1780s, and later in Paris.
Brother of Stefano Mandini.

Mandini, Stefano 1750–1810

Tenor in *Figaro* and other Mozart works in 1780s, Vienna. Possibly related to Giuditta Mandini, who sang in *Don Giovanni*.

Manfredini, Vincenzo 1757–1799

Successful touring Italian composer, violinist. His brother, Giuseppe (c. 1735–1790?), was a castrato.

Mann, Johann Christoph 1726–1782

Viennese instrumental composer.

Manna, Gennaro 1715–1779

Neapolitan opera composer whose works were known to Mozart.

Manservi, Rosa c. 1750–1800?

Soprano who sang Sandrina in Munich premiere of *La finta giardiniera* (1775). Sang in Vienna in 1780s.

Manservi, Teresina c. 1749–1800?

Soprano, sister of above, who sang Serpetta in *La finta giardiniera* premiere.

Mansfeld, Johann Georg 1764–1817

Member of family of prominent Viennese artists and engravers of music; brother of J. E. Mansfield (1738–1796), engraver.

Manzuoli, Giovanni 1725–1782

Italian castrato who sang in *Ascanio* premiere, Milan (1771), and publicized Mozart's music.

Mara, Gertrud Elisabeth 1749–1833

German touring soprano much appreciated in England. Mozart heard her qualities but preferred Lucrezia Agujari or Aloysia Weber.

Marchand, Gretl 1768–1800

Singer in several of Mozart's compositions. Daughter of Theobald Marchand, Munich theater director and Freemason; sister of Leopold's pupil, Heinrich Marchand (1769–1812); married to Franz Danzi (1763–1826).

Marchesi, Luigi 1755–1829

Italian male soprano active in Vienna in 1780s.

Marchetti-Fantozzi, Maria   1767–1807

Prague soprano, sang Vitellia in *La clemenza di Tito* premiere (1791); also sang in *Don Giovanni.*

Mareschalchi, Madalena   c. 1770–1800?

Prague soprano from 1790, also active in Vienna. (Related to Munich dancer?)

Mariani, Girolamo   c. 1740–1790?

Italian dancer active with Le Picq in Milan, and Mannheim.

Maria Carolina, Queen of the Two Scilies   1752–1814

Warmly welcomed Mozart to Naples.

Maria Theresia, Empress of Austria   1717–1780

A kindly, determined ruler who preferred Gluck and Haydn to Mozart, and generally was untouched by the arts.

Marinelli, Karl von   1744–1803

Playwright, actor, director of Leopoldstadt Theater, Vienna, in 1780s.

Mariottini, ——— c. 1750–1810?

Italian singer active in Vienna in 1780s.

Marivaux, Pierre Carlet de   1688–1763

Stylish French playwright who influenced Beaumarchais and the entire theatre world.

Marmontel, Jean-François   1723–1799

French writer whose *Les Incas* inspired Naumann's opera *Cora* (1799), and attracted Mozart, who however did not set a text by Marmontel.

Marpurg, Philipp Wilhelm   1718–1795

Esteemed composer and theorist, active in Berlin.

Martin, Jean Paul   1741–1816

French composer of popular works played when Mozart was in Paris.

Martin, Philipp Jakob   c. 1750–1800?

Director of concerts at the Mehlgrube, Vienna, where his friend Mozart often played.

Martin y Soler, Vicente 1754–1810

Spanish opera composer active in Italy; in Vienna in the 1780s, and later in Russia.

Martinez, Marianne von 1744–1812

Composer and pianist, pupil and friend of Joseph Haydn.

Martinelli, Gaetano c. 1750–1800?

Dresden composer of *La schiava liberata* (1777), a forerunner of *Die Entführung*.

Martini, Padre Giovanni Battista 1706–1784

Italian composer, theorist, maestro in Bologna. Esteemed friend and teacher of Mozart and many others.

Martini, J. P. A. (Schwarzendorff) 1741–1816

German composer of Italian descent active in Paris, for whose Viennese singspiel, *Il burbero di buon cuore*, Da Ponte wrote the text.

Mašek, Winzens 1755–1831

Prague opera and instrumental composer, pianist, publisher-arranger of *Figaro* (1787).

Masi, Maria c. 1750–1800?

Soprano active in Cremona in 1770s, where Mozart heard her (related to Masi the composer?)

Massoneau, Louis 1766–1848

French violinist and composer active in Germany.

Mattei, Stanislas 1750–1825

Bolognese instrumental composer.

Mattheson, Johann 1681–1764

Esteemed German poet; author of text of Anhang, C.8.25.

Maulberstch, Anton 1724–1796

Important Viennese painter and etcher, also active in Prague.

Maurer, Franz 1767–1831

Maurer, Franz   1767–1831
Singer active in Vienna from 1780s. Sang in *Die Zauberflöte*.

Mayer, Anton   c. 1750–1800?
Esterházy oboist in 1780s who played with Mozart.

Mayer, Friedrich Sebastian   1775–1835
Actor and bass singer with Schikaneder company from 1793. Married Josepha Weber in 1797 after her first husband, Karl Hofer, died.

Mayer, ——— c. 1750–1800?
Munich theatre director.

Mayr, Andrade   c. 1750–1800?
Violinist at Salzburg court in 1770.

Mayr, Johann Joseph   1740–1790
Salzburg printer of opera and theatre programs.

Mayr, Johann Simon   1763–1845
German opera and instrumental composer mostly active in Italy and Paris.

Maximilian III, Elector of Bavaria   1727–1777
Commissioned Mozart to compose *La finta giardiniera* (1775).

Mazziotti, Giuseppe   c. 1740–1790?
Castrato active in London when Mozart was there (1764).

Mazzo, Giovanni   1748–1790
Engraver, and stage and costume designer for *Lucio Silla* in Milan premiere (1772).

Mazzocci, D.   c. 1740–1790?
Leader of traveling company for whom Mozart composed K. 209 in Salzburg (1775).

Mazzola, Caterino   1740–1806
Saxon court poet and librettist for operas by Naumann, Paisiello,

clemenza di Tito.

Mechel, Christian von 1737–1817

Swiss artist, engraver active also in Italy, Paris, etc. Executed engravings of Carmontelle, etc.

Mecklenburg, Duke Georg August zu 1730–1785

Fellow Freemason, for whom Mozart composed K. 477 (also in memory of Count Franz Esterházy von Galántha).

Meder, Johann Gabriel c. 1735–1782

Viennese instrumental composer of symphonies, etc.

Mederitsch, Johann (also known as Ludwig Gall) 1752–1835

Viennese composer, conductor, pupil of Mozart (1783), who helped spread Mozart's music after Mozart's death.

Meisl, Karl 1775–1853

Collaborator of E. Schikaneder.

Meissner, Joseph 1724–1795

Salzburg singer in *La finta semplice,* etc. Later a theatre manager.

Meissner, August Gottlieb 1735–1807

Fellow Freemason. Librettist for Joseph Schuster and Franz Seydelmann in Dresden; worked with Koželuh and Süssmayr in Vienna; translator of works by Joseph Haydn.

Melani, Alessandro 1639–1703

Composer of *L'Empio punito,* "first 'Don Giovanni' opera," produced in Rome (1669).

Melschek, ——— c. 1750–1800?

Vienna friend, 1780s.

Mendel, Arthur 1905–1979

American musician, editor Breitkopf Mozart Edition (1956).

Menilglaize, Chevalier de c. 1740–1790?

French composer of a version of "La belle Françoise." cf. K. 300d.

Mergéry, Louis   c. 1760–1820?

Friend, French dancer active in Vienna in 1780s; collaborated with Mozart on a masquerade.

Merschner, C. F.   c. 1750–1800?

Successful "silhouettist" of prominent Viennese.

Mesmer, Dr. Anton   1734–1814

Long-time Viennese friend of Mozart family, in whose garden *Bastien und Bastienne* may have been premiered (1769). The Mesmers were music-lovers, but fickle connections, and also friendly with Righini, etc. Fellow Freemason.

Mestrino, Niccolo   1748–1790

Italian composer, violinist, active in Esterháza and Paris.

Metastasio, Pietro (real name Trapassi)   1698–1782

With Apostolo Zeno (1668–1750) probably the outstanding name among 18th-century librettists. His activity centered in Vienna; many of his texts were set by Mozart.

Metzger, Georg   1746–1793

Mannheim flutist and instrumental composer whom Mozart knew.

Meyer, Wilhelm   1759–1840

Librettist for the Viennese composer Johann Schenk, and translator of Shakespeare.

Meytens, Martin van   1695–1770

Stockholm painter who became a favorite artist of Empress Maria Theresia.

Miča, Frantisek Adam   1746–1811

Moravian symphony and opera composer, conductor active in Graz and Vienna.

Micelli, Caterina   c. 1760–1800?

Prague soprano active in 1780s and 1790s. Sang Donna Anna in premiere of *Don Giovanni* (1787).

Michaelansky, Joseph   c. 1740–1780?

Salzburg tenor in 1770s.

Michaud, J. B.   c. 1740–1789
Parisian publisher of early editions of Mozart's music.

Michel, Virgil (Joseph)   1745–1810?
Mannheim violoncellist, also active in Munich as an opera composer.

Mienzi, Daniella   c. 1750–1800?
Sang Celia in *Lucio Silla*, Milan premiere (1772).

Migazzi, Count C. B. A. 1714–1803
Vienna patron.

Miglivacca, Gianambrogio   1720–1791
Saxon court poet and librettist for Hasse, Gluck, Traeta, Myslivecek; also active in Milan, Vienna.

Miksch, Johann   1765–1845
German baritone active in Dresden.

Miller, Johann Martin   1750–1814
Text poet for K. 367a (349).

Millico, Giuseppe   1739–1812
Italian male soprano and composer, active at Vienna court in 1770s.

Mingotti, Regina Valentini   1722–1808
Soprano, pupil of Porpora in Naples, later active in Vienna, etc.; married to impressario Pietro Mingotti.

Mizler, Lorenz Christoph   1711–1778
Esteemed German music theorist and editor of Fux's *Gradus ad Parnassum*, which Mozart used.

Molière, Jean Baptiste Poquelin   1622–1673
France's great comic playwright in the age of Louis XIV, whose *Don Juan* and other plays Mozart read.

Molina, Tirso de (Gabriel Télles)   1571–1641
Spanish monk, reputed originator of "Don Giovanni" story.

Moline, Pierre Louis 1739–1820

French man of letters, translator of Gluck, Mozart, etc., and librettist of Anfossi, Cimarosa, Paisiello, Edelmann.

Mölk, Franz Felix von 1714–1776

Salzburg court chancellor, whose son courted Nannerl, and whose daughter attracted Wolfgang. Nothing came of either attraction.

Moll, ——— c. 1760–1820?

Bass, sang "Speaker" in Vienna premiere of *Die Zauberflöte.*

Möller, Heinrich Ferdinand 1745–1798

The Mozarts enjoyed his popular plays, produced by Schikaneder.

Mombelli, Domenico 1755–1838

Vienna tenor married to Luisa Laschi, Countess in *Figaro* premiere.

Momigny, Jerome Joseph de 1762–1842

Belgian composer, theorist who wrote on Mozart and Haydn. Active as Parisian publisher.

Monn, Georg Matthias 1717–1750

Important pre-classic symphonist and organist at Vienna's Karlskirche.

Monsigny, Pierre Alexandre 1729–1817

French opera composer; with Rigel, LeDuc, Grétry, and others, an influence on Mozart's style after 1778.

Montani, Giovanni c. 1740–1800?

Milan printer of *Mitridate* program (1770).

Montecuculli, Marquis François de 1767–1827

Amateur oboist, patron, pupil of Mozart (1784–1791?); fellow Freemason.

Monvel, Jacques Marie Boutet de 1745–1812

Actor, dramatic author, and French collaborator of Dézède, Champein, Dalayrac, etc.; also active touring.

Monza, Carlo 1740–1801

Milan theatre and sacred composer Mozart met in 1771. For an early Milan performance of *Figaro*, Monza "recomposed" Acts III and IV.

Morbili, Duke Nicola Giuseppe c. 1720–1790?

Librettist for Cafaro's opera *La disfatto di Dario* (1756). Revised by Paisiello, Traeta, and Tommaso Giordani (1730–1806) for Milan in 1789 with textual changes by Angioli; text used by Mozart in his "Mentre di lascio," K. 513.

Moreau, J. M. 1741–1814

French artist and stage designer also active in Vienna in 1780s.

Morella, Francesco c. 1760–1820?

Sang Don Ottavio in Vienna first performance of *Don Giovanni,* as well as other Mozart roles.

Morelli, Domenico c. 1750–1800?

Dancer in *Lucio Silla,* Milan (1772). Possibly related to dancer Elisabeth Morelli, and Maddalena Morelli (1727–1800), an Italian poet who admired Mozart.

Morelli, F. c. 1750–1800?

Italian composer, and librettist for Astarita, etc.

Moretti, Ferdinando c. 1750–1800?

Italian librettist for Bianchi, Cherubini, Cimarosa, Himmel, Sarti, Martin, Tarchi.

Morgnoni, Bassano c. 1750–1800?

Tenor in Milan premiere of *Lucio Silla* (1772).

Mörike, Eduard 1804–1875

Important German Romantic writer and poet whose short story "Mozart auf der Reise nach Prag" first appeared in 1853 in a Stuttgart periodical. (Frequently reprinted and translated.)

Moser, Franz Joseph 1717–1792

Well-known German theatre director active in Augsburg, Mannheim, etc. in 1770s and 1780s.

Moser, Jacobus 1751–1800

Sang Priest in Salzburg premiere of *Die Schuldigkeit* (1767).

Motta, Francesco c. 1740–1790?

Costume designer for premiere of *Lucio Silla*, Milan (1772).

Muffat, Gottlieb 1690–1770

Keyboard musician active in Vienna, whose works Mozart knew.

Müller, August Eberhard 1767–1817

Weimar composer, theorist, conductor, and keyboard player of Mozart's concertos, for which he wrote a guide to their performance. Also in Haydn circle.

Müller, Johann (Schröter) 1738–1815

Viennese actor, poet, author of text to several numbers of *Bastien und Bastienne* (most of the text was adapted from the French by Weiskern). Fellow Freemason.

Müller, Josepha Hortensia c. 1770–1820

Daughter of above, piano pupil of Mozart c. 1785; she married painter Heinrich Füger in 1791.

Müller, Silverius 1745–1812

Viennese church and instrumental composer.

Müller, Wenzel 1767–1835

Prolific Viennese composer and conductor, whose *Kaspar der Fagottist* (with text by Joachim Perinet) was produced in 1791.

Müllner, Josepha (later Frau Gollenhofer) 1770–1823

Viennese harpist who performed at a concert with Mozart in 1788.

Münter, Friedrich 1761–1830

Fellow Freemason in Vienna.

Muschietti, Pietro c. 1740–1800?

Male soprano, sang Arbate in the premiere of *Mitridate* K. 74(87), Milan (1770).

Müthel, Johann Gottfried 1728–1788

German composer of keyboard music and songs.

Mysliveček, Josef 1737–1781

Bohemian composer of Italian operas active in Italy, Munich, Vienna. Warm friend of Mozart.

Nägeli, Hans Georg 1773–1836

Swiss composer, writer, publisher who stated Mozart's music was too modern. Nägeli's works were confused with those of Mozart.

Nardini, Pietro 1722–1793

Composer, violinist admired by Leopold and Wolfgang. With Tartini, St. Georges, and Boccherini an apparent influence on Mozart's music for violin.

Nassau-Weilburg, Princess Caroline von 1743–1793

Heard Mozart as a boy in England. Later a keyboard pupil in Mannheim (1777).

Natorp, Nanette 1766–1791

With her sister, Babette Natorp Jacquin (1769–1844), a pupil of Mozart from 1787. Both performed Mozart's music in public.

Naumann, Johann Gottlieb 1741–1801

Fellow Freemason; Dresden composer in many forms, whose *Osiris* (1782) with libretto by Mazzola perhaps was one of the inspirations of *Die Zauberflöte.*

Navoigille, Guillaume 1745–1811

French composer whose works (and those of his brother) were played at the Concert Spirituel when Mozart was in Paris.

Neefe, Christian Gottlob 1748–1798

German composer, conductor, arranger who taught Beethoven in Bonn. Neefe's *Adelheit von Veltheim,* with libretto by Friedrich Wilhelm Grossmann (1780), was one of several operas preceding *Die Entführung* which was devoted to a Turkish theme. Fellow Freemason.

Neidl, Johann H. 1776–1832

Viennese artist and engraver.

Nenzini, Santo c. 1760–1810?

Bass singer active in Vienna from 1790, previously in Esterháza.

Neruda, Johann Baptist Georg   1707–1776
Czechoslovakian instrumental composer and violinist, also active in Dresden.

Nesslthaler, ——— c. 1740–1800?
Viennese stage designer of *Die Zauberflöte*.. Relative of Salzburg painter, Andreas Nesslthaler (c. 1770–1820?) who painted Joseph Haydn.

Neubauer, Franz Christoph   1760–1795
Czechoslovakian opera and instrumental composer and violinist active in Vienna and Germany in 1780s. Collaborator of Schickaneder.

Neumann, Johann Leopold   1748–1818
Dresden secretary to Saxon State Council; opera librettist and translator; patron and friend of the Dučeks.

Nicolai, Christoph Friedrich   1733–1811
Berlin musician with whom Gebler discussed music for his *Thamos* in the 1770s.

Niccolini, Carlo   c. 1740–1790
Castrato who sang with Mozart in Florence (1770), etc.

Niemetschek, Franz Peter   1766–1849
Czechoslovakian professor who knew Mozart, and published a brief biography in 1798.

Niklas, Sophie Semler   c. 1760–1810?
German soprano who sang Constanze in *Die Entführung* and other roles in Berlin in 1780s. Member of a musical family who knew Mozart.

Nilson, J. E.   1721–1788
Engraver of Aloysia Weber's portrait. Friend of Mozart.

Nissen, Georg Nikolaus von   1765–1826
Danish diplomat, second husband of Constanze Weber Mozart. Author of first comprehensive biography of Mozart, published posthumously by Breitkopf & Härtel.

Noailles, Duke Louis de c. 1740–1790?

Gracious melomane host of Mozart in Saint-Germain in 1778.

Nohl, K. Fr. Ludwig 1831–1885

Important Mozart researcher; author of *Mozarts Leben,* etc.

Nopitsch, Christoph F. W. 1758–1810

Organist, theorist, and instrumental composer from Nuremberg.

Nostitz, Count Franz Anton 1706–1787

Friend and patron of Mozart; relative of Count Nepomuk Nostitz, operetta composer.

Nottebohm, Martin Gustav 1817–1882

Viennese collector of Mozart autographs, author of *Mozartiana,* editor of Breitkopf Mozart Edition (1877–1882).

Nouseul, Johann Joseph 1742–1821

Viennese singing actor who performed Monostatos in *Die Zauberflöte* premiere (1791).

Novello, Vincent 1781–1861

English composer, writer, and founder of Novello and Company, publishers. Mozart admirer and collector; he and his wife went to Salzburg to meet Nannerl and Constanze.

Noverre, Jean-Georges 1727–1810

Great French choreographer, active also in Vienna, Milan, Stuttgart, London. Choreographer of Mozart's *Ascanio* (1771) and *Les petits riens* (1778). (Married Marie-Louise Sauveur, c. 1750–1810.)

Novotny, Ferenc 1749–1806

Hungarian church and instrumental composer and organist at Esterháza.

Oettingen-Wallerstein, Count Ernst von 1748–1802

Admirer and patron of Mozart from 1770, as were others in his family.

Ollivier, Michel-Barthelémy 1712–1784

French painter of "Prince de Conti's Drawing Room," with the singer Jélyote and Mozart at the harpsichord (1764).

Onofrio, Giuseppe   c. 1750–1810?
Tenor singing Aufidio in Milan premiere of *Lucio Silla* (1772).

d'Ordonez, Carlo   1734–1786
Spanish instrumental composer active in Vienna; fellow Freemason.

Orsi, Angelo   c. 1740–1800?
Italian violinist who performed with Mozart in Mantua (1770).

Orsler, Joseph   1772–1806
Vienna court violoncellist, composer, chamber player. Friend of Mozart; attended funeral.

Ostad, Fr.   ?
Composer whose works Mozart knew.

Ottani, Bernadino   1735–1827
Successful composer whose works Mozart heard in Bologna.

Overbeck, Christian   1735–1821
Text poet of Mozart songs, K. 596, 598 (1791).

Ozi, Etienne   1754–1813
French instrumental composer, and publisher, who played bassoon in the Concert Spirituel. Member of a musical family.

Paar, Prince Wenzel Johann   1719–1792
Viennese friend and patron of Mozart. Fellow Freemason.

Pachta, Count Johann von   1760–1822
Prague patron for whom Mozart composed K. 509.

Paganelli, Giuseppe Antonio   1710–1763
Italian vocal and instrumental composer also active in Germany and Spain, whose music Leopold taught young Mozart.

Paisiello, Giovanni   1741–1816
Important Italian composer whose works were performed throughout Europe. Mozart wrote several arias to be inserted in his operas.

Paladini, Giuseppe c. 1710–1770?

Milanese vocal and instrumental composer whose music Leopold taught to young Mozart.

Pálffy, Countess Josepha 1765–1810?

Vienna patron and piano pupil in 1782. Prince Joseph Pálffy (1764–1827) was also a patron, and a fellow Freemason.

Pallavicini, Count Gian Luca 1697–1773

Bolognese patron of Mozart in 1770.

Pallotta, Matero c. 1730–1790?

Italian composer, also active in Vienna.

Palmini, Elena Rosa c. 1760–1810?

Probably sang K. 255, Innsbruck (1776; Carlo Saramondi, tenor, sang K. 256.)

Palomba, Giuseppe c. 1750–1810?

Collaborator with Fioravanti and Valentino, and librettist for Cimarosa's opera *I due baroni*, for which Mozart composed K. 578, an aria used in Vienna production (1789).

Pampini (or Pampani), Antonio Gaetano 1705–1775

Roman vocal composer whose music Leopold taught young Mozart.

Paneck, Johann Baptist c. 1760–1810?

Opera conductor and composer active in Austrian Empire cities from 1789 (collaborator with F. X. Girzik).

Panny, Joseph c. 1780–1840?

Salzburg violinist, and collector of Mozart manuscripts.

Panzacchi, Domenico de 1733–1805

Italian tenor who sang Arbace in Munich premiere of *Idomeneo* (1781).

Paradeiser, Carl 1747–1775?

Melk composer of symphonies and other instrumental works.

Paradies, Maria Theresia 1759–1824

Blind Viennese composer and keyboard pupil of Mozart, for whom he composed K. 456 (1782).

Paradies, Petro Domenico 1707–1791

Italian composer who settled in England whose works Mozart knew; teacher of Linley.

Parhamer, Ignaz 1715–1786

Important Viennese educator and melomane.

Parini, Giuseppe 1729–1799

Librettist for Mozart's *Mitridate* and *Ascanio*.

Paris, ——— c. 1750–1810?

Sang Nardo in *La finta giardiniera* premiere, Munich (1775).

Paris, Anton? 1739–1809

Salzburg court organist (1777).

Parke, W. T. 1762–1847

English musician and writer who praised Mozart's operas, but not his other music.

Partsch, Placidus c. 1760–1810?

Viennese musician and editor of Mozart compositions published by Alberti.

Pasqualati, Joseph 1733–1799

Salzburg violinist, and collector of Mozart manuscripts.

Pasquini, Giovanni Claudio 1695–1763

Prolific librettist, active in Vienna and Dresden, collaborating with Bonno, Hasse, Caldara. Mozart used his text in K. 295, an aria for Anton Raaf.

Passy, Joseph 1758–1809

Viennese fellow Freemason and friend.

Pasterwitz, Father Georg 1730–1803

Cleric, composer of symphonies and other instrumental music appreciated by Mozart. Early teacher of Süssmayr.

Pater, Johann Ferdinand c. 1720–1780?

Munich chamber musician and copyist.

Pauler, Desideria von c. 1750–1800?

Amateur singer who appeared in concert with Mozart and Josephine Auernhammer (1782).

Pauersbach, Joseph von c. 1740–1800?

Austrian writer, librettist whose work Mozart knew; director of the Esterháza-marionette theatre.

Peisser, Franz X. c. 1740–1800

Mozart family friend from Vienna.

Perelli, Domenico c. 1750–1800?

Italian librettist for Cimarosa, Gazzaniga, etc. Member of a musical family.

Perez, Davide 1711–1778

Neapolitan composer whose music Mozart appreciated when he heard it in London (1764).

Pergolesi, Giovanni Battista 1710–1736

Important Italian composer whose music Mozart knew.

Perillo, Salvatore c. 1730–1790?

Venetian opera composer of *La finta semplice* (1764).

Perinet, Joachim 1763–1816

Viennese lawyer and prolific librettist for Wenzel Müller, etc.

Perini, Carolina, Anchulina c. 1770–1820?

Prague alto who sang Annio in *La clemenza di Tito* premiere (1791).

Perotti, Giovanni Domenico   c. 1740–1800?

Roman composer whose music Leopold appreciated.

Perwein, Ignaz   1758–1812

Salzburg organist, teacher, friend of the Mozart family.

Pescetti, Giovanni   1704–1766

Venetian composer, organist, pupil of Lotti, whose music Leopold taught young Mozart.

Pesch, Karl August   1730–1793

German composer, violinist Mozart met in Frankfurt (1763).

Peters, Carl Friedrich   1779–1827

Leipzig musician, associated as publisher with Ambrosius Kühnel.

Petit, ——— c. 1710–1754

Composer whose music Leopold appreciated. (Related to bassoon player, or horn player, in Concert Spirituel, Paris?)

Petran, Franz   c. 1750–1810?

Czechoslovakian text poet for K. 471 (1785); fellow Freemason.

Petri, Johann   1738–1790?

German singer and theorist.

Petroni, Franz   c. 1750–1810?

Tenor who sang Belfiore in *La finta giardiniera* premiere in Munich (1775).

Petrosellini, Giuseppe (Abbate)   1727–1799

Poet active in Germany, Russia, Vienna as librettist for Accorimboni, Anfossi, Paisiello, Piccinni, Salieri, etc. Texts for Mozart include K. 196, 424b, 256.

Peyerl, Elise   1761–1800

German soprano, who with her husband, tenor Johann Nepomuk, sang Mozart canons, K. 559, 560.

Pfeiffer, Carl Hermann   1769–1829

German artist, engraver, active in Leipzig.

Philidor, François André Danican   1726–1795

French opera composer who had an influence on Mozart.

Pian, Antonio di   1784–1851

Important Italian stage designer of Mozart productions in the early 19th century.

Piantanida, Giovanni   1705–1782

Italian composer and violinist centered in Verona.

Piccinelli, Marianna (called La Francesina)   c. 1750–1790?

Italian singer (née Soleri de Vesian) active in Vienna in 1780s, with her husband Antonio Francesco Piccinelli.

Piccinni, Nicola   1728–1800

Famous Italian composer active throughout Europe, for several of whose operas Mozart wrote arias for insertion.

Pichl, Wenzel   1741–1805

Bohemian composer, violinist, and copyist, also active in Vienna and Italy.

Pichelberger, Friedrich   c. 1750–1810?

Viennese double bass player and member of Schikaneder circle.

Pichler, Johann   1765–1806

Engraver active in Vienna in 1780s. Colleague of Franz Wrenk (1766–1830) and F. X. Müller (1756–1837).

Pichler, Caroline von   1769–1843

Austrian pianist who received "inspiration" from playing four hands with Mozart (1790), and who wrote useful memoirs abour her artistic family relationships.

Picinelli, Clémentine   c. 1740–1780?

French soprano who sang at one of Mozart's concerts, Paris (1764).

Pietragrua, Xaver   c. 1740–1800

Violoncellist Mozart knew in Mannheim in 1770s.

Pietscher, Maria Anna 1732–1805
Viennese friend in 1780s.

Pinottini, Teresa Agnesa 1720–1795
Italian opera composer Mozart met in 1770.

Pinzger, Andreas 1740–1817
Violinist active in Salzburg in 1770s.

Pio, Antonio c. 1750–1800?
Italian opera composer and conductor active in Ravenna and Venice whose work was known to Mozart.

Piovene, Agostino c. 1690–1760?
Venetian opera librettist for Orlandini, Gasparini, Handel, Mysliveček, and others.

Pirker, Marianne 1717–1782
Prominent German soprano.

Pirkmayer, Friedrich c. 1740–1790?
Salzburger who mentioned Mozart in his diary.

Pitocchio, Francesco c. 1740–1800?
Italian opera and instrumental composer, also active in Dresden and Vienna in 1780s.

Pitoni, Giuseppe 1657–1743
Italian composer of a melody Mozart adapted in both *La Betulia* and *Die Zauberflöte*.

Pizzini von Thürberg, Baron Gian Giulio 1719–1779
Veronese music patron who was Mozart's host in 1771.

Platania, Ignazio c. 1740–1800?
Italian opera composer whose music Mozart heard in 1770s.

Platzer, Josef 1751–1806
Member of family of outstanding Prague stage designers whose work was also seen in Vienna (*Figaro, Don Giovanni*, etc.).

Plazzeriani, Barbara c. 1755–1810

Wife of Leutgeb, heir to her father's cheese business in Vienna.

Pleyel, Ignaz 1757–1831

Successful Austrian composer, pupil of Haydn, who went to Paris; also publisher, and piano maker.

Ployer, Barbara von (later Frau Bojanovich) 1765–1811

Daughter of a Viennese patron (and fellow Freemason), one of Mozart's best keyboard pupils in Vienna (1784). Mozart performed with her, and composed several concertos for her. Haydn also composed for her.

Plümicke, Karl Martin c. 1730–1790?

Playwright, whose *Lanassa* (performed by Johann Böhm's traveling company) was produced with music by Mozart, including K. 184, and perhaps music from *Thamos* (K. 345). Also librettist for Karl Hanke (c. 1740–1790?), etc.

Podleská, Thekla Batka 1764–1852

Bohemian singer of Mozart roles in Prague and Vienna in 1780s, who also had a collection of Mozart manuscripts.

Podstatzky, Count Leopold von c. 1740–179-?

Austrian nobleman from Olmütz friendly to the Mozart family.

Pohl, Wilhelm c. 1750–1800?

Viennese song composer active in 1780s.

Polzelli, Luigia 1760–1832

Soprano in whom Joseph Haydn had a particular interest.

Poggi, Domenico c. 1740–1791

Singer at Vienna court opera, originally scheduled to perform in *La finta semplice*; cancelled because of intrigue.

Pokorny, Gotthard 1728–1794

Bohemian composer, organist, violinist, also active in Vienna; father of Magdalena Hofdemel.

Ponziani, Felice c. 1750–1800?

Singer active in Prague and Leipzig in 1780s, performing Leporello in *Don Giovanni*, and other Mozart roles.

Porpora, Niccolò 1686–1766

Italian composer, also active in London, Bremen, and Vienna (where Joseph Haydn worked with him).

Porro, Pierre Joseph 1759–1831

Parisian publisher of early editions of Mozart's music.

Porta, Nunziato c. 1750–1810?

Librettist whose texts were set by Sarti, Joseph Haydn, etc.

Posch, Leonard 1750–1831

Artist, engraver active in Vienna and Berlin.

Potter, Cipriani 1792–1871

English composer who edited Mozart's "complete" piano works for Coventry, beginning in 1836.

Potterie, Ferdinand de la c. 1760–1810?

Mannheim piano pupil of Mozart in 1777.

Pozzi, Carlo c. 1750–1800?

Italian composer who, with Angelo Tarchi and Giovanni Paisiello, "recomposed" sections of *Le nozze di Figaro* for an Italian production. Also active in England and Russia.

Prati, Alessio 1746–1788

Italian opera composer, also active in Munich, Paris, etc., whose music Leopold Mozart knew.

Prato, Vincenzo dal 1756–1828

Castrato who sang Idamante in Munich *Idomeneo* premiere (1781).

Praupner, Vaclav 1745–1807

Composer, violinist, organist in Vienna, and friend of Mozart.

Predieri, Luc'Antonio 1688–1769

Italian opera and church composer whose works Mozart knew.

Preindl, Joseph 1756–1823
Composer, organist, choirmaster at Vienna's Saint Stephen cathedral.

Preisig, ——— c. 1760–1820?
Stage designer for last scene of *La clemenza di Tito* (1791), Prague premiere; Pietro Travaglia designed the first three scenes.

Preisler, Johann Georg 1757–1808
German artist, engraver who worked for Breitkopf & Härtel, etc.

Preu, Friedrich c. 1750–1800?
German opera composer active in Dresden and Leipzig in 1770s and 1780s whose work Mozart knew. Collaborator of Bretzner.

Prinz, Johann Friedrich 1775–1819
Flutist who performed with Mozart in Dresden (1789).

Proney, Baron Alexander 1760–1839
Viennese fellow Freemason.

Puchberg, Johann Michael 1741–1822
Freemason and close Viennese friend from 1784, who lent Mozart considerable sums, most of which were never repaid.

Pufendorf, Anna Posch von 1757–1843
Soprano who performed Ilia in the Vienna performance of *Idomeneo* (1786). Wife of Konrad von Pufendorf.

Pugnani, Gaetano 1731–1798
Italian composer of operas and instrumental works and violinist, active in London when Mozart was there.

Pugnetti, ——— c. 1760–1810?
Italian bass singer, active at Vienna court opera in 1780s.

Pulini, Baron von 1760–1820?
Tenor who performed Idamante in the Vienna performance of *Idomeneo* (1786).

Punto, Giovanni (Johann Wenzel Stich)   1746–1803

Bohemian composer, horn player, also active in Germany and Paris. Mozart composed Anh. C.14.01 (297b) with Punto in mind for the horn solo.

Puthon, Baron Johann von   1745–1816

Viennese merchant, fellow Freemason, patron of Mozart.

Puttini, Francesco   c. 1740–1800?

Librettist for Anfossi in Rome (1776), *La vera costanze*. Haydn and Travaglia adapted the libretto for use in 1779.

Quaglio, Lorenzo   1730–1805

Stage designer for Munich premiere of *Idomeneo* (1781). His brother Joseph (1745–1828) collaborated on the Vienna (1788) and Mannheim (1789) productions of *Don Giovanni*, and the Munich premiere of *Die Zauberflöte*.

Quallenberg, Elisabeth   c. 1750–1810?

Longtime friend of Mozart, wife of Munich clarinettist.

Quantz, Johann Joachim   1697–1773

Berlin composer, harpsichordist for Friedrich II (der Grosse). Quantz's music was known to Leopold.

Quénédy, E.   1756–1830

Active French artist who made likenesses of musicians (including Mozart and Haydn) in several media.

Querfurth, Franz   c. 1740–1790?

German instrumental composer of symphonies.

Raab, Marie Anna   c. 1740–1800?

Longtime landlady of Mozart family in Salzburg, related to Dr. Ignaz Raab of Vienna.

Raaff, Anton   1714–1797

Celebrated German tenor also active in Italy and Paris. A good friend of Mozart, he sang the title role in the Munich premiere of *Idomeneo* (1781).

Racine, Jean 1639–1699

Distinguished French playwright, author of *Mitridate.*

Rackemann, F. C. 1735–1795?

Berlin composer whose music Leopold taught young Mozart.

Ragué, Louis Charles c. 1755–1794?

French composer (also known in London), whose music was popular when Mozart was in Paris.

Ramm, Friedrich 1744–1811

Important German oboist who played in Munich premiere of *Idomeneo* (1781); Mozart wrote a solo for him in K.368b.

Rathgeber, Valentin 1682–1750

Augsburg composer whose works Mozart knew.

Ratschky, Franz Joseph von 1757–1810

Fellow Freemason in Vienna, and text poet of K. 468.

Raupach, Hermann Friedrich 1728–1778

German composer and keyboard player, also active in Paris and Russia. Mozart adapted Raupach works for his early concertos: K. 37, 39, 41.

Rautenstrauch, Johann 1746–1801

Austrian poet and writer, collaborator of Süssmayr.

Rauzzini, Venanzio 1746–1810

Member of musical family, composer and castrato who sang in Mozart's *Lucio Silla* (1772), and for whom Mozart wrote "Exsultate Jubilate," K. 165. Settled in London in 1774.

Redwen, ——— c. 1760–1810?

Danseuse in Munich premiere of *Idomeneo* (1781).

Reicha, Joseph 1750–1795

Czechoslovakian composer, violoncellist, friend of Mozart family, uncle of Anton Reicha (1770–1836).

Reichardt, Johann Friedrich 1752–1814

German composer, conductor, writer; he appreciated Nanette von

Schaden's playing of Mozart keyboard works in Augsburg (1790).

Reichsiegel, P. Florian   1735–1793

Austrian singspiel composer active in 1770s, friendly with the Mozart family.

Reinecke, Carl   1824–1910

German composer, pianist, member of Breitkopf Mozart Edition editorial board (1877–1883).

Reiner, Felix   1732–1783

Munich bassoon player whom Mozart knew.

Rellstab, Johann Carl Friedrich   1759–1813

German opera composer, and publisher of Mozart's music, mostly active in Berlin and Hamburg.

Reuling, Karl Ludwig   c. 1740–1800?

German singspiel librettist and translator active in 1770s, whose works Mozart saw in Munich.

Reutter, Johann Adam Karl Georg   1708–1772

Viennese composer, and conductor at Saint Stephen cathedral.

Ricci, Pasquale   1733–1817

Italian composer active in Como whose music Mozart knew, particularly the canons.

Richard, ———   c. 1750–1810?

French composer and bassoon player in the Concert Spirituel from the 1770s.

Richault, Charles Simon   1780–1860

Paris publisher, whose firm issued Mozart first editions.

Richter, Franz Xaver   1709–1789

Strasbourg composer, also active on tour.

Richter, Georg Friedrich   1750–1789?

Viennese composer, pianist, at whose concerts Mozart played. (Related to Philipp Richter, collaborator of Schikaneder?)

Riedsel, Carl F.   1769–1824

Artist, engraver active in Vienna and Leipzig from 1780s.

Riedsel, Joseph Hermann von   1740–1785

Prussian ambassador to Vienna who admired *Die Entführung*.

Rieger, Gottfried   c. 1720–1800?

Austrian instrumental composer.

Riepel, Joseph   1709–1782

German instrumental composer active in Regensburg and Vienna.

Rietz, Julius   1812–1877

Composer, conductor active in Dresden, who edited eight operas in the Breitkopf Mozart Edition (1877–1883).

Rigel, Henri-Joseph   1741–1799

German composer active in Paris from 1770. A "French" influence on Mozart, and Haydn.

Righini, Henriette Kneisel   1767–1801

Soprano, active in Mozart roles in Berlin from 1790; second wife of Vincenzo Righini.

Righini, Vincenzo   1756–1812

Tenor and Italian composer of *Il convitato di Pietra*, Vienna (1777), also active in Mainz. First married to Anna Lehritter (1762–1793). Attended Mozart's funeral.

Rigler, Franz Xaver   c. 1740–1796

Viennese composer in Hatzfeld circle.

Rinaldo da Capua   1705–1789

Roman opera composer, also active in Paris. Teacher of Salzburg composer Friedrich Wilhelm Rust.

Ringmacher, Christian Ulrich   1742–1781

Berlin music distributor of works by Bach, Handel, Haydn, Pergolesi,

Quantz, Rameau, Stamitz, Vivaldi, etc. Valuable for identifying (through his catalogues) over 600 works by Mozart's contemporaries.

Riotte, P. J. c. 1760–1811
Instrumental composer active in Vienna.

Ritter, Georg 1748–1808
Mannheim composer and touring bassoon player, for whom Mozart composed a solo in C.14.01 (297b).

Robineig von Rottenfeld 1750s on
Salzburg family friendly to the Mozarts.

Rochlitz, Johann Friedrich 1769–1842
Leipzig writer on music (including Mozart), founding editor of *Allgemeine musikalische Zeitung.*

Rodolphe, Jean Joseph 1730–1812
French composer in Royal service who offered Mozart the position of Versailles organist in 1778.

Roeser, Valentin 1735–1782
German-born horn player and composer of instrumental music also active in France; translator of Leopold Mozart's *Violinschule* into French, published by LeMenu (1770).

Rolla, Alessandro 1757–1841
Italian instrumental composer and violinist also active in Vienna.

Rolle, Johann Heinrich 1716–1785
German opera and instrumental composer, conductor, centered in Magdeburg and Leipzig.

Röllig, Karl Leopold 1761–1804
Viennese composer of attractive concertos for several wind instruments who was also very active in Germany.

Romani, Felice c. 1740–1800?
German singspiel composer active in Vienna in 1780s.

Romberg, Andreas c. 1767–1821

German instrumental composer, also active in Vienna.

Rosa, Joseph (Roos) 1726–1805

Director of Viennese Imperial Picture Gallery, friend of the Mozarts.

Rosa, Pietro c. 1740–1790?

Director of touring company in 1770s; personnel included Rosa Palmini, Andrea Chiappini, Carlo Seramondi.

Orsini-Rosenberg, Count Franz Xaver Wolf 1723–1796

Director of Vienna court theatres from 1776.

Roser, Franz de Paula 1779–1830

Composer (and piano pupil of Mozart in 1789); his musician father, Johann Georg Roser (1740–1797), attended Mozart's funeral.

Rosetti (Rössler), Anton 1750–1792

Prague composer, conductor, later active in Berlin, etc., whose music Mozart knew.

Rossi, Felice (?) c. 1750–1810?

Tenor who appeared in Munich premiere of *La finta giardiniera* (1775): later a poet.

Rossmäsler, Johann August c. 1760–1830

Artist, engraver of frontispiece for K. 621, and other early editions of Mozart published by Breitkopf & Härtel.

Roth, W. A. T. 1720–1765

German composer whose music Leopold taught young Mozart.

Rothfischer, Paul 1746–1785

Composer, conductor, violinist in service of Princess Nassau-Weilburg whom Mozart met in Mannheim, and liked.

Rousseau, Jean Jacques 1712–1778

French philosopher, and composer of *Le Devin du village* (1752), etc.

Rück, Ulrich   c. 1770–1820?

German pianist whose Mozart performances evoked warm praise in 1790s.

Rudorff, Ernst   1840–1916

Berlin composer, collector of Mozart manuscripts, member of editorial board of Breitkopf Mozart Edition (1877–1883).

Rugietz, ———   c. 1740–1790?

German instrumental composer of symphonies in 1770s.

Rupp, Martin von   1748–1819

Solo horn in Vienna, 1782–1806. Colleague of Eisen, Schmidt, Hörmann, and the Steinmüller brothers.

Ruprecht, Anton   1750–1806

Tenor in Munich opera from 1770s, member of musical family, including brother Joseph (trumpeter).

Ruprecht, Martin   1758–1800

Singspiel composer active in Vienna in 1780s.

Rust, Jakob (Giacomo)   1739–1796

German composer, conductor, active in Salzburg in 1770s.

Rutini, Giovanni Maria   1723–1797

Florentine opera and instrumental composer, also active in Austria and Germany, etc.

Ryba, Jakub   1765–1815

Prolific Bohemian composer of vocal and instrumental works.

Saal, Ignaz   1761–1836

Bass singer at the Vienna court opera in the 1780s, who performed under Mozart in *Messiah* (1789).

Sacchi, Regina   1764–1823

Italian violinist, also active in Paris and Germany, married to Conrad Schlick. Her playing is said to have pleased Mozart.

Sacchetti, Vincenzo 1759–1829

Italian stage designer active in Vienna and elsewhere in Mozart opera productions (probably after Mozart's death).

Sacchi, Giovenale 1726–1789

Milan musical theorist respected by Mozart.

Sacchini, Antonio 1730–1786

Popular Italian composer, several of whose operas Mozart saw.

Sacco, Johanna c. 1750–1800?

Viennese actress in premiere of *Der Schauspieldirektor*.

Sagredo, Berberigo c. 1650–1720?

Italian author Mozart read.

Saint-Georges, Chevalier de 1734–1799

French instrumental composer whose music Mozart heard in Paris.

Saint–Huberty, Antoinette 1756–1812

French soprano who also toured, whom Mozart heard sing Gluck at the Concert Spirituel.

Salamoni, Giuseppe c. 1750–1800?

Dancer in Milan premiere of *Lucio Silla* (1772).

Saldo, Wenzel c. 1750–1800?

Violinist active at Salzburg court in the 1770s.

Salern, Count Joseph von 1718–1805

Director of Munich opera; friendly with Mozart.

Sales, Pompeo 1729–1797

Italian opera and instrumental composer, also active in Munich and London. Leopold taught his music to young Mozart.

Salis-Seewis, J. G. von 1762–1834

Writer, librettist, text poet for K. 530 (also for Schubert and others).

Salieri, Antonio 1750–1825

Italian composer at Vienna court, unfriendly to Mozart, but attended his funeral. Freemason (?)

Sallaba, Matthias von 1754–1813

Physician to Mozart in Vienna.

Sallins von Lamezon, Count Joseph c. 1750–1810?

Viennese patron of Mozart's concerts.

Salomon, Johann Peter 1745–1815

German violinist and promoter of the music of Haydn in London, where he also conducted Mozart symphonies from 1786.

Sambach, Christian 1715–1795

Viennese artist, engraver, collaborator of Maulbertsch.

Samber, Johann Baptist 1654–1717

Salzburg composer whose music may have touched Mozart.

Sammartini, Giovanni Battista 1700–1775

Important Milanese composer, whose music Mozart knew.

Santi, Alfonso c. 1750–1800?

Italian opera composer whose work Mozart knew.

Saporiti, Teresa 1763–1839?

Sang Donna Anna in Prague premiere of *Don Giovanni,* and also performed in Italy and Germany. Married to Codecasa in 1783 (?)

Saramondi, Carlo c. 1750–1800?

Singer touring with Palmini in the 1770s; sang K. 256.

Sarti, Giuseppe 1729–1802

Opera and instrumental composer active in Vienna and other European centers.

Sartori, M. c. 1740–1790?

Italian soprano, also active in London with Mozart.

Sattler, Johann Tobias c. 1720–1774

German composer of original incidental music for Gebler's play, *Thamos*. Later Gebler commissioned Mozart to write new music, which was more effective, according to Gebler and Mozart. (Freemason?)

Sauer, Ignaz 1759–1833

Viennese music publisher active from 1790s.

Saüerle, Michael c. 1750–1810?

Munich hornmaker.

Savioli, Count Louis Aurèle de c. 1740–1788

Composer, music director in Mannheim in 1770s.

Scarlatti, Giuseppe 1723–1777

Italian opera and church composer active in Rome and Vienna; grandson of Alessandro, but not son of Domenico Scarlatti.

Schacht, Theodor von 1748–1823

German vocal and instrumental composer active in Regensburg and Vienna.

Schachtner, Johann Andreas 1732–1795

Close friend of Mozart family. Trumpeter, violinist, violoncellist, text poet of K. 336, librettist for *Zaide* (after Franz Joseph Sebastiani, c. 1740–1790?); translator of *Idomeneo* into German.

Schack, Benedict 1758–1826

Bohemian composer and tenor active in Vienna. Sang in several of Mozart's works.

Schack, Elisabeth Weinhold c. 1770–1820

Sang Third Lady in Vienna premiere of *Die Zauberflöte* (1791). Married to above.

Schaden, Nanette von 1763–1834

Augsburg pianist, praised by Reichardt, married to Wilhelm von Schaden (any relation to Nanette Natorp or Mademoiselle Jeunehomme?).

Schall, Claus Nielsen   1757–1835
Danish conductor and composer of instrumental music, whom Mozart met in Prague.

Schall, Johann Eberhard Friedrich   1742–1790
Text poet of K. 529.

Schalz, Franz Karl   c. 1750–1821
Tenor at the Salzburg court in the 1770s.

Schauf, Jean   1757–1827
Pressburg publisher of Mozart from 1780s.

Schelhammer, Joseph   c. 1760–1820?
Baden musician, colleague and successor of Mozart's friend Anton Stoll.

Schellinger, Johann   c. 1750–1810.
Austrian music copyist for Haydn, etc.

Schenk, Johann   1753–1836
Viennese composer of singspiels, who saw and applauded *Die Zauberflöte*; a teacher of Beethoven.

Schetky, F. G. C.   1737–1824
German touring composer and violoncellist, whose music Leopold knew.

Schick, Margarethe Hamel   1773–1809
German singer of Mozart roles who appeared in Frankfurt with Mozart; also active in Mainz and Berlin.

Schickaneder, Emanuel (der Jungere)   1751–1812
Austrian actor, singer, theatre director, librettist, producer of *Die Zauberflöte*, in which he alternated with Wittmann as Papageno; friend of Mozart and fellow Freemason; married to Eleanore Arthe.

Schikaneder, Urban   1746–1818
Singer, elder brother of Emanuel.

Schikaneder, Nanette c. 1770–1818

One of "Three Boys" in *Die Zauberflöte* (with Mathias, Tuscher, and Handelgruber).

Schiedenhofen, Joachim von 1747–1823

Salzburg friend of Mozart family, and writer of an informative diary.

Schiller, Friedrich von 1759–1805

Famous German playwright whose works Mozart read.

Schindler, Katherina Leithner 1755–1788

Singer active in Vienna in 1780s. In 1777 she married actor-manager J. B. Bergopzoomer (1742–1804).

Schindler, Philipp Ernst 1723–1793

Painter of miniatures, father of Joseph Lange's first wife, Anna (1757–1779).

Schink, Johann Friedrich 1755–1795?

Fellow Freemason; perceptive German writer in several periodicals, whose articles often praised Mozart's music.

Schinkel, Karl Friedrich 1781–1841

Famous Berlin artist who designed the 1816 revival of *Die Zauberflöte*.

Schinn, Johann Georg c. 1760–1810?

Salzburg musician, pupil of Johann Michael Haydn.

Schleiss, Ferdinand c. 1750–1810?

Viennese musician, fellow Freemason.

Schlichtegroll, Adolph Heinrich von 1765–1822

Viennese philologist, librarian, friend, and fellow Freemason who wrote Mozart's obituary in 1793.

Schlick, Johann Konrad 1759–1825

German composer of instrumental music and violoncello player whose music Leopold knew.

Schlittersberg, Augustin Veith von 1751–1811

Fellow Freemason. Text poet for K. 483.

Schmid, Ernst Fritz   1904–1960
Distinguished Mozart scholar from Augsburg.

Schmidt, ——— c. 1760–1820?
Horn player active in Vienna in 1780s.

Schmidt, Anton   c. 1760–1820?
Viennese violinist, friend of Mozart.

Schmidt, Balthasar   1705–1749
Nuremburg instrumental composer whose works Leopold taught young Mozart.

Schmidt, Ferdinand   1693–1756
Viennese church composer and conductor.

Schmidt, Gottfried Heinrich   c. 1760–1820?
Singer alternating with Dauer as Pedrillo in Vienna premiere of *Die Entführung* (1782), later a theatre manager.

Schmidt, Johann Gottfried   c. 1764–1803?
Leipzig artist who decorated Breitkopf & Härtel Mozart early editions.

Schmidt, Johann Michael   1720–1792
Instrumental and church composer in Augsburg. Friend of Mozart and Haydn. Also active elsewhere.

Schmidt, Joseph   c. 1750–1808
Cloister symphonist of Eberbach.

Schmidt, Klamer Eberhard Karl   1746–1824
Text poet for K. 519.

Schmitt, Alois   c. 1870–1930?
Editor of K. 417 (427), version first performed Dresden c. 1901.

Schmitt, Joseph   1734–1791
Viennese symphony composer, and keyboard player.

Schmittbauer, Joseph Aloys   1718–1809

German instrumental and vocal composer and organist known to Leopold.

Schmutzer, Jacob   1733–1811

Viennese engraver and artist friend of Joseph Lange and Mozart.

Schneider, Franz   1737–1812

Austrian "cloister" composer of religious and instrumental works.

Schneider, Georg Laurenz   1766–1855

German composer at Coburg court whose work Mozart knew. (Related to Viennese poet?)

Schobert, Johann   c. 1720–1767

German composer active in Paris whose symphonies and other works interested the young Mozart.

Scholze, Johann Sigismund   1705–1750

Austrian composer whose works Leopold taught young Mozart.

Schönfeld, Baron Johann F. von   c. 1750–1821

Prague publisher of a few Mozart works.

Schonmayer, Frau   c. 1760–1810?

Singer active in Vienna in 1780s.

Schopenauer, Arthur   1788–1860

German philosopher who admired the music of Mozart.

Schott, Bernard   1748–1809

Founder of important Mainz publishing house.

Schrattenbach, Sigismund von   1698–1771

Archbishop of Salzburg, 1753–1771.

Schreyvogel, Joseph   1768–1832
Director of major Vienna theatres (beginning c. 1814).

Schröder, Friedrich Ludwig   1744–1816
Viennese actor, producer/translator of Shakespeare, Da Ponte; friend of Mozart.

Schröter, Johann Samuel   1750–1788
Warsaw composer of instrumental music who settled in England, whose music Mozart appreciated. His sister Corona (1751–1802) was a composer and singer. The widow of his brother, composer Johann Heinrich Schröter, was a good friend of Joseph Haydn.

Schubart, Daniel   1739–1791
German text poet for Baron von Dalberg, and libretto translator active in Vienna. Writer of articles praising the music of Mozart.

Schubauer, Johann Lukas   1749–1815
Composer of singspiels performed in Austria and Germany in 1780s; the score of one was in Mozart's estate.

Schultz, Johann Abraham Peter   1747–1800
Austrian composer whose music Leopold knew (related to painter?).

Schultz, Josepha Rabenau   1734–1786
Well-known Austrian singer and actress in 1770s.

Schulz, Christian   1759–1820?
Nuremburg musician, editor of first Mozart Breitkopf & Härtel editions.

Schulz, Frau   c. 1755–1800?
Mozart's piano pupil in 1787 (?), later applauded in Russia.

Schuster, Joseph   1748–1812
Dresden composer of operas, sacred music, and instrumental works, whose chamber music Mozart appreciated; his Janissary music is also remembered. Traveled to Italy.

Schütze, Stephan   1771–1839
Member of Schikaneder circle who collaborated on *Die Zauberflöte*.

Schwan, Christian Friedrich 1733–1815

Important north German librettist for F. A. Holly (1747–1783), O. von Berlin (1753–1817), C. L. Diester (1757–1822), Otto Kospoth (1753–1817), Nicole Mühle (c. 1750–1795), Friedrich Preu (c. 1750–1795); also translator for Audinot, Duni, Monsigny.

Schwanberger, Johann 1740–1800?

German operatic and instrumental composer, conductor, harpsichordist who studied with Saratelli and Latilla in Italy.

Schwankhardt, Johann Daniel c. 1750–1800?

Friend and fellow Freemason in Vienna.

Schwarz, Anton c. 1750–1800?

Violist Mozart knew in Mannheim and Munich.

Schwarz, Benedikt 1750–1795

Viennese musician and writer who wrote admiringly of Mozart's piano playing.

Schwarzenberg, Prince Johann Nepomuk 1742–1789

Vienna patron, melomane, lover of Mozart's music; member of Swieten circle.

Schweigl, Ignaz c. 1750–1803

Viennese composer, violinist, publisher.

Schweitzer, Anton 1735–1787

Instrumental and theatre composer who set texts of Wieland; active in Mannheim and Weimar.

Schwenke, Christoph Friedrich Gottlieb 1767–1822

Hamburg composer, conductor, and editor of several Mozart works published by Günther & Böhme, Hamburg.

Schwindel, Friedrich 1737–1786

German instrumental composer, follower of the Mannheim school.

Schwingenschuh, Anna von c. 1750–1800?

With her daughter Lisette, a Viennese friend of Mozart in 1791.

Scirolli, Gregorio   1722–1781

Conductor and instrumental composer active in Naples (when Mozart was there), and Palermo.

Scolari, Giuseppe   1720–1770

Italian opera and instrumental composer whose works were performed in Milan, Venice, Vienna, Dresden, etc.

Sebastiani, Franz Joseph   c. 1740–1790?

Librettist of *Das Serail*, which Schachtner adapted for Mozart's *Zaide*.

Sedaine, Jean Michel   1719–1797

French dramatist and librettist, many of whose works were adapted for German operettas.

Seeau, Count Joseph Anton von   c. 1720–1799

Manager, Munich National Theatre (1778–1799), friend of Mozart.

Seidl, Ferdinand   c. 1740–1800?

Salzburg concertmaster in 1770s.

Seinsheim, Count Maximilian   1751–1803

Noble Munich enthusiast of Mozart's *Idomeneo*; fellow Freemason.

Seipp, C(?)   c. 1750–1810?

Austrian artist, member of a theatrical family.

Seizer, Sebastian   c. 1750–1810?

Viennese publisher in 1780s.

Séjan, Nicolas   1743–1800

French composer, keyboard performer, teacher, whose music Mozart knew.

Sellitti, Giuseppe   1700–1777

Italian opera composer; active in Paris.

Serini, Giuseppe   1710–1760?

Cremona composer active in Vienna, whose music Leopold taught young Mozart.

Serrarius, Thérèse 1762–1810?

Mannheim piano pupil of Mozart in 1777.

Sertor, Gaetano c. 1760–1810?

Text poet for K. 416, etc., and librettist in Munich and Vienna from 1770s for Martin y Soler, Anfossi, Bianchi. (Also singer?)

Sessi, Marianne 1776–1847

Singer (also pianist) active in Vienna in 1790s.

Seuche, Joseph 1702–1790

Viennese church composer.

Seve, Barbara c. 1755–1810?

Soprano active in Vienna in 1780s (singing Constanze in *Die Entführung*): previously active in Mannheim.

Seydelmann, Franz 1748–1806

Dresden opera, instrumental, and religious composer whose works Mozart heard.

Seyfried, Ignaz von 1776–1841

Mozart pupil (1790) and assistant, later opera composer and conductor.

Seyler, Abel 1730–1800

Librettist and director of traveling opera company Mozart heard in Mannheim (1777). Married to Sophie Sparmann (1738–1789).

Sgrilli, Cosimo c. 1760–1810?

Prompter at Vienna court opera, 1780s.

Sichling, L. c. 1770–1820?

Artist, engraver active in Austria.

Sickingen, Count Otto von 1755–1836

German ambassador at whose Paris establishment Mozart's *Paris Symphony* was first heard (1778).

Sidra, Matthias Joseph c. 1760–1820?

Bass singer active in Vienna in 1780s.

Sieber, Jean-Georges 1738–1822

German-born horn player and publisher active in Paris from 1765 (as a performer, later as a publisher).

Siebig, Ludwig 1775–1807

German composer; early biographer of Mozart.

Sieger, H. c. 1750–1800?

Munich lawyer-merchant, friendly to Mozart (1780).

Siegl, ——— c. 1750–1800?

Munich keyboard player, pupil of Mozart (1777).

Silbermann, Johann Andreas 1712–1783

Member of Strasbourg family of organ and keyboard instrument makers and players.

Silverstolpe, Fredrik Samuel 1769–1851

Swedish diplomat in Vienna who knew Constanze and Nissen from 1798, and collected Mozart manuscripts.

Simonetti, Luigi c. 1760–1820?

German tenor in Bonn who promoted and sang in performances of Mozart operas in 1790s.

Simrock, Nikolaus 1752–1834

German horn player and publisher at Bonn.

Sohier, C. J. B. 1728–1759

Lille symphony composer known to Leopold.

Soliman, Angelo 1721–1798

Distinguished fellow Freemason of Vienna.

Solzi, Adamo c. 1740–1800?

Male soprano in *Ascanio* premiere, Milan (1771).

Sonnenfels, Joseph von 1733–1817

Well-connected writer, fellow Freemason; friendly with Gottsched,

Emperor Joseph II, Lessing, Mozart, etc.

Sonnleithner, Christoph von 1734–1786
Viennese church and instrumental composer.

Sonnleithner, Joseph 1765–1835
Viennese court official, son of above. Collector of musicians' portraits, etc.

Sonnleithner, Leopold 1797–1873
Published Da Ponte's words for K. 577 and 579 in his own memoirs. Good friend of Schubert.

Souter, ———— 1760–1810?
Tenor in Vienna, 1790s.

Spängler, Franz Anton 1757–1811
Viennese composer and tenor (?) who sang Mozart roles.

Späth, Franz Anton 1714–1786
Early organ, fortepiano, and organ maker of Regensburg.

Späth, Franz Xaver 1750–1808
Salzburg bridegroom of Elisabeth Haffner (1753–1784).

Spaun, Count Felix von c. 1740–1790?
Viennese, fellow Freemason.

Spaur, Count Franz Joseph 1725–1797
Innsbruck judge, member of family sponsoring Mozart's Innsbruck, and other, concerts.

Spehr, Johann Peter c. 1770–1860?
Braunschweig publisher of an unfinished "Complete Mozart Edition."

Sperger, Johannes 1750–1812
German instrumental composer and performer active in Vienna.

Spielmann, Baron Anton von 1738–1813

Member of Swieten circle and in Prince Kaunitz' Council (at whose establishment Mozart performed in 1783).

Spindler, Franz Stanislaus 1763–1819

German singspiel composer whose works were popular in Munich and Vienna in 1780s.

Spitta, Philipp 1841–1894

Musicologist, member of Breitkopf Mozart Edition editorial board.

Spitzeder, Franz Anton 1735–1796

Salzburg tenor who sang in Salzburg premieres of *Die Schuldigkeit* and *La finta semplice,* and was a keyboard pupil of Mozart.

Spohr, Ludwig 1784–1859

German composer who later produced many Mozart works.

Sporck, Count Johann Wenzel 1724–1804

Director of Vienna court chamber music. In 1768 he investigated Leopold Mozart's complaint over Affligio's intrigue against Mozart's *La finta semplice,* but did not arrange a Vienna performance.

Springer, Vincent c. 176?–1810?

With brother Anton, performed Mozart's works calling for basset horn, in Prague and Vienna from the 1780s.

Stadler, Anton 1753–1812

Clarinet and basset horn player, for whom Mozart composed K. 498, 581, 622. Fellow Freemason.

Stadler, Johann c. 1747–1819

Clarinet and basset horn player (brother of above?).

Stadler, Abbate Maximilian 1748–1833

Austrian composer, organist, teacher, friend of Haydn and Mozart and Constanze (whom he helped sort and publish music left in Mozart's estate). Stadler's niece (?) Elisabeth was Mozart's theory and keyboard pupil in 1784 (related to above?).

Stadler, Mathias 1744–1800?

Performed role of Oebalus in *Apollo et Hyacinthus* in Salzburg premiere (1767).

Stage, Conrad Heinrich c. 1730–1790?

Augsburg bookseller known to Leopold Mozart.

Stamitz, Carl 1745–1801

Mannheim instrumental composer, member of musical family, also active in Paris and London.

Stampa, Claudio c. 1750–1800?

Milan librettist who may have collaborated on Mozart's *Ascanio*.

Starck, Abbé Johann (also Storck) c. 1750–1800

Mainz organist, conductor who made an unauthorized piano reduction of *Die Entführung* published by Schott in 1785.

Starke, ———— c. 1770–1820?

Sang one of the Three Slaves in *Die Zauberflöte* premiere in Vienna.

Starzer, Joseph 1726–1787

Viennese composer, conductor at court; member of the Swieten circle.

Steffan, Joseph Anton (Joseph Antonín Štepán) 1726–1797

Viennese church and instrumental composer and harpsichordist active in Vienna.

Steglich, Rudolph 1886–1976

Mozart authority.

Stegmann, Carl David 1751–1800

Dresden composer, violinist, and conductor of *Così*, etc. (Mainz, 1791).

Stegmayer, Matthäus 1771–1820

German opera composer active in Vienna, etc. from 1790.

Stein, Anton c. 1750–1800?

Viennese professor of poetics and later classical literature, a friend whose works Mozart read.

Stein, Johann Andreas 1728–1792

Augsburg piano maker and friend, whose daughter, Nanette, was briefly a keyboard pupil of Mozart (1777), and who later carried on the piano-making business with her husband in Vienna.

Steiner, Sigmund Anton 1773–1838

Vienna publisher.

Stephanie der Jungere, Johann 1741–1800

Active actor and librettist and translator for composers in Vienna. Translated Shakespeare.

Sterkel, Johann Franz Xaver 1750–1817

Mannheim composer, pianist, also active in Mainz, whose music was appreciated by Leopold Mozart and Joseph Haydn.

Stetten, Paul von c. 1750–1810?

Augsburg pianist, poet and critic who praised Mozart, and performed Mozart's *Concerto for Three Keyboards* (the Lodron concerto), K. 242 with Mozart and Johann Michael Demmler; also wrote text for a Demmler cantata.

Stierle, Franz Xaver c. 1750–1800?

Actor in Böhm's traveling theatre company who translated *La finta giardiniera* into German for Böhm. Several members of the Stierle family (friends of the Mozarts) appeard in the opera.

Stock, Dora (Doris) 1760–1831

Artist from Dresden who drew the latest portrait of Mozart that has survived (1789?).

Stolberg-Wernigerode, Count Heinrich zu c. 1710–1770?

Composer-editor of several sacred songs Leopold taught young Mozart. Member of musical and literary circles.

Stoll, Anton 1748–1805

Baden choirmaster and good friend for whom Mozart composed K. 618.

Storace, Nancy (Anna) 1766–1817

Important English soprano active in Vienna in 1780s, where she sang works of her brother and others, particularly Mozart; married briefly to a composer, violinist J. A. Fisher.

Storace, Stephen 1747–1805

English composer friendly with Mozart in Vienna in 1780s, when he was a pupil of Mozart. Brother of above. Later published first edition of one work of Mozart.

Strack, Joseph Killian von 1724–1793

As valet to Emperor Joseph II, he was in charge of court chamber music. Although in 1781 Mozart composed K. 375 especially to gain his favor, he never became friends with him.

Strasser, Johann c. 1730–1800?

German composer, violinist, active in Mannheim, Munich, and Vienna (?).

Streicher, Franz Nicolas 1738–1800?

Austrian artist who may have painted Mozart. Friend of Robinigs.

Streicher, Johann Andreas 1761–1833

Viennese pianist and piano maker, who after marrying Nanette Stein moved the Stein firm from Augsburg to Vienna.

Strinasacchi, Regina 1761–1839

Italian touring violinist, married to Johann Konrad Schlick, who performed K. 454 with Mozart in 1784. Her repertoire also included Giornovichi, Cambini, and Saint-Georges.

Strobach, Johann Joseph 1731–1794

Prague conductor of Mozart operas, etc., in 1780s.

Stumpf, Johann Andreas 1769–1846

Musician based in London, harp maker, collector of Mozart manuscripts.

Stuppi, G. c. 1770–1830?

Portrait engraver, active in Vienna.

Sturm, Christoph Christian   1740–1786
Text poet of K. 597.

Suardi, Felicita   c. 1750–1800?
Italian soprano, sang Cinna in Milan premiere of *Lucio Silla*, K. 135 (1772).

Sukowaty, Wenzel   1747–1810
Vienna court copyist who sold copies of *Die Entführung* in 1785, etc.

Sulzer, Johann George   1720–1779
Swiss philosopher, also active in Berlin. Mozart knew members of his family, although perhaps not the philosopher.

Summer, Georg   c. 1750–1810?
Organist and music master to the Royal family in Vienna—a post Mozart coveted.

Süssmayr, Franz Xaver   1766–1803
A pupil (1790), assistant, and follower of Mozart, and of Salieri.

Swieten, Baron Gottfried van   1733–1803
Minor composer, ambassador, court librarian, and important Vienna melomane whom Mozart met in 1768, and whose circle he joined in 1781. Mozart's interest in Handel, Bach, etc., was greatly expanded by his contact with van Swieten. Fellow Freemason.

Tag, Christian Gotthilf   1735–1811
Dresden vocal composer, and fellow Freemason.

Talon, Pierre   1721–1785
French instrumental composer active when Mozart was in Paris (1778).

Tanucci, Marquis Bernardo   1688–1783
Friendly contact in Naples (1770).

Tapray, Jean François   1738–1814
French composer, organist and pianist active in Paris when Mozart was there (1778).

Tarade, Théodore 1731–1819

French opera and instrumental composer and violinist active in Paris when Mozart was there (1778).

Tarantini, Pasquale 1740–1794

Italian opera composer and conductor Mozart met in Naples.

Tarchi, Angelo 1760–1814

Italian composer active throughout Europe. He abbreviated and recomposed Acts III and IV of *Figaro* for a Monza production in 1787 (one of only two 18th-century Italian productions of *Figaro*).

Tartini, Giuseppe 1692–1770

Important Italian composer for violin whose works Mozart respected.

Tassi, Niccolo c. 1740–1790

Italian opera librettist for Guglielmi, Sacchini, etc., whom Mozart met in 1771. (Not to be confused with Torquato Tasso, many of whose poems inspired librettists.)

Tausch, Jakob 1740–1817

Court clarinettist when Mozart was in Munich and Mannheim.

Telemann, Georg Philipp 1681–1767

Important German composer, about whom Mozart knew little.

Teller, Gottlieb Ephraim 1754–1810?

Singer active in Austria in 1770s and 1780s, along with his wife, Marie Louise (Schurian) Teller, known to the Mozarts.

Tenducci, Giusto Ferdinando 1736–1790

Castrato, for whom Mozart composed K. 315b. Also sang for J. C. Bach.

Terradellas, Domingo 1711–1751

Neapolitan opera composer, also active in England.

Terrasson, Abbé Jean 1670–1750

French author of *Sethos* (1721), a novel on Egyptian mysteries popular with Freemasons; translated, it was a source for *Die Zauberflöte*.

Tesi, Vittoria 1700–1775

Famous Italian singer known to the Mozarts, living in retirement in Vienna.

Tessé, Countess Adrienne Catherine 1741–1814

Dedicatee of Mozart's early clavier sonatas (K. 8 and 9), published in Paris during his first visit.

Teyber, Anton (also spelled Teiber) 1756–1822

Composer, organist; played quartets with Mozart in Dresden, and also sang bass in Baron van Swieten's concerts. Long-time friend of the Mozart family.

Teyber, Elisabeth 1744–1816

Soprano, active in Vienna court opera in 1780s.

Teyber, Franz 1756–1810

Vienna singspiel composer, court conductor and violinist.

Teyber, Matthäus 1711–1785

Minor Viennese composer, father of Elisabeth, Anton, Franz.

Teyber, Thérèse 1765–1830

Viennese soprano married to Ferdinand Arnold. Active in 1780s; studied keyboard with Mozart, performed Blonde (*Die Entführung*) and Zerlina (*Don Giovanni*).

Thiennes de Rumbeke, Countess Marie Karoline (née Cobenzl) 1755–1812

Viennese patron and keyboard pupil of Mozart in 1780s.

Thonus, J. P. von c. 1750–1810?

Leipzig publisher active from 1770s; issued first edition of K. 196.

Thorwart, Johann 1737–1813

Auditor of Vienna court theatres, associated with Count Orsini-Rosenberg; "guardian" of Constanze Weber.

Thuille, Francesco c. 1750–1800?

Munich printer of *Idomeneo* libretto (1781).

Thun, Count Johann Joseph 1711–1788

Member of Viennese noble family, patrons of Mozart. Fellow Freemason.

Thun, Countess Wilhelmine von 1744–1800

Well-connected Viennese pupil, and patron of Mozart. Friend of Emperor Joseph II.

Tibaldi, Giuseppe 1719–1780?

Italian tenor admired by Mozart and Leopold. Sang in Milan premiere of *Ascanio* (1771).

Tiedge, Christoph August von 1752–1841

Contemporary poet, whose German verses were later fitted to Mozart's music. (Friend of Beethoven.)

Tinti, Baron Anton c. 1740–1790?

Viennese noble violinist who (with his brother Bartholomäus, violoncellist) performed K. 458, 464, 465 with Haydn (violin) and Mozart (viola). Leopold Mozart was present. Both Tintis were Freemasons.

Tischbein, Johann Heinrich Wilhelm 1751–1829

German artist, friend of Goethe, member of artistic family, one of whom painted Mozart (possibly from life).

Tischer, Johann Nikolaus 1707–1774

German composer whose works Leopold taught young Mozart and his sister, Nannerl.

Tissot, Auguste 1728–1797

Writer who met the young Mozart in Lausanne and wrote an article on the prodigy.

Todeschi, Baron Giovanni Battista 1730–1799

Rovereto host to Leopold and Wolfgang Mozart (1770).

Toeschi, Carlo Giuseppe 1723–1788

Italian composer, violinist, also active in Mannheim.

Tomasek, Jan Vaclav   1774–1850
Prague composer who helped maintain Mozart performance practice.

Tomaselli, Giuseppe   1758–1836
Salzburg singer, teacher, member of musical family friendly with the Mozarts.

Tomasini, Aloisio Luigi   1741–1808
Composer, violin pupil of Leopold Mozart, long-time colleague of Joseph Haydn at Esterháza.

Tomisch, Franz   1759–1796
Viennese composer, pupil of Haydn.

Tommasi, Dr. Antonio   c. 1740–1790?
Secretary of Verona Accademia Filharmonia, which elected Mozart to membership in 1771.

Torrefranca, Fausto   1883–1955
Important Italian musicologist in late 18th-century music.

Torricella, Christopher   1715–1798
Viennese publisher, and fellow Freemason.

Tost, Johann   c. 1740–1810?
Moravian merchant, violinist; patron of Haydn and Mozart.

Touchemoulin, Joseph   1727–1801
German instrumental composer and violinist active in Paris, where Mozart probably heard his music. Brother of well-known graphic artist, G. F. Touchemoulin.

Tozzi, Antonio   1736–1812
Italian composer, pupil of Padre Martini, also active in Mannheim and Munich.

Traeg, Johann   1747–1805
Vienna music publisher and dealer, beginning in 1770s.

Traëta, Tommaso 1727–1779

Italian composer, also active in Paris, London, Vienna, and Russia, whose music Mozart knew.

Trattner, Johann Thomas von 1717–1798

Viennese publisher, whose second wife, Thérèse Nagel (1758–1793), was a keyboard pupil and friend of Mozart in 1780s.

Travaglia, Pietro c. 1760–1820?

Austrian stage designer for *Der Schauspieldirektor* and *La clemenza di Tito*, also active in Esterháza as designer and librettist.

Treitschke, G. F. c. 1776–1842

Vienna librettist, theatre director who appreciated Mozart's works.

Triebensee, Joseph 1772–1846

Prague composer, conductor, oboist, arranger of Mozart operas; also active in Vienna.

Tritto, Giacomo 1733-1824

Italian opera composer, of *Il convitato di Pietra, Don Giovanni* (1783), etc., also known in Vienna.

Troger, Ludwig c. 1740–1790?

Milan host to Mozart in 1770s.

Tschudi, Baron Jean de 1734–1784

Swiss librettist for Gluck, Salieri, etc.

Tuček, Jan 1743–1783

Prague composer, also active in Vienna, whose operas were known to Mozart.

Tuma, Franz Ignaz Anton 1704–1774

Bohemian composer of sacred works and symphonies, active in Vienna.

Türreschmiedt, Karl 1753–1797

Potsdam horn player, friendly with Mozart in 1789.

Tuscher, Mathilda   c. 1775–1825
One of "Three Boys" in *Die Zauberflöte* premiere, 1791.

Ugarte, Count Johann   1748–1796
Patron of Mozart, he replaced Count Rosenberg-Orsini as director of Vienna court opera, 1790–1791.

Ulibisheff (Oulibicheff), Alexander   1794–1858
Enterprising pioneer Russian Mozart scholar.

Ulbrich, Maximilian   1752–1814
Viennese singspiel and instrumental composer active from 1770s.

Umlauf, Ignaz   1756–1796
Austrian composer and conductor, assistant to Salieri.

Unterkoffler, Andreas   c. 1740–1800?
Male soprano singer in Salzburg in the 1770s.

Unterberger, Ingnaz   1748–1797
Artist, fellow Freemason in Vienna.

Unzelmann, Friederike Flittner   c. 1768–1835?
German soprano who sang Donna Anna (*Don Giovanni*), Countess (*Figaro*), Constanze (*Die Entführung*), in Berlin from 1780s.

Unzelmann, Karl Wilhelm   1753–1832
German bass who sang title role in *Figaro* and Leporello (*Don Giovanni*) in Berlin in 1790s. Married to above.

Uslenghi, Stefano   c. 1740–1790?
Mozart's host in Rome (1770).

Uttini, Francesco   1723–1795
Instrumental and vocal composer mostly active in London and Stockholm. Related to tenor who sang with Mozart in Mantua (1770)?

Uz, Johann Peter   1720–1796
Text poet, K. 47e (53). Also text poet for Wolfgang, Jr., (*Die Nacht*).

Vachon, Pierre 1731–1803

Lyric and instrumental composer active in Paris when Mozart was there (1778), later in Berlin.

Valentini, Giovanni c. 1680–1770?

Opera composer whose works Mozart heard in Naples (1770).

Valentini, Michele 1704–1797

Cremona composer whose *La clemenza di Tito* Mozart heard (1770).

Valesi, Giovanni (Johann Wallishauser) 1735–1811

German tenor active in Italy, Mannheim, Munich. Sang in *Idomeneo* premiere, Munich (1781).

Valloti, Padre Francesco Antonio 1697–1780

Padua composer and organist Mozart met in 1771.

Vanhal, Johann Baptist (also Wanhal) 1739–1813

Important Bohemian composer active in Vienna.

Vanschenz, Joseph c. 1750–1810?

Violinist active at Vienna court in 1780s.

Varesco, Abbate Giambattista 1736–1813

Salzburg chaplain, text poet for *Idomeneo* (after Danchet), and *L'oca del Cairo* (?).

Varese, Anna c. 1750–1800?

Italian soprano, sang Ismene in Milan premiere of *Mitridate* (1770).

Vendôme, Marie Charlotte c. 1744–1786

Paris publisher of first editions of K. 6, 7, 8, 9, etc.

Vento, Mattia 1735–1776

Italian composer, also active in London where Mozart heard his music.

Vestris, Gaetano 1729–1808

Great Franco–Italian dancer; performed in *Les petits riens* (1778).

Victoire, Madame Louise M. T. de Bourbon   1733–1799

Vivacious daughter of Louis XV to whom Mozart dedicated his first keyboard and violin sonata.

Viguerie, J. B.   1761–1819

Parisian publisher of early editions of Mozart's music.

Villeneuve, Louise (Aloysia)   c. 1765–1810?

Soprano active in Vienna in 1780s, for whom Mozart composed several arias, and the role of Dorabella in *Così*. (Related to director of Strasbourg theatre?)

Villeroi, Frl.   c. 1760–1810?

Studied K. 246 with Leopold Mozart in June 1778?

Vinci, Leonardo   1690–1730

Italian instrumental and opera composer—influence on Handel, and Mozart?

Viotti, Giovanni Battista   1753–1824

Important Italian composer for violin, whose works Mozart knew.

Vismes du Valgny, Anne Pierre Jacques De   1749–1814

Director of Paris Opéra.

Vogel, Abbé Cajetan   1750–1794

Prague musician, arranger of Mozart operas for keyboard.

Vogel, Johann Christoph   1756–1788

Nuremberg composer and horn player, whose works Mozart probably heard in Paris. Cherubini collaborator.

Vogl, Johann Michael   1768–1840

Sang Mozartean roles in Vienna in 1790s, later a friend of Franz Schubert.

Vogler, Abbate Georg Joseph   1749–1814

Mannheim composer and keyboard player, pupil of Padre Martini and Mysliveček. Mozart met him in 1777.

Vogt, F. D. 1750–1826?

Parisian publisher of early editions of Mozart's music.

Vogt, Peter 1745–1800?

Dancer in Vienna, Prague; ballet master in Böhm's touring company. Friend of Mozart.

Volkert, Franz 1767–1845

German instrumental and stage composer, conductor, active in Vienna from 1780s.

Voltaire, François Arouet 1694–1778

Famous French philosopher, whose writings Mozart read.

Voltolini, Josef c. 1750–1800?

Director of traveling opera company performing *Die Entführung* in Augsburg, etc., 1791.

Vontherton, Josephus 1750–1800?

Performed Zephyrus in Mozart's *Apollo et Hyacinthus*, K. 38 in Salzburg premiere. Later librettist for Michael Haydn.

Voss, Johann Heinrich c. 1760–1820?

Poet, whose verse was later fitted to Mozart melodies.

Vulpius, Christian August 1762–1827

German writer, librettist for Dittersdorf. Brother-in-law of Goethe. Translated *Figaro* into German in 1788.

Wafeneder, Joseph c. 1750–1800?

Violinist at the Salzburg court in the 1770s.

Wagenseil, Georg 1717–1777

Viennese court composer in many forms. His music was appreciated by Mozart.

Wahr, Karl 1745–1800?

Director of traveling company, producing *Die Entführung* and other works. Also active in Vienna.

Waldberg zu Wolfegg, Count Anton   c. 1740–1821
Noble Augsburg melomane who presented Mozart in concert in 1777.

Waldersee, Paul von   1831–1906
Member of Breitkopf Mozart Edition editorial board (1877–1883); scholar, collector.

Waldstätten, Baroness Martha Elisabeth   1744–1821
Viennese close friend, patron, pianist, and pupil of Mozart.

Wall, R.   c. 1750–1810?
Viennese artist-etcher in 1780s.

Walsegg-Stuppach, Count Franz Georg   1763–1827
Through his estate manager, Franz Anton Leitgeb (1744–1812), he commissioned Mozart to compose a *Requiem* in 1791.

Walter, Anton   1752–1826
Viennese piano maker whose fortepianos were favored by Mozart in his maturity.

Walter, Joseph   c. 1755–1800?
Tenor, actor active in Vienna from 1780s.

Wánski, Jan   1762–1830
Polish composer, violinist.

Wappler, Christian Friedrich   1711–1807
Vienna publisher, fellow Freemason.

Wassmuth, Johann Georg Franz   1710–1766
Würzburg court composer, conductor, whose "Schlitterfahrt" (1753) was once believed to be by Mozart.

Weber, Adelheid   c. 1729–1807
Sister of Fridolin Weber (father of Aloysia, Josepha, Constanze, Sophie).

Weber, Aloysia   1760–1839
Sister of Constanze. Brilliant soprano who sang in four of Mozart's operas, and many other works. Married Joseph Lange.

Weber, Carl Maria von 1786–1826

Important German composer, son of Franz Anton Weber and Genoveva Brenner Weber.

Weber, Constanze (later Mozart; later Nissen) 1762–1842

Sister of Aloysia, daughter of Fridolin and Maria.

Weber, Edmund 1766–1828

Brother of Fridolin. Pupil of Joseph Haydn.

Weber, Franz Anton 1734–1812

Brother of Fridolin, husband of Genoveva Brenner, father of Carl Maria.

Weber, Fridolin 1733–1779

Musician, pupil of Joseph Haydn, husband of Maria, father of four daughters, including Constanze.

Weber, Genoveva Brenner 1760–1798

Wife of Franz Anton. Sang Constanze (*Die Entführung*) and other roles from 1780s in various towns.

Weber, Josepha (later Hofer; later Mayer) 1758–1819

Sister of Constanze. Soprano who sang in many Mozart works.

Weber, Maria 1727–1793

Wife of Fridolin Weber, mother of Constanze, etc.

Weber, Sophie (later Haibel) 1763–1846

Sister of Constanze.

Weber, Bernard Anselm 1766–1821

Composer, conductor, critic favorable to Mozart's music.

Weber, Gottfried 1779–1839

Composer, flutist, writer of controversial (skeptical) pamplets on Mozart's *Requiem*.

Weger, A.   1767–1832

Artist active in Dresden and Austria who made and engraved Mozart and Haydn portraits?

Weidmann, Joseph   1743–1810?

Important Viennese actor, librettist (for Umlauf, Barta, etc.) who performed a speaking role in *Der Schauspieldirektor*. Brother of dramatist, Paul Weidmann.

Weigl, Joseph   1740–1820

Austrian violoncellist at Vienna Court (also at Esterháza). His son, Thaddaus (1776–1844) was also a composer, conductor, publisher in Vienna.

Weigl, Joseph   1766–1846

Viennese composer, conductor, also active in Germany. Son of above, pupil of Salieri. Member of Swieten circle. Admired Mozart and conducted many of his works.

Weinbrenner, Joseph von   1728–1807

Viennese merchant, educator, patron; fellow Freemason.

Weinlig, Christian Ehregott   1743–1813?

Religious and instrumental composer, conductor, active in Leipzig and Dresden; fellow Freemason.

Weiser, Ignaz von   1701–1785

Salzburg official. Text poet of K. 35, and also for Leopold Mozart. Grandfather of Josepha Duček.

Weiskern, Friedrich Wilhelm   1710–1768

Adaptor-librettist of *Bastien und Bastienne,* etc.

Weiss, Anna Maria   c. 1755–1831

Soprano active in Vienna from 1770s.

Weiss(e), Christian Felix   1726–1804

Text poet, K. 472, etc.

Wendling, Augusta ("Gustl")   1756–1794

Pianist, alto singer, former mistress of Elector Theodor when Mozart met her in Mannheim (1777).

Wendling, Franz Anton   1729–1786

Violinist in service of Mannheim Elector, later in Munich. Married to Elisabeth, below.

Wendling, Dorothea Spurni   1736–1811

Soprano who sang Ilia in Munich premiere of *Idomeneo* (1781).

Wendling, Elisabeth Sarselli   1746–1786

Soprano who sang Electra in Munich premiere of *Idomeneo* (1781). Married to Franz Anton Wendling, above.

Wendling, Johann Baptist   1720–1797

Instrumental composer, flutist, active in Mannheim and Munich. Married to Dorothea, above. Brother of violinist Karl. Fellow Freemason.

Wendt, Joseph von   1745–1801

Vienna oboist active in 1780s, arranger of music from *Die Entführung, Figaro, Così,* etc.

Wenzel, Johann   c. 1750–1810?

Prague organist, publisher of piano version of K. 366, 543, etc.

Werner, Karl   c. 1750–1810?

Viennese physician and friend of Mozart.

Wernhammer, Johann Georg   c. 1760–1810?

Bass who sang in *Die Entführung,* etc., in Donaueschingen.

Werther, F. A. C.   c. 1750–1810?

Poet, translator, whose text Mozart set in K. 365a.

Wessely, Karl   1768–1826

German composer, conductor.

Wetzlar von Plankenstein, Baron Raimund   1752–1810
Patron, landlord, and friend of Mozart in Vienna. Son of Baron Karl
Wetzlar.

Wider, Johann   1707–1797
Host to Mozart in Venice in 1770s.

Widerkehr, Jacques   1729–1823?
Strasbourg-born instrumental composer active in Paris.

Widl, Father Rufinus   1731–1798
Collaborator on *Apollo et Hyacinthus*.

Wieland, Christoph Martin   1733–1813
Important German author whose works Mozart read, and whose
works formed the bases of operas by Schweitzer, Wenzel Müller,
Wranitzky, etc. The tale *Die Zauberflöte*, was published in a collection
of works mostly by Wieland, but actually was by August Jakob
Liesbeskind (c. 1740–1800?). Also translated Shakespeare.

Wieland, Johann Adam   1733–1813
Collaborator on *Die Schuldigkeit*.

Wildburg, Philipp von   c. 1750–1800.
With his wife, a Viennese friend of Constanze and Mozart.

Wilder, Victor   1835–1892
French musician, librettist, writer, member of Breitkopf Mozart Edition
editorial board, 1877–1883.

William V, Prince of Orange   1748–1795
Melomane ruler of Netherlands when Mozart visited in 1764.

Williamson, T. G.   c. 1730–1800?
London musician who published K. 10 and other works in 1764.

Willmann, Walburga   1769–1835
Vienna pianist, pupil of Mozart who performed his music in 1780s. Her
brother Max was a violoncellist; her sister Magdalena was a singer.

Wilson, Bernard E. c. 1910–1980?
American editor of Breitkopf Mozart Edition reprint (1956).

Wimmer, Jakob Anton 1725–1793
Salzburg collaborator on text of *Die Schuldigkeit.*

Winckler, T. F. c. 1760–1810?
Author of biographical notice on Mozart in France, 1801. (Also translator, librettist?)

Winkler, C. E. c. 1750–1800?
Symphonist, pupil of Joseph Haydn (?).

Winter, Felice 1742–1772
Salzburg bass singer who performed Simone in Salzburg premiere of *La finta semplice* (1769). (Related to Felix Winter, who sang Speaker and was stage manager for Vienna *Die Zauberflöte* premiere?)

Winter, Peter von 1755–1825
German composer active in Mannheim, Munich, Vienna, etc.

Winter, Sebastian 1743–1815
Barber-valet of Leopold Mozart, and also a musician.

Wittassek, Johann 1770–1839
Prague composer, pianist, pupil of Duček and Koželuh, who performed Mozart's concerto, K. 466 and other works with success.

Woberzill, Thomas c. 1740–1800?
Conductor and violinist at Vienna court in the 1780s.

Wohanka, Cl.
Composer whose music Mozart knew.

Wolf, Ernst Wilhelm 1735–1792
German singspiel and instrumental composer, active in Weimar and Berlin, whose music Mozart knew.

Wolfegg, Count Anton 1729–1820
Musician, cleric, admirer of Mozart's music. Fellow Freemason.

Wölfl, Joseph Johann   1773–1812

Piano pupil of Mozart in Vienna (1790). Later composer and conductor for Schikaneder.

Woschitka, Franz Xaver   1727–1790

Composer, violoncellist at Munich court; friend of Mozart in 1777.

Wranitzky, Paul   1756–1808

Moravian composer, violinist active in Vienna; pupil of Mozart; fellow Freemason. Brother Anton (1761–1820) was also an active musician in Vienna.

Wüllner, Franz   1832–1902

German composer, Wagner conductor, editor of Breitkopf Mozart Edition, 1877–1883.

Würm, Fräulein (also Würben, Wrbna)   c. 1770–1820?

Viennese pupil of Mozart, for whom he composed K. 485.

Würtemberg, Prince Ludwig   1731–1795

Noble melomane Mozart met in Lausanne.

Yost, Michel   1754–1786

French composer and clarinettist active in the Concert Spirituel when Mozart was in Paris.

Yppold, Franz d'   1730–1790

Salzburg official, unsuccessful suitor for the hand of Nannerl.

Zahradniezek, Joseph   c. 1750–1810?

Viennese artist, engraver; fellow Freemason.

Zappa, Francesco   1730–1790

Italian composer, violoncellist, active in London, Holland, and Switzerland, whom Leopold did not admire.

Zechner, Johann Georg   1716–1778

Viennese church and instrumental composer.

Zelenka, Jan Dismas   1679–1745
Czechoslovakian composer of instrumental music.

Zelter, Carl Friedrich   1758–1832
German composer and teacher in Berlin, who knew many of Mozart's compositions; friend of Goethe.

Zeno, Apostolo   1668–1750
Important librettist. Mozart used his text in K. 61c, and possibly in K. 469.

Zeyl, Count Ferdinand von   1719–1786
Bishop of Chiemsee. Musical connoisseur and patron of Mozart. Fellow Freemason.

Ziani, Marc-Antonio   1653–1715
Venice-born composer of popular operas and church music, active in Vienna.

Zichy, Countess Anna Khevenhüller-Metsch   1759–1809
Viennese piano pupil and good friend of Mozart.

Ziegenhagen, Franz Heinrich   1753–1806
Text poet for K. 619; fellow Freemason.

Ziegler, Joseph   1722–1767
Viennese church and theatre composer, and violinist.

Zilcher, ———   c. 1750–1800?
Viennese composer.

Zimmerman, Anton   1741–1781
Pressburg instrumental composer and organist; also active elsewhere.

Zinck, Benedict   1743–1801
North German instrumental composer and organist.

Zingarelli, Nicola   1752–1837
Neapolitan opera, instrumental, and church composer; also active in Paris and Vienna.

Zini, Saverio   c. 1740–1790?
Italian librettist for Cimarosa, Guglielmi, Paisiello, etc.

Zingoni, Giovanni Battista   c. 1740–1790?

Tenor and instrumental composer mostly active in Holland and England.

Zinzendorf, Count Karl von   1739–1813

Noble Viennese friend and patron of Mozart who appreciated his music, but often criticized it.

Zistler, Joseph   1744–1794

Austrian conductor, violinist, friend of Mozart and Joseph Haydn; fellow Freemason.

Zitterbarth, Bartolomäus   1751–1806

Collaborator of Schikaneder; fellow Freemason.

Zoffany, John   1725–1810

German portraitist, mainly active in England, who may have painted Mozart.

Zöhrer, Franz   1749–1800

Conductor in Regensburg; fellow Freemason.

Zonca, Giovanni   1728–1809

Italian bass singer active in Mannheim and Munich, whose voice Mozart appreciated.

Zucchinetti, G. B.   1730–1801

Milanese chapel master of Monza cathedral whose music Mozart heard in 1770.

Zugeisen, Joseph   c. 1750–1800?

Tenor active at the Salzburg court in the 1770s.

Zulehner, Carl   c. 1760–1830

German church composer and arranger of *Don Giovanni* and *Thamos* piano-vocal scores for Schott. Also music publisher.

Zumsteeg, Johann   1760–1802

German vocal composer mostly active in Stuttgart; good friend of Schiller.

APPENDIX I

Pupils (Chronological List)

K—keyboard; TH—composition; V—voice.
See also Section V, for those whose numbers are italicized.

1771–1776
Salzburg

1. Ignaz Leutgeb (1745–1811)—K
2. Franz Anton Spitzeder (1735–1796)—K
3. Countess Antonia Lützow (1738–1780)—K

1777
Munich

4. Maria Theodora von Branca (c. 1760–1810?)—K
5. Maria Anna von Hamm (c. 1765–1810?)—K
6. Josepha Freysinger (c. 1760–1810?)—K
7. Juliana Freysinger (c. 1755–1810?)—K

Augsburg

8. Nanette Stein (c. 1760–1810?)—K

1777–1778
Mannheim

9. Rosa Cannabich (c. 1760–1810?)—K
10. Ferdinand de la Potterie (c. 1760–1810?)—K
11. Thérèse Pierron Serrarius (1762–1810?)—K
12. Princess Caroline von Nassau-Weilburg (1743–1793)—K
13. Aloysia Weber (1760–1839)—V, X
14. Josepha Weber (1758–1819)—V
15. Christian Danner (1745–1803)—TH

1778
Paris

16. Mademoiselle A. de Guines (c. 1760–1810?)—TH

1779
Salzburg

17. Numerous choirboys

1781
Vienna

18. Baroness Martha Waldstätten (1744–1821)—K
19. Countess Marie Thiennes de Rumbecke (1755–1812)—K
20. Countess Wilhelmine von Thun (1744–1800)—K
21. Josepha Auernhammer (1758–1820)—K
22. Prince Karl Lichnowsky (1755–1814)—K
    (son-in-law of Countess Thun)
23. Thérèse Nagel von Trattner (1758–1793)—K

1782
Vienna

24. Countess Anna Marie von Zichy (1759–1809)—K
25. Count Ludwig Cobenzl (c. 1765–1810?)—K
26. Countess Josepha Pálffy (1765–1810)—K

1783
Vienna

27. Maria Theresia von Paradies (1759–1824)—K
28. Ludwig Gall (1752–1835)—K

1784
Vienna

29. Barbara von Ployer (1766–1811)—K,TH
30. (Elisabeth?) Stadler (c. 1765–1810?)—K,TH
31. Anton Eberl (1765–1807)—K

1785
Vienna

32. Thomas Attwood (1765–1838)—TH

1786
Vienna

33. Count August Hatzfeld (1756–1787)—Violin?
34. Michael Kelly (1762–1826)—V
35. Johann Nepomuk Hummel (1778–1837)—K, TH
36. Stephen Storace (1747–1805)—TH
37. Marianne (Babette) Natorp (1769–1844)—K
38. Nanette Natorp (1766–1791)—K

39. Marianne Henikstein (c. 1770–1820?)—K
40. Marianne Walburga Willmann (1769–1835)—TH
41. Baron Gottfried von Jacquin (1767–1792)—TH
42. Franziska von Jacquin (1769–1853)—K
43. Franz Freystädtler (1768–1841)—TH
44. Frau (Rosa?) Schulz (c. 1760–1810?)
    There are at least three possible candidates for the identity
    of "Frau Schulz"
    1. Rosa Cannabich (1760–1810?)
    2. Josepha Rabenau (1755–1795?)
    3. Maria Zauner (1730–1783?)

1788
Vienna

45. Josepha Müller (c. 1770–1820?)—K
46. Ludwig van Beethoven (1770–1827)—TH
47. Anton Liste (1774–1832)—K

1789
Berlin

48. Henriette Baranius (1768–1853)—V

1790
Vienna

49. Dr. Joseph Frank (c. 1765–1810?)—K
50. Magda Pokorny Hofdemel (1766–1810?)—Violin, K ?
51. Philipp Karl Hoffmann (1769–1842)—K
52. Franz Xaver Süssmayr (1766–1803)—TH
53. Joseph Eybler (1765–1846)—TH
54. Anton Wranitzky (1761–1820)—TH
55. Ignaz von Seyfried (1776–1841)—TH
56. Franz de Paula Roser (1779–1830)—K

57. Karl Anton Göpfert (1768–1818)—K
58. Caroline Pichler (1769–1843)—K
59. Joseph (Johann) Wölfl (1773–1812)—K
60. Franz Seraph von Destouches (1772–1844)—K

APPENDIX II

Patrons, Vienna, 1784 (Alphabetical List)

See Section 5 for further information on those whose number is italicized.

1. Aguilar, Marquis Conde de la Torre c. 1740–1790? (Spanish Ambassador in Vienna, 1779–1784)
2. Aichelburg, Regine Wetzler von
3. Althan, Countess Eleonore Batthyány
4. Apponyi, Count Anton (1751–1817) and Countess Thérèse
5. Arnstein, Nathan von 1743–1833
6. Auersperg, Prince Karl 1750–1822
7. Auersperg, Princess Maria Josepha Trautson
8. Auersperg, Prince Adam 1721–1795
9. Auersperg, Count Karl 1750–1822
10. Auersperg, Count Wilhelm
11. Bánffy, Count Georg
12. Batthyány, Count Anton c. 1720–1799
13. Bedekovich von Kumur, Franz (Anton?) 1755–1825
14. Béothy, Councillor Joseph
15. Béothy, Frau "Betty" (wife of above)
16. Binnenfeld, Johann Adam
17. Born, Ignaz von 1742–1791
18. Braun, Baron Karl Adolf von
19. Braun, Johann Gottlieb von
20. Burkhardt, Baron

21. Burkhardt, Baroness
22. Chotek, Count Johann Rudolf 1748–1800?
23. Czernin, Count Johann 1757–1845
24. Dalberg, Baron Johann Friedrich Hugo 1752–1812
25. Deglmann, Baron Bernhard c. 1740–1790?
26. Dietrichstein, Count Joseph c. 1740–1810?
27. Ditmar, Baron Gottfried Rudolf von c. 1740–1800?
28. Drossdik, Johann Baptist von c. 1740–1800?
29. Dzierzanowsky, Count Michael (?)
30. Edlenbach, Benedikt von 1748–1800?
31. Ehrenfeld, Joseph Frech von
32. Engelsperg, Frau von (wife of Joachim von Engelsperg)
33. Engeström, Baron Lars von c. 1740–1800?
34. Erdödy, Count Ladislas c. 1750–1810? (brother of Count Peter or Count Sigismund)
35. Esterházy, Count Franz 1715–1785?
36. Esterházy, Count Johann 1747–1796
37. Esterházy, Countess Maria (?)
38. Fechenbach, Baron Karl Philipp Ferdinand
39. Fichtl, Johann Baptist von c. 1720–1790
40. Finta, Baron Joseph von 1732–1802
41. Fries, Count Johann 1719–1785
42. Gebsattel, Baron
43. Gleichen, Baron Heinrich c. 1740–1800?
44. Golicyn (Galitsin), Prince Demetrius 1720–1794
45. Gontard, Baron Johann Jakob c. 1760–1819
46. Graneri, Count Peter c. 1740–1800?
47. Greiner, Franz Sales von 1731–1798
48. Grezmüller (the elder), Erasmus von
49. Grezmüller (the younger), Johann Nepomuk
50. Hall, Baron Theodor
51. Häring, Johann Baptist von 1760–1818
52. Harrach (the elder?), Count Johann Nepomuk 1756–1829
53. Harrach, Count Ernst 1757–1838
54. Hartenstein, Franz Zacharias von 1734–1796
55. Hatzfeld, Countess Maria Anna Hortensia Zierotin
56. Henikstein, Adam Adalbert, Honig von 1740–1811
57. Hentschell, Leonard von

58. Herberstein, Count Bishop Johann Karl 1719–1787
59. Herberstein, Count Joseph Franz Stanislaus 1757–1816 (?)
60. Herberstein, Count Joseph
61. Herberstein, Count Nepomuk Johann 1727–1809
62. Hess, Frau Kannegieser von (wife of Joachim von Hess, 1740–1801?)
63. Hess, Frau Maria Theresia Leporini von c. 1740–1798 (wife of Franz Joseph von Hess)
64. Hochstetter, Baron Gottfried von
65. Hoyos, Count Johann Leopold Innozenz 1728–1796
66. Izdenczy, Joseph
67. Jacobi, Konstantin (later Baron Klöst) 1745–1816
68. Jacomini, Herr
69. Jahn, Ignaz von c. 1740–1800?
70. Jungwirth, Baron Franz
71. Kaunitz, Prince Dominik 1739–1812
72. Kees, Franz von 1720–1795
73. Keglevich, Count Joseph 1729–1800
74. Khevenhüller, Count Joseph 1709–1784 and Countess Karolina
75. Kluszewsky, Count
76. Knecht, Johann Anton von
77. Koller, Count Franz Xaver
78. Kollonitz, Count Karl Joseph 1730–1804
79. Kuefstein, Count Johann F. 1752–1818
80. Lamezan, Count Joseph von
81. Lewenau, Joseph Arnold von 1755–1829
82. Lichnowsky, Princess Christine Thun c. 1720–1790?
83. Liechtenstein, Prince Alois 1759–1805
84. Lobkowitz, Prince Joseph 1725–1802
85. Lüewald, Ferdinand von
86. Lutz, Peter von 1754–1809
87. Madruzzi, Baron Joseph von
88. Mandelslohe, Baron Lunikshausen von
89. Margelick, Frau von (wife of Joseph von Margelick)
90. Marschall von Biberstein, Count
91. Martini, Baron Karl 1726–1800
92. Mayenberg, Anton Joseph von

93. Mecklenberg, Duke Georg August   1730–1785
94. Montecuculli, Marquis François de   1767–1827
95. Morton, Lord George
96. Müller, Johann Christian von
97. Nádasty, Count Franz   1745–1802
98. Neipperg, Count Leopold Johann   1728–1792
99. Neuhold, Frau von (wife of Joseph von Neuhold)
100. Nevery, Alexis Leopoldus von
101. Nimptsch, Count Joseph   1755–1838
102. Nimptsch, Frau von (wife of above)
103. Nostitz, Count Joseph   1706–1787
104. Nostitz, General Friedrich Moritz von   1728–1796
105. Nostitz, Count Franz Anton   1720–1787?
106. Oettingen, Count Philipp   1759–1826
107. Oeynhausen, Count Philipp   c. 1740–1810
108. Ott, Joseph von
109. Paar, Prince Wenzel   1744–1812?
110. Paar, Prince Wenzel Johann   1719–1792
111. Pálffy, Prince Joseph   1764–1827
112. Palm, Prince Karl Joseph   1749–1814
113. Palm, Princess Maria   1746–1802
114. Passowitz, Countess
115. Passthory, Alexander von
116. Pentzenstein, Johann Penzeneter von
117. Pergen, Count Johann   1725–1814
118. Ployer, Agent Gottfried Ignaz von   c. 1740–1800?
119. Podstatzky, Count Joseph
120. Poncet, Frau von
121. Prandau, Baron Franz   1751–1811
122. Prandau, Baron Joseph
123. Pufendorf, Anna von   1757–1843
124. Puthon, Johann von   1745–1816
125. Raab, Dr. Ignaz   1743–1811
126. Rosty, Colonel Ignaz von
127. Rottenhahn, Count Heinrich   1737–1809
128. Salburg, Count Christoph   1732–1806
129. Sauer, Count Wenzel Ferdinand   1718–1793
130. Sauer, Countess (wife of above)
131. Sauer, Countess (wife of Count Kajetan)

132. Schaffgotsch, Countess Maria Kollnitz 1744–1802
133. Schleinitz, Wilhelm von c. 1750–1810?
134. Schwab, Philipp J. 1750–1811
135. Schwarzenberg, Prince Johann 1742–1789
136. Seilern, Count August 1717–1801
137. Seilern, Count Joseph 1737–1809
138. Smitmer, Jakob von
139. Soltyk, Count August
140. Sonnenfels, Joseph von 1733–1817
141. Sonnfeld, Leopold von
142. Starhemberg, Countess Wilhelmine Neipperg
143. Sternberg, Count Franz
144. Sternberg, Count Adam
145. Sternberg, Count Grundacker 1737–1802
146. Stöckel, Frau von (wife of Franz Xaver Stöckel, art dealer, 1756–1810?)
147. Stockmayer, Baron Jakob von
148. Stopford, Lord James
149. Streeruwitz, Johann Nepomuk von
150. Swieten, Baron Gottfried van 1733–1803
151. Thun, Countess Wilhelmine Uhlefeldt 1744–1800
152. Trattner, Thérèse Nagel von 1758–1793 (wife of the printer, Johann von Trattner, 1717–1798?)
153. Türkheim, Frau von (wife of Ludwig von Türkheim)
154. Ugarte, Count Johann Wenzel 1748–1796
155. Ugarte, Countess Maria Josepha (wife of above)
156. Urmenyi, Joseph von 1741–1825
157. Vasseg, Count Edmund Maria
158. Vockel, Baron Friedrich
159. Waldstein, Count Franz de Paula 1759–1823
160. Waldstein, Count Georg 1743–1791
161. Waldstein, Countess Marie Elisabeth Uhlefeldt 1747–1791
162. Waldstetten, Baroness Martha 1744–1821 (wife of Baron Hugo Waldstetten)
163. Weinbrenner, Joseph von 1728–1807
164. Wetzlar, Baron Karl 1716–1799
165. Wetzlar, Baron Raimund 1752–1810
166. Wilczek, Count Franz Joseph 1748–1834
167. Winkler, Baron Joseph Johann von

168. Wölker, Lazarus von
169. Wrbna, Count Joseph   1738–1809
170. Wrbna, Count Eugene   1728–1789
171. Wrbna, Count Louis
172. Würtemberg, Prince Ferdinand
173. Yriarte, Don Domingo (Secretary, Spanish Embassy in Vienna)
174. Zichy, Count Karl   1753–1826
175. Zichy, Count Stefan   1757–1841
176. Zinzendorf, Count Karl von   1739–1813
177. Zois, Baron Joseph   1741–1800?

APPENDIX III

Alphabetical List of Characters in Mozart's Works

Aceste—priest of Venus—tenor
  Ascanio in Alba, K. 111.
Achior—prince of the Ammonites—bass
  La Betulia liberata, K. 74c (118).
Agenor—noble friend of Alexander in love with Tamyris—tenor
  Il re pastore, K. 208.
Alexander—king of Macedonia—tenor
  Il re pastore, K. 208.
Don Alfonso—a mature philosopher—bass
  Così fan tutte, K. 588.
Allazim—a Christian turned Mohammedan—bass
  Zaide, K. 336b.
Count Almaviva—Spanish nobleman—bass
  Le nozze di Figaro, K. 492.
Countess Almaviva (Rosina)—his wife—soprano
  Le nozze di Figaro, K. 492.
Amintas—shepherd in love with Elisa—male soprano
  Il re pastore, K. 208.
Amital—noble Israelite woman—soprano
  La Betulia liberata, K. 74c (118).
Don Anchises—lord of Lagonero, in love with Sandrina—tenor
  La finta giardiniera, K. 196.
Donna Anna—fiancée of Don Ottavio—soprano

Don Giovanni, K. 527.

Annius—friend of Sextus, in love with Servilia—soprano
  La clemenza di Tito, K. 621.

Antonio—gardener at Almaviva's estate—bass
  Le nozze di Figaro, K. 492.

Apollo—guest of Oebalus—alto
  Apollo et Hyacinthus, K. 38.

Arbace—adjutant of Idomeneo—tenor
  Idomeneo, K. 366

Arbate—governor of city of Nymphea—male soprano
  Mitridate, K. 74a (87).

Arminda—niece of Anchises, fiancée of Belfiore (formerly in love
with Ramiro)—soprano
  La finta giardiniera, K. 196.

Ascanio—grandson of Venus, fathered by Aeneas—male soprano
  Ascanio in Alba, K. 111

Don Asdrubale—brave officer loved by Bettina—tenor
  Lo sposo deluso, K. 424a (430).

Aspasia—fiancée of King Mitridate—soprano
  Mitridate, K. 74a (87).

Aufidio—governor, friend of Silla—tenor
  Lucio Silla, K. 135.

Auretta—chambermaid to Pantea—soprano
  L'oca del Cairo, K. 422.

Barbarina—daughter of Antonio—soprano
  Le nozze di Figaro, K. 492.

Barmherzigkeit—Mercy—soprano
  Die Schuldigkeit des ersten Gebotes, K. 35.

Dr. Bartolo—physician in Seville—bass
  Le nozze di Figaro, K. 492.

Don Basilio—music master in Almaviva's household—tenor
  Le nozze di Figaro, K 492.

Bastien—Shepherd—tenor
  Bastien und Bastienne

Bastienne—Shepherdess—soprano
  Bastien und Bastienne, K. 46b (50).

Count Belfiore—ex-fiancé of Violante, now betrothed to Arminda
  La finta giardiniera, K. 196.

Belmonte—lover of Constanze—tenor

Die Entführung aus dem Serail, K. 384.

Bettina—vain young niece of Bocconio—soprano
Lo sposo deluso, K. 424a (430).

Biondello—town plutocrat—tenor
L'oca del Cairo, K. 422.

Blondchen—English maid of Constanze—soprano
Die Entführung aus dem Serail, K. 384.

Bocconio Papparelli—stupid fiancé of Eugenia—bass
Lo sposo deluso, K. 424a (430)

Boy—Spirit in service of Sarastro—treble (also Second and Third Boy)
Die Zauberflöte, K. 620.

Buff—actor—speaking role
Der Schauspieldirektor, K. 486.

Cabri—co-leader of Betulia—soprano
La Betulia liberata, K. 74c (118).

Calandrino—nephew of Pantea, in love with Lavina—tenor
L'oca del Cairo, K. 422.

Carmi—co-leader of Betulia—soprano
La Betulia liberata, K. 74c (118).

Cassandro—overbearing landowner—bass
La finta semplice, K. 46a (51).

Cecilio—condemned senator—male soprano
Lucio Silla, K. 135.

Celia—sister of Silla, ruler of Rome—soprano
Lucio Silla, K. 135.

Celidora—daughter of Pantea, in love with Biondello—soprano
L'oca del Cairo, K. 422.

Cherubino—page of Almaviva—soprano
Le nozze di Figaro, K. 492.

Chichibio—majordomo of Pippo, lover of Auretta—bass
L'oca del Cairo, K. 422.

Cinna—Roman patrician, friend of Cecilio—soprano
Lucio Silla, K. 135.

Christian—lukewarm, later zealous Christian—tenor
Die Schuldigkeit des ersten Gebotes, K. 35.

Christgeist—Christianity—tenor
Die Schuldigkeit des ersten Gebotes, K. 35.

Colas—shepherd, and village soothsayer—bass

Bastien und Bastienne, K. 46b (50).

Commendatore—father of Donna Anna—bass
Don Giovanni, K. 527.

Constanza—Constancy—soprano
Il sogno di Scipio, K. 126.

Constanze—Spanish Lady captured by Pasha—soprano
Die Entführung aus dem Serail, K. 384.

Don Curzio—lawyer—tenor
Le nozze di Figaro, K. 492.

Despina—ladies' maid—soprano
Così fan tutte, K. 588.

Dorabella—younger of two sisters, fiancée of Ferrando
Così fan tutte, K. 588.

Eiler—banker—speaking role
Der Schauspieldirektor, K. 486.

Electra—daughter of King Agamemnon of Argos—soprano
Idomeneo, K. 366.

Elisa—Phoenician in love with Amintas—soprano
Il re pastore, K. 208.

Donna Elvira—lady from Burgos, abandoned by Don Giovanni—
soprano
Don Giovanni, K. 527.

Emilio—Scipio's real father—tenor
Il sogno di Scipione, K. 126.

Eugenia—Roman lady faithful to Asdrubale—soprano
Lo sposo deluso, K. 424a (430).

Farnace—elder son of king, in love with Aspasia—male soprano
Mitridate, K. 74a (87).

Fauno—shepherd—male soprano
Ascanio in Alba, K. 111.

Ferrando—officer, fiancé of Dorabella—tenor
Così fan tutte, K. 588.

Figaro—valet of Almaviva—bass
Le nozze di Figaro, K. 492.

Fiordiligi—older of two sisters, fiancée of Guglielmo—soprano
Così fan tutte, K. 588.

Fortuna—Fortune—soprano
Il sogno di Scipione, K. 126.

Fracasso—Hungarian officer, lodging with Cassandro—tenor

La finta semplice, K. 46a, (51).
Frank—impressario—speaking role
Der Schauspieldirektor, K. 486.
Gerechtigkeit—Justice—soprano
Die Schuldigkeit des ersten Gebotes, K. 35.
Gervasio—tutor of Eugenia, suitor of Metilda—bass
Lo sposo deluso, K. 424a (430).
Giacinta—older sister of Cassandro—soprano
La finta semplice, K. 46a (51).
Don Giovanni—licentious young Spanish nobleman—bass
Don Giovanni, K. 527.
Giuditta—widow of Manasses, daughter of Merari—alto
La Betulia liberata, K. 74c (118).
Giunia—fiancée of Cecilio—soprano
Lucio Silla, K. 135.
Gomatz—son of Sultan, in love with Zaide—tenor
Zaide, K. 336b (344).
Guglielmo—officer, fiancé of Fiordiligi—bass
Così fan tutte, K. 588.
Hammon—priest loyal to Menos (Sethos)—speaking role
Thamos, K. 336a (345).
Herz—actor—speaking role
Der Schauspieldirektor, K. 486
Madame Herz—singer—soprano
Der Schauspieldirektor, K. 486
Hyacinthus—son of Oebalus—treble
Apollo et Hyacinthus, K. 38.
Idamante—son of Idomeneo—male soprano/tenor
Idomeneo, K. 366.
Idomeneo—King of Crete—tenor
Idomeneo, K. 366.
Ilia—daughter of Priam, King of Troy—soprano
Idomeneo, K. 366.
Ismene—daughter of King of Parthia—soprano
Mitridate, K. 74c (87).
Klaas—sailor in service of Belmonte—speaking role
Die Entführung aus dem Serail, K. 384.
Madame Krone—actress—speaking role
Der Schauspieldirecktor, K. 486.

Lady (First)—in service of Queen of the Night—soprano (also Second Lady and Third Lady)
Die Zauberflöte, K. 620.
Leporello—personal valet of Don Giovanni—bass
Don Giovanni, K. 527.
Lavina—companion of Celidora—soprano
L'oca del Cairo, K. 422.
Man in Armour—subject of Sarastro—tenor (also second Man in Armour—bass)
Die Zauberflöte, K. 620.
Marcellina—Lady in waiting at Almaviva Estate—soprano
Le nozze di Figaro, K. 492.
Marzio—governor, friend of Farnace—tenor
Mitridate, K. 74c (87).
Masetto—fiancé of Zerlina—bass
Don Giovanni, K. 527.
Melia—daughter of Oebalus—treble
Apollo et Hyacinthus, K. 38.
Metilde—singer and dancer in love with Asdrubale—soprano
Lo sposo deluso, K. 424a (430).
Mirza—virgin, faithful to Phero
Thamos, K. 336a (345).
Mitridate—king of Pontus, fiancé of Aspasia—tenor
Mitridate, K. 74a (87).
Monostatos—evil Moor in service of Sarastro—tenor
Die Zauberflöte, K. 620.
Nardo—see Roberto.
Ninetta—maid of Giacinta—soprano
La finta semplice, K. 46a (51).
Oebalus—king of Sparta—tenor
Apollo et Hyacinthus, K. 38.
Osmin—a slave trader—bass
Zaide, K. 336b (344).
Osmin—custodian of Pasha's estate—bass
Die Entführung aus dem Serail, K. 384.
Don Ottavio—fiancé of Donna Anna—tenor
Don Giovanni, K. 527.
Ozia—son of Micah, governor of Betulia—tenor
La Betulia liberata, K. 74c (118).

Pamina—daughter of Queen of the Night—soprano
  Die Zauberflöte, K. 620.
Donna Pantea—wife of Pippo, now known as Sandra—soprano
  L'oca del Cairo, K. 422.
Papagena—lover of Papageno, first disguised as old lady—soprano
  Die Zauberflöte, K. 620.
Papageno—birdcatcher—bass
  Die Zauberflöte, K. 620.
Pedrillo—former servant of Belmonte, now in Pasha's service—
tenor(baritone)
  Die Entführung aus dem Serail, K. 384.
Madame Pfeil—actress—speaking role
  Der Schauspieldirecktor, K. 486.
Don Pippo—lord of an Italian seaport, in love with Lavina—bass
  L'oca del Cairo, K. 422.
Polidoro—timid younger brother of Cassandro—tenor
  La finta semplice, K. 46a (51).
Priest (First)—in service of Sarastro—non-singing role (Second
Priest—tenor; Third Priest—bass)
  Die Zauberflöte, K. 620.
Priest (I & II)—acolytes of Apollo—bass
  Apollo et Hyacinthus, K. 38.
Publio—Scipio's adopted father—tenor
  Il sogno di Scipione, K. 126.
Publius—captain of the guard—bass
  La clemenza di Tito, K. 621.
Pulcherio—woman-hating friend of Bocconio—tenor
  Lo sposo deluso, K. 424a (430).
Queen of the Night—mother of Pamina—soprano
  Die Zauberflöte, K. 620.
Cavalier Ramiro—rejected suitor of Arminda—male soprano
  La finta giardiniera, K. 196.
Roberto—Violante's servant, disguised as her cousin, Nardo—bass
  La finta giardiniera, K. 196.
Rosina—sister of Fracasso—soprano
  La finta semplice, K. 46a (51).
Sandrina—see Violante
Sarastro—high priest of the sun—bass
  Die Zauberflöte, K. 620.

Scipione—Roman warrior—tenor
   Il sogno di Scipione, K. 126.
Pasha Selim—suitor of Constanze—speaking role
   Die Entführung aus dem Serail, K. 384.
Serpetta—maid of Anchises, in love with him—soprano
   La finta giardiniera, K. 196.
Servilia—sister of Sextus, in love with Annius—soprano
   La clemenza di Tito, K. 621.
Sextus—friend of Titus, in love with Vitellia—soprano
   La clemenza di Tito, K. 621.
Sifare—successful suitor of Aspasia—male soprano
   Mitridate, K. 74a (87).
Madame Silberklang—singer—soprano
   Die Schauspieldirektor, K. 486.
Lucio Silla—Roman dictator—tenor
   Lucio Silla, K. 135.
Silvia—nymph related to Hercules, fiancée of Ascanio—soprano
   Ascanio in Alba, K. 111.
Simone—valet of Fracasso—bass
   La finta semplice, K. 46a (51).
Slave—(First, also Second, and Third) in service of Sarastro—non-singing roles
   Die Zauberflöte, K. 620.
Sultan Soliman—eastern potentate—tenor
   Zaide, K. 336b (344).
Speaker—priest in service of Sarastro—non-singing role
   Die Zauberflöte, K. 620.
Susanna—maid of Rosina, fiancée of Figaro—soprano
   Le nozze di Figaro, K. 492.
Tamino—foreign prince—tenor
   Die Zauberflöte, K. 620.
Tamyris—shepherdess (princess in disguise) in love with Agenor—soprano
   Il re pastore, K. 208.
Thamos—king of Egypt—speaking role, as are six other roles in this play by Gebler for which Mozart composed interludes and choruses, K. 336a (345).
   Thamos, K. 336a (345)

Tharsis—virtuous daughter of Menes
   Thamos, K. 336a (345).
Titus—emperor of Rome—tenor
   La clemenza di Tito, K. 621.
Venus—goddess of love—soprano
   Ascanio in Alba, K. 111.
Violante—former fiancée of Belfiore, disguised as Sandrina—
soprano
   La finta giardiniera, K. 196.
Vitellia—ambitious daughter of former emperor—soprano
   La clemenza di Tito, K. 621.
Vogelsang—singer—tenor
   Der Schauspieldirektor, K. 486.
Madame Vogelsang—actress—speaking role
   Der Schauspieldirektor, K. 486.

Identifiable Locales in Mozart's Works

Alba, near Rome
   Ascanio in Alba, K. 111.
Betulia, Judea
   La Betulia liberata, K. 74c (118).
Crete
   Idomeneo, K. 366.
Egypt
   Thamos, König in Aegypten, K. 336a (345).
   Die Zauberflöte, K. 621.
Italy
   L'oca del Cairo, K. 422.
   Così fan tutte, K. 588: Naples, or Venice, or Trieste.
Lacedaemonia, Greece
   Apollo et Hyacinthus, K. 38.
Lagonero, Italy (Lagonegro?)
   La finta giardiniera, K. 196.
Leghorn, Italy
   Lo sposo deluso, K. 424a (430).

Lydia (Italy)
  Apollo et Hyacinthus, K. 38.
Numidia, Africa
  Il sogno di Scipione, K. 126.
Ponto, Greece
  Mitridate, K. 74c (87).
Rome
  Lucio Silla, K. 135.
  La clemenza di Tito, K. 621.
Seville (surroundings)
  Le nozze di Figaro, K. 492.
  Don Giovanni, K. 527.
Sidon, Phoenicia
  Il re pastore, K. 208.
Turkey
  Die Entführung aus dem Serail, K. 386.
  Zaide, K. 336b (344).

APPENDIX IV

Organizations Concerned with Mozart and His Music.

Societies/workshops, some with regular or irregular bulletins. List compiled from published and unpublished sources, including Internationale Stiftung Mozarteum, Salzburg, and *Mitteilungen der ISM*. Dates of founding and officers named when known. Formal and informal groups are included (some of which may be inactive presently). Alphabetized by city.

AMSTERDAM, HOLLAND (see also ZEIST)
The Mozart Society (Reorganized, 1930)
Directors: Mr. and Mrs. Hermann Paschier (1980)

ANSBACH, GERMANY
Mozart Gemeinde (1902)

ARNSBERG, GERMANY
Mozart-Gesellschaft Arnsberg (1979)
Oberstudienrat Manfred Hörr (1986)
Kettelburgstrasse 23
D-5760 Arnsberg 1

ATHENS, GREECE

Mozart-Society Athens (1953?)
President: Professor Ida Margaritis (1986)
Nereidon 3
Athens—P. Phaliron

ATLANTA, GEORGIA, U.S.A

Pro-Mozart Society of Atlanta, Georgia (1965?)
Director: Mrs. Beatrice L. Senn (1986)
4558 Roswell Road, Apt B2
Atlanta, Georgia 30342

AUGSBURG, GERMANY

Deutsche Mozart Gesellschaft e. V. (1951?)
President: Professor Dr. Erich Valentin (1986)
Karlstrasse 6
D-8900 Augsburg
Publishes *Acta Mozartiana* since 1954 (Quarterly)

Mozartgemeinde Augsburg
Studiendirektor: Helmut Haug (1986)
Friedrich Maurer-Weg 22
D-8900 Augsburg 22

BAD AIBLING, GERMANY

Mozartgemeinde Südostbayern
President: Professor Dr. Erich Valentin (1986)
Maillingerstrasse 8/12
D-8202 Bad Aibling

BADGASTEIN, GERMANY

Mozart Gesellschaft (1902)

BAD ISCHL, AUSTRIA

Mozart-Gemeinde (1962)

BARCELONA, SPAIN

Associació Amies de Mozart Barcelona
President: Professor Josep M. Bosch (1986)
Jesús i Maria, 4, torre
Barcelona-22

BASEL, SWITZERLAND

Mozart-Gemeinde Basel
President: Ernst Neuner (1986)
C. F. Meyerstrasse 60
CH-4059 Basel

BAYREUTH, GERMANY

Mozart-Gemeinde Bayreuth (1969?)
F. Schmidt, Notar (1986)
Maxstrasse 8
D-8580 Bayreuth

BERLIN, GERMANY

Mozart Gesellschaft (1894)
Publications

BERN, SWITZERLAND

Mozart Gesellschaft (1898)

BLOOMINGTON, INDIANA, U.S.A.

Mozart Society (1965)

BONN, GERMANY

Mozart Gesellschaft (1902)

BOSTON AND CHICAGO, U.S.A.

Salzburger Society (1937, now inactive)

BREMEN, GERMANY

Mozartgemeinde (1933) (1967)
President: Elly Helms (1958)

BRÜNN, AUSTRIA
Mozart Gesellschaft (1902)

BRUSSELS, BELGIUM
Les amis de Mozart (1898)

BUDAPEST, HUNGARY
Mozart Society and Mozart Youth Club (1902) (1926)

BUENOS AIRES, ARGENTINA
Mozarteum Argentino (1967)
President: Jeannette Arate de Arize (1986)
Buenos Aires, Rodriguez Pena 1882

CANNES, FRANCE
Les amis de Mozart (1966)

CELLE, AUSTRIA
Mozart Gesellschaft (1902)

CHICAGO, ILLINOIS, U.S.A. (see under Boston)

CHRISTIANA, NORWAY
"Mozart Workshop" (1898)

COBLENZ, GERMANY
Mozart Gesellschaft (1955)

COLOGNE, GERMANY
Mozart Gesellschaft (1902) (1953)

DALLAS, TEXAS, U.S.A.
"Mozart Workshop" (1965)

DETROIT, MICHIGAN, U.S.A.
Pro Mozart Society of Greater Detroit (1967)
Director: Mrs. Marguerite Kozenn Chajas
14511 Rosemary
Oak Park, Michigan 48237

DORTMUND, GERMANY
Mozart-Gesellschaft Dortmund e. V. (1967)
Director: Peter Wiegmann (1986)
Schwanenwall 8-10
D-4600 Dortmund 1

DRESDEN, GERMANY
(1898, with over 1600 members in 1900)
Mozart Gesellschaft
Occasional publications

DÜSSELDORF, GERMANY
Mozart Gesellschaft (1902)

FRANKFURT, GERMANY
Mozart-Gesellschaft Frankfurt e. V. (reorganized 1902)
Director: Frank Stähle (1986)
c/o Stiftung Dr. Hochs Konservatorium
Eschersheimer, Landstrasse 4
D-6000 Frankfurt

FÜRTH, GERMANY
Mozart Gesellschaft (1902)

GRAN, AUSTRIA
Mozart Gesellschaft (1902)

GRAZ, AUSTRIA
Mozartgemeinde Graz (1902)(1953)
Director: Dr. Manfred Ortner
Musikwissenschaftliches Institut der Universität Graz
8010 Graz, Mozartgasse 3

HAMBURG, GERMANY
Mozart-Gemeinde (1902)

HEILIGENKREUZ, AUSTRIA
Mozart Gesellschaft (1902)

HILDESHEIM, GERMANY
Mozart-Gemeinde Hildesheim e. V. (1981)
Director: Joachim Stepp
Bahnhofsallee 40
D-3200 Hildesheim

IGLAU, AUSTRIA
Mozart Gesellschaft (1902)

INNSBRUCK, AUSTRIA
Mozartgemeinde Innsbruck (1955)
Director: Herwig Widmoser
Maria Theresienstrasse 8
8020 Innsbruck

KARLSRUHE, GERMANY
Mozart Gesellschaft (1902)

KLAGENFURT, AUSTRIA
Mozartgemeinde Klagenfurt (1935)
Director: Frau Britte Zechner
Kramergasse 2-4
9020 Klagenfurt

KØBENHAVN (COPENHAGEN), DENMARK
"Mozart Workshop" (1898)

KÖNIGSBERG, GERMANY (now Kalingrad, U.S.S.R.)
Mozart Gesellschaft (1902)

LEIPZIG, GERMANY
Mozart Gesellschaft (1902)

LENINGRAD (see Saint Petersburg)

LINDAU-BREGENZ, GERMANY

Mozart Gemeinde (1987)

LISBON, PORTUGAL

Mozarteum (1969)

LONDON, ENGLAND

Mozart Society (1898)

Haydn-Mozart Society (1946?)
Harry Blech, Music Director
70 Leopold Road, Wimbledon
London SW 19 7 J Q, England
Publication: Haydn-Mozart Newsletter

LÖRRACH, GERMANY

Mozart Gesellschaft (1902)

LUDWIGSBERG, GERMANY

Mozart Gesellschaft (1969)

LUDWIGSHAFEN, GERMANY

Mozart Gemeinde (1969)

LUXEMBOURG

"Pro Mozart" (1957)

LYON, FRANCE

Mozarteum de France à Lyon (1967)
23, rue Tramassac
Lyon 5, France

MAINZ, GERMANY

Mozart Gesellschaft (1902)

MANNHEIM, GERMANY

Mozartgemeinde Kurpfalz e. V.
(including Ludwigsberg & Heidelberg) (1902)
Geschäftsführer: Gert Ulrich
Tattersallstrasse 39
D-6800 Mannheim 1

MARBURG, GERMANY

Mozart Gesellschaft (1902)

MIAMI BEACH, FLORIDA, U.S.A.

Mozart Society (1965)
Professor Marie-Louise Mansfeld-Leeds
2800 Fairgreen Drive
Miami Beach, Florida, 33140

MILAN, ITALY

Società Mozart (1958)

MOSCOW, U.S.S.R

Mozart Society (1967)

MUNICH, GERMANY

Mozart-Gemeinde München e. V. (1902)
Richard-Wagner Strasse 75
Professor Otto Winkler (1986)

NEUBERG/DONAU, GERMANY

Neuberger Mozartgemeinde
Dr. Fritz von Philipp
Karlsplatz A 14
D-8858 Neuberg/Donau

NEW ORLEANS, LOUISIANA, U.S.A.

"Mozart Society Workshop" (1965)

NEW YORK, NEW YORK, U.S.A.

Friends of Mozart, Inc. (1974)
President: Mrs. Erna Schwerin
Box 24, F.D.R. Station
New York, New York, 10150
Concerts, publications.

The Mozart Festival Orchestra, Inc. (1957)
Director: Dr. Baird Hastings
33 Greenwich Avenue
New York, New York 10014
Concerts, occasional publications, etc.

NORTH RYDE, NEW SOUTH WALES 2113, AUSTRALIA

The Sydney Mozart Society (1986)
President: David Worobin
22 Warwick Street
North Ryde, NSW 2113

NUREMBERG, GERMANY

Mozart-Verein von 1829, e. V. Nürnberg
Dr. Hermann Thorwart
Rechtanswalt
Karolinenstrasse 31-33
D-8500 Nürnberg

OBERLIN COLLEGE, OHIO, U.S.A.

Mozart Society (1958)
Oberlin College, Ohio, U.S.A. 44074

OFFENBACH, GERMANY

Mozart Gesellschaft (1955)

OLMÜTZ, GERMANY

Mozart Gesellschaft (1902)

ORLEANS, FRANCE

Association Mozart
M. Marcel Dupont
L'Alouette, Vouzon
F-41600 Lamotte-Beuvon

PARIS, FRANCE

Association Française des Amis de Mozart et de Maîtres Classiques
(1898)
Guy Mollat du Jourdin
54, rue du Général Delestraint
F-75016, Paris

PRAGUE, CZECHOSLOVAKIA

Mozartova obeč v CSSR
Präsidentin: Jitka Snízková
Vizepräsident: Dr. Frantisek Sauer
Postovni Schranka 8
CSSR—Prag 5
(1902; reorganized 1927; issues bulletins)

REGENSBURG, GERMANY

Mozart Gemeinde Regensburg e. V. (1967)
Dr. Liselotte Reiter
Margaretenau 36
D-8400 Regensburg

REIMS, FRANCE

Association Mozart (1970)

ROME, ITALY

Società Mozart

ROTTERDAM, HOLLAND

Mozart Society (1902)

SAALFELDEN, AUSTRIA

Mozart Gesellschaft (1902)

SAINT GALL, SWITZERLAND
Association Mozart (1925)

ST. LOUIS, MISSOURI, U.S.A.
Mozart Society (1902)

SAINT PETERSBURG, RUSSIA (now Leningrad, U.S.S.R.)
Mozart Society (1898)

SALZBURG, AUSTRIA
Mozarteum (1880)
Leiter der wissenschaftlichen
Abteilung: Dr. Rudolph Angermüller
A-5024 Salzburg, Austria
Library, unique archives, series and other publications.

SANTA FE, ARGENTINA
Mozarteum de Santa Fe
President: Olilia Fayé de Rocca
Suavedra 2257

SANTA FE, NEW MEXICO, U.S.A.
Mozart Society

SAO PAULO, BRAZIL
Mozartéum do Brasil
rue Francisco Perotti, 628
Sao Paulo, Brazil

SARAJEVO, YUGOSLAVIA
Mozart Society (1970)

SCHWETZINGEN, GERMANY
Mozart Gesellschaft Schwetzingen (1969)
Präsident: Dr. Richard Treiber
Schillerstrasse 2
D-6830 Schwetzingen

SEA ISLAND, GEORGIA, U.S.A.

The Mozart Society of Glynn County (1967)
Mrs. Artiss de Volt-Zacharias
P.O. Box 202
Sea Island, Georgia 31561

SEATTLE, WASHINGTON, U.S.A.

Mozart Society (1981)

STUTTGART, GERMANY

Mozartgemeinde Stuttgart (reorganized 1926)
Dr. Wilhelm Hofmann
Carl-Benz-Strasse 8
D-7141 Beilstein

SYDNEY, AUSTRALIA

Mozart Society

TEPLITZ, AUSTRIA

Mozart Gesellschaft (1902)

TETSCHEN-LIEBWERD, AUSTRIA

Mozart Gesellschaft (1902)

TOKYO, JAPAN

Nippon Mozart Society (1957)
President: Professor Keisei Sakka
Seijo 2-11-4
Setegaya-ku
Tokyo 157
Issues bulletins.

TORONTO, ONTARIO, CANADA

Mozart Society (1984)
Peter E. Sandor
250 Heath Street, We, No. 403
Toronto, Ontario M 5 P 3 L A

TRAUNSTEIN, GERMANY
Mozart Gesellschaft (1902)

TRIER, GERMANY
Mozart Gesellschaft (1955)

TROPPAU, AUSTRIA
Mozart Gesellschaft (1902)

VANCOUVER, BRITISH COLUMBIA, CANADA
Vancouver Mozart Society (1979)
Joachim Petrick
P.O. Box 4823
Vancouver, British Columbia

VIENNA, AUSTRIA
Mozartgemeinde Wien
Professor Dr. Erik Werba
Wipplingerstrasse 4
1010 Vienna
Publications: *Wiener Figaro* (since 1931, not regular)

Wiener Mozartgemeinde
Fritzi Schlesinger-Czapka
Hadikgasse 106
1140 Vienna

VORALBERG, AUSTRIA
Mozart-Gemeinde (1973)

WIESBADEN, GERMANY
Mozart Gesellschaft Wiesbaden e. V. (1967)
Kurt Breuer
Kirchgasse 24
D-6200 Wiesbaden 1

WOLFSBERG/KÄRNTEN, AUSTRIA
Mozart Gesellschaft (1951)

WÜRZBURG, GERMANY

Mozart Gesellschaft (1902)

ZEIST, NETHERLANDS

Nederlandse Mozart Vereniging
(formerly, Mozart Society of Holland)
President: Herman Passchier (1986)
Bethanieplein 17
NL 3701 EM Zeist

ZERBST, GERMANY

Mozart Gesellschaft (1902)

ZITTAU, GERMANY

Mozart Gesellschaft (1902)

ZNAIM, AUSTRIA

Mozart Gesellschaft (1902)

ZURICH, SWITZERLAND

Mozart-Gesellschaft Zürich (1945)
Präsident: Dr. Rudolf Türler
Lenzwiesstrasse 16
CH-8702 Zollikon-Zürich

ZWEIBRÜCKEN, GERMANY

Mozart-Gemeinde (1987)

Serial Publications Devoted to Mozart

Acta Mozartiana (Augsburg, 1954–), Quarterly, Erich Valentin, ed.
Karlstrasse 6, Augsburg, Germany D-8900.

Mostly short articles; occasionally deep, useful summaries
(German).

Bulletin de la société d'études mozartiennes (Paris, 1930–1932).

Short-lived yearbook; includes a list of Mozart autographs at the Institut de France, Paris (French).

Jahresbericht des Internationalen Stiftung Mozarteum in Salzburg (1881, intermittent), J. E. Engl and R. Kiesel, eds.

Report on early activities at the Mozarteum (German).

Mitteilungen der Internationale Stiftung Mozarteum (Salzburg, 1918–1921; 1950–), Rudolph Angermüller, ed., Geza Rech, ed. emeritus. A-5024 Salzburg, Austria.

Presently an annual with brief incisive historical, biographical, bibliographical, musical articles (mostly German).

Mitteilungen—Mozart Gemeinde (Berlin, 1895–1925), Rudolf Genée, editor-founder; later editor, Fritz Rückward.

Mozart Jahrbuch (Munich, 1923, 1924, 1929), H. A. Abert, ed.

Neues Mozart Jahrbuch (Regensburg, 1941–1943), Erich Valentin, ed.

Mozart Jahrbuch (Salzburg, 1950–). A-5024 Salzburg, Austria.

Currently a yearly publication edited by the Internationale Stiftung Mozarteum, and Rudolph Angermüller, with important biographical, historical, bibliographical, musical articles (mostly German).

Neue Mozart Ausgabe (Kassel: Bärenreiter, 1955–). Heinrich Schütz Allee 31, D-3500 Kassel-Wilhelmshöhe, Germany.

Prefaces and valuable critical commentaries (German).

Wiener-Figaro, Mitteilungen der Mozartgemeinde. Wipplingerstrasse 4, 1010 Vienna, Austria. (Vienna, 1931–) .

Publication intermittent (German).

Other Music Publications with
Articles on Mozart

Readers will find additional information and useful periodicals by consulting the *New Grove Dictionary of Music and Musicians,* volume 14, Periodicals: pp. 407–535; also Marco (#539).

Acta Musicologica (Kassel, 1931–), Quarterly, Friedrich Lippmann, ed. (c/o Bärenreiter).

Each number has a focus: an opera, a year, a person, etc.

Allgemeine musikalische Zeitung (Leipzig, 1798–1848).

First numbers have reminiscences of Mozart by Rochlitz and other contemporaries (German).

Journal of the American Musicological Society (Philadelphia, 1948–) Three times a year, Anthony Newcomb, ed. Department of Music, University of California, Berkeley, California 94720.

Occasional authoritative aricles on Mozart (English).

Analecta Musicologica (Bonn, 1953–) 5300 Bonn, Germany.

Good source of articles (mostly German).

Archiv für Musikwissenschaft (Stuttgart, 1918–), Quarterly, Hans Eggebrecht, ed. Postfach 347, Birkenwaldstrasse 44, D-7000, Stuttgart, Germany.

Important music journal (German).

L'Avant-Scène Opéra (Paris, 1977–), Monthly, Alain Dualt, Michel Pazdo, eds. 16 Rue des Quatre-Vents, F-75006 Paris, France.

Each issue devoted to one opera (French).

Berlinische Musikalische Zeitung (Berlin, 1805– ?) Johann Friedrich Reichardt, founder-editor.

Important early German journal, successor to Reichardt's *Musikalische Kunst Magazin*, 1782–1791.

College Music Symposium (Boulder, Colorado, 1961–) Boulder, CO 80302, U.S.A. Annual, Jan Herlinger, ed. Journal of College Music Society.

Occasional authoritative articles on Mozart (English).

Denkmäler deutscher Tonkunst (Leipzig, Breitkopf & Härtel, 1892– 1931), Max Seiffert, ed.

Selected volumes devoted to music and commentary on Mozart's contemporaries (German).

Denkmäler der Tonkunst in Bayern (Braunschweig: Litolff, 1900– 1938), Adolf Sandberger, ed.

Selected volumes devoted to music and commentary on Mozart's contemporaries (German)

Denkmäler der Tonkunst in Österreich (Vienna: Universal, 1894–), Guido Adler, founder.

Selected volumes devoted to music and commentary on Mozart's contemporaries (German).

Mitteilungen der Internationalen Gesellschaft für Musikwissenschaft (Freiburg, Switzerland, 1928–?), Dr. F. Wagner, director.

(French, German.)

Monthly Musical Record (London, 1871–1960).

Occasional authoritative articles on Mozart (English).

Music and Letters (Oxford, England, 1920–). Quarterly, Nigel Fortune, John Whenham, eds. Music Dept., University of Birmingham, Birmingham, B15 2TS, England.

Occasional authoritative articles on Mozart (English).

The Music Review (Cambridge, England, 1940–?). CB3 9DR. Quarterly, A. F. L. Thomas, ed.

Occasional authoritative articles on Mozart (English).

The Musical Quarterly (New York City, 1915–). Eric Salzman, ed. 866 Third Avenue, New York, NY 10022.

Occasional authoritative articles on Mozart (English).

Musikerziehung (Vienna), Quarterly, Franz Blasi, ed. Österreichischer Bundesverlag, A-1010 Vienna, Austria.

Frequent articles on matters Mozartean (German).

Die Musikforschung (Kassel, Bärenreiter, 1948–). Quarterly, Martin Just and Wilhelm Seidel, eds.

Occasional authoritative articles on Mozart (German).

Neue Zeitschrift für Musik (Mainz, Schott, 1834–1919; 1955–) Ernst Thomas, ed. Postfach 3640, Weihergarten/D-6500 Mainz, Germany.

(German).

Notes (Canton, Massachusetts, American Music Library Association, 1943–). Monthly, Michael Ochs, ed. P.O. Box 487, Canton, MA 02021 U.S.A.

Occasional reviews on Mozart (English).

Opera Quarterly (Chapel Hill, North Carolina, U.S.A., 1982–), Irene Sloan and Sherwin Sloan, eds. 5934 Rod Avenue, Woodland Hills, CA 91367.

Often center on one theme. Occasional articles on Mozart (English).

Opera (London, 1950–) Rodney Milnes, ed. 1A Mountgrove Road, London, N5 2LU, England.

Includes articles, and opera translations (English).

Österreichische Musikzeitschrift (Vienna: Bauer Verlag, 1946–) Monthly, Elisabeth Lafitte, ed. Hegelgasse 13, A-1010 Vienna, Austria.

Most issues contain material on Mozart (German).

Revue de musicologie (Paris, 1922–), Christian Meyer, ed. 2 Rue Louvois F-75006 Paris, France.

Occasional articles on Mozart (French).

La Revue Musicale (Paris, 1920–), M. Richard, ed. 7 Place St. Sulpice, F-75006 Paris, France.

Occasional articles on Mozart (French).

Schweizerische Musikzeitung (Zurich, Switzerland 1879–?)

Occasional articles on Mozart (mostly German).

Studien zur Musikwissenschaft (Tutzing, Germany, 1924–?)

(German.)

Zeitschrift für Musikwissenschaft (Leipzig, Germany 1918–1936).

(German.)

INDEX OF AUTHORS,
EDITORS, AND TRANSLATORS

Abbott, Elizabeth	A/E	669
Abert, A. A.	A	748, 882
Abert, Hermann	A/E	604, 748, 844, 938
Abraham, G.	A	545, 774
Adkins, Cecil	A/E	516
Aigner, Theodor	A/E	716
Alberti, C. E. R	A/E	605
Albrecht, Hans	A/E	825
Albrecht, O. E.	A/E	738
Algatzy, Anton	A/E	556
Allanbrook, W. J.	A/E	883, 966
Allrogen, Gerhard	A/E	748, 1017
d'Amico, Silvio	A/E	517
Anderson, Emily	A/E	557
Anderson, Judith	A/E	720
André, August Hermann	A/E?	668
Angermüller, Rudolph	A/E	546–551, 584, 585, 689, 722, 723, 739, 917, 959, 967, 979, 1018
Armitage-Smith, J. N. A.	A/E	982
Arnold, I. E. F. K.	A/E	740
Asov, Erich H. Müller von	A/E	558, 741, 742
Autexier, P. A.	A/E	586
Babitz, Sol	A/E	826
Babler, O. F.	A/E	572
Bachmann, Alberto	A/E	518
Badura-Skoda, Eva	A/E	1031
Badura-Skoda, Paul	A/E	1031
Baker, Richard	A/E	606
Balk, H. W.	A	953
Ballantine, Christopher	A/E	884

Ballin, E. A.	A/E	877
Ballola Carli, Giovanni	A/E	840
Banat, Gabriel	A/E	103
Bär, Carl	A/E	735
Barrington, Daines	A/E	607
Bartha, D.	A	846
Batley, A. M.	A/E	983
Bauer, Anton	A/E	519
Bauer, Wilhelm	A/E	559
Baumann, Thomas	A/E	520
Beales, Derek	A	573
Beaumarchais, P. A. C. de	A/E	968
Beck, Sidney	A/E	108
Becker, Felix	A/E	27
Belmonte, Carola Groag	A/E	695
Bergin, Thomas	A/E	669
Besch, Lutz	A/E	614
Beyle, Marie Henri (Stendhal)	A/E	574
Bianchi, Luigi	A/E	688
Biancolli, Louis	A/E	743
Birsak, Kurt	A/E	1062
Blaiklock, Mary	A/T	640
Blaschitz, Mena	A/E	744
Bleiler, Eileen	A/E	939
Blom, Eric	A/E/T	592, 608, 610, 969
Blum, Fred	A/E	521
Blume, Friedrich	A/E	553, 745, 774, 777
Blümml, E. K.	A/E	696, 984
Bolongaro-Crevenna, H.	A/E	587
Bory, Robert	A/E	25
Bossarelli, Francesco	A/E	746
Bouillon, E.	A	925
Bouvier-Lapierre, S.	A	925
Brandstetter, Gabriele	A	926
Branscombe, Peter	T	610
Breydert, Frédéric	A/E	885
Britten Festschrift		528
Broder, Nathan	A/E/T	612, 777
Brook, Barry S.	A/E	522, 523, 588
Brown, Maurice	A/E	847, 878
Broyles, Michael	A/E	848
Brukner, Fritz	A/E	985
Brunel, P.	A	925
Burk, J. N.	A/E	609
Burney, Charles	A/E	524
Busoni, Ferruccio	A/E	747
Buszin Festschrift		528

Carolan, Monica	A/E	557
Carr, Francis	A	697
Carse, Adam	A	589
Casaglia, Gherardo	A/E	Page 27
Chailley, Jacques	A	986
Chantavoine, Jean	A	849
Charlton, David	A	590
Chesnut, J. H.	A	567
Churgin, Bathia	A	597
Clapham, John	A	850
Clark, Windeyer	T	943
Cobbett, Walter William	A/E	1011
Cole, M. S.	A/E	988
Coolidge, A. D.	T	672
Cowden, R. H.	A	525
Crankshaw, Edward	A	575
Crawford, G.	A	528
Croll, Gerhard	A/E	748, 954
Cross, Eric	T	579
Csampai, Attila	A	940, 955, 970, 987
Curzon, Henri de	A/E	560
Dalchow, Johannes	A	736
Danckwardt, Marianne	A	839
David, Ernest	A	698
Davis, Shelley	A	841
Dazeley, G.	A	1063
Dean, Winton	A	591
Dearling, Robert	A	1019
Della Croce, Luigi	A	1020
Del Mar, Norman	A	960
Dennerlein, H.	A	1032
Dent, E. J.	A	100, 886
Deutsch, Otto Erich	A/E	26, 559, 561, 610, 731, 748, 749, 774, 777
Dickinson, Alis	A/E	516
Dietrich, M.	A	937
Disault, M.	A	925
Dobias, V.		846
Downes, Edward	A	975
Dru, Alexander	T	615
Duckles, Vincent	A	526, 527
Durant, Ariel	A	576
Durant, Will	A	576
Dussour, M.-A.	A	925
Dutronc, J.-L.	A	925
Ebisawa (Bin E. Bisawa)	A	751

Eckelmayer, J. A.	A	989
Eckstein, P.	A	545
Eibl, J. H.	A/E	559, 610, 611, 724
Einstein, Alfred	A/E	107, 130, 592, 612, 613, 752, 972, 1012
Eisen, Cliff	A	610, 648, 753
Eisley, I.	A	1033
Eitner, Robert	A	527
Emerson, John	A	754
Engel, Hans	A	712, 748, 774, 828, 887, 916, 1021
Engerth, Ruediger	A	649
Engländer, Richard	A	127, 674, 684, 755
Etheridge, David	A	1064
Ewens, F. J.	A	673
Faber, Marian	T	620
Fairleigh, James	A	1034
Farmer, H. G.	A	756
Feder, G.	A/E	961
Federhofer, H.	A	650, 651, 961
Felinski, Zenon	A	1056
Fellerer, Karl Gustav	A	699, 700, 837, 846, 868
Ferguson, L.	K	1035
Ferrari, Virgilio	A	652
Finscher, Ludwig	A	718, 937
Fischer, H. C.	A	614, 1107
Fischer, L.	A	865
Fischer, Wilhelm	A	528, 687, 748
FitzLyon, April	A	670
Floros, Constantin	A	757, 782, 903
Flothuis, Marius	A	865, 865A, 1023
Flotzinger, Rudolf	A	1036
Forman, Denis	A	1037
Fortassier, P.	A	846
Franken, F. H.	A	737
Freyhan, Michael	A	992
Friedrich, G.	A	937
Gagla, G.	A/E	937
Gallini, Natale	A	1038
Geiringer, Karl	A	593, 675, 774
Gelhorn, Peter	T	938
Gerboth, Walter	A	528
Ghéon, Henri	A	615
Gheusi, J.	A	925
Giazotto, Remo	A	616
Giegling, Franz	A	545, 918

Gieseking, Walter	A	1039
Girdlestone, Cuthbert	A	1040
Gishford, A.	A	528
Glöckner, H. P.	A	937
Gloede, Wilhelm	A	927
Glück, Franz	A	681
Goedbé, Samuel	E	570
Göhler, Georg	A	829
Goldovsky, Boris	A	888, 928
Gombrich, E. H.	A	929
Gorke, Manfred	A	121
Görner, Rüdiger	A	713
Goslick, Siegfried	A	782
Gottron, Adam B.	A	653, 1041
Gounod, Charles	A	943
Graf, Max	A	758
Grand Larousse	A/E	529
Granturco, Carolyn	A	889
Grasberger, Franz	A	993
Green, H.	A	1118
Green, Richard	A	530
Gribenski, Jean	A	531
Grosse Brockhaus	A	532
Grout, D. J.	A	533
Gruber, Gernot	A	903, 961, 994
Guellette, A.	A	925
Gugitz, Gustav	A	617
Haas, Robert	A	618, 683
Haberkamp, Gertraut	A	759
Hadamowsky, Franz	A	619
Hafner, Otfried	A	760
Haggin, B. H.	A	1042
Hall, Monika	A	110
Hamburger, Paul	A	879
Hammer, Karl	A	761
Harris, L.	A	975
Hastings, Baird	A	570, 852, 962, 975
Hausner, Henry	A	710, 721, 725, 995
Heartz, Daniel	A/E	890, 891, 903, 919, 944, 961, 962
Heinzelmann, Josef	A	690
Hennessee, Don	A	534
Hermann, Hildegard	A	711
Hertzmann, Erich	A	777
Hess, E.	A	748, 846
Heuss, Alfred	A	853, 963
Hickman, Roger	A	594

Hildesheimer, Wolfgang	A	620
Hill, George R.	A	1006
Hirschberg, Jehoash	A	964
Hitze, Wilhelm	A	562
Hixon, D. L.	A	534
Hocquard, J.-V.	A	925, 930
Hoffman, E. T. A.	A	945
Holland, Dietmar	A	970, 987
Holmes, Edward	A	621
Honolka, Kurt	A	691
Hopkinson, Cecil	A/E	762
Hortschansky, K.	A	937
Howard, Patricia	A	595
Hrabussay, Zoltán	A	763
Hümmeke, Werner	A	1013
Hummel, Walter	A	654, 701, 702
Hutchings, Arthur	A	596, 774, 1043, 1044
Hutchinson, J. T.	T	943
Inzaghi, Luigi	A	688
Irmer, Otto von	A	1044A
Jahn, Otto	A	622, 748
Jancik, Hans	A	678
Jenkins, Newell	A	597
Jeurisson, Herman	A	1065
Johansson, Carl	A	764
John, Nicholas	A/E	931, 996
Jonas, Oswald	A	1045
Jost, C.	A	937
Kaiser, Joachim	A	892
Kaperl, Otto	A	1057
Kaut, Josef	A	765
Kecskeméti, István	A	726, 727, 854
Keller, Hans	A	774
Keller, Hermann	A	830
Keller, Otto	A	554
Kelly, Michael	A	623
Kelterborn, Rudolf	A	855
Kennard, Joseph	A	577
Kerner, Dieter	A/E	869
Keys, Ivor	A	624
Killer, Hermann	A	893
King, A. H.	A	104, 528, 557, 680, 766–769, 1007, 1014
Kingdon-Ward, Martha	A	1066
Kirkendale, Warren	A	1008
Klein, Herbert	A	866
Knocker, Editha	E/T	598

Köberle, Adolf	A	625
Köchel, Ludwig von	A/E	Page 28, 748
Köhler, K.-H.	A/E	110, 125, 128, 770, 771
Kolbin, Dmitri	A	772, 1058
Komorzynski, Egon	A	703, 870, 1067
Koprowski, Richard	A	812
Korisheli, Wachtung	A	856
Kozma, T.	A	975
Kramer, Kurt	A	626, 694, 932
Kretschmar, H.	A	748
Kristek, Jan	A	946
Krummel, D. W.	A	773
Kunz, Otto	A	1119
Kunze, Stefan	A	867, 894, 903, 947, 986
Laborde, J. B. de	A	535
Lach, Robert	A	568
Landon, H. C. Robbins	A/E	676, 732, 774–776, 846
Lang, P. H.	A/E	777
Larsen, J. P.	A	677, 748, 774
LaRue, Jan	A	112, 528, 536
Lauer, Erich	A	569
Lebermann, Walter	A	1059
Leeson, D. N.	A	1015, 1068
Lequin, Frank	A	671
Lert, Ernst	A	895
Lesure, François	A	122, 655
Leux, Irmgard	A	686
Levarie, Siegmund	A	973
Levin, R. D.	A	1068
Lewicki, Rudolph	A	778
Le Winter, R.	A	925
Lichtenthal, Pietro	A	627
Liebner, Janos	A	896, 961
Lippmann, Friedrich	A	656, 903
Livinston, Arthur	A	669
Loewenberg, Alfred	A/E	537
Loft, Adam	A	897
Lombard, A.	A	925
Lorenz, Franz	A	1047
Lowinsky, Edward	A	777
Lowrie, W.	T	714
Luethy, Walter	A	857
Lühning, Helga	A	903, 920
Lunde, A. E.	A	871

Luoma, R. G.	A	779
MacIntyre, B. C.	A	872
Mackerras, Charles	A	831
Magnus, M.	T	935
Mahling, C. H.	A	903
Mainka, Jürgen	A	898
Major, Ervin	A	780
Malbos, P.	A	925
Mandyczewski, E.	A/E	132
Mann, William	A	899
Marco, Guy A.	A	538, 539
Marethe, Ursula	A	704
Marguerre, Karl	A	728, 1016, 1069
Marignano, N. Medici di	A/E	628
Martinoty, J.-L.	A	925
Marx, K. J.	A	106
Massin, Brigitte	A	629
Massin, Jean	A	629
Matthews, Denis	A	117
Mayor, A. H.	A	Page 167
Meissner, A. G.	A	685
Melkus, Eduard	A	1060
Mendel, Arthur	A/T	612
Merkling, Frank	A/E	975
Metastasio, Pietro (Trapassi)	A	578
Meyer, Reinhart	A	900
Mies, Paul	A	832
Mila, Massimo	A	880
Milligan, Thomas	A	781
Mishkin, H. G.	A	1048
Mitchell, Donald	A/E	528, 774
Moberly, R. B.	A	901, 921, 1004
Moldenauer, Hans	A	102
Mooser, A. R.	A	902
Mooser, Robert	A	540
Mozart, Leopold		Pages 28, 73–74; 598
Mozart, Wolfgang		Pages 28, 73–76; 570
Müller, A. E.	A	1049
Münster, Robert	A	630, 785, 1024, 1025
Muraro, Maria	A	904
Murr, S.	A	925
Musiol, Karl	A	786–788
Nef, Albert	A	933, 956
Nettl, Paul	A	113, 733, 975
Neumann, F.	A	833, 961, 1050
Neumann, Hans	A	118
Neville, D. J.	A	922

Newman, Ernest	A	905
Newman, W. S.	A	1051
Newsom, Jim	A	107
Nielsen, Carl	A	791
Niemetschek, Franz Xaver	A	631
Nissen, Georg Nikolaus von	A	632
Noble, Jeremy		610
Nohl, Ludwig	A	633
Noske, Frits	A	906
Nottebohm, M. G.	A	792
Novello, Mary Sabilla	A/E	628
Novello, Vincent	A/E	628
Nowak, Leopold	A	793
Nys, Carl de	A	846
Očadlík, Mirko	A	843
Oldman, Cecil	A	528, 571, 794
Ollivier-Smith, Martine	A	976
Orel, Alfred	A	795, 981, 997
Ortheil, Hanns-Josef	A	563
Osborne, Charles	A	907
Ostoja, Andrea	A	657
Oulibischeff, A. D.	A	634
Patzak, Julius	A	834
Paumgartner, Bernhard	A/E	561, 635, 748, 835
Payne, E. F. J.	T	717
Pečman, R.	A/E	545
Pesková, Jitrenka	A	796
Pestelli, Giorgio	A	579
Pfannhauser, Karl	A	797
Pierpont Morgan Library Staff		798
Pirrotta, Nino	A	908
Pisarowitz, K. M.	A	719
Pizka, Hans	A	111
Plath, Wolfgang	A	748, 799–801, 873
Pohl, C. F.	A	636
Postolka, Milan	A	679
Procházka, Rudolph von	A	637
Prodhomme, J. G.	A	638
Protz, Albert	A	957
Racek, J.	A	802
Raeburn, Christopher	A	803
Raeburn, Michael	A	803
Rainer, Werner	A	599
Rech, Geza	A/E	551, 564
Rehm, W.	A	903
Reich, Nancy B.	A	804
Reijen, Paul W. van	A	805

Richner, Thomas	A	1052
Riedel, J.	A	528
Ringer, Alexander	A	580
Robinson, Michael	A	909
Rochlitz, J. F.	A	639
Roe, Stephen	A/E	784
Rolland, Romain	A	640
Rosen, Charles	A	859
Rosenberg, Alfons	a	581, 948, 998
Rosenberg, Richard	A	1053
Rosenthal, Karl	A	874, 910
Rudolf, Max	A	911
Ruf, Wolfgang	A	977
Ruhnke, M.	A	903
Rushton, Julian	A	949
Russell, Charles C.	A	950
Ryskamp, Charles	A	115
Sadie, Stanley	A/E	555
Saint-Foix, Georges de	A	647, 1026
Sandberger, Adolf	A	693
Sandt, Alfred	A	980
Schaal, Richard	A	541, 806
Schachter, Carl	A	118
Scharnagel, August	A	807
Schenk, Erich	A	545, 641, 846
Scheurleer, Daniel	A	529, 642
Schickling, Dieter	A	729
Schiedermair, Ludwig	A	565
Schlichtegroll, Friedrich	A	643
Schlosser, J. A.	A	808
Schmid, E. F.	A	100, 658, 659, 692, 748, 777, 842, 846
Schmieder, Wolfgang	A	809
Schneider, Constantin	A	601
Schneider, Hans	A/E	810
Schneider, Otto	A/E	546, 556, 999
Scholz, Janos	A	Page 167
Schönig, Heinz	A	660
Schopenauer, Arthur	A	717
Schrade, L.	A	748
Schuler, Heinz	A	705
Schünemann, Kurt	A	845
Schurig, Arthur	A	566, 644, 707
Schwarz, Vera	A	682
Schweizer, H. J.	A	958
Schwerin, Erna	A	566
Sechter, Simon	A	1027

Senn, Walter	A	571A
Serwer, Howard	A/E	677
Shaw, Bernard	A	811
Shaw, Watkins	A/E	117
Shamgar, Beth	A	860
Sheehy, Eugene	A/E	542
Siegmund-Schulze, Walther	A	838, 861
Simpson, A. T.	A	1120
Singer, I.	A	836
Smart, Fiona	A/e	557
Smith, Erik	A	1028
Smith, Herbert	A	756
Smith, P. J.	A	583
Somfai, László	A	961
Sommer, Susan	A	812
Sonneck, Oscar G. T.	A/E	543
Spink, Reginald	T	791
Spitzer, John	A	1070
Squire, W. B.	A	813
Stadler, Maximilian	A	875
Stahelin, Lucas E.	A	661
Stefan, Paul	A	951
Steibel, Harold	A	1071
Steinpress, Boris	A	814, 815
Steptoe, Andrew	A	934
Sternfeld, Frederick	A	603, 777
Stevens, J. R.	A	1054
Stowell, Robin	A	544
Strauss, H.	A	662
Strauss, Richard	A	935
Surian, E.	A	912
Szabolcsi, Bence	A	816, 913
Tagliavini, L. F.	A	846
Taling-Hajnali, Maria	A	862
Tangeman, R. S.	A	876
Tanimura, Ko	A	1000
Terry, Charles	A	602
Thieme, Carl	A	1029
Thieme, Ulrich	A/E	27
Thomson, Katherine	A	734
Tischler, Hans	A	1055
Tobin, J. R.	A	863
Tondorf, F. J.	A	914
Torrefranco, Fausto	A	645
Tovey, D. F.	A	817
Townsend, Pauline	T	622
Turner, J. R.	A	112, 115

Tyrrell, John	A/E	545
Tyson, Alan	A	130, 131, 818, 923, 936, 978, 1030
Ujfalusay, J.	A	864
Valbrega, C.	A	846
Valentin, Erich	A	100, 715, 952
Vaughan, Denis	A	1001
Verchaly, A.	A	846
Vetter, Walther	A	819
Vieuille, M.-F.	A	925
Vill, Susanne	A/E	937
Virneisel, Wilhelm	A	119
Volkmann, H.	A	663
Walin, S.	A	846
Walter, Bruno	A	1002
Wandruszka, Adam	A	924
Waters, E. N.	A	820
Weaver, W.	A	975
Webster, James	A/E	677
Wegele, Ludwig	A/E	708, 709
Weinmann, Alexander	A	821, 822
Weinstock, Herbert	T	986
Wellesz, Egon	A	603
Wendelin, Lidia	A	664
Werba, Erik	A	881
Werner, K.	A	937
Westphal, N.	A	937
Whitwell, David	A	1015
Winkler, T. F.	A	646
Winston, Clara	T	641
Winston, Richard	T	641
Wirth, H.	A	846
Wise, Rosemary	A/E	545
Witzmann, R.	A	682
Wlček, Walter	A	730
Wolf, E. K.	A	823
Wolff, Christian	A	865
Würtz, Roland	A/E	665
Wurzbach, C. v.	A	824
Wyzewa, Théodore de	A	647, 746, 1003
Zaloba, Jiri	A	796
Zaslaw, Neal	A	1009
Zenger, Max	A	26
Ziffer, Agnes	A	603A
Zingel, H. J.	A	1010
Zingerle, Hans	A	528

INDEX OF NAMES

Adlgasser, A. C.	(composer)	599, 601
Alberti, Ignaz	(artist-publisher)	46
Albrechtsberger, J. G.	(composer)	667
Allgemeine Musikalische Zeitung	(publisher)	47
André, Johann	(composer, publisher)	30, 48
Artaria	(publisher)	31, 49
Bach, J. C.	(composer)	602
Bach, J. S.	(composer)	593
Bambini, Eustacio	(composer)	950
Beaumarchais, P. A. Caron de (see also *Le nozze di Figaro* in Index of works)	(writer)	968
Beethoven, Ludwig van	(composer)	836
Bianchi, G. B.	(publisher)	50
Bossler, H. P.	(publisher)	51
Boyer, Pascal	(publisher)	52
Breitkopf & Härtel	(publisher)	29, 45
Breitkopfische Musikhandlung	(publisher)	53
Bureau des Arts et d'Industrie	(publisher)	54
Cappi, Johann	(publisher)	55
Carmontelle, L. C. de	(artist)	2–4
Chabal, J. L.	(publisher)	44
Chappell, Samuel	(composer, publisher)	56
Chemische Druckerei	(publisher)	33
Cianchettini & Sperati	(publisher)	57
Coventry, Charles	(publisher)	43
dalla Rosa, Saverio	(artist)	6
Da Ponte, Lorenzo	(colleague)	669, 670
De Jean, Dr. Ferdinand	(flutist)	671
della Croce, J. N.	(artist)	10
Diabelli, Anton	(composer, publisher)	58
Diesbach, G. E.	(publisher)	59

Ditters von Dittersdorf, Karl	(composer)	672
Eberl, Anton	(composer)	673
Eybler, Joseph	(composer)	710, 711
Falter, M.	(publisher)	60
Fischietti, Domenico	(composer)	674
Frey, J. J.	(publisher)	38
Gluck, C. W.	(composer)	592, 595, 687
Goethe, J. W. von	(writer)	113
Goldoni, Carlo	(dramatist)	577, 944
Gombart, G.	(publisher)	61
Gottlieb, Anna	(singer)	703
Götz, J. M.	(publisher)	62
Gräffer, Rudolph	(publisher)	63
Grétry, André	(composer)	590
Günther & Böhme	(publisher)	64
Handel, George Frideric	(composer)	591, 837, 838
Haslinger, Tobias	(publisher)	35
Haydn, F. J.	(composer)	675–677, 839
Haydn, Michael	(composer)	678
Heina, Madame G.	(publisher)	66
Heydenreich, Joseph	(composer, publisher)	65
Hofdemel, Magdalena Pokorny	(pupil)	697
Hoffmeister, F. A.	(composer, publisher)	32, 67
Hummel, J. J.	(publisher)	68
Hummel, J. N.	(pupil)	1024
Imbault, J. J.	(publisher)	69
Janet & Cotelle	(publisher)	37
Jommelli, Niccolò	(composer)	840
Joseph II	(monarch)	575
Kierkegaard, Søren	(philosopher)	712–714
Koželuh, Leopold	(composer)	619, 1005
Krafft, Barbara	(artist)	24
Krausstschen Buchladen nächst Burg	(publisher)	70
Kreusser, Peter Anton	(composer)	680
Kurzböck, Joseph	(musician, publisher)	71
Lang, J. C.	(composer)	841
Lange, Joseph	(actor, artist)	11, 705
Launer, Mme.	(publisher)	41
Leuckart, F. E. C.	(publisher)	72
Lorenzoni, Pietro Antonio	(artist)	1
Löschenkohl, Hieronymous	(artist)	12–14, 681, 682
Lotter, J. J.	(publisher)	73
Lyser, J. P.	(poet)	715
Magasin de musique	(publisher)	28
Majo, G. F.	(composer)	840

Name	Role	Page
Maria Theresa	(monarch)	575
Mayr, J.	(publisher)	74
Mederitsch, Johann (Gallus)	(composer)	716
Mesmer, Anton	(friend)	(see *Cosi fan tutte* in Index of Works)
Metastasio, P.	(librettist)	578
Mollo, Tranquillo	(publisher)	75
Monsigny, Pierre	(composer)	842
Montani, Giovanni	(publisher)	76
Mozart and family (self-publisher)		84
Mozart, Carl (son)		702
Mozart, Constanze (wife)		566
Mozart, Leopold (father)		707, 708
Mozart, Marianne Thekla (cousin)		709
Mozart, Nannerl (sister)		701
Mozart, W. A. (son)	(composer)	702
Müller, Wenzel	(composer)	683
Musenalmanach	(publisher)	77
Musikalische Magazin	(publisher)	78
Mysliveček, Josef	(composer)	843
Naumann, J. G.	(composer)	684, 685
Neefe, C. G.	(composer)	686
Nissen, G. N.	(writer)	632
Ollivier, M. B.	(artist)	5
Paisiello, Giovanni	(composer)	844
Peters, C. F.	(publisher)	79
Piccinni, Nicola	(composer)	687
Pleyel, Ignaz	(composer, publisher)	39, 1005
Posch, Leonard	(artist)	15–21
Rellstab, J. K. F.	(publisher)	80
Richault, C. S.	(publisher)	42
Rolla, Alessandro	(composer)	688
Salieri, Antonio	(composer)	689, 690
Sammartini, G. B.	(composer)	586, 597
Schikaneder, Emanuel	(colleague)	691
Schmiedt & Rau	(publishers)	81
Schobert, Johann	(composer)	845
Schönfeld, J. F. von	(publisher)	82
Schopenauer, Arthur	(philosopher)	717
Schott, Bernhard	(publisher)	83
Sieber, Jean-Georges	(publisher)	36, 85
Simrock, Nikolaus	(publisher)	34, 86
Societa Tipografica	(publisher)	87
Spehr, J. P. (see Magasin de musique)	(publisher)	28

Stadler, Maximilian	(musician)	718, 719, 875
Steiner, S. A.	(publisher)	40
Stock, Doris	(artist)	22
Storace, Stephen	(composer, publisher)	88, 720
Süssmayr, F. X.	(pupil)	723–730
Swieten, Baron van	(patron-musician)	692
Taubstimmen Institut (F. Seizer)	(publisher)	89
Thonus, J. P.	(publisher)	90
Thuille, F. G.	(publisher)	91
Torricella, Christoph	(publisher)	92
Traeg, Johann	(publisher)	93
Traeta, Tommaso	(composer)	693, 840
Varesco, G. B.	(poet)	694
Vendôme, Marie (and family)	(publisher)	94
Wappler, C. F.	(publisher)	95
Weber, Aloysia	(relative, singer)	704
Weigl, Joseph	(composer)	721
Weingand, J. G.	(publisher)	96
Wenzel, Johann	(musician, publisher)	97
Williamson, Thomas G.	(musician, publisher)	98
Ziegenhagen, F. H.	(publisher)	99

INDEX OF WORKS

Ascanio in Alba	916
Bastien und Bastienne	917
Clemenza di Tito, La	918–924
Così fan tutte	925–937, 1072–1075
Don Giovanni	938–952, 1076–1079
Entführung aus dem Serail, Die	953–958, 1080–1083
Finta giardiniera, La	959
Finta semplice, La	975
Idomeneo	960–964, 1084–1087
Lambach Symphony	1017
Masonic Music	733, 734
Masses	See Religious Music
Mitridate	965
Nozze di Figaro, Le	966–978
Petits riens, Les	979, 980
Religious Music	868
Thamos	981
Zauberflöte, Die	982–1002

ABOUT THE AUTHOR

Dr. Baird Hastings is a 1939 graduate of Harvard. His teachers include: Barry S. Brook, Louis Fourestier, Boris Goldovsky, Bernhard Paumgartner, Yella Pessl. He has taught at Trinity College and The Juilliard School, and lectured at Emerson College, Hartt College, Harvard University, Queens College, Tufts University. He is the author-compiler of eight books and many articles and reviews (a number involving the arts of France). In addition to being the founder-conductor of The Mozart Festival Orchestra, he has been guest conductor at the New York State Theater and music advisor of The Eglevsky Ballet and has conducted The American Symphony, The Hartford Symphony, The Queens Philharmonic. He was the recipient of a scholarship to Tanglewood, a Regents Scholarship, and a Fulbright Fellowship to France. He has collaborated with Virgil Thomson, the Royal Academy of Music, Lincoln Kirstein, Alexandra Danilova.